Interprofessional Relations in Health Care

Edited by

Keith Soothill, Lesley Mackay, Christine Webb

D0140818

Edward Arnold
A member of the Hodder Headline Group
LONDON   MELBOURNE   AUCKLAND

© 1995 Edward Arnold

First published in Great Britain 1995

British Library Cataloguing in Publication Data

Available upon request

ISBN 0–340–59806–9

Typeset in 10/11 pt Times by Anneset, Weston-super-Mare, Avon.
Printed and bound in Great Britain for Edward Arnold, a division
of Hodder Headline PLC, 338 Euston Road, London NW1 3BH
by Mackays of Chatham PLC, Kent.

Contents

List of Contributors

Stephen Ackroyd
Organisational Consultant and Senior Lecturer, Department of Behaviour in Organisations, Management School, Lancaster University

Nils-Holger Areskog
Professor of Clinical Physiology at Linköping University, Sweden, Founding Dean of the Faculty of Health Sciences, and currently President of the European Network for Development of Multiprofessional Education in Health Sciences (EMPE)

Alan Beattie
Head of Department, Health Studies and Human Sciences, St Martin's College, Lancaster

John Carpenter
Senior Lecturer at the Tizard Centre of Social Care, University of Kent at Canterbury

Tom Chapman
Deputy Head of School of Health Studies, Edge Hill College of Higher Education

Richard Cole
Senior Manager working in Surrey Social Services, and a research student at Surrey University

Julie Dockrell
Lecturer in the Department of Social Psychology, London School of Economics

Peter Funnell
Head of Cross-College Programmes Unit, Suffolk College, Ipswich, and Trustee of the Centre for the Advancement of Interprofessional Education

Janet Gill
Senior Lecturer in Social Work in the School of Health and Social Work, Suffolk College, Ipswich

June Greenwell
Honorary Research Fellow, Department of Applied Social Science, Lancaster University

Geoff Harding
Senior Research Fellow, Jocelyn Chamberlain Unit, Department of Public Health Sciences, St George's Hospital Medical School, London

Christine Henry
Professor at the University of Central Lancashire heading the Professional Ethics Unit

John Horder
Retired general practitioner, past-president of the Royal College of General Practitioners, and currently Chairman of the National Centre for the Advancement of Interprofessional Education

Richard Hugman
Senior Lecturer in the Department of Applied Social Science, Lancaster University

Kevin Kendrick
Senior Lecturer in Philosophy and Health Care Ethics at Liverpool John Moore's University

John Ling
Senior Lecturer in Health Studies in the School of Health and Social Work, Suffolk College, Ipswich

Anna Lorbiecki
Lecturer in the Department of Management Learning, Management School, Lancaster University

Lesley Mackay
Senior Research Fellow, School of Education, Leeds University

Eileen McLeod
Lecturer in the Department of Applied Social Studies, Warwick University

Michael Perides
Senior Manager working in Surrey Social Services, and a research student at Surrey University

Jane Sandall
DoH-funded Doctoral Research Fellow in the Department of Sociology, Surrey University

Keith Soothill
Professor of Social Research in the Department of Applied Social Science, Lancaster University

Kevin Taylor
Lecturer in Pharmaceutics, School of Pharmacy, University of London

Mary Thomas
Macmillan Lecturer, Macmillan Education Resource Unit, Centre for Medical Education, University of Dundee

Christine Webb
Professor of Nursing in the School of Nursing Studies, University of Manchester

Anne Williams
Lecturer in Nursing in the School of Nursing Studies, University of Manchester

Gail Wilson
Lecturer in Social Policy and the Elderly, London School of Economics

Part A

Introduction

Throughout the world, health issues are coming to the fore in a variety of ways. From the sadly familiar concerns of ill-health derived from a basic dearth of social and economic resources, to the consideration of a more effective health care delivery for the richest nation in the world, health care issues are certainly on the agenda. Although the medical profession remains the dominant occupational group in the provision of health care, there are an increasing number of health care professions claiming much more of the action. How they all work together — or fail to do so — will be one of the critical questions in the coming decade or so. The tradition of health care professionals functioning independently and autonomously or, alternatively, working to the beck and call of the medical profession is both breaking down and being challenged. The difficulties of working interprofessionally are legion but the issues need to be confronted.

In this volume we set the scene in Part A by examining the context in which questions of interprofessional working are emerging. Mackay, Soothill and Webb suggest that paradoxically the present 'may be the worst yet the best of times to address professional working practices'. This apparent paradox underpins many of the issues and contradictions in moving forward to develop more satisfactory interprofessional relations. For those who support such moves, the scope at a time of radical change is enormous, while for others the time of turbulent change is the very time when one should try to ensure that the glories of the past are not lost.

Beattie in 'War and peace among the health tribes' provides a striking metaphor to explain the past and as a basis for understanding current boundary conflicts and boundary changes in the health field. Certainly the question remains open as to whether it will be war or peace among the health tribes in the next decade or so.

The three remaining parts of this volume are each distinctive, but the boundaries — like interprofessional working! — are often difficult to delineate. Part B focuses on *The Reality of Current Interprofessional Working* where examples of both the difficulties and some successes are delineated. The reality of the present is difficult to mask, but the hopes and aspirations of those committed to interprofessional education strongly emerge in Part C, *Education and Training for Working Together*. Finally, in Part D, *Underlying Issues Examined*, our contributors focus on issues which are now part of contemporary reality. While morale, partnerships, and professional ethics remain as pertinent topics, the emergence of the client (or customer, patient, or user) as a stakeholder in the proceedings has been a useful reminder for everyone as to what ultimately the health care game is all about.

1 Troubled times: The context for interprofessional collaboration?

Lesley Mackay, Keith Soothill and Christine Webb

There has been a surge of interest in interprofessional working in recent years. That interest has been spurred by concerns with quality, both inside and outside the health care system. Many initiatives have been taken in a variety of settings to improve the ways in which colleagues from different professional backgrounds can work together effectively. Each one of us prides ourself on our own knowledge base and it often requires an act of will to recognize the skills and expertise which colleagues in other occupations have to offer. Working 'interprofessionally' means crossing occupational boundaries, setting aside the 'rightness' of our view of health care and having a willingness to listen to what colleagues from another occupation are saying. It is hard enough to work well 'intraprofessionally' with one's own colleagues without the added difficulty of communicating with those who have been trained in a different tradition.

Most practitioners who work in health care are trained to function both independently and autonomously. Learning to work as part of a team is not easy. And learning to work with many different types of professionals in a multidisciplinary team can be extremely difficult. There are numerous barriers to working interprofessionally or multiprofessionally. There are barriers of ascribed and perceived occupational status; barriers of occupational knowledge and the perceived importance of that knowledge for health care; barriers of fear, even distrust, of the perspectives of other occupational groups. Yet many have tried and are continuing to make the effort to work together effectively as a team.

These efforts are being made in a range of environments each presenting its own difficulties and additional barriers to joint working. Hospitals with their long-established traditions of occupational hierarchies present particular difficulties. There are non-teaching and teaching hospitals, large and small hospitals, rural and metropolitan hospitals — each with its own atmosphere and practices. Working in the community is no easier, with the additional constraints of covering a dispersed geographical area. Again, 'the community' is a catch-all phrase which encompasses the wild islands of Scotland to the claustrophobic existence of the inner-city high-rise block of flats.

Attempts to improve the quality of health service need to be supported by changes in training and education. But learning to learn with colleagues from other disciplines is not easy. Positive attitudes to inter- and multiprofessional working are best engendered during pre-qualification education, before the recruits receive the traditional view of working. There are, of course, disputes as to whether it is better to establish a sound body of knowledge and an occupational identity before presenting the alternative and differing perspectives of other occupational groups.

The variety of occupations involved in health care is tremendous and there is a remarkable diversity in the composition of groups working in any area. Each has its own view of 'the patient' and its own view of 'the solution'. Each profession has been given its own 'spectacles' through which to view the world. Reconciling these differing perspectives cannot ever be easy. There are social workers, radiographers, midwives, general practitioners, occupational therapists, district nurses, consultants and junior doctors, nurses, dietitians, health visitors, physiotherapists and others too numerous to mention. There are also voluntary workers and those who work in 'alternative' medicine and therapies. Most importantly of all, there are the patients, their relatives and their carers whose views of the health care in which they participate have only relatively recently been sought.

There has been continuing interest in fostering multiprofessional working from some dedicated practitioners, and additional strength has recently been given to the arguments for collaborative working. Firstly, there have been a number of cases, so much loved by the mass media, when there have been failures of communication between different groups of carers so that patients/clients have suffered unnecessarily. Secondly, there has been increasing awareness of the need to improve the quality of care for patients and clients. Thirdly, the need to improve the effective use of resources in health and social care systems has been identified. Demand for health care has been rising and continues to rise. There seems to be no limit to our ability to 'consume' health care. The need to use the available resources carefully and to maximum effect has resulted in a variety of initiatives. These initiatives have focused on the division of labour between professional and occupational groups, so that, for example, nurses are being encouraged to take over tasks previously the responsibility of junior doctors. In the community, on the other hand, there has been a shift in responsibility from nurse to social worker in the care of the long-term dehospitalized patient/resident living in local authority accommodation.

These changes are taking place when there are serious problems of morale within the whole arena of health care. Essentially these problems are caused by pressures on resources, both financial and human. Attempts to control the rocketing costs of health care have affected every single aspect of the NHS. Restrictions in the types of drugs prescribed, contracting out of numerous activities from laboratory services to cleaning, the reintroduction of plush private 'hotel' facilities, the delegation of 'budget-holding' to ward and unit level — these are just a few of the changes which the concerns with cost have generated. Indeed, the National Health Service is an exciting place to be working these days. Reorganization has followed reorganization. Today the extent of change and the number of changes are breath-catching, designed as they are to fundamentally alter the nature of the health service.

The movement to community care of patients previously living in mental hospitals, general practitioner budget-holders, the changing staff-mix in acute hospital wards, reductions in the hours worked by junior doctors, higher bed occupancy rates and increased use of operating theatres are just a few of the factors which have affected the day-to-day work of professionals in the NHS.

In an effort to improve the quality of care, the attempt has been made to engender a spirit of competition within the NHS through the creation of hospital trusts, independent organizations which are in competition with other hospitals, as well as through the distinctions being made between the purchasers and providers of services.

Underpinning all the changes buffeting the NHS are other more subtle pressures. Recent governments have mounted sustained attacks on the established and emerging professions. The power of the professional groups to determine their own conditions of work, their own standards of service and to monopolize their area of competence has not been appreciated by governments which wish to assert the primacy of 'the market'. National pay scales unresponsive to local labour markets and pay scales which do not reward or foster the pursuit of excellence and which do not discriminate between the committed and the lack-lustre, may soon be a thing of the past. For good or perhaps mostly ill, localized pay agreements are increasingly likely to be on the agenda. The financial advantages to the organization which is one of the largest employers in Europe are obvious.

Privatization of much of the care recently undertaken under the umbrella of the NHS has affected the employment position of the professionals. They can now choose between working in the private or the public sector. They have the chance to work in independent care homes for the elderly and in private hospitals. It is a choice, it must be said, which does not appeal to everyone who works in health care. Nevertheless, the choice means variations: in pay, conditions of employment, place of employment, etc.

There have also been attempts to control the professional groups within the health service which have been primarily directed towards reducing autonomy and increasing financial accountability. Professionals are being scrutinized as never before. Whether in the guise of bed occupancy rates, medical audit, operating theatre usage or staffing ratios, the freedom of professionals to determine their own working practices has been reduced.

The benefit to the consumer of the health services has been one of the major claims in the government's rhetoric in defending the changes in the NHS. The benefit to the consumer has hinged on the notion of quality. While the patient's charter may have attracted the mockery of some observers, there has nevertheless been a sea-change in the attitudes and atmosphere in many NHS hospitals. There is a greater willingness to provide information, to reduce waiting times in outpatient departments and for surgery, to treat the patients and their relatives as valued clients rather than as objectified 'cases'. Information is still being withheld from patients, sometimes with good reason for doing so (but often not). Not yet are all patients active participants in decisions regarding their own care but at last the effort is being made.

Nevertheless, as mentioned earlier, simply working with other professionals presents many difficulties. Members of each occupational group have their own distinctive view of the patient. Indeed, that is one of the aspects of being 'professional'. Each group brings different skills and different solutions to the health care problem with which they are presented. In some decisions, the contribution of one occupational group needs to be of primary concern and of incidental interest only in others. Flexibility is needed, therefore, in the decision-making process.

The facts of life must not, however, be ignored. The dominant occupational group in the provision of health care continues to be the medical profession. It is doctors who retain final and legal responsibility for patients. Doctors enjoy undoubted supremacy in the management and direction of the health care team. Without doctors' goodwill to listen, the contributions of other professionals can be marginalized. Interprofessional working, in other words, is a question of the redistribution of power in health care. Other than in the interests of patients there seems little reason why doctors should accede to demands to power-share. Why should one professional group embark on a process of decision-making which reduces its power and makes decision-making a slower and more laborious process? The sometimes strident and resentful demands for equality from members of other occupational groups must strike a harsh note for doctors who are only too aware of the burden of responsibility they have to bear. Why should a dominant profession want to give up its hard-won right to autonomy? The answer is that some members of the medical profession may not want to do so but increasingly will have to do so. Many of the recent changes in the NHS have focused on the activities of doctors.

The medical profession has offered a constant challenge to governments seeking to contain the costs of health care. In answer to that challenge recent governments have introduced concepts such as accountability, efficiency and value-for-money into the vocabulary of the health service. These are not empty concepts but ideas which are in the process of transforming the health service. By replacing professional ideas and ideals of performance with those of the government (and called managerial values), the dominance of professionals has been weakened. Whether professionals have been seen as failing to give value for money or failing to put patients first, the outcome has been the reduction of professional autonomy. Primarily through the initiatives seeking efficiency and effective use of resources, the activities of professionals are now circumscribed.

Another way in which the power of professionals is being eroded is being effected in the management of the NHS. The consensual management of the 1970s and early 1980s, in which the views of various professional groups were heard, has been jettisoned in favour of 'executive' management. Attempts to make the service more 'manageable' have resulted in changes in the management structure, the number of management tiers, the reporting structure, the style of management and the type of manager. Short-term contracts and performance bonuses ensure that a softly-softly approach for today's manager is unworkable.

Specifically this has resulted in the introduction of general management; i.e. non-professionally based management. Seldom are any health professionals to be found in such roles. No longer is management acting to defend a particular corner of the service, but is to view each corner dispassionately and without favour. It is a move which has not enjoyed particular favour within the health service, and has broadly been argued against on the basis of 'what can such a manager know about health care when s/he has never been involved in it?'.

Perhaps more importantly for interprofessional working has been the introduction of the concept of budget-holders. These individuals are responsible for the budget of a unit, a group of wards, suite of theatres, outpatient clinics, etc. These budget-holders have a direct management responsibility for the budget of their patch. Obviously the professional background of each manager may affect their priorities in decision-making. But the budget-holder is solely, not jointly, responsible for meeting a budget target. It is a system of management which by its nature, rather than by the personalities or professional backgrounds of individuals, may create additional strains in interprofessional working relationships.

In the midst of this turbulent environment emerges the movement to stimulate interprofessional cooperation and working: to ensure that those providing health care work as a team. It is a concept enjoying considerable popularity at the moment. Yet curiously it is a concept which runs counter to government policies for the provision of health care. The movement could hardly have emerged at a less auspicious time.

How, for example, can professionals hope to cooperate when accepted working practices, divisions of labour, organizational structures, accountabilities and decision-making are all being subjected to radical change? Yet perhaps because so many fundamental changes are taking place, established and entrenched attitudes can be challenged. This may be the worst yet the best of times to address professional working practices. Under attack from many directions, professionals may find they have more in common than they thought. Only colleagues know the stresses and strains of working in the highly emotional environment of health care. Members of these diverse occupational groups have much in common. Attempts to improve interprofessional collaboration and team-working may well be the antidote to the disorientating changes in the NHS.

Against all odds, attempts at interprofessional working are being made. There are many who refuse to consider it: the old ways of working are hard to change. Collaboration and participation can be frustrating and time-consuming, adding to the burdens of already overstretched staff. But there are those for whom interprofessional and multiprofessional working is an article of faith; they believe the health care they provide can be improved by the active participation of colleagues. After all, interprofessional working is an ideal which essentially seeks to ensure that the best interests of the patient are protected. It is a never-ending process in which the patient, relatives and carers will increasingly have to be involved, making their own contribution to decisions affecting their lives. Interprofessional working is, therefore, only a step on the way to fully informed decision-making in the care of patients.

Interprofessional collaboration requires a willingness to listen and to hear what others are saying. It requires some bravery to stand aside from one's own professional group. It also requires a continuing acknowledgement of the contribution which others have to make. Attempts to foster interprofessional working reflect a maturity of perspective lacking in most areas of enterprise in the late twentieth century.

2 War and peace among the health tribes

Alan Beattie

Recent interest in tribalism in the health professions

Not long after the National Health Service Training Authority was established in the early 1980s, its Chief Executive identified as a priority the need for 'multiprofessional education' across occupational boundaries, observing that 'there is far too much "tribalism" in the NHS for its own good' (Dearden, 1985). In the past decade, this vivid anthropological metaphor can be heard being used more and more frequently by managers and academics (and even professional practitioners themselves) in and around the NHS. In fact it seems to have become a favoured image among many who are faced with the multiple and conflicting specialisms that are to be found in the institutions of the modern state. Becher (1989) has developed a sociological analysis of British higher education establishments in terms of 'tribes and territories'; an American management consultant has offered a comprehensive guide to identifying and resolving 'tribal conflicts' within large organizations (Neuhauser, 1988); and a cultural anthropologist has constructed a framework for dealing with multiple and conflicting viewpoints among what he calls 'the energy tribes' — the numerous expert groups engaged in disputes about nuclear power, its benefits, its hazards and its alternatives (Thompson, 1984). Like these other authors, I find the 'tribes' metaphor intriguing and attractive, and I believe it is worth exploring as a basis for understanding current boundary conflicts and boundary changes in the health field. As in other areas of anthropological inquiry, it can help us to construct a 'critique of institutions and the culture of professionals' (Marcus and Fischer, 1986, p. 154). But we can use it, like other powerful metaphors (as noted by Morgan, 1986), not only to 'read and understand' but also to 'manage and design' the health institutions that we work within.

At the present time, traditional boundaries between occupational groups in health care appear to be under attack as never before.

In central government, there is a growing belief that all skills and roles across all professions in the NHS need to be reviewed. This was clearly signalled by the Department of Health in its White Paper on the reform of the NHS:

> 'There have been many developments in recent years in the better use of nursing staff, but the Government believes that there is still scope for more progress at local level . . . Local managers, in consultation with their professional colleagues, will be expected to re-examine all areas of work to identify the most cost-effective use of professional skills. This may involve a re-appraisal of traditional patterns and practices. Examples include the extended role of nurses to cover specific duties normally undertaken by junior doctors in areas of high technology care and in casualty departments.' (DoH, 1989, p. 15)

Concerns about 'tribalism' have gathered momentum precisely at a time when the political economy of 'education for the health professions' has become much more visible as a result of new management structures and financial constraints in the NHS, in particular the purchaser/provider split and arrangements for the commissioning of 'training' as part of workforce planning (Beattie, 1993a). The demand for newly qualified health professionals is now firmly linked to predicted personnel and skill-mix requirements defined within the workforce plans of health authorities, and within the business plans of NHS management units and trusts. These in turn depend on health care contracts procured in the marketplace which are much affected by current cuts and closures in services. These moves towards the 'mixed economy of welfare' (together with the decline in the size of the labour pool for demographic reasons) are dramatically reducing total student intakes, and putting at risk many of the taken-for-granted areas of specialization in health care — or demanding that students shift (relocate) between different specialisms. Another pressure in this context is the rapid growth of training programmes for health care workers controlled by NCVQ — the National Council for Vocational Qualifications — largely outside the control of the mainstream professions. As a result, the established education schemes for the mainstream health professions are increasingly 'taking their chances' alongside (and competing for business with) other vocational training agencies outside the traditional NHS system. As a recent Discussion Paper from the Royal College of Nursing puts it:

> 'The NCVQ framework has great appeal to managers and politicians faced with increased demands for complex health care services, and seeking measures to contain costs.' (Beattie, 1993a, p. 8)

Within the professions these developments may be seen as not exclusively a managerial or economic matter, but as also a new challenge to the professional imagination. The General Secretary of the Royal College of Nursing (herself a former general manager in the NHS) has argued that interprofessional education 'should be at centre-stage in the debates around NHS reforms', and that it is unfortunate that education has largely been absent from these debates so far, because it is clear that 'the health professions will have to learn to relate to one another in new ways' (Hancock, 1990).

Equally from a consumer viewpoint, the historic boundaries between the health professions seem to be increasingly open to challenge. At the same conference at which Christine Hancock was speaking, Michael, Lord Young — founder of the Consumers' Association, of the College of Health, etc. — asked the question (from the Chair, and 'as a layman . . . an iconoclastic mouse in tiger country'):

> 'Why are there so many professions? Is the growth of professional specialisation inevitable for the rest of human history? Or may the trend be beginning to reverse, and a measure of fusion starting to emerge? Could we perhaps be moving now towards one profession of medicine — a profession of many parts, but one profession?' (Young, 1990)

In what follows I will pursue the 'tribes' metaphor in an attempt to illuminate the ways in which the traditional boundaries between the health professions have arisen, and ways in which they may be redrawn in the not-too-distant future.

Where do tribal boundaries in health care come from?

In the nineteenth century, the medical and nursing professions evolved separately for reasons that were deeply bound up with the class divisions and gender barriers of Victorian Britain (Abel-Smith, 1960; Gamarnikow, 1978; Whittaker and Olesen, 1967); and the boundaries between them reflected prevailing cultural codes surrounding social selectivity, sponsorship and chaperonage. But research by social psychologists, sociologists and social anthropologists since the 1950s has drawn attention also to the profound impact of specialist training schools on the sense of identity and the values of the separate health professions. Most investigations have been carried out on medicine and nursing, and all those who have studied traditional forms of preparation for these health professions recognize that it is a significant 'secondary socialization' experience: it initiates the individual student into new sectors of the social world and into the criteria of 'success' that are distinctive for each sector. Merton, working within a 'functionalist' perspective, identified the significance of medical schools in the transmission of a unique 'culture', in the following terms:

> 'It is their function to transmit the culture of medicine and to advance

that culture. It is their task to shape the novice into the effective practitioner of medicine, to give him the best available knowledge and skills, and to provide him with a professional identity so that he comes to think, act and feel like a physician. It is their problem to enable the medical man to live up to the expectations of the professional role long after he has left the sustaining value-environment provided by the medical school.' (Merton, 1957, p. 7)

Hughes, working within an 'interactionist' perspective, likewise points to the processes by which the social environment of the medical school leads to the acquisition of a distinct occupational culture:

'The education of the members of the medical profession is a set of planned and unplanned experiences by which laymen, usually young and acquainted with the prevailing lay medical culture, become possessed of some part of the technical and scientific medical culture of the professions . . . Medical education becomes the learning of the more complicated reality on all these fronts.' (Hughes, 1956, p. 22)

Davis (and Olesen, 1963, 1968) has described the equivalent (but different) initiation rituals through which schools of nursing encourage the identity changes entailed in the transition into the occupational culture of nursing:

'. . . a transition from a relatively diffuse and open collegiate youth culture to one much more narrowly age-graded and sexually segregated; a transition from a milieu in which the occupational identities of fellow-students are still largely unformed, or at best highly tentative and experimental, to one in which shared activities, round-of-life and student status are articulated almost wholly in terms of membership of a distinct occupational category; a transition from a setting characterised by a diverse multiplicity and overlap of student ties, interests and associations, to one in which there is a single and overruling tie. The tie is that of being a class of occupational novices together, subjected at the same point in time and in near identical sequence to a common set of experiences, pressures and choices . . . a guild-like association of colleague apprentices.' (Davis, 1972, p. 13)

Studies of this sort, within functionalist and interactionist perspectives, yield many socio-anthropological insights into the cultural fabric of specialist professional training schools: the interplay between the affective life and sense of identity of the student and the moral ordering of the school; the central place of ritual and ceremony; the processes of doctrinal conversion and the transmission of institutionally approved imagery and language; the power of hidden or tacit and informal messages alongside the formal educational activities of the school. But, as Atkinson (1983, 1985) has observed, research into socialization processes within educational institutions was pointed in a new direction by the work of Bernstein, which drew on structuralist perspectives to focus on the question of 'boundaries' — how social groupings, or domains of knowledge, are kept apart.

Bernstein's central concern is with how a society 'selects, classifies, distributes, transmits and evaluates the educational knowledge it considers to be public' (Bernstein, 1971, p. 47). One of the most fruitful of his ideas is the distinction between two fundamental types of curriculum, the 'collection code' and the 'integrated code' (Bernstein, 1971). In the collection code, subjects are taught separately, and no criteria are permitted which might allow comparison of different subjects. The only source of unity in such a course of study is the timetable, which specifies an unchallengeable ritual sequence. This perpetuates the absolute purity of separate areas of study — in itself it conveys messages about power and hierarchy, and defines what things shall be kept apart. Numerous studies have indicated the significant effects of adherence to a collection code within traditional professional training schools. In English medical schools, Armstrong (1977, 1980) suggests that strong classification and separation of subjects within preclinical education foster strong subject loyalties and serve to segregate the 'sacred' knowledge of the profession from profane, mundane knowledge. In a series of studies in a Scottish medical school, Atkinson (1977, 1981) shows how segmentation into totally separate specialist areas of knowledge and experience serve to reproduce the distinct professional ideology of medicine. In a medical school in Denmark, Jacobsen (1981) finds that knowledge is arranged in tightly classified units of space and time, perpetuating a hierarchical structure of knowledge and a hierarchical set of social relationships. In an Australian medical school, Colditz and Sheehan (1982) note that basic science subjects (physics, chemistry, zoology) are taught within a strict collection code — although some other subjects (preventive medicine, medical sociology) are less obviously so.

In hospital training schools in Ireland, Treacy (1987a,b) found that a collection code was pervasively established in nursing education. She reported that as a result, students' dominant experience is one of powerlessness, uncertainty and depersonalization, and that they learn to 'get by' through obedience, deference and subservience, through compliance and conformity — she calls this the status of being 'in the pipeline'. In a study of nurse education in Scotland, Melia (1987) identified 'compartmentalization' and 'segmentation' as the principal features of the system. She observes that different segments promote their own version of the nature of nursing work, and have different expectations of the socialization process. Students cope with this by 'fitting in' with whatever is required at the time (Melia, 1987, p. 182); and she notes the tensions that this creates when the nursing 'tribe' (with its own internal differences) comes into contact with other 'tribes':

'. . .when it comes to its dealings with other health care disciplines the group must be able to produce and rely upon a united front . . . the students learn not to expose the differences as they pass between segments during their training — instead they "fit in" and move on.' (Melia, 1987, p. 183)

A historical account by Jolley (1987) concludes that:

'. . . the curriculum in nurse education . . . was up to the early 1960s, a subject-centred curriculum based on a medical model [which] closely approximated to Bernstein's collection-type curriculum with separate subjects clearly bounded and insulated from each other. Classification, the degree of boundary maintenance between subjects was strong . . .' (Jolley, 1987, p. 10)

So in the light of Bernstein's 'structuralist anthropology of education', we can see that specialist training schools for the health professions — like many state and private schools, particularly boarding schools (Kapferer, 1981; Donald, 1985; Hargreaves, 1977), and like teacher training colleges (Walker, 1983) — have been able to exert a powerful controlling influence over the consciousness, language, values and sense of identity of their students. It is in these segregated seminaries, and in the everyday rituals of learning through which they create separate and distinctive ways of thinking and ways of relating, that the 'tribalism' in health care is originated and perpetuated anew in every cohort and generation of student professionals. Adapting Becher's analysis of 'tribes and territories' in higher education (Becher, 1989, 1990), we can characterize the traditional pattern of medical school training as one dominated by 'partition', associated with the development of high social distance, and cosmopolitan loyalties; while the traditional pattern of training in schools of nursing has been one dominated by 'patronage', associated with a strong focus on task completion ('getting through the work') and local loyalties.

Could the boundaries between health professions be redrawn?

The opposite type of curriculum which Bernstein (1971) identified has a very different set of characteristics and social consequences. In the integrated code, the emphasis is not on the autonomy and separation of subjects, but on the active connections between them. The purity rule is rejected, and the governing principle here is 'things shall be put together' — in the interests of 'relevance' and the capacity of a programme to justify itself to others. Knowledge is organized in themes and the timetable is structured to support the exploration of such themes. The boundaries between areas of study are seen as entirely provisional and can be suppressed or dismantled; and new, flexible combinations can be devised. Bernstein further suggests that the two types of curriculum bear a cyclical relationship to each other, such that when an integrated curriculum is in place, there may be a progressive redefinition of boundaries, to reconstitute a collection curriculum. In turn, when a collection curriculum is in the ascendancy, a progressive collapse of boundaries may again produce an integrated curriculum, and so on (although it should be emphasized that this is a recursive 'spiral', not a closed loop: when boundaries are re-established, they are in a different place). This is illustrated in Fig. 2.1.

The integrated code is always seen as a bearer of 'dangerous knowledge' (Johnston, 1978) by those who are firmly located within the collection code, because impure, weakly classified learning, with a variety of open options and combinations, offers the threat of transgressing familiar social and moral boundaries. It is likely to be the focus of complaint and resistance. Indeed, the collapse of boundaries and the shift to an integrated code is the way in which — if they can survive the attacks of 'traditionalists' — new subjects or disciplines may begin to emerge and may make it to becoming a 'proper subject' in their own right, as in such examples as microbiology (Jamous and Peloille, 1970); biochemistry; environmental studies (Goodson, 1981, 1983). The emergence of just such integrated curriculum codes in the field of health studies is (I suggest) a powerful force for transcending the tribalism of the health professions.

Indeed, amidst the turmoil of political change in the delivery of public services in Britain in the past decade, it has perhaps been easy to overlook the fact that within the higher education system, the conditions have been put in place which do make possible a radical challenge to traditional professional boundaries in health care. A major influence has been the 'Project 2000' reforms in the initial

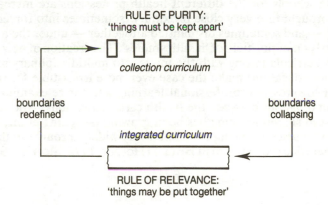

Fig. 2.1 The curriculum cycle

preparation of nurses, which although first and foremost concerned with putting a 'new division of labour' in nursing care firmly on the agenda, were clearly seen also by the UKCC to have far-reaching longer-term implications for professional boundaries beyond nursing:

> 'New ideas and new structures could in the long term mean that the CFPs (common foundation programmes) pioneered for nursing, midwifery and health visiting could form the basis for a common foundation for shared learning with other health workers. This could be a step on the road to common foundation programmes for all health workers and to health manpower development along the lines envisaged by the WHO.' (UKCC, 1986, p. 47)

Other features of the Project 2000 reforms — such as the wholesale incorporation of hospital-attached schools of nursing and midwifery into mainstream higher education, student status during initial preparation, and the coupling of professional registration to an academic Diploma award — all underline the fact that a decisive shift has occurred in education for the health professions. We can now take it for granted that new physiotherapists, occupational therapists, radiographers, dietitians and other 'professions supplementary to medicine' will have been educated to degree level, and that new nurses will have been educated at least to Diploma level and increasingly also to degree level. Moreover, with the unification of the higher education system, all of these professions now receive academic awards from the university sector, so that the previous and longstanding state of affairs, in which the health professions encompassed between them an absurdly heterogeneous and disparate collection of academic qualifications, is vanishing very fast indeed. The situation now is that initial qualifying courses for all the health professions require study for university awards, and with concurrent changes in departmental boundaries within higher education institutions, the erstwhile separate training schools for the different health professions are increasingly being brought into very close proximity (sometimes into forced marriages) — and sometimes dismantled altogether — under the aegis of the newly emerging field of 'health studies'. The creation of new health studies curricula (along with the move into multidisciplinary settings in higher education) make the case ever more irresistible for shifting further towards interprofessional learning and for re-examining the division of labour between the health care occupations. And indeed, interest in shared learning has been growing fast (Ling et al., 1990), and new courses are being developed very widely throughout the professional education system in Britain (Horder, 1992; Storrie, 1992).

What might new boundaries between health professions look like?

Studies in the structuralist anthropology of education show us that transformations in the structuring of educational knowledge can be expected to be strongly linked to changes in cultural values and social arrangements. In this light, the recent growth of interprofessional health studies can be seen as part of a far-reaching shakeup of the belief systems that underlie the traditional division of labour in health. Elsewhere (Beattie, 1991, 1993b) I have argued that it has been possible for some time now to envisage a realignment of the boundaries of health work, in terms of four contrasting models of 'practice paradigms':

- *The biotechnological model of health*, which focuses on 'mechanical defects' in the individual human being, and sets out to rectify these in the light of the biomedical sciences and technologies.
- *The biographical model of health*, which focuses on troublesome life events that are personally significant for the individual, and aims to help the person develop strategies for coping with these.
- *The ecological model of health*, in which the concern is with the risks and hazards of human environments, and which seeks social intervention to reduce risks and protect the vulnerable.
- *The communitarian model of health,* in which social groups and social movements mobilize to share their health concerns and which engage in cooperative advocacy and campaigning for change.

A number of colleagues and myself have documented some of the role conflicts and dilemmas that are created by the push and pull around these poles of strategic thinking about intervention in health — in studies of the work of family planning nurses (Beattie and Durguerian, 1980; Durguerian, 1982), of general nurses (Keyzer, 1985, 1986, 1988), and of health visitors (Twinn, 1989). Similar contrasts at the 'extremes of patient work' — between high technology care and psychosocial care — have been noted by Melia (1987). And — quite independently — Aroskar (1982) has identified a not dissimilar scheme of four alternative and conflicting 'mind-sets' in nursing: 'health care as medical cases'; 'health care as the patient's right to relief from pain'; 'health care as a commodity requiring administration'; and 'health care as the promotion of wellbeing in a cooperative community'.

From the point of view of structural anthropology, each of the different models of health can be seen as a manifestation of a different form of 'cultural bias' (see Douglas, 1970, 1978, 1982, 1986) or a distinct 'cultural mandate' (Crawford, 1984). Each of the four different approaches to health employs a distinct 'explanatory framework', each finds its justification in a different set of institutional values and social interests, and within each 'paradigm of practice' social relationships are structured in a distinctive way (Beattie, 1993b). And each of the four health belief systems identified here may find favour in different factions or subgroups among the health occupations — in ways that run completely across the traditional 'tribal boundaries' between the mainstream professions — as can be seen currently in the case of health promotion (Beattie, 1991). In these circumstances, the opportunities are growing for different health workers to come together — to learn together and/or to work together — on tasks or projects within the terms of a particular health model precisely because they share a commitment to the same 'cultural mandate'. I am inclined to think that these developments may prefigure a completely different ordering of the division of labour, where common ground between erstwhile separate professions will become more significant than traditional differences. In this scenario, common ground would be defined in terms of shared definitions of priority needs and tasks, and shared definitions of clients and targets; while roles and standards of good practice would be defined and agreed on the basis of the simple question: who does what best in this particular health project or programme?

Towards a new republic of health

As new areas of interprofessional and multidisciplinary research and new subject combinations arise within health studies in universities, they will be able to stimulate and ratify the emergence of entirely new coalitions and ways of working in practice settings. Thompson (1976, 1979) offers an insight into the dynamics of situations of rapid and potentially radical change such as this, which suggests a highly plausible scenario for the future of interprofessional health studies. This predicts that (of course) individuals and official bodies who remain loyal to the traditional tribal boundaries will join together and seek common cause to oppose the redrawing of boundaries. For instance, referees for research proposals or research papers are often themselves likely to be firmly located within traditional discipline boundaries; course validation procedures may be linked to traditional professional bodies. Thus, certain projects may be approved because they fit in with traditional 'tribal' interests, while other projects (those that challenge the dominant boundaries) may be disapproved of, being castigated and rubbished as disruptive or 'unrealistic'. So we can expect that attempts to bring the tribes together and to define new maps of the territory will generate discomfort and resistance, and will encounter serious criticism and opposition.

So the future which faces interprofessional education in health will be turbulent and problematic. Values and power relations are very different in each camp, emotional investment is high, and therefore interpersonal conflicts and troubles are extremely likely (Zeeman, 1979). As a result, one aspect of any serious efforts at sustained interprofessional education that will undoubtedly need the utmost care and attention is the psychodynamics of personal stress and anxiety (Beattie, 1993c; Woodhouse and Pengelly, 1991). For those involved to a substantial degree in interprofessional initiatives, action at this 'micro' level — to provide personal and emotional support — will be imperative.

But the very possibility of making a transition from traditional tribal boundaries in health to a different division of labour, will itself depend on action also at a 'macro' level. If the traditional classes and castes of the health professions are to be replaced by new health cadres and health teams, a great deal of energy and imagination will need to go into the design of new managerial systems to support them. Such new structures might be along the lines of the 'adhocratic' organization which Hales (1993) argues is superior to traditional professional specialization as a way of overcoming the rigidities of bureaucracies, and of achieving flexibility and creativity in organizations:

> 'In essence, adhocratic organisation involves the pursuit of innovation, problem-solving and responsiveness to situational demands through the creation of a loose federation of temporary work units, or teams, in which technical expertise and creativity are given free rein. The system rests upon . . . a fluid division of labour, based on situational expertise [which] is a way of deploying experts which reconciles the particular, bounded nature of technical expertise with complex, unpredictable and open-ended work. The basic unit is the task force or project team, constituted on an *ad hoc*, fluid and temporary basis. Teams form to deal with a particular task . . .' (Hales, 1993, p. 165)

If such managerial arrangements could be developed on a substantial scale we might move rapidly towards the kind of 'decentralized democratic occupational politics' that is envisaged by several recent commentators on the place of the professions in the modern state in western countries (Collins, 1979; 1990, pp. 16–17). Beyond this turning point we might see a form of organization of health work that could dispel the doubts that legitimately arise about calls for multiprofessional collaboration, for example:

'. . .without changes in existing forms of power, the prospect of greater unity amongst caring professions could have negative implications'. (Hugman, 1991, p. 222)

Such new arrangements might meet the challenge to the professions (Murphy, 1990) that has been posed frequently in the literature of social administration for over a decade:

> 'The relationship between the professions and the public should be seen as one of partnership — partnership with clients, partnership with society, and partnership with other professionals.' (Wilding, 1981)

> 'Professionals are today on the defensive — their heyday has passed. People in such a position do not react positively to proposals that they further share their power. [But] the advancement of the interests of public service professionals can imply the enhancement of public services. Alliances between professionals and the public to defend services provide a good basis for the development of the partnerships advocated by Wilding.' (Hill, 1982)

The ideas I have presented here are an attempt at what Morgan (1986) calls 'imaginization' — using metaphor deliberately and systematically to read, rewrite and redesign social arrangements. The picture of the territory of health that I have sketched here has many features in common with other visions of 'post-Fordist' and 'post-modernist' society — it acknowledges that health is and will remain a vigorously 'contested concept', that there will continue to be a plurality of competing views and values related to health, and that complexity and contradiction will be a constant challenge to all efforts at organizational development and social planning for health. Redrawing the traditional boundaries between the health professions will (I suggest) move us towards a new 'republic of health':

> '. . . the republican ideal is of a separation of powers where each source of power is strong — rejecting the notion that the power of one might be accomplished by the weakening of the others.' (Braithwaite, 1993, p. 5)

Acknowledgements

I should like to thank colleagues who provided me with useful references during the preparation of this chapter: David Brunton, Frank Ledwith and Keith Soothill.

References

Abel-Smith B (1960) *A History of the Nursing Profession*. London: Heinemann.

Armstrong D (1977) The structure of medical education. *Medical Education*; **11**: 244–248.

Armstrong D (1980) Health care and the structure of medical education. In: Noack H (Ed.), *Medical Education and Primary Health Care*. London: Croom Helm.

Aroskar MA (1982) Are nurses' mind-sets compatible with ethical practice? *Topics in Clinical Nursing*; **4**: 22–32.

Atkinson P (1977) Professional segmentation and students' experience in a Scottish medical school. *Scottish Journal of Sociology*; **2**: 71–85.

Atkinson P (1981) Bernstein's structuralism. *Educational Analysis*; **3**: 85–96.

Atkinson P (1983) The reproduction of professional community. In: Dingwall R, Lewis P (Eds), *The Sociology of the Professions: Doctors, Lawyers and Others*. London: Macmillan.

Atkinson P (1985) *Language, Structure and Reproduction*. London: Methuen.

Beattie A (1990) *New Initiatives in Education for Teamwork in Primary Health and Community Care*. London: Centre for the Advancement of Interprofessional Education, LSE (newsletter 2).

Beattie A (1991) Knowledge and control in health promotion: a test case for social policy and social theory. In: Gabe J, Calnan M, Bury M (Eds), *The Sociology of the Health Service*. London: Routledge.

Beattie A (1993a) *Teaching in a Different World: Frameworks for the Future Preparation of Teachers of Nurses, Midwives and Health Visitors*. London: Royal College of Nursing (discussion paper).

Beattie A (1993b) The changing boundaries of health. In: Beattie A, Gott M, Jones L, Sidell M (Eds), *Health and Wellbeing: a Reader*. London: Macmillan.

Beattie A (1993c) Healthy alliances or dangerous liaisons? The challenge of working together in health promotion. In: Leathard A (Ed.), *Going Interprofessional: Working Together for Health and Welfare*. London: Routledge.

Beattie A, Durguerian S (1980) *Occupations, Organisations and Ideologies in Family Planning: A Case Study in the Sociology of Knowledge*. London: DHSS (research report).

Becher T (1989) *Academic Tribes and Territories*. Milton Keynes: SRHE/Open University Press.

Becher T (1990) Professional education in a comparative context. In: Torstendahl R, Burrage M (Eds), *The Formation of the Professions: Knowledge, State and Strategy*. London: Sage.

Bernstein B (1971) *Class, Codes and Control, Vol 1*. London: Routledge.

Braithwaite J (1993) Criminalization, decriminalization and republican theory. Plenary Paper, 11th International Congress on Criminology, Budapest, 1993.

Colditz GA, Sheehan M (1982) The impact of instructional style on the development of professional characteristics. *Medical Education*; **16**: 127–132.

Collins R (1979) *The Credential Society: An Historical Sociology of Education and Stratification*. London: Academic Press.

Collins R (1990) Changing conceptions in the sociology of the professions. In: Torstendahl R, Burrage M (Eds), *The Formation of the Professions, State and Strategy*. London: Sage.

Crawford R (1984) A cultural account of health: control, release, and the social body. In: McKinlay JB (Ed.), *Issues in the Political Economy of Health Care*. London: Tavistock.

Davis F, Olesen VL (1963) Initiation into a women's profession. *Sociometry*; **26**: 89–101.

Davis F (1968) Professional socialization as subjective experience: the process of doctrinal conversion among student nurses. In: Becker HS (Ed.), *Institutions and the Person*. Chicago: Aldine.

Davis F (1972) *Illness, Interaction and the Self*. Belmont, Calif: Wadsworth.

Dearden B (1985) *Annual Report of the National Health Service Training Authority*. Bristol: NHSTA.

DoH (1989) *Working for Patients*. London: HMSO.

Donald J (1985) Beacons of the future: schooling, subjection and subjectification. In: Beechey V, Donald J. *Subjectivity and Social Relations*. Milton Keynes: Open University Press.

Douglas M (1970) *Natural Symbols: Explorations in Cosmology*. Harmondsworth: Penguin.

Douglas M (1978) *Cultural Bias*. London: Royal Anthropological Institute (Occasional Paper 35).

Douglas M (Ed.) *Essays in the Sociology of Perception*. London: Routledge.

Douglas M (1986) *How Institutions Think*. London: Routledge.

Durguerian S (1982) *A Study of the Role and Training of Family Planning Nurses*. PhD thesis, University of London Institute of Education.

Gamarnikow E (1978) Sexual division of labour: the case of nursing. In: Kuhn A, Wolpe AM (Eds), *Feminism and Materialism*. London: Routledge.

Goodson I (1981) Becoming an academic subject: patterns of explanation and evolution. *British Journal of Sociology of Education*; **2**: 163–180.

Goodson I (1983) Defining and defending the subject: geography versus environmental studies. In: Hammersley M, Hargreaves A (Eds), *Curriculum Practice: Some Sociological Case Studies*. Lewes: Falmer.

Hales C (1993) *Management through Organisation*. London: Routledge.

Hancock C (1990) Education for teamwork. In: Beattie A (Ed.), 1990, *op cit*.

Hargreaves D (1977) Power and the paracurriculum. In: Richards C (Ed.), *Power and the Curriculum*. Driffield: Nafferton.

Hill M (1982) Professions in community care. In : Walker A (Ed.), *Community Care: the Family, the State and Social Policy*. Oxford: Blackwell/Robertson.

Horder J (1992) A national survey that needs to be repeated. *Journal of Interprofessional Care*; **6**: 73–74.

Hughes E (1956) The making of a physician. *Human Organization*; winter: 21–25.

Hugman R (1991) *Power in Caring Professions*. London: Macmillan.

Jacobsen B (1981) Collection-type and integrated-type curricula in systems of higher education: an empirical and theoretical study. *Acta Sociologica*; **24**: 25–41.

Jamous H, Peloille B (1970) Changes in the French university hospital system. In: Jackson JA (Ed.), *Professions and Professionalization*. Cambridge: Cambridge University Press.

Johnston K (1978) Dangerous knowledge: a case study in the social control of knowledge. *Australian and New Zealand Journal of Sociology*; **14**: 104–112.

Jolley M (1987) The weight of tradition. In: Allan P, Jolley M (Eds), *The Curriculum in Nursing Education*. London: Routledge.

Kapferer J (1981) Socialization and the symbolic order of the school. *Anthropology and Education Quarterly*; **12**: 258–274.

Keyzer D (1985) *Learning Contracts, the Trained Nurse, and the Implementation of the Nursing Process: Comparative Case Studies in the Management of Knowledge and Change in Nursing Practice*. PhD thesis, University of London Institute of Education.

Keyzer D (1986) Concepts of care: a way of life. *Nursing Practice*; **1**: 190–195.

Keyzer D (1988) Challenging role boundaries: conceptual frameworks for understanding the conflict arising from the implementation of the nursing process in practice. In: White R (Ed.), *Political Issues in Nursing, Vol 3*. London: John Wiley.

Ling J, Funnell P, Gill J (1990) Shared learning. *Nursing Times*; **86**: 65–66.

Marcus GE, Fischer MMJ (1986) *Anthropology as Cultural Critique: An Experimental Moment in the Human Sciences*. Chicago: University of Chicago Press.

Melia KM (1987) *Learning and Working: The Occupational Socialization of Nurses*. London: Tavistock.

Merton RK (1957) Some preliminaries to a sociology of medical education. In: Merton RK, Reader G, Kendall PL (Eds), *The Student Physician*. Cambridge, Mass: Harvard University Press.

Morgan G (1986) *Images of Organization*. London: Sage.

Murphy R (1990) Proletarianization or bureaucratization: the fall of the professional? In: Torstendahl R, Burrage M (Eds), *The Formation of the Professions: Knowledge, State and Strategy*. London: Sage.

Neuhauser P (1988) Tribal thinking patterns. In: *Tribal Warfare in Organizations*. Cambridge, Mass: Ballinger.

Storrie J (1992) Mastering interprofessionalism — an enquiry into the development of masters programmes with an interprofessional focus. *Journal of Interprofessional Care*; **6**: 253–259.

Thompson M (1976) Class, caste, the curriculum cycle and the cusp catastrophe. *Studies in Higher Education*; **1**: 31–46.

Thompson M (1979) The geometry of credibility. In: *Rubbish Theory*. Oxford: Oxford University Press.

Thompson M (1984) Among the energy tribes: a cultural framework for the analysis and design of energy policy. *Policy Sciences*; **17**: 321–329.

Treacy MP (1987a) Some aspects of the hidden curriculum. In: Allan P, Jolley M (Eds), *The Curriculum in Nursing Education*. London: Routledge.

Treacy M (1987b) *'In the Pipeline': A Qualitative Study of General Nurse Training with Special Reference to Nurses' Role in Health Education*. PhD thesis, University of London Institute of Education.

Twinn S (1989) *Change and Conflict in Health Visiting Practice*. PhD thesis, University of London Institute of Education.

UKCC (1986) *Project 2000: New Preparation for Practice*. London: UKCC.

Walker M (1983) Control and consciousness in the college. *British Educational Research Journal*; **9**: 129–140.

Whittaker E, Olesen VL (1967) Why Florence Nightingale? *American Journal of Nursing*; **67**: 2338–2341.

Wilding P (1981) *Socialism and the Professions*. London: Fabian Society (Fabian Tract 473).

Woodhouse D, Pengelly P (1991) *Anxiety and the Dynamics of Collaboration*. Aberdeen: Aberdeen University Press.

Young M (1990) Partnership and the professions (Chairman's closing remarks). In: Beattie A (Ed.), 1990, *op cit*.

Zeeman EC (1979) A geometrical model of ideologies. In: Renfrew C, Cooke KL (Eds), *Transformations: Mathematical Approaches to Culture Change*. London: Academic Press.

Part B

Part B

The Reality of Current Interprofessional Working

Exploring the reality of current interprofessional working is complex, for there are many sites and situations where one could focus upon the effectiveness — or otherwise — of interprofessional relationships. However, with the implementation in 1993 of the National Health Service and Community Care Act 1990, collaboration between professionals and between service agencies has come right to the fore. The development of community care in the United Kingdom provides a new and crucial context in which the reality of a policy of collaborative working can be considered. Indeed, collaboration between professionals and service agencies is the linchpin of the whole enterprise. This development is particularly fascinating for it provides the context in which health and social care mixes have been and are continuing to develop.

Hugman focuses specifically on the ways in which various occupational groups have defined and responded to interprofessional boundaries between health and social care. In fact, Hugman suggests that the new community care policies present a challenge to health and social care professions to develop fresh ways of defining their skills, knowledge and values around the newly defined tasks of purchasing and providing rather than around their formal professional identities.

Chapman, Hugman and Williams begin to provide the empirical evidence which is so desperately needed to consider the problems and possibilities of effective collaborative working. The will to make collaboration in community care a reality is identified as a necessary first step, but their example demonstrates how the structures can move into place to enable a shift from an emphasis on individual agency responsibility to that of taking joint responsibility for community care. The possibilities at the local level are clearly shown and the authors rhetorically ask whether central government can focus its own social policy to act as a supportive partner in the collaborative effort.

While Chapman, Hugman and Williams tend to focus on the importance of the introduction of appropriate structures, Cole and Perides — both managers in the field — stress the emerging conflict between the professional culture and the organizational culture. They stress the enormous emerging pressures on first-line staff and the consequent responsibility of senior managers to recognize and understand the impact of changes upon their staff. New demands upon managers mean the development of new skills.

Carpenter focuses on the *Caring for People* Joint Training Project set up in June 1990 with the objective of identifying the organizational requirements and training needs for the implementation of the community care reforms. There are many lessons which can be learned about interagency collaboration from this series of pilot projects, but Carpenter warns that it is as yet by no means clear whether many health authorities and local authorities are willing to make a commitment to the kind of interagency working piloted in the series of initiatives which he describes. The actual outcome will become clearer with the passage of time but, most importantly, Carpenter is beginning to demonstrate that success is potentially achievable.

The analysis of the impact on managers of changes in health and social care which Cole and Perides consider more generally and which Carpenter relates more specifically to the development of community care is taken a stage further by Lorbiecki in considering clinical work. She notes how clinicians have been encouraged to become more actively involved in the management of their hospital units as a means of implementing the recent NHS reforms. Interestingly, she considers whether this produces a convergence or collision of interests in the perspectives of the medical profession and managers. Furthermore, because clinical management includes a devolution of managerial responsibility, the *collision* of interests which has traditionally been an issue between clinicians and managers may also become a source of inbuilt tension between clinical directors and their consultant colleagues.

Finally, Harding and Taylor remind us that the efficient delivery of health services to the public relies on cooperation between members of the health care team. While the concept of an integrated health centre was first formulated in the Dawson Report of 1920, only in recent years has there been a steady increase in the number of health centres having integral pharmacies. However, very little is known of the impact that inclusion of a pharmacy in a health centre has on the interprofessional relations between pharmacist and general practitioners. Harding and Taylor suggest that against a historical backcloth of antipathy between medical and pharmaceutical professions, health centre pharmacists have been pioneers in establishing bridges between the professions — especially in establishing good working relationships. But they also stress that much work remains to be done, particularly in a restructured health service.

3 Contested territory and community services: Interprofessional boundaries in health and social care

Richard Hugman

Introduction

With the implementation in 1993 of the National Health Service and Community Care Act 1990, much attention has been paid to the working relationships between the various agencies involved in service provision. Indeed, that issue is of vital importance and is addressed in Chapters 4 and 6 of this volume. However, the relationships between the different professional groups involved also are crucial to the outcome of these policy developments. In Chapter 2, Beattie explores professionalism using an analytic framework derived from social anthropology. In this chapter I want to concentrate on the more concrete ways in which various occupational groups have defined and responded to interprofessional boundaries between health and social care, placing the claims made by each group on the basis of their occupational skills and knowledge within the organizational and policy contexts of community care.

The discussion will focus on two examples of the areas in which health and social care mixes have been and are continuing to develop. The first is that of services for older people as the predominant users of home-based care services, a phenomenon evident both in the UK and across the European Community (Jamieson, 1990; Anderson, 1992). The other example is that of child care which provides a point of comparison as a major arena of welfare state services (Fox Harding, 1991; Parton, 1991). These service areas are both integral parts of the development of the welfare state since 1948, although I will argue that they represent two somewhat different patterns in the contested boundaries between health and social care, and demonstrate different potential for interprofessional working. Issues in services for younger people with disabilities, for people with learning difficulties and for people with mental health needs also are relevant (Grant, 1986; Robinson, 1989; Sheppard, 1991), but will not be considered in detail although some parallels will be drawn briefly.

Professionalism as demarcation

This chapter takes as its starting point the contested nature both of the nature of professions (their skills, knowledge and values) and of the object of their interventions (the areas of life in which they intervene).

The boundaries between professional groups are developed and maintained through claims to competence in dealing with specific problems, and in this process differences rather than similarities tend to be stressed (Johnson, 1972; Parkin, 1979; Hugman, 1991). For analytic purposes such distinctions may be very helpful, and for managers and practitioners it is necessary to set clear boundaries so that responsibilities are explicit. Yet, through the process of professionalizing, occupational groups who may share much in common or who may complement the skills and knowledge exercised by each other are separated rather than united. This may at times lead to debates at the level of individual practice about questions such as whether assisting someone who requires help to have a bath is a health or social care task. The current jocular answer to this, based on whether disinfectant or bubble-bath oil is added to the water, obscures the practical reasoning about such a demarcation, which is that the context of a practice will create a logic for the division of labour that is only partly related to the nature of the occupational groups concerned. In other words, a bath may be a health or social service depending on whether it is provided at home or in an institution, on which agency has key responsibility for the individual person, and on the availability of local resources, at least as much as on the skill content of the qualification held by the person providing the bathing service.

So, first I will examine in more detail some particular boundary issues between health and social care professions as these have developed during the period of the National Health Service in the UK (that is, post-1948). I will then focus on contemporary questions raised by the implementation of the community care legislation (and the responses of professionals and their employing agencies to these) and aspects of the division of labour in child protection. In conclusion I will explore some possibilities for the reshaping of professional boundaries and the constructive use of overlap between different occupational groups.

The background of boundary disputes

Contemporary disputes over the boundaries between health and social care have their origins in the organizational divisions of the early NHS and local government in the immediate post-war period of the late 1940s and 50s. However, these were not simply representative of the divide between health on the one hand and social services on the other. At that time the NHS employed medical and psychiatric social workers while the Health and Welfare Departments of the local authorities were headed by the Medical Officer of Health and included district nurses, along with other health professionals, as well as social workers and other social care staff (Younghusband, 1978; Land, 1991).

More distinct from the vantage point of history was a legislative and policy divide in the creation and expansion of a range of services. Looking back, the National Health Act 1946 and the National Assistance Act 1948 can be regarded as operating in parallel in shaping what I would like to term the 'first generation' welfare state organizations, with the former providing the framework for what in the 'second generation' was to become the domain of health professionals and the latter the territory of social care. One example of this is to be seen in the allocation of responsibility for residential services for adults in need to the local authorities (in Part III of the National Assistance Act), at the same time as some former Poor Law facilities were handed to the health services to become geriatric hospitals. Although both came under the aegis of doctors, as medical superintendents and medical officers of health, the local authority services were from the outset perceived primarily as a social care rather than a nursing resource, even though nurses were employed in large numbers as officers-in-charge of residential homes. Between these two pieces of legislation therefore was seeded the divide which in more recent years has grown into the separation of nursing homes from social care homes in both the popular and professional consciousness.

In the arena of child care, a clear split between health and social professionals can be seen in the boundaries which came to separate child care officers from health visitors (Younghusband, 1978; Dingwall, 1980). Child care officers focused on instances of particular difficulty while health visitors were concerned with the general population of young children as a whole. This emphasis set the scene for social work to be defined as the lead profession in child protection work. As with services for adults, in the 'first generation' of welfare state organizations the structural foundations for the separation of health and social services for children were already in place.

The point at which the various strands of development were brought together can be seen in the major reorganizations of the early 1970s. Beginning with the unification of social work and the creation of Social Services Departments (1968 in Scotland where the term Social Work

Departments is used, and 1971 elsewhere), this process was completed in 1974 with the restructuring of local authorities and the reorganization of the NHS. Out of this series of changes a full separation between health and social services was wrought. For example, all hospital social workers were now employed by the local authority, medical officers of health lost their management responsibilities for home help and related services and became (for the most part) community physicians, while any community nursing staff employed by the local authority were transferred to the NHS. The divisions begun some 25 years earlier had been completed, in what I am identifying as the 'second generation' of welfare state health and social services organization.

Organization pressures and problems

Notwithstanding this bifurcation in early development, both the health and social services agencies have continued to face many common problems of organization. Indeed, at their point of origin the 'second generation' agencies, though outwardly very different, were often modelled on similar concepts, drawing on the same body of research (Rowbottom et al., 1973, 1974). A major element of these conceptual concerns was to delineate the areas of capacity of each occupational group in relation to others so that the 'best fit' might be achieved. That this approach might have been overly technical is a pertinent criticism, because often it appeared to ignore the contested nature of professional claims to 'capacity', namely that public acceptance of ability to take autonomous responsibility for specified tasks is not self-evident but the outcome of claims by occupational groups (Wilding, 1982; Hugman, 1991). However, it did begin to address the problems of the relationship between health and social services agencies and to identify the necessity for dialogue. Unintentionally (perhaps) this mechanistic analysis of organization pointed to the arbitrariness of such divisions by highlighting the continuing significance of the question of communication and the need for professions to work together despite their designation as either 'health' or 'social'. For example, in situations of discharge from a geriatric ward, admission to residential care from the community of an elderly person, or investigations into suspected child abuse, the liaison between doctors, nurses, health visitors, social workers and others were and continue to be of vital importance (Marshall, 1990; Fox Harding, 1991).

Following two reports by Griffiths (1983, 1988), several policy documents (DoH, 1989a, 1991a,b) and legislation (NHS and Community Care Act, 1990), we are now in the era of what may be termed the 'third generation' of health and social services organizations. This has been developed out of a concern not so much to find the best technical organization of professionals, but rather of the most efficient, effective and economic ways of managing them to produce health and social services both in institutions and in the community (Audit Commission, 1986; Cousins, 1987; Klein, 1989; Pollitt, 1993). Indeed, one of the most profound characteristics of NHS 'third generation' organization is to subsume professional action under the management process rather than seeing management as administration to support professionals (Cousins, 1987; Strong and Robinson, 1990; Dent, 1993). In some senses this is less of a dramatic change for Social Services Departments, where management since 1974 has been hierarchically superordinate to professional practice; but even in this context there is a qualitative shift as management, previously recruited mostly from social work, increasingly is defined as a separate occupational grouping with its own skills, knowledge and values (Bamford, 1990). On both sides of this divide there are indications that a compromise around the defence of the technical control of work by professionals in return for acceptance to the broader resource control by managers may be emerging (Klein, 1989; Bamford, 1990; Hugman, 1991).

In these conditions the boundaries between health and social care professionals may become increasingly important both for practitioners and for managers. Practitioners may be expected to wish to maintain their hold over work which has high professional status (however this is defined) while managers will be seeking to limit the responsibility of their own services to those which ensure an efficient, effective and economic return on resource use. As interprofessional work is less easy to control, because of potentially divided loyalties (Grant, 1986), these arenas appear to be a potential location of contest as new spheres of influence and authority become established. The image of a debate over the definition of a bath as a health or social service ceases to be quite so ephemeral and becomes more obviously a microcosm of wider issues in which costs as well as skills, knowledge or values play a part.

Conflict or cooperation in the contemporary context?

In order to explore this potential in more detail I want to return to the two issues of community care for elderly people and interventions in child welfare as major areas of work for both health and social services. I will examine each and indicate some general issues arising from them before proceeding to look at the possibilities of interprofessional boundaries shifting in response to the new policy and organizational pressures.

Elderly people

Under the NHS and Community Care Act 1990, the key responsibility for the assessment of need for elderly people and their carers (as for all adults in need of assistance in ordinary living) has been placed on the local authorities (s. 47). However, the legislation does not specify *how* need is to be assessed or *by whom* (Wilson, 1993). These issues have been elaborated in the guidance published by the Department of Health, developing a particular interpretation of the idea of 'care management' in which needs are identified and then a 'package of care' is purchased and monitored (DoH, 1991a,b). The particularity of this interpretation is that the assessment and organization of services is separated from their provision in a much sharper way than in the earlier experiments with 'case management' (Challis et al., 1990; Huxley, 1992; Wilson, 1993). In other models the case manager both assessed and arranged a package of care but at the same time might continue to provide some direct service input beyond the monitoring now envisaged by the DoH.

What of the specific role which may be required in the new order of community care? The practice within the new role of the care manager may be summarized as a list of tasks (Lawson et al., 1991):

- case finding (the identification of people in need of assessment);
- assessment of need and capacity (jointly with the service user and informal carers);
- care planning (jointly with the service user and appropriate colleagues, including the management of devolved budgets);
- provision of a care package (including purchase of service and coordination with informal care);
- monitoring and reviewing (with all interested parties, especially the service user);
- case closure.

Some of these tasks require skills to which a variety of claims are made by health and social care professions as they now perceive themselves (Challis et al., 1990; Dant and Gearing, 1990; Wilson, 1993). These include assessment of need, coordination between services and monitoring. However, as Wilson's research demonstrates, the practice of these skills tends to be directed towards the primary professional group and the defence of existing career paths rather than towards the emerging interprofessional group (1993, pp. 115–6). This is buttressed by the separate organizational hierarchies to which each group is accountable. I will return to this point below.

Following the application of the DoH guidance (1991a), Social Services Departments have been seeking ways to distinguish between the 'purchasing' and 'providing' functions and to allocate these to designated professional staff. In practice there is a national variation (see, for example, Carpenter et al., 1991) but the underlying principle is the same: the future for all professional work lies on one side or other of the purchaser/provider divide (Allen, 1992).

For the purposes of this discussion, the main implication of the purchaser/provider split will be in the relationships between different professional groups, especially home care organizers, nurses, occupational therapists and social workers. Much of this will hinge on the perceptions of the relative skills each group is able to exercise in the assessment of need, the management of resources in purchasing a care package, or in providing the identified services (Dant and Gearing, 1990). For example, to what extent will an assessment for an elderly person be based on the physical dimensions of need (capacity to feed, dress, use the toilet, mobility and so on), the personal and interprofessional dimensions (family relationships, other sources of support, the attitude of the older person), external aspects of need (finance, housing) or a combination of all three. Some combination seems the most likely outcome, but with what balance and, given any specific balance, which profession has the most appropriate skills to make an assessment and manage a care package? Who then have the most appropriate skills to meet the needs identified?

One possible source of decision-making about the future roles of the professions in community care will rest with the perceptions senior managers in local authority Social Services Departments have of home care organizers', nurses', occupational therapists' or social workers' abilities to act as care managers or as providers (Kubisa, 1990). Yet to what extent will such perceptions be based on an appraisal of the appropriateness of one group in preference to another in terms of general levels of skill, knowledge and values, or will they be reflections of prejudice? There are, I suggest, three reasons why none of these groups *as groups* should be considered as having prior claims over others in this field.

First, none of these professions can be said to have prioritized services for elderly people within their collective world views. Even home care organizers, who have tended as a group to work predominantly with older people, may regard other types of work as more challenging (Dexter and Harbert, 1983). It has been argued that this follows from the more widespread antipathy to old age as a positive or desirable object of professional attention, because of the perception of the types of need involved and an assumed lack of potential for positive outcomes (Emery, 1981; Biggs, 1989; Scrutton, 1989; Slevin, 1991). Occupational ageism of this kind is evident in all professional groups. On these grounds a choice is not compelling.

Second, negative attitudes are reflected in the low proportions of qualified staff who make a career in services for elderly people their first choice (Chandler et al., 1986; Howe, 1986). Much of the service provision for older people is reliant on unqualified or ancillary staff.

As a consequence, the numbers of qualified professionals who could take on a key role within community care *ab initio* could be expected to be limited.

Third, although each professional group lays claim to a perspective on need which is necessary for a full assessment, none may be regarded as sufficient. The balance between physical, personal, interpersonal and external factors within the framework of any one profession will be affected by the general ethos of that group. If elderly people are to have a complete assessment available across a range of perspectives, this cannot be guaranteed in itself by membership of any one profession.

So in summary, the collective values, skills and knowledge of any one occupational group do not immediately suggest themselves as paramount. However, there are many individual members of each of the three professions most likely to become care managers or providers for elderly people who have the necessary expertise, knowledge base and value orientation (Dant and Gearing, 1990). Research which has demonstrated the general antipathy of these professions to work with older people has shown also that there are minorities who have made a positive selection of this area of work (Emery, 1981; Chandler et al., 1986; Howe, 1986; Slevin, 1991). Given demonstrable capacity in other aspects related to the developing roles, these individuals could form the pool of recruitment both as purchasers and providers. For this minority in each profession the area of common ground in skills, knowledge and values is likely to be (at least potentially) as great if not greater than that shared with other members of their profession. The point is that the basis of selection as care managers or service providers arises from the requirements of the emerging roles and not from any presumption about one professional qualification in relation to others.

Children

I have noted above that there are some similarities between the services for elderly people and those concerned with child welfare, and especially child protection, in relation to organization and interprofessional boundaries as these pertain to communication and cooperation. Indeed, it is these issues (the type, quality, manner and timing of information exchange) which have featured in the major public enquiries into child protection cases where serious problems occurred (Hallett and Stevenson, 1980; Fox Harding, 1991).

Yet, at the same time there are some important differences. Dingwall has argued that the creation of unified Social Services Departments and the allocation to them of primary responsibilities in child protection work effectively limited the development in the UK of the health visiting profession through strengthening that of social work (1980, p. 126). This situation has not prevented health visiting from continuing to be defined principally in relation to child welfare but has taken the form of a generalized assessment, monitoring and advisory role for families with children aged under five years (Twinn, 1991). However, the Health Visitors' Association advised its members not to undertake the keyworker role in cases of child abuse as the primary legal responsibilities rest with Social Services Departments and so are exercised by social workers (Dingwall et al., 1983). Moreover, there is a concern to maintain the identity of the health visitor as primarily concerned with serving the needs of children and their families, and a surveillance role is seen to compromise this (Twinn, 1991). Health visitors continue to monitor situations in which children are deemed to be at risk and to liaise with social workers, but they do so from the basis that their work is focused on child health and early development and is provided to all families with young children.

In comparison with services for elderly people, this pattern of development appears to be one in which the interprofessional boundaries of skills, knowledge and values are interlocking rather than overlapping. Yet it is possible to see this position as one derived not from a recognition of difference in professional formation but as based entirely on the ascription of legal authority in the organizational location of social workers *vis à vis* health visitors. In other words, it is because the legislative responsibilities, for example in the Children Act 1989, empower Social Services Departments that social workers are seen as the primary group in child protection work rather than health visitors or other professionals. It is the contextual development of social work and health visiting that has tended to emphasize their complementary rather than overlapping roles in child welfare work (Fox Harding, 1991). The skills and knowledge base of both health visiting and social work has through two decades been based on this division of labour (Dingwall et al., 1983).

At the same time it is possible to define the core of both professions in this field in similar terms. Assessment skills — especially in relation to risk factors, knowledge of child development and family dynamics, skills in intervention in families, antidiscriminatory values and legal knowledge — are required of both professions (Parton, 1991). So, at a time when the discrete identity of social work is under question and the use of terms such as 'child protection worker' becoming more common, the extent to which each has gained an irrevocably separate identity may be no more well established than in the various fields of services for adults.

Redrawing the boundaries?

The examples of interprofessional boundaries which have been considered here represent the opposite ends of a continuum between the actual recruitment of nurses and occupational therapists into areas which for several decades have been occupied by social workers (the assessment of elderly peoples' needs as the basis for the allocation of social care resources) and an area in which such a blurring of boundaries seems much less probable (child protection).

Other service areas may also be placed on this continuum. In the field of learning difficulties, there has been recruitment of nurses into Social Services Departments as well as the development of joint working structures and training programmes (Grant, 1986; Carpenter et al., 1991). As these are also community care services, it might be expected that they could be placed close to services for elderly people in this respect. In contrast, mental health services — which may be seen also as an aspect of community care — could be described as being located somewhere in the middle of such a continuum, as there are increasing claims by community psychiatric nurses (CPNs) that they could enact the legal responsibilities currently the preserve of approved social workers (ASWs) (Sheppard, 1991). As was previously the case in the child protection field with regard to health visitors, however, the response of social workers (and others) is less than fully supportive on the CPNs' claim, in regarding the mix of social and legal factors in the ASWs' role much more as the province of social work. (It may also be that those areas of social work that are based on statutory responsibilities are more heavily defended by social work as a profession because they have been the most professionalized; in common with nursing they are also those areas which attract larger proportions of men (Howe, 1986; Robinson, 1989).) So while joint training and an interchange of jobs is taking place in the area of learning difficulties and may do so shortly in services for elderly people, blurred boundaries in the mental health and child care fields are less foreseeable.

So far I have been suggesting that the possibilities of redrawing boundaries between health and social care professions are grounded in the organizational framework of practice, including statutory responsibilities. However, in all these contexts the professionals' responses appear to be based on a tendency to emphasize their own skills, knowledge and values and at the same time to be concerned about maintaining a work environment (including careers) which are conducive to the current position. This may be quite plausible, in that one must have confidence in one's own capacities to engage in this work and few people with good job prospects actively seek unemployment. However, this 'inward looking' aspect of professionalism may militate against the flexibility that current dramatic changes in services demand.

The barriers to the reshaping or breaking down of interprofessional boundaries may arise from a wish to defend that which is valued in the existing formation of home care, nursing, occupational therapy, social work or other care professions. I also would now want to deny the extent to which these various groups do actually have different approaches to assessment, intervention and evaluation. This is nowhere more clear than in recent research which reinforces awareness of the very diverse ways in which the idea of 'counselling' is used to refer to a spectrum from directive information and advice giving to non-directive therapy (Scrutton, 1989; Allen and Hogg, 1993; Wilson, 1993). What is at issue, however, is that, by failing to engage in a *rapprochement* in the form of a careful consideration of what each other has to offer in terms of new services, and what each has to learn from the others, the various health and social care professions are at risk of abandoning their influence over the shape of new services entirely to managers (although some managers might find this a desirable outcome) (Cousins, 1987; Strong and Robinson, 1990; Pollitt, 1993).

The likelihood of redrawing boundaries between health and social care professionals appears, therefore, to be grounded within the historical baggage of occupational and agency identity to which each group currently adheres. Such attachments might be expected to increase rather than decrease in the context of dramatic change, at least during the early stages (Mackay, 1989; Robinson, 1989). Yet it will only be through a radical reappraisal of such identities that a professional rather than a purely organizational response to current pressures for change will be constructed.

Conclusions

I began this discussion by noting that professionalism is about occupational differences and boundaries. The present divisions between health and social care professions are shaped not only by claims to specific combinations of skills, knowledge and values but also by three distinct phases in the organizational and policy developments of the welfare state. This development has reinforced the sense of separateness between professional groups whose origins have much in common (Hugman, 1991).

The new community care policies present a challenge to health and social care professions to develop fresh ways of defining their skills, knowledge and values around the tasks of purchasing and providing rather than formal professional identities. Because of the major organizational restructuring which is following from the implementation of the NHS and Community Care Act 1990, this may also have a consequential impact on the more statutory services currently within the responsibilities of Social Services Departments, most notably child care and child protection. However, in that area the indications of potential for change are less clear.

In looking at the overlap between health and social care professions we are, I suggest, facing a new professional mix and the possibility of new professions emerging. The construction of a 'care manager' role which cuts across the boundaries is a clear case in point, and Griffiths (1988, pp. 25–6) refers also to the idea of a 'community care worker' who would be ancillary rather than professional. The former role could well be a logical outcome of the reseating between home care organizers, nurses, occupational therapists and social workers which is taking place in the early 1990s, while the latter would (if it is created) most obviously come out of an amalgamation between home care workers, nursing assistants and therapy aides. The drive for or against, however, is likely to come from the professionally qualified groups as they begin to identify the contribution they can make and their interests in the new order.

In defending their existing strengths the health and social care professions are exercising appropriate caution. One regrettable result of rapid change can be the rejection of every facet from the past, the good along with the bad. However, there is much potential for valued professional roles within the new framework and each profession has much to contribute to its further development. The question remains whether these professions can take an active part and so enhance the growth of community-based health and welfare services.

References

Allen I (Ed.) (1992) *Purchasing and Providing Social Services in the 1990s: Drawing the Line*. London: Policy Studies Institute.

Allen I, Hogg D (1993) *Work Roles and Responsibilities in Genito-urinary Medicine Clinics*. London: Policy Studies Institute.

Anderson R (1992) Health and community care. In: Davies L (Ed.), *The Coming of Age in Europe*. London: Age Concern.

Audit Commission (1986) *Making a Reality of Community Care*. London: HMSO.

Bamford T (1990) *The Future of Social Work*. London: Macmillan.

Biggs S (1989) Professional helpers and resistance to work with older people. *Ageing and Society;* **9**: 43–60.

Carpenter J, Onyett S, Smith H, Williams J, Peck E (1991) *Caring for People Joint Training Project Report*. Bristol: NHS Training Directorate.

Challis D, Chesterman J, Traske K, von Abendorf R (1990) Assessment and case management: some cost implications. *Social Work & Social Sciences Review*; **1**: 147–162.

Chandler JT, Rachal JR , Kazelskis R (1986) Attitudes of long-term care nursing personnel toward the elderly. *Gerontologist*; **26**: 551–555.

Children Act (1989). London: HMSO.

Cousins C (1987) *Controlling Social Welfare*. Brighton: Wheatsheaf.

Dant T, Gearing B (1990) Keyworkers for elderly people in the community: case managers and care coordinators. *Journal of Social Policy*; **19**: 331–360.

Dent M (1993) Professionalism, educated labour and the state: hospital medicine and the new management. *Sociological Review*; **41**: 244–273.

Department of Health (1989a) *Working for Patients*, Cm.555. London: HMSO.

Department of Health (1989b) *Caring for People*, Cm.849. London: HMSO.

Department of Health (1991a) *Care Management and Assessment: Managers' Guide*. London: HMSO.

Department of Health (1991b) *Care Management and Assessment: Practitioners' Guide*. London: HMSO.

Dexter M, Harbert W (1983) *The Home Help Service*. London: Tavistock.

Dingwall R (1980) Problems of team-work in primary care. In: Lonsdale S, Webb A, Briggs T (Eds), *Teamwork in the Personal Social Services and Health Care*. London: Croom Helm.

Dingwall R, Eekelaar J, Murray T (1983) *The Protection of Children: State Intervention and Family Life*. Oxford: Blackwell.

Emery G (1981) Cognitive therapy and the elderly. In: Emery G, Hollon SD, Bedrosian RC (Eds), *New Directions in Cognitive Therapy*. New York: Guilford Press.

Fox Harding L (1991) *Perspectives in Child Care Policy*. London: Longman.

Grant G (1986) Towards joint teams with joint budgets? The case of the all-Wales strategy. In: Chant J (Ed.), *Health and Social Services: Collaboration or Conflict?* London: Policy Studies Institute.

Griffiths R (1983) *Letter to the Secretary of State*. London: Department of Health and Social Security.

Griffiths R (1988) *Community Care: Agenda for Action*. London: HMSO.

Hallett C, Stevenson O (1980) *Child Abuse: Aspects of Interprofessional Cooperation*. London: George Allen & Unwin.

Howe D (1986) *Social Workers and their Practice in Welfare Bureaucracies*. Aldershot: Gower.

Hugman R (1991) *Power in Caring Professions*. Basingstoke: Macmillan.

Huxley P (1992) Social services assessment and case management: getting it right. *Journal of Mental Health*; 1: 285–294.

Jamieson A (1990) Informal care in Europe. In: Jamieson A, Illsley R (Eds), *Contrasting European Policies for the Care of Older People*. Aldershot: Avebury.

Johnson TJ (1972) *Professions and Power*. London: Macmillan.

Klein R (1989) *The Politics of the National Health Service*, 2nd edn. London: Longman.

Kubisa T (1990) Care manager: rhetoric or reality? In: Allen I (Ed.), *Care Managers and Care Management*. London: Policy Studies Institute.

Land H (1991) The confused boundaries of community care. In: Gabe J, Calnan M, Bury M (Eds), *The Sociology of the Health Service*. London: Routledge.

Lawson R, Davies B, Bebbington A (1991) The home-help service in England and Wales. In: Jamieson A (Ed.), *Home Care for Older People in Europe*. Oxford: Oxford University Press.

Mackay L (1989) *Nursing a Problem*. Milton Keynes: Open University Press.

Marshall M (1990). *Social Work with Old People*, 2nd edn. London, Macmillan.

National Assistance Act (1948). London: HMSO.

National Health Act (1946). London: HMSO.

National Health Service and Community Care Act (1990). London: HMSO.

Parkin F (1979) *Marxism and Class Theory: a Bourgeois Critique*. London: Tavistock.

Parton N (1991) *Governing the Family: Child Care, Child Protection and the State*. Basingstoke: Macmillan.

Pollitt C (1993) *Managerialism and the Public Services*, 2nd edn. Oxford: Blackwell.

Robinson J (1989) Nursing in the future: a cause for concern. In: Jolley M, Allan P (Eds), *Current Issues in Nursing*. London: Chapman & Hall.

Rowbottom R, Balle J, Cang S, Dixon M, Jaques E, Packwood T, Tolliday H (1973) *Hospital Organisation*. London: Heinemann.

Rowbottom R, Hey A, Billis D (1974) *Social Services Departments*. London: Heinemann.

Scrutton S (1989) *Counselling Older People*. London: Edward Arnold.

Sheppard M (1991) *Mental Health Work in the Community: Theory and Practice in Social Work and Community Psychiatric Nursing*. London: Falmer.

Slevin O (1991) Ageist attitudes among young adults: implications for a caring profession. *Journal of Advanced Nursing*; **16**: 1197–1205.

Strong P, Robinson J (1990) *The NHS Under New Management*. Buckingham: Open University Press.

Twinn SF (1991) Conflicting paradigms of health visiting: a continuing debate for professional practice. *Journal of Advanced Nursing*; **16**: 966–973.

Wilding P (1982) *Professional Power and Social Welfare*. London: Routledge & Kegan Paul.

Wilson G (1993) Conflicts in case management. *Social Policy and Administration*; **27**: 109–123.

Younghusband E (1978) *Social Work in Britain 1950–1975*. London: George Allen & Unwin.

4 Effectiveness of interprofessional relationships: A case illustration of joint working

Tom Chapman, Richard Hugman and Anne Williams

Introduction

Collaboration between professionals and between service agencies is now regarded as a cornerstone of the development of community care in the UK (Hardy et al., 1992; Knapp et al., 1992). However, only recently have the mechanisms of collaboration been subject to empirical evaluation, raising questions about why joint planning and joint working between services seems to function more effectively in some districts than in others (Hudson, 1992).

This chapter addresses the need to consider empirical evidence through the detailed exploration of one case example. Setting this single instance in the broader context of policy development, the problems and possibilities of effective collaborative working are considered.

The policy context

Collaboration between health authorities and local authorities became a major policy objective following the 1974 reorganizations of health and local government (Hunter and Wistow, 1987; National Audit Office, 1987; Wistow et al., 1990). At that stage it included the establishment of joint consultative committees, overlapping membership between authorities, and joint planning teams. However, the mechanism for joint planning and service provision was then focused chiefly on the use of joint funding arrangements, introduced in 1976, which tended to be used for relatively small-scale specific projects. Joint finance was used to provide monies for health authorities to be spent mainly on personal social services projects for people with learning disabilities and elderly people, after discussion and negotiation between the two authorities. However, as Wistow et al. (1990) note, joint-funded projects frequently became the responsibility of one agency through a lack of longer-term planning, resource problems for one partner (often the local authority), organizational complexity or their use as short-term developmental funding. So despite the introduction of a system which necessitated working together, few successful joint ventures could be reported (Ham, 1992). Differences in organizational structure and political hostility between certain health authorities and local authorities thwarted joint planning in many parts of the country. Furthermore, differences in planning processes, authority boundaries, budget cycles, and ways of working, presented considerable obstacles to even the best of intentions.

The recognition that health policy is intrinsically intertwined with social policy gained further ground through the 1980s as arguments for a concerted approach to health problems became even more prominent (Hunter and Wistow, 1987; Ham, 1992). At the level of central government a succession of reports charting the uneven and slow progress of community care continued to lay stress on the significance of collaboration in the 'mixed economy of care', which was at the foundation of government social policy. A particularly damning report by the Audit Commission (1986) pointed to the existence of 'perverse incentives' discouraging local authorities from even using joint finance. Instances of local authorities being penalized by rate-capping for exceeding spending targets acted as a major disincentive to engage in difficult interagency projects.

The government responded to the strong criticism contained in the Audit Commission report by commissioning Sir Roy Griffiths to review policy and make recommendations. Griffiths (1988) advocated that local authorities should be given the lead role in community care, becoming the purchasers of services, and the coordinators of service provision. It was proposed that local authorities should be given the responsibility for assessing people's needs for residential care, which was to be paid for by a means-tested allowance made available through the social security system.

Most of Griffiths' recommendations were contained in the White Paper *Caring for People* (DoH, 1989), which identified local authorities as 'lead agencies' in delivering community care. Local authorities were given the responsibility of identifying the need for community services, and preparing joint plans with district health authorities. In the area of joint planning and joint funding, the White Paper stated that existing funding arrangements should be reviewed in order to assess their impact on collaboration between health and local authorities.

The White Paper proposals led to the National Health Service and Community Care Act 1990, which was due to take effect on 1 April

1991, introducing the new system of community care together with NHS reforms. In some senses these changes went beyond the previous scope of joint work, adding housing and other agencies to the range normally expected to contribute to this process (Rao, 1991, p. 4). The emphasis also was now firmly on personal social services as local authorities were identified as the primary agency responsible, with the key roles of enabling, coordination and purchasing of services (*ibid.*, p. 13). In the event, the full introduction was phased in between 1991 and 1 April 1993, in order to lessen the impact of community care on local government finance through levels of the community charge (now council tax) (Henwood et al., 1991).

The organizational context

The policy development of the 1980s was influenced also by a number of community care experimental projects, principally those which built on the practice of 'case management' (Challis and Davies, 1986; Huxley, 1992; Knapp et al., 1992). Although focused on various groups of service user need, these schemes shared a common basis in attempting to create services which were flexible for the service user at the point of delivery and which were able to overcome the institutional boundaries between large agencies. It is not the purpose of this chapter to discuss the practice of case management, which has been undertaken elsewhere (Davies and Missiakoulis, 1988; Holloway, 1991; Huxley, 1992). In relation to the discussion here, the most important finding from evaluative research has been the wide variety of organizational models. Knapp and colleagues have summarized these as five types (1992, p. 238):

- The '*unitary agency*' *model*, in which a single agency has responsibility for service development even though funding and initial planning may have been shared.
- The '*semi-independent agency*' *model*, in which a scheme is run through a separate organization which may be a voluntary body or consortium.
- The '*lead agency*' *model*, in which one agency takes the lead to manage a development but to which others contribute during the project's work.
- The '*joint agency*' *model*, in which a bilateral responsibility between two agencies for leading and managing a scheme was implemented.
- The '*multi-agency*' *model*, in which several agencies shared together in responsibility and management of a project.

Although the research of the PSSRU in Kent, the Nuffield Institute in Leeds, the King's Fund Institute in London and others demonstrated the success of projects based on this variety of forms, they often remained local and small-scale, involving not entire agencies but specific parts of organizations. Moreover, less powerful organizations such as voluntary sector agencies and service user groups at times might find themselves excluded from policy and planning or even management (Hadley and Hugman, 1992; Knapp et al., 1992; Barnes, 1993). This tended to focus the process on the concerns and interests of the larger statutory bodies.

As the NHS and Community Care Act 1990 has made clearer the expectations for joint planning and wide consultation amongst interested agencies and groups, it remains to be seen which types of joint working arrangements are developing to meet these requirements. So in the remainder of this chapter we examine in detail one illustrative case example, to consider the influences and decisions which have shaped a particular community care planning model and to explore some of the issues which arise from this one model.

Collaboration in community care workshops

As a first phase of a research project into the process of joint planning (JP) and joint working (JW), a one-day workshop was held at Lancaster University in August 1990. It was anticipated that as collaboration between different agencies in the provision of health and social care became a statutory duty under the NHS and Community Care Act 1990, these agencies would have identified a range of key issues in the development of joint approaches. To consider these issues, agencies from the north of England were brought together to make comparisons between the various models of collaborative planning and service provision and to consider general themes which were emerging.

Since collaboration is essential in order to bring about the intended seamless service (Griffiths, 1988; DoH, 1989), two important prerequisites to effective collaboration were anticipated: firstly, a recognition of the arbitrary and artificial divide between 'health care' and 'social care'; and secondly, a genuine willingness on the part of health and social services professionals to work together. Since it is part of the conventional wisdom of the sociology of occupations that the defence of professional autonomy is a major obstacle to interprofessional collaboration (Kane, 1980), a major objective of the workshop was to ascertain whether or not such defences were revealed in debate, and to note their potential effects in either helping or hindering the process of joint working at various levels of operation.

The process of the workshop was to engage professionals who had some first-hand experience of interprofessional collaboration in identifying opportunities for, and barriers to, effective collaboration.

The purpose of the debate was made clear to the participants, and it was stressed that at this stage the researchers were interested only in identifying issues, rather than finding solutions to problems. In essence, the workshop was an attempt to ground future research in the perceptions and views of professionals who already had considerable insight and experience. It was considered to be important that the conceptual framework and the design of the project should emerge from the professionals themselves, rather than be superimposed 'from the outside' — that is, derived solely from consultative documents, official reports and other government publications.

This one-day workshop brought together 21 invited participants, drawn from top and middle management as well as 'grass roots' levels, from the following authorities:

Cumbria Social Services   Salford Health Authority
Lancashire Social Services   Salford Social Services
Lancaster Health Authority   Sheffield Family & Community Services
Rochdale Health Authority   Tameside Social Services
Rochdale Social Services

From the proceedings of this event, the following *opportunities* for effective collaboration were identified:

(a) Joint resourcing was consistently viewed as a major motivating factor in promoting serious efforts to collaborate. Many examples were provided of how joint consultation exercises seldom led to any actions which had practical effects. The necessity of exercising proper managerial control over scarce resources invariably provided a stimulus for taking joint management seriously.

(b) Many participants pointed out that their initial reservations about the efficacy of JW disappeared as their experience of it developed. A common theme was that JW enabled the identification of common values, which they had not anticipated. Indeed, many had been surprised to discover that value systems were often closer than they had imagined. Several participants stressed that the processes by which they came to realize that they shared many common values had been an important prerequisite to the realization that JW could provide a real sense of 'satisfaction' and 'stimulation'.

(c) It was in the planning of care programmes involving different agencies that many practitioners working at the operational level felt that real progress was achieved. The need to concentrate on the interests of clients was cited frequently as something which focused people's minds on meeting objectives, and on 'getting the job done'.

(d) Somewhat surprisingly, there seemed to be common consent that joint appointments to particular posts according to managerial skills, and regardless of professional background, were highly desirable. Such posts would signal 'serious intent to work together', and serve to mark the end of 'professional preciousness as a kind of restrictive practice'. Since decisions regarding the professional qualifications required for posts are taken at a senior level, it was noticeable that there appeared to be positive encouragement for such appointments from the senior managers present.

In contrast, the following *barriers* to effective collaboration also were identified:

(a) There was a failure on the part of some participants in joint planning and joint working to recognize the existence of differences in 'culture' between health and social services. Whilst both agencies increasingly operate within a 'business culture', the concept is different in each. For example, the form of separation between purchasers and providers in health is different from that in social services. Many examples were cited of joint plans that had gone awry because key individuals had been insufficiently sensitive to different working cultures. Different views on, and interpretations of, 'people power' had also created some difficulties in joint working.

(b) The need to embrace joint working was introduced at a time of considerable structural change in both health and social services. People were being expected to change attitudes, habits, conventions, and working practices when morale was historically low, and anxiety and stress generally high.

(c) Professional differences were mentioned though, significantly, few participants dwelt on these at any length. This seemed to reflect a general feeling that these had been exaggerated in the past. One participant expressed the view that there was no alternative to 'getting on with the job of negotiating differences away'.

(d) Some senior managers pointed to logistical barriers to effective collaboration, in particular the fact that authority boundaries were not coterminous. That this resulted in considerable problems for many was generally agreed.

(e) Since joint working was still something of a novelty for most managers, collaborative and innovatory projects were frequently thwarted by resourcing difficulties. Quite frequently such difficulties arose from lack of 'laid-down policy guidelines and procedures'. It was suggested by one participant that 'where public money is involved people take fewer chances'.

(f) Poor communication was mentioned by some participants. It was notable that the examples given mostly referred to communication difficulties within their own agency. The general feeling seemed to be that 'communication is always a problem', albeit less of one when people feel that their reputation for efficiency is important to them.

(g) The absence of 'overall coordination' was frequently cited as a barrier to effective collaboration. Insufficient attention at central government department level had been given to determining and disseminating guidance on who had the responsibility for supplying many of the services, in addition to health and social services, individuals require in order to prevent admission into residential care.

(h) Whilst the internal market within the health service makes a certain sense, it should be recognized that the social services could not go outside their authority. Furthermore, their use of the private sector is either encouraged or prevented according to local political pressure. The shortfall between DSS and private market costs puts providers at risk if they choose to maintain existing staff costs, even in a traditionally low-wage sector.

The first workshop was followed by a second in July 1991 at which a smaller group were invited to consider in more detail the issues raised from the first workshop. The group which met on the second occasion comprised representatives from the District Health Authorities, Family Health Services Authorities and Social Services Departments of Lancaster, Rochdale and Salford. The discussion focused on the opportunities and barriers to successful collaborative working as they now appeared, and in particular the involvement of policy-makers, managers, professionals and service users in the joint processes. From this discussion three key areas were identified as crucial indicators in evaluating any concrete instances of collaborative work:

- planning (structures and procedures);
- training (for all participants);
- working (practices at service delivery level).

The following case illustration explores each of these key areas in the example of community care developments in Rochdale. This locality was selected for two reasons. The first was that in the course of the workshops it had become clear that collaboration was relatively advanced compared with some other localities. Secondly, Rochdale had already been part of a national survey in which it had been identified as having both a strong multidisciplinary structure and a relatively high level of service user involvement (Carpenter et al., 1991). Not only does this report provide the basis for placing our single case study in its wider context, but it also enables it to be located conceptually as both a 'multi-agency' approach (Knapp et al., 1992) and as 'multi-tier' (Hardy et al., 1992).

Rochdale: a case illustration

It is clear, both from previous studies and documentation (Carpenter et al., 1991; Rochdale, 1993), and from the authors' various encounters with persons involved in community care in Rochdale, that two major imperatives guide its 'multi-agency/multi-tier' approach. First, issues in community care must be jointly conceptualized between agencies; and second, plans should be user-focused (recognizing that these two imperatives are not mutually exclusive). Data from interviews with representatives of those charged with implementing community care in Rochdale highlight the opportunities and potential barriers to the planning, training and working processes in respect of upholding these imperatives.

Planning

Rochdale's first Joint Community Care Plan was published in April 1992. This was the first time that the various agencies (Borough Council, Health Authority, Health Care NHS Trust, Voluntary Sector and Family Health Services Authority [FHSA], had come together to say jointly how they intended to work with each other, and to prepare for changes in the way services would be provided after April 1993. The second Joint Community Care Plan, *Working Together* (Rochdale, 1993), notes how many more people have become involved in the planning process. It also emphasizes the intention to provide a plan for action. This intention has seemingly become reality as reflected in the words of Rochdale's Community Care Coordinator when he says:

'We've been able to put a tool in place which will move services forward, which will actually create real cooperation, rather than just being words on a piece of paper.'

How has this been achieved in Rochdale? At an instrumental level, the planning process has been coordinated by a group called the Community Care Steering Group. The group is chaired by the Chief Executive of the FHSA, and it includes the Deputy Director of Social Services, the Social Services Community Care Planning Officer, the Community Care Coordinator (who acts at the interface between health and social care agencies), a representative of the voluntary sector, the Director of Nursing, the NHS Trust Community Director, the Director of Public Health and the Assistant General Manager from the FHSA. This is the group that has solved and resolved problems, and pushed strategies and initiatives forward. The group reports to the chief officers of the planning team (Director of Social Services; Chief Executive, Health Care Trust; Chief Executive, Health Authority; General Manager, FHSA; Chief Officer, Age Concern, on behalf of the Voluntary Sector; and the Secretary of the Community Health Council).

Each agency has its own implementation group which further feeds into the planning process, and it is useful to note how opportunities for collaboration are facilitated structurally even at this level, insofar as it is possible for agencies to have representation on each other's teams. By way of example, the Community Care Coordinator explains: 'I am a member along with my colleagues of the social services community care implementation team, but I also chair the Trust's implementation team'.

A further key feature of the approach to planning in Rochdale is that users of services must be involved. Structurally, here, the main avenue for involvement appears to be the recently launched 'partnership groups'. As stated in *Working Together*:

> 'Each partnership group represents the interests of a particular group of users, and the groups bring together users and carers as well as representatives from all organisations. The partnership groups are * Children and Families * Older People * Learning Disabilities * Physical Disabilities * Mental Health * Drug Misuse * Alcohol Misuse' (Rochdale, 1993, p. 23)

Of course, membership of a group does not guarantee an active voice, and user voices are, historically, less powerful than the voices of professionals (Collins and Stein, 1989). The partnership groups, however, are required to have users as chair-people so that, for example, the disabilities group is chaired by a disabled person. Further, an external review group monitors the degree to which users and carers are involved in planning processes.

The outcomes of the partnership groups include newsletters and publicity about community care and, not least, the community care plan itself. The following comment reflects the extent of user participation in this respect:

> 'This year the community care plan has been written [by], or rather all material has come from, the partnership groups. So staff from all the agencies together with users and carers have produced the material.'

Opportunities for joint planning are taken and used creatively. However, the authors were keen to explore the extent to which barriers to effective collaboration might still exist. In answer to the question, what would you identify as the major blocks to planning, the following response was made:

> 'A major concern all along has probably been finance officers. Whether or not they would have the imagination to really acknowledge progress by practitioners, planners, managers, users and carers. Whether they'd really be able to come up with the financial systems necessary to really put community care onto a proper inter-agency basis.'

When explored, it became apparent that here was an example of 'cultural' tension in the sense of business culture versus the culture of care. The problem is recognized in Rochdale, as indeed it is elsewhere (Bamford, 1990), and steps are being taken to address the problem. However, where before blocks to action were about differences in organizational and professional politics and culture, now the arguments are about inflexibility in respect of resourcing community care.

In summary, Rochdale has clearly signalled the intention to produce collaborative community care plans. Collaboration for Rochdale means putting in place structures that allow agencies and users to conceptualize issues jointly. Barriers to the success of this strategy exist, notably around finance. However, the impression given is that the barriers are not insurmountable. What is required is the building of relationships which is, as one spokesperson said, 'the real test of how successful community care is going to be'. The following discussion illustrates how Rochdale is setting about the task of building relationships through training.

Training

A coordinated move towards joint training was initiated in 1991, and it has been influenced by the following principles as outlined in *Working Together*:

> 'Training activities will be geared to the requirements of national community care legislation and the Rochdale Community Care Plan. The strategy "will be built on the concept of public service to the community". Equal opportunities legislation and local equal opportunities policies "will be reflected in everything we do". Importantly training will reflect the needs of users of services and their carers. Training will be based on standards that are achievable and appropriate to the organisations involved and training effectiveness will be monitored to ensure the successful implementation of the community care for people in Rochdale.' (p. 130)

How are these principles being put into practice? Training on a joint multidisciplinary basis is facilitated structurally through the Working Together Joint Trainers Group. Prior to the setting up of the group, joint training did occur, mainly in terms of seminars aimed to challenge institutionalized behaviour. For example, 'a couple of trainers would go out to GP surgeries to give them basic awareness training about community care'. By contrast, the newly convened Joint Trainers Group's approach has been to identify training needs across agencies, and to work out ways of providing the training. As one member puts it, 'when we've got to train 200 people to be care managers, we can only do this collaboratively'. The group has recently been extended to include representatives from the voluntary sector and the independent sector, and currently there is a move to include a service user.

A major development in 1992 was the production of 'cascade training packs'. These packs provide a foundation course which looks at community care legislation and guidance from a variety of perspectives including those of users and carers, professionals, the independent sector and so on (Rochdale, 1993, p. 130). The pack has already been used, following briefing sessions with key managers. A key point here is that 37 representatives from the Pakistani community and the Bangladeshi community have attended cascade training sessions which have been offered in Bengali, English and Urdu.

As one spokesperson explained, it is the intention to use the packs on a multidisciplinary basis, by locality. For example, the coordinator reported that training on care assessment was provided for:

'[. . .] all the people from Middleton who are care managers. For example, district nurses, health visitors, community practice nurses, and social workers have been training together.'

This approach will be developed to include:

'[. . .] awareness training for reception staff . . . from primary health care teams, social services offices, from health centres. Again these will take place on a locality basis and on a multidisciplinary basis. Similarly, training will be provided for the chief executives.'

It appears that the principles of joint work, user-focused care and equal opportunities are guiding the training programme. Further we see in practice the theory posited at the 1991 workshop, namely that user-focused approaches help disparate practitioners in getting the job done. But what are the barriers to achieving success in the domain of joint training? In answer to this question, one person interviewed suggests 'differences in culture'. This was elaborated by another respondent who said:

'I suppose the blocks have been, well they are not so much blocks as interests really, the differences between the social service culture, you know . . . which is something around, well the idea of "let's talk about our feelings" and the health service culture which is "let's see a bit of action here, let's actually get on and get stuck in".'

This respondent went on to say that, while one is no more persuaded by the latter than the former, the two imperatives reflect possible tensions in approach. It was added that such tensions are to be had in any complicated project, and while differences in professional cultures are potential barriers, differences can be exploited and used constructively. The following example was given:

'A district nurse will go in with a form, a scale, a tool to do a specialist assessment on a client, whereas a social worker tends not to use them. Closer contact could lead to a lot of sparks, or it could allow people to learn from each other. I'd hope that the district nursing sister will have realised, well actually there is another way of doing assessments apart from working from the form. And I hope the social worker would realise there is another way of, well, not being so spontaneous, and a bit more organised.'

It was suggested that the latter approach would be a way of using difference constructively to provide a better service, in addition to the potential for joint training sessions to provide a forum for building relationships between personnel from different organizations. This was reflected in the following statement:

'The best example, I think, is one of the assessment care management training (sessions). All the staff from the trust and the local authority were from the same locality, and we were exchanging telephone numbers at the end of the meeting, so that was a bit of an indication that it was a really successful event in terms of building up relationships which would be the real test of how successful community care is going to be.'

So, in summary, the structures for joint training for community care are in place. The intention is to involve users in the near future. A potential barrier to effective joint training has been identified as difference in professional cultures. As noted above, this seeming barrier can be exploited to provide an opportunity for different professionals to learn from each other. However, closer learning and working relationships do engender corresponding tensions and frustrations (as well as opportunities) as indicated in the following discussion.

Working

The early indication is that, despite barriers, working together in coordinated ways towards effective community care is happening in Rochdale. First, people who a few months ago may never have met are now in the same room twice a week making decisions about how money should be spent between the agencies:

'Senior operational managers, budget-holders are now meeting and making decisions about how finance should be committed. So that means that people, for example, from the trust and from social services can meet and say we'll meet those needs, we'll put extra resources into this or that area, and they will start looking at individual assessments of people in a target group who need admission into nursing and health care [. . .]

The primary care manager for district nursing and the care manager, from the trust, for geriatric medicine would not, before, have sat down with the deputy director of social services to make decisions about how money should be spent, whether or not they can put more or less time into an individual patient's care arrangements, or whether that person should or shouldn't go to a nursing home.

> Before now they would not have had that focus at all. We didn't have the mechanism before.'

A major block to joint working in this respect is the under-resourcing of this extra activity undertaken by NHS staff. Staff involved are 'very, very overstretched' which 'certainly tests people's good-will'.

A second way in which people across agencies are working more cooperatively is through the implementation of the local assessment care management arrangements, where practitioners are working towards common documentation, procedures and guidelines. This means closer work between practitioners (e.g. district nurses and social workers) at the ground level, through, for example, weekly meetings to decide who should be the care manager, or what process should be followed in an emergency.

A potential block here would seem to be cultural, as indicated below:

> 'You know, distrust and hostility which exists between nursing staff and local authority staff, and the stereotypes which are built up. Training has helped to break this down but we still need to do more work on this.'

Why is this the case?

> 'There are different backgrounds and protocols, if you put areas of work under a microscope.'

The following example illustrates how trying to put the idea of joint work into practice conflicts with the professional imperative to take individual responsibility for a problem:

> 'There is the classic example of the district nurse who spent a whole afternoon trying to get through to a social services department. Not so much trying to get them to answer the 'phone, but to get them to take responsibility for somebody. She made nine 'phone calls, and everybody gave her good reasons why the person she wanted wasn't them.
>
> This conflicts, I think, with the local view within the health service of, you know, a patient who is in difficulties and is referred to a primary health care team. Then you go out yourself and visit and check it out for yourself, rather than pass the buck to other people.'

The point being made here is that the district nurse was trying to practise a cooperative approach to health care. However, the process of trying to do this was both in conflict with her view of good practice and, indeed, was a source of frustration. 'Close cooperation', it is observed, 'opens up the potential for friction'.

Relatedly, professional boundaries are changing. This, in turn, carries anxieties, as the following comment indicates:

> 'Social work staff, I think are under pressure at the moment because

they feel the whole nature of social work is changing . . . what their role is and how it has changed from what it used to be.'

However, despite difficulties, joint work is practised and has its successes as the following comment on the work of joint commissioning indicates:

'The joint commissioning work was specifically to work out how we were going to commission residential nursing home care. The groups involved service users and carers as well as managers and practitioners from all agencies, representatives from the independent sector, particularly representatives of the private nursing sections.'

Both practical and conceptual issues were tackled jointly:

'Throughout the whole process we sat down with people and worked through the issues . . . There were a lot of issues to be resolved . . . for example, installation of vertical lifts and the timescale allowed for installation, the fitting of dormer windows. And issues of quality and standards of care. Together, we got them resolved with compromise on all sides. We worked alongside people who were going to use the services directly, or people who were caring for people who use the services directly, as well as, obviously, practitioners.'

As illustrated, collaboration offers potential for productive work in community care. It also opens up areas of friction which must be confronted and resolved for effective interprofessional relationships.

Conclusions

The will to make collaboration in community care a reality in Rochdale is evident. This has both inspired and, in turn, facilitated structural elements such as the setting up of joint planning, training and working groups which can be defined as 'multi-agency' in the terms discussed above. The structures are now in place for enabling a shift from an emphasis on individual agency responsibility to that of taking joint responsibility for community care. At the same time, structural barriers exist, notably (as indicated in the first workshop) the fact that authority boundaries are not coterminous. However, as indicated, such barriers are not halting jointly conceptualized plans for community care, nor joint innovations for implementing care.

Changes in working structures have fostered a climate where cultural differences can be taken seriously. Joint responsibility for community care does not necessarily mean homogeneity, in the sense of producing a professionally undifferentiated approach to care. Rather, as indicated in the preceding discussion on training, it is important to recognize professional differences and, indeed, professionals have much to learn from each other in a 'multi-tier' framework. Similarly, moves to include users in planning, training and working together with professionals and managers so far has been productive. Indeed, it is possible at this stage to suggest that 'multi-tier' should be taken to mean not only the inclusion of a wide range of hierarchical levels from within agencies, but also those who are 'external' to the agencies (who, in another sense, do not form a 'tier' as such).

Rochdale is an example of a particular approach to implementing changes in community care. This 'multi-agency' approach is not, as we have noted, the only possible solution. However, it appears to be an indicator of a system which has strong potential for change. Community care is, however, in its infancy. Will the systems set up be flexible enough to withstand changing workloads? As a key spokesperson comments:

> 'The proof of the pudding will be in five or six month's time. At present the workload for those in the community is manageable, but will it be in five or six month's time? This is a challenge for co-working and balancing budgets between agencies.'

Joint planning, training and working present an ongoing challenge for Rochdale, as they do for other localities. However, opportunities have been positively exploited, and they continue to be developed. Barriers are monitored, and they are confronted, for example, in training programmes. The experience of 'working together' in Rochdale has been shared with other localities. Indeed Rochdale's reputation for sharing experiences can be taken as an indicator of a capacity for collaboration. What remains to be seen is whether or not central government can engage in its own social policy and act as a supportive partner in the collaborative effort.

Acknowledgement

We would like to thank Roisin Miller for her enthusiastic participation in the project and for comments on ideas presented here.

References

Audit Commission (1986) *Making a Reality of Community Care*. London: HMSO.

Bamford T (1990) *The Future of Social Work*. London: Macmillan.

Barnes M (1993) Introducing new stakeholders. *Policy & Politics*; **21**: 47–58.

Carpenter J, Onyett S, Smith H, Williams J, Peck E (1991) *Caring for People Joint Training Project Report*. Bristol: NHS Training Directorate.

Challis D, Davies B (1986) *Case Management in Community Care*. Aldershot: Gower.

Collins S, Stein M (1989) Users fight back: collectives in social work. In: Rojek C, Peacock G, Collins S (Eds), *The Haunt of Misery*. London: Routledge.

Davies B, Missiakoulis S (1988) Heineken and matching processes in the Thanet Community Care Project: an empirical test of their relative importance. *British Journal of Social Work*; **18** (suppl.): 55–78.

Department of Health (1989) *Caring for People: Community Care in the Next Decade and Beyond*, Cm. 849. London: HMSO.

Griffiths R (1988) *Community Care: Agenda for Action*. London: HMSO.

Hadley R, Hugman R (1992) Organisational change in a turbulent climate. *Social Work & Social Science Review*; **3**: 205–226.

Hardy, B, Turrell A, Wistow G (1992) *Innovations in Community Care Management*. Aldershot: Avebury.

Ham C (1992) *Health Policy in Britain: The Politics and Organisation of the National Health Service*, 3rd edn. London: Macmillan.

Health and Social Services and Social Security Adjudication Act (1983). London: HMSO.

Henwood M, Jowell T, Wistow G (1991) *All Things Come (To Those Who Wait?)*. London: King's Fund Institute.

Holloway F (1991) Case management for the mentally ill: looking at the evidence. *International Journal of Social Psychiatry*; **37**: 2–13.

Hudson B (1992) Community care planning: incrementalism to rationalism. *Social Policy and Administration*; **26**: 185–200.

Hunter D, Wistow G (1987) *Community Care in Britain*. London: King's Fund.

Huxley P (1992) Social services assessment and care management: getting it right. *Journal of Mental Health*; **1**: 285–294.

Knapp M, Cambridge P, Thomason C, Beecham J, Allen C, Darton R (1992) *Care in the Community: Challenge and Demonstration*. Aldershot: Ashgate/PSSRU.

Kane RA (1980) Multi-disciplinary teamwork in the United States. In: Lonsdale S, Webb A, Briggs T (Eds), *Teamwork in the Health and Personal Social Services*. London: Croom Helm.

National Audit Office (1987) *Community Care Developments*. London: HMSO.

National Health Service and Community Care Act (1990). London: HMSO.

Rao N (1991) *From Providing to Enabling*. York: Joseph Rowntree Foundation.

Rochdale (1993) *Working Together: Rochdale's Community Care Plan*. Rochdale: Rochdale MBC/DHA/FHSA.

Whitely P (1990) Side by Side? *Social Services Insight*; 6 June: 20.

Wistow G, Hardy B, Turrell A (1990) *Collaboration Under Financial Constraint: Health Authorities' Spending of Joint Finance*. Aldershot: Avebury/CRSP.

5 Managing values and organizational climate in a multiprofessional setting

Richard Cole and Michael Perides

Introduction

There is nothing new or radical about community care. The concept has been with us for many years. However, what is radical is the legislative framework that has been constructed to implement community care, namely the National Health Service and Community Care Act 1990. The thinking behind this legislation has had and will continue to have a profound impact upon the way health and social care are delivered and the manner in which those working in health and social care operate. The legislation that sets out the implementation of care in the community is the culmination of profound changes in social policy and is the product of the three White Papers entitled *Caring for People, Working for Patients* and *The New GP Contract* (DoH, 1989a,b, 1990).

The impact of this social policy legislation emphasizes the need for health care practitioners to re-examine their roles and relationships. Doctors, nurses, social workers, occupational therapists, managers and other health and social service professionals must find new ways of working together that may involve crossing traditional professional boundaries in order to create and deliver services to meet consumers' needs. It is clear that professional isolationism is neither acceptable nor appropriate and if maintained will not meet the challenges and changes that health and social care continue to face.

Recent developments have been advanced from the perspective of classical economic theory. Structural reforms based on a market norm seem to offer a superficially attractive solution, in that it is envisaged that improvements can occur as a result of reliable and natural laws of economics in which customers and providers find efficient solutions to their respective needs and constraints. This, of course, remains to be proven. What is clear is that the environment in which the provision of health and social care takes place is generating conflict between purchasers and the providers, as well as between the professional disciplines. This conflict results from a naive perception of how the two roles should interrelate. The naivety arises from the assumption that purchasers and providers will have a commercial relationship that will confine itself to the buying and selling of products. This assumption does not consider the nature of the product nor does it consider the historical relationship between the professional disciplines prior to their separation into purchasers and providers. Hage (1989), in an unpublished paper, argues that market mechanisms do not fit easily into health care settings. This is because doctors decide who gets what treatment, the patient does not choose the doctor on the basis of value-for-money, and the patient cannot easily challenge the quality of the product.

This situation is not surprising when one recognizes the role change demanded on the part of both provider and purchaser. The provider is now required not only to consider their clinical treatment of the patient, but also to take account of their performance in relation to set parameters which may not relate to their clinical performance. Many previously extraneous factors have become relevant; for example, the costs both in time and equipment, the quality of the service in relation to agreed standards, the impact of service level agreements on the economic viability of the organization, as well as their contribution to the overall success of the organization. These growing demands on the professional are overlaid by the rise of the consumer power manifested in the right of consumer choice.

This emphasis on consumer choice is a central theme of the legislation. Furthermore, as part of the promotion of the consumer voice, appeal mechanisms and explicit complaint procedures, consumers are being enabled to challenge professional decisions. These additional pressures contribute to the continual erosion of professional autonomy as perceived by health and social care professionals themselves.

Likewise purchasers are required to consider variables other than clinical efficiency when purchasing the service. Their specifications must also be conscious of value-for-money and consumer choice. Purchasers are subject to the same feelings of professional erosion as their provider colleagues.

Given the magnitude of these changes, both real and imagined, in the daily lives of professionals, it is not surprising that organizational structures are constantly shifting to find the right balance. An alternative approach is one of continuing change or evolution as opposed to revolution, using as a model the way in which Japanese organizations manage the issue of change. Essentially, some Japanese organizations are identified as being comfortable with the notion of 'small steps' and continuously developing their organizations through building on workers' contributions. In contrast, the western approach to organizational development is characterized by dramatic and sweeping changes. The basic distinction is well illustrated in the study of the Matsushita organization by Pascale and Athos (1981). This study looked at a number of manufacturing and service organizations operating both in Japan and the USA and compared the involvement of workers in the management of each organization. Essentially the Japanese organizations saw their workforce as having a much wider role in the organizational life than simply producing the product or providing the service. There was seen to be an expectation that the workers would contribute to the development of the organization and in doing so provide the incremental steps for achieving the overall strategy. The Japanese required total organizational commitment to create an organizational culture that focused on consistently producing quality products or service and continually looking to improve that quality.

The theme of this chapter is to explore the idea of whether the concept of organizational cultures can be used to assist health and social care organizations better to manage the changes they are facing as a result of central government's view of how health and social care should be managed and delivered. It will be argued that the idea of an organizational culture is particularly helpful in organizations that are labour-intensive and where the achievement of organizational goals is highly dependent upon the interrelated activities and commitment of its workforce.

Historical perspective on contemporary issues

Whilst notions of health and social care have their origins in the belief that the state has an obligation to provide for the health and care needs of the nation, increasingly this belief is being challenged. The style of many health and social services organizations has been, and to some extent remains, that of large bureaucratic systems. These systems have developed along particular cultural lines shaped by both organizational culture and professional culture. In particular, professional culture has always been eminently powerful and resistant to change. Ackroyd et al. (1989) have identified the typical management context of public sector service as one of 'controlled management'. In essence, 'controlled management' is characterized as being highly defensive of existing modes of working whereby considerable autonomy is extended to practitioners. It is in this context that much of the impact of 'marketplace' thinking has to be considered.

In recent times we have witnessed significant changes in social service organizations. In some cases there is evidence of a shift from a centralized approach to a devolved system where control and decision-making have been pushed closer to the customer. The issue for senior managers has been to judge how far one can allow decisions about the allocation of resources to move down the chain of command without appearing to lose control over the general strategy.

Our own study focuses directly on the ways in which health and social service organizations invest in their workforces.[1] We are attempting to evaluate how this contributes to their ability to create and develop services. In addition, we are constructing research tools that will enable us to understand the impact of the investment on the organization by tracing how far the culture was penetrated through the role structure of the organization. We intend to focus on the impact senior managers have on the dissemination of the culture through the organization and to identify the prevailing subcultures at various points in the structure. We have also designed a consumer perception instrument which helps to gather views about the quality of the service. We used the data collected to measure the organizations' ability to establish and deliver services.

Our study has demonstrated that the concept of organizational culture is recognized with varying degrees of understanding by senior managers. In fact, the task of working within the constraints of the organizational culture is, in our view, pivotal to the successful management of the important challenges facing managers in implementing the changes arising from the care in the community legislation.

Schein (1985) argues that organizational culture is the key to organizational excellence. However, definitions proffered by Baker (1980), Haralambos (1986) and McClean and Marshall (1983) settle for the notion that organizational culture is a set of shared meanings that make it possible for members of the organization to understand their organization and to act accordingly within their organization.

In our view the organizational culture is, therefore, better understood as a dynamic process continually interacting and shaping itself according to the strength and relative influence of both internal and external factors.

Organizational culture is thus seen by Schein (1987) as a multi-faceted phenomenon whose component parts can coexist. He argues in his book *The Art of Managing Human Resources* that culture goes beyond the norms and values of a group in that it is more than the

---

[1] The study was undertaken between 1990 and 1992 and involved three local authority social service departments and three district health authorities, all of which were located in South East England. The sample size taken from each organization was 20% of the total population of the organization and our response rate was 52%. These samples were given a questionnaire to complete and were subsequently followed up with an interview. The total population of each organization consisted of between 400 and 500 individuals.

ultimate outcome derived from repeated success and a gradual process of taking things for granted. Organizational culture, he suggests, is perpetually being formed in the sense that there is constantly some kind of learning going on about how to relate to the environment and manage internal affairs.

Contemporary issues

The most obvious impact of the current social and health care legislation is the resulting conflict between purchasers and providers. This is perhaps most pronounced within the social services when colleagues, who formerly worked together, find themselves in roles that they perceive to be on opposing sides of the fence. This situation is not so apparent in health settings because the split between purchasers and providers essentially separated planners from practitioners and was not dividing practitioners as in the social services.

A further crucial difference is that health purchasers tend to carry out their purchasing function by considering the needs of a geographically defined population. The health care needs of their target population are generally predictable through the use of health indices applied to the population in question. This is done through the mechanism of large block contracts. A consequence of this approach is that the health purchaser will have little or no contact with individual users of the service, making issues such as quality control and user participation difficult to establish.

In contrast to this, social service purchasers come from a background of social work *practice* rather than from a planning perspective, as is the case with their health counterparts. There is a further distinction between health and social service purchasers, in the manner in which they interact with the user of the service. Social service purchasers will assess individual need and purchase services accordingly.

These purchasing decisions form an individual care plan for the user. The aggregation of many such plans informs the overall planning process within social services departments, whereas health purchasers need to base their plans on statistical predictions. Within the social services approach to planning there is, in our view, a greater potential for the user of the service to influence the service itself.

Whilst conflict exists in both organizations, the nature of this conflict is very different. From our research, it has emerged that the conflict within health authorities results from the fact that many of the purchasing decision-makers are drawn from non-clinical backgrounds. This inevitably leads to a perception that hitherto sacrosanct clinical decisions are being challenged by managerial staff who may have different agendas arising from their contractual commitments as well as economic considerations. This is further complicated by the manner in which health service purchasers operate. They have to consider service levels rather than the needs of a particular individual. While health care purchasers are sometimes drawn from clinical practice, we have no evidence that this significantly alters the situation in one direction or another.

Conversely, the situation within the social services departments throws up different issues. Here the newly formed purchasers and providers are very likely to have come from similar backgrounds and have undergone similar training. This produces dissonance of a different nature and one that is more to do with clashes of professional judgement. This manifests itself in the need to claim 'clinical autonomy' as a justification for disregarding the view of a former colleague.

The switch in emphasis from a needs-orientated service to a service constrained by cash-limited budgets brings into focus the different objectives of those concerned with the delivery of the service as opposed to those responsible for the management of the service. The conflict is often expressed as a clash between the professional dominance of the accountant and the practitioner which leads the observer to believe that the conflict is beginning to take a similar form in social services to that in health settings.

In both health and social services, the situation is exacerbated by the fact that the political imperative prevents a full market economy from developing. The prominence of the NHS in the public eye is one such imperative, as is the need for local authority politicians to maintain their established provider services.

Traditionally, local authority politicians have highlighted local services as being an indicator of the success of the political activity and the overall direction of their party policies. It is, therefore, arguably in their interest to maintain a high level of local provision for which they can claim responsibility and consequently their success. This stance militates against the externalization of services through the development of market economics in both health and social care.

A similar conflict arises in the degree to which the hospital trust can be allowed to be seen as operating outside the NHS. This is a delicate issue and one that has a serious impact on how the services operate. The challenge within this situation is to transform the conflicts that nationally exist within the marketplace into creative tension that stimulates competition without damaging the embryonic relationship between the new purchasers and providers.

A further source of conflict arises from the patient or client. The power base of the patient has been strengthened by the emphasis on consumer rights as expressed in citizens' charters aimed at raising the standard of public services and increasing consumer choice. This has encouraged users of health and social care services to expect to influence the way in which services are provided and developed. In this way, the customer must be seen as an interactive partner with the professional. In turn, the professional no longer has absolute power to dictate what is right or wrong in a particular situation, but needs to be able to offer information and a range of options upon which the basis of a choice can be established. Clearly, this will take time to establish in the repertoire of professionals. However, it is important to note that the standards which the charters seek to establish are set by the very people who are responsible for purchasing and providing the service. In effect this situation appears to give little real meaning to the standards and their relation to the needs and wishes of the users.

Interestingly the standards that are set by the purchasers and providers are often no higher than current service levels. At the same time they do not represent significant challenges to those responsible for the service and do nothing to extend the quality and effectiveness of the service. Indeed, the razzmatazz that accompanies the launch of charters can often mask the real issues. Glossy pamphlets do not make the trains run on time. More importantly, it is the commitment of workers and first-line managers that carries through the desired standards and thus can be directly related to the level of investment made by the organization in its people. This investment in first-line managers is endorsed in the recent CBI study *Focus on the First Line* (CBI, 1992).

When looking at the current situation, it is difficult to obtain a coherent overview. In effect, the level to which local authorities have responded to care in the community varies enormously. It is clear that there are those who believed that potential changes in central government might bring a reversal of policy and have used this as a justification for inactivity. At best, this approach is naive. The rate and degree of change in health and social services has been such that a change of political direction at Westminster would have little impact on the current ethos of health and social care because the professionals implementing the changes have become convinced of the need to change by the requirements of the legislation.

Given the degree of variation in the way in which local authorities have prepared for the changes generated by the care in the community legislation, it is not surprising that many local authorities appear ill-equipped to put into practice the key principles that convey to their consumers the fact that they understand what is needed to address the legislation. Consequently much needs to be done by these local authorities in establishing the right framework to deliver care in the community.

The emergence of the fund-holding GP has highlighted the same lack of preparedness by health authorities to adapt their approach to purchasing and providing. The way in which the GP fund-holder purchases services is analogous to that of social service purchasers.

In turn, health authorities may become marginalized and, therefore, less influential in planning and purchasing of local services. This leaves the way clear for GP fund-holders and local authority social service purchasers to strengthen their working relationships and to form partnerships in the purchase of both health and social care in local communities.

Managing the organizational climate

Health and social services must recognize the opportunities that are open to them in order to move forward successfully. The opportunities lie in the investment senior managers make in their workforce. This investment cannot be made simply through training and education programmes as promulgated by the modern human capital investment theorists, such as Hage et al. (1988). In pursuing the idea of investment in the human capital of an organization, its workforce must recognize the values an organization wishes to promote. In addition, there must be clear statements about the direction and purpose of the organization which can be understood by the workforce.

However, the approach taken by the human capital school does not address the issue of the influence which these value systems can have on the culture of the organization and the importance of developing attitudinal change in relation to customer care. We would argue that this traditional view of human capital investment reinforces professional culture rather than organizational culture.

The use of training in the traditional sense tends to establish skills that are particular to a specific profession, such as counselling skills in social work practice, or surgical techniques in medicine. These skills tend to promote the insular nature of professions, and as a consequence produce a professional culture that relates only to those in the profession. Both local authority social services departments and health authorities have workforces that comprise a range of such professionals. In order to bring the workforce into a coherent group that can identify with the organization as a whole, a culture needs to be established in both local authority social services departments and health authorities that transcends the narrow professional cultures. This culture we would describe as the 'organizational culture'. This culture is established on the basis of common values and aims that the organization holds.

Professional cultures are profession specific. They can promote neither cultural diffusion within the organization nor corporate direction, and will do very little in establishing a human resource plan that will prepare and equip the workforce with the required skills to meet the challenge of change. In effect, a professional culture appears to be an 'arrested culture'.

The creation of an innovative climate within the organization is one in which there is continual awareness of both internal and external changes and tries to find solutions in a changing environment. Such a culture is described by Boulding (1981) where success involves the 'survival of the fitting' and not just the 'survival of the fittest'. In other words, health and social services managers need to take into account the needs of their own workforce and match those to the needs of the task the organization has to carry out.

Organizational cultures can manifest themselves in different ways. For example, the level of self-actualization within an organization would provide a key to the type of culture within that organization. In this example the use of self-actualization refers to the ability of an individual to assess a situation and respond independently without direct reference to a superior but within the framework of the organization's activity. The degree of self-actualization is linked to the level of devolved management. Conversely, the heavy use of procedure manuals within the organization would indicate a centralized culture where the power and autonomy is vested in a small number of senior managers placed at the centre.

In our research we found that in organizations where the dominant culture was a professional one there was little evidence of innovation, and generally professionally trained staff demonstrated less flair than their non-professional colleagues. This was equally true of first-line managers, which is consistent with the CBI study (1992). Clearly this outcome raised issues of trust in the system and demonstrated a propensity to rely heavily on set procedures and a tendency to abide by the rules and regulations of the organization regardless of the situation they were facing. By contrast, those staff such as residential care assistants, auxiliary nurses, assistant occupational therapists, social work assistants and domestics in our research organizations who were not professionally trained showed high levels of self-actualization in that they were looking for innovative ways of delivering their hands-on care. This group also displayed significantly higher levels of morale than their professional colleagues. These findings are supported by the work of Strauss et al. (1978), who demonstrated that lay personnel working extensively with or near the patients are likely to have more impact on the treatment of those patients and, therefore, gain greater job satisfaction which is used as the measure of their morale.

Our findings are significant as the organizations in which the staff were operating were undergoing radical changes as a result of the community care legislation. Here one can conclude that a value system was operating between these particular workers. However, we found no evidence of an explicit statement of values or aims made by the senior managers of the organization. Conversely, in other organizations that were part of our study there were explicit statements about the values and aims of the organization. These had been constructed by senior managers and placed on walls and noticeboards throughout the organization without explanation or any identifiable method of integrating the aims and values into the existing organizational culture. The result was that there was no discernable influence on the way the workforce provided the service. This finding supports our belief that the existence of explicit value statements and proclamations about the aims of the organization are not sufficient in themselves to influence the organizational culture. In brief, there needs to be a commitment by senior managers to be actively pursuing ways in which the explicit values of the organization are reflected in the behaviour of the workforce.

In addition to this commitment from senior managers there needs to be a recognition of the role that the consumers have and their influence on the way in which services are provided. This influence is well documented in the work of Peters and Waterman (1982). Their work demonstrates that an understanding of the needs of consumers and a desire to meet those needs will be better achieved if the importance of the consumer is an explicit part of the organizational culture. Alongside the need to understand the role of the consumer is the issue of quality. The work of W. Edward Deming in relation to the importance of quality is well demonstrated in the success of Japanese products in particular in the electronics and automobile industries. Swiss (1992) argues the need to adapt Deming's work in order to take account of issues of service provision rather than simply focusing on product manufacturing. Swiss concludes that total quality management can be adapted to public sector services by adopting the major features of an orthodox approach — these are consumer feedback, performance monitoring, continuous improvement and worker participation.

Indications from our research suggest that the key to achieving these features is effective information flow. This is not just communication, but the timeliness, quality, quantity and nature of the information. How this moves around the organization is pivotal to its success.

From our own work we found a significant number of people (65% of the sample population) in the health and social care organizations studied who considered that the information flow within their organization was poor and did not assist the communication process whatsoever. It was in these organizations that information tended to be via the written word, rather than through face-to-face meetings. This prevented people from understanding the context in which the information was given and its relationship with previous information and their working situation. In times of rapid change the type and level of information flow becomes even more critical. A successful example of this was the use of 'briefing sessions' following meetings when important events were discussed. Line managers throughout the organization actively sought briefings with their staff to ensure that current issues were successfully communicated and understood.

Further examples of the power of communication can be found in the use of custom and practice. A particularly powerful perception held about health and social care services is the supremacy of the doctor. Indeed it is likely that the public will assume that the 'doctor' is responsible for the service and indeed controls the service. This leaves the public impotent in lodging their complaints, as in the absence of other information they may assume the person to complain to is the very person about whom they wish to complain. The antidote to this is to broadcast the structure of the service and to be clear about the values and the aims of the organization, including the process of complaint. However, this path is not trouble-free. The organization's value statements nicely framed, hung on walls do not guarantee that the values are understood throughout the organization or by the public for whom they are intended. In our experience these statements are often coined by senior management who do not ensure that the values are diffused throughout the organization. It is this level of diffusion that is critical in the matter of information flow. We found that the critical impact of this lack of information flow was that the staff within the organizations studied did not understand where the organization was going in terms of its overall direction. There was considerable confusion about the overall strategy and how and what individuals could do to contribute. There was little evidence that the direction the organization wished to take had been diffused through the structure, and whilst there was evidence that some managers had been active in this sphere it was at best patchy. In essence there was an emphasis upon promoting the external image of the organization at the expense of ignoring the needs of those working within it.

Of equal importance in understanding the issues for public sector organizations is the matter of recognition. Traditionally, public sector organizations have been limited in their ability to reward and recognize their personnel when compared with their private sector counterparts. Performance-related pay is a relatively new activity in health and social care and is largely restricted to senior management. The organizations that we have studied were no exception. There was little that was offered other than basic salary and management acknowledgement of good work which was confined to those managers whose style promoted this action rather than the corporate culture.

The future: what are the basic dilemmas?

The next decade will see the health and social care services working closer together to deal with changes. If they are to be successful, the future managers of these services must recognize and accept some fundamental issues within the organizational climate in which they work. Furthermore, there must be recognition that both health and social care services are organizations that provide services for people that are delivered by people. By internalizing the fact that investment in the workforce must go beyond the traditional concepts of training and education, managers will enable their staff to take on the roles that will lead to success and, therefore, survival.

Health and social care professionals are moving through role changes. They will need to decide whether they remain in 'practice' for which they were trained and continue to maintain their skills, or whether they wish to embrace the new world in which there is a marriage between clinical practice and business ethics. This remains unresolved for these professionals.

Our study has highlighted the emerging conflict between the professional culture and the organizational culture. It is clear that organizations that consisted of a collection of cultures each of which identified with a particular profession and which adhered to a strict hierarchy are being subsumed by an overarching culture that has little or no allegiance to any particular profession. The organizational culture will generate its own influence that will challenge the traditional roles of professionals and reduce their respective power bases, and consequently their level of influence on the functioning of the organization.

Managers must look towards becoming leaders. In doing so they will need to promote a strong team spirit without stifling individual initiative, and create well-defined strategies and credible policies which accommodate an entrepreneurial climate. The imperatives here are the fact that public sector organizations will increasingly become the subject of public scrutiny as they move more into partnerships with their consumers. This will require them to develop and establish robust quality audit systems that take account of a range of consumer opinion and are set against explicit quality standards. This will undoubtedly place enormous pressures on first-line staff and it is, therefore, the responsibility of senior managers to ensure that they understand the impact on their staff and invest in them in a way that will ensure that both the staff and the organization move forward in harmony with their consumers.

Clearly, these concepts are not new and may appear obvious. However, our research has demonstrated that in the real world they are conspicuous by their absence. Their simplicity belies the fact that consciously managing values in an organization is time-consuming, difficult, and demands that managers develop new skills and risk sharing the fact that they do not have a monopoly on wisdom. In conclusion, health and social care organizations are both labour-intensive and, therefore, the success of both is dependent upon the skills of the workforces. Each member of the workforce will have something to offer that adds value to the enterprise of the whole organization.

References

Ackroyd S, Hughes JA, Soothill K (1989) Public sector services and their management. *Journal of Management Studies*; **26**: 603–619.

Baker E (1980) Managing organisational culture. *Administrative Quarterly*; autumn: 57–61.

Boulding KE (1981) *Evolutionary Economics*. Beverly Hills: Sage.

Confederation of British Industry (1992) *Focus on the First Line — The Role of the Supervisor*. London: CBI.

Department of Health (1989a) *Caring for People*. London: HMSO.

Department of Health (1989b) *Working for Patients*. London: HMSO.

Department of Health (1990) *The New GP Contract*. NHS (General Medical and Pharmaceutical Services). Updated by NHS (General Medical Services) Regulations 1992.

Hage J (1989) Investment in human capital or powerful interest group: the case of the medical profession in Britain, France and the United States from 1890–1970. For more details of this study contact Prof. Jerald Hage, Department of Sociology, University of Maryland, College Park, Maryland, USA.

Hage J, Garnier MA, Fuller B (1988) The active state: investment in human capital and economic growth. *American Sociological Review*; **53**: 824–837.

Haralambos M (1986) *Sociology: A New Approach*. Ormskirk, Lancashire: Causeway Books.

McClean A, Marshall J (1983) *Intervening in Cultures*. Bath: University of Bath (working paper).

National Health Service and Community Care Act (1990). London: HMSO.

Pascale R, Athos A (1981) *The Art of Japanese Management*. New York: Warner Books.

Peters PJ, Waterman RH (1982) *In Search of Excellence*. New York: Harper & Row.

Schein E (1985) *Organisational Culture and Leadership*. San Francisco: Jossey-Bass.

Schein E (1987) *The Art of Managing Human Resources*. Oxford: Oxford University Press.

Strauss A, Schatzman L, Ehrlich D, Butcher R, Sabshin M (1978) The hospital and its negotiated order. In: Salaman G, Thompson K (Eds). *People and Organisations*. Harmondsworth: Longman.

Swiss JE (1992) Adapting total quality management to government. *Public Administration Review*; **52**: 356–362.

6 Implementing community care

John Carpenter

Introduction

Successive governments have exhorted health and welfare agencies to work together in the best interests of clients/patients with, according to the Audit Commission (1986), not a great deal of success. Problems identified by the Commission included poor mechanisms for interagency collaboration and entrenched attitudes. The community care reforms outlined in the 1989 White Paper *Caring for People* and subsequently enacted as the NHS and Community Care Act were seen in part as a response to these obstacles. The new legislation requires greater consumer involvement, a shift to services based on people's needs, and a *joint* approach to the planning and delivery of services by health authorities, local authorities, voluntary organizations and the private sector.

In this chapter I will consider some of the lessons learned about interagency collaboration from a series of pilot projects concerned with the implementation of the community care reforms.

Caring for People Joint Training Project

The *Caring for People* Joint Training Project was set up in June 1990 with the objective of identifying the organizational requirements and training needs for the implementation of *Caring for People*. (For a full report, see Carpenter et al. (1991a,b).) Obviously these two elements are inextricably linked — it is impossible to define training needs without knowing fairly clearly what you are trying to achieve. The White Paper had outlined the broad goals of the policy but was short on specifics. The policy guidance which followed in draft form in June 1990, and which was subsequently published in November that year, sensibly made it clear that the government did not intend to be prescriptive (Department of Health, 1990). This was an important message: because needs are different in different places, so too should be the services designed to meet those needs, and the structures to support them. Further, new models of service, and particularly joint approaches, are always built on existing services and political structures. Failure to take these into account leads to suspicion, competitiveness and inefficiency.

The approach

The project, which was coordinated and funded by the NHS Training Directorate (NHSTD) and the Social Services Inspectorate (SSI) of the Department of Health, took place in seven areas in England, covering a representative range of rural, urban and inner-city areas with different demographies and of various political complexions. The brief specified that the work undertaken should be truly joint: the focus was to be not merely on interagency cooperation (e.g. with good liaison and cross-referral between the agencies) but also on the creation of joint care systems, whereby different disciplines and agencies would work together to provide joint assessment and care. At least two agencies (health and social services) were to be involved and there was specific encouragement to engage the participation of Family Health Service Authorities (FHSAs), GPs and representatives of service users and carers.

In considering factors which influenced the success of these projects, it is important to note that all began with meetings between project managers from the NHSTD and SSI and senior managers in the respective health authorities and social services departments. Whilst it is true to say that there was at least some contact between the agencies in the seven areas, the project was the catalyst which brought them together in order to engage in joint work. At these meetings, broad objectives were agreed and *core groups* consisting of representatives of the agencies — typically middle managers — were established. As I will discuss later, the commitment, or otherwise, of senior managers is significant. The core groups each had the services of a consultant appointed and paid for by the NHSTD/SSI. The consultants came from the Universities of Kent and Newcastle, the King's Fund College and LBTC: Training for Care. The role of the consultants was also seen as important, and will be discussed below.

Each area was allowed to focus on one aspect of the community care reforms although this did not prohibit work in other related areas. Thus, one of the projects aimed to develop proposals for a new joint planning structure which separated the purchaser and provider functions of health and local authorities (one of the key elements of the NHS and Community Care Act). Others were concerned with arrangements for the joint assessment and care management for elderly people and people with disabilities. One project had as its focus the development of joint mental health services for black and minority ethnic groups living in an inner-city.

There was a wide variation between the areas in the extent of their previous experience of joint training and service development. Most groups established a subgroup to assess training needs in relation to the project and to devise programmes to meet training needs. However, as all the participants were quick to recognize, their involvement in the project was in itself a form of interprofessional and interagency training.

Developing working relationships

The first point to make about interagency working is that it takes time. This may seem so obvious that it hardly needs stating; however, in the experience of this project, shortage of time was the greatest impediment. Thus, for almost all participants, involvement in interagency project work was additional to their usual managerial or professional tasks. Not only did this make arranging meetings difficult, it also put participants under pressure when having to complete tasks between meetings. As one professional complained: 'My manager says that this project is really important to the way we're going. But if it's so important, why doesn't she allow me the time to put into it?' The irony was that the manager usually felt the same way about *her* manager.

Such sentiments were most likely to be expressed when a project was going through a sticky patch. In the worst situations, attendance at meetings dropped and participants could barely conceal their irritation with each other, implying either blame for failing to deliver the goods or resenting the pressure under which they were being put. Nevertheless, as one group summarized their experience:

> 'Joint working takes a lot of time and investment at the individual and institutional levels. It is very hard work, and very messy. With endurance and persistence it is likely to succeed, provided account is taken of the inherent tensions in the process of coming together.'

This sense of 'messiness' was a common experience:

> 'We found ourselves constantly trying to make order out of the messiness that comprises effective joint working. We had to learn how to allow members to find their own level of required structure in order to be able to contribute most effectively. We wanted to value diversity and difference. There were, for example, difficult decisions to be made about how meetings were to be run. We had to learn that comfort was sometimes at the expense of someone else's discomfort and that we had to find ways of managing that discomfort.'

Even in areas where there had been long-term contact between agencies, members in fact knew very little about the ways in which other agencies worked, the constraints on action and how decisions were made. For example, health service managers consistently overlooked the role and power of local authority elected council members and tended to think that social services colleagues were being unnecessarily slow and cautious when they stressed the importance of 'bringing the members on board'. Conversely, social services staff appeared to be shocked at times by the 'gung-ho' attitude of health service colleagues, particularly those who were involved in the formation of the new, independent business-style NHS Trusts. The political sensitivity required, for example, to present proposals to Labour councillors who had expressed themselves as being ideologically opposed to aspects of the new legislation (e.g. the 'mixed economy of care'), was not, they felt, appreciated.

These differences in culture were compounded with differences in language and interpretation. For example, in at least one of the project groups, health service managers viewed Department of Health guidance on *Caring for People* as just that — guidance. Social services managers, by contrast, seemed to regard it as prescriptive, perhaps reflecting the perceived consequences of failing to follow 'guidance' on child care procedures.

Differences in the understanding of terminology were a particular source of difficulty when they were unrecognized. Thus, much attention in *Caring for People* is focused on 'assessment' as the initial step in care management. District nurses, social workers and GPs all undertake assessment. However, the process, context and outcome of these assessments differ markedly between the three professional groups. As the project group members discovered, such differences need to be explored and understood before assessment — and especially mutlidisciplinary assessment — can be sensibly discussed.

The following comments on the importance of language were noted at a meeting of one of the groups: 'The main problem when two services come together is which language we're going to use. We have to get a language of integration'; and, in the realization of the fact that *Caring for People* had itself introduced a new terminology (e.g. 'needs-led assessment', 'care' — or was it 'case'? — 'manager'): 'Can you come up with a glossary of terms?'

Managing change

The new approach to interagency working envisaged in the projects required considerable organizational changes. Various approaches to the management of change were identified, some being more successful than others. In one project, the approach was described as: senior managers set the mission and the aims, and created the structure (and then moved on to new jobs!); middle managers from health and social services were told to implement and practitioners were expected to change practice. Not surprisingly, the middle managers were reported as wondering: 'Whose mission is this?'; 'Where are they now?'; 'Does it still count?'; 'Can we make sense of this project?'; and 'Are we allowed to change it?' The practitioners, not surprisingly, said they were more than a little confused.

In contrast, in another project the senior managers gave no direction, leaving the middle managers with almost total autonomy and with practitioners not initially being involved. This was equally unhelpful as the middle managers began to ask: 'How did we get into this?'; 'How much autonomy do we really have?'; and 'What should we do first?'.

In both projects the middle managers crucial to successful implementation of *Caring for People* felt disempowered and the practitioners either uninvolved or imposed upon. The creation of a clear mission and aims at the top of organizations is not sufficient; rather, all levels need to become involved so that there is a shared investment in achieving the organization's objectives (Beckhard and Harris, 1987). Further, involving a cross-section of 'stakeholders' when developing new ways of working helps to ensure the relevance and feasibility of proposals. This is even more important when a number of different organizations are involved.

In order to promote organizational change, Beckhard and Harris (1987) argue, it is essential to have a 'critical mass' of people with energy and influence, but also a suitable organizational structure within which to work. The following case study illustrates how this was achieved in the Medway area of Kent.

The Medway Project

The initial agreement for the work of the Medway Project was drafted by senior managers in health and social services, together with the NHSTD project manager and middle managers from the two authorities. These managers recruited colleagues to form an interagency working group (subsequently known as the Core Group). The original goals of the project were very ambitious, involving plans for developing interagency planning structures as well as an area-wide joint assessment and care management service. Doubts about the capacity of the Core Group to effect the proposed changes quickly emerged, particularly in relation to the time that group members could give the project.

Confronted with the likely collapse of the whole project, the group then redefined the tasks of the project and agreed a 'bottom up' approach to the development of a joint care management system in one part of the area, the Isle of Sheppey. The following mission was formulated for the service:

'To provide a comprehensive and integrated service designed to support people with disabilities to live in their own homes in the community, which is sensitive to the strengths and needs of carers, which prevents unnecessary admission to hospital, and promotes easy access to residential care if this becomes necessary.'

It was considered that the best approach to designing such a service would be through an interagency group of practitioners and their managers together with representatives of carers' organizations. Accordingly, a group (the Sheppey Group) was convened which included a district nurse, health visitor, nursing managers for general and elderly services, a GP, a social worker (care manager) and social services managers for elderly and disability services. The local organizer of the Carers' National Association joined the group. The remit was to develop a proposal based on their experience of working together.

Developing proposals

The group was facilitated by one of the consultants through a series of workshops and meetings which proceeded through the following agenda:

1. Clarification of aims and expectations.
2. Brainstorming ideas on joint care management and visions for the future.
3. A small group exercise looking at strengths and weaknesses of the present service; the contribution of the carers' representative was particularly useful here.
4. A presentation on 'core requirements' of care management: publicizing information; assessment; care planning; implementation; monitoring'; and reviewing (Department of Health, SSI, 1991).
5. A small group exercise aimed at drawing up recommendations to achieve the core requirements. Here it was necessary for participants to share information about their skills and knowledge and to consider how these could be pooled. In addition, representatives from the different disciplines were asked to clarify their particular roles and duties in order that a shared model of care could be developed which satisfied the requirements of each agency.
6. At the second meeting, feedback on a draft report prepared by the consultants. This drew out some further recommendations.
7. Prioritizing the recommendations.
8. An exercise examining the experience of a prospective service user progressing through the proposed system. This identified

some previously unconsidered obstacles to joint working, such as differences in entitlement to service and whether a charge was involved.

9. Planning of presentation of the model to the Core Group.

The group proposed that the existing services for older people, people with physical disabilities and learning difficulties be re-organized as a multidisciplinary team of health and social services staff with a common base and operational policy. The multidisciplinary team would operate a core record-keeping system, collecting information on both met and unmet needs. This information would be fed up to a joint management board comprising health and local authority managers. The team would share common budgets for purchasing the support of assistants (presently nursing assistants and care assistants).

Creating structures for change

Following the successful presentation of the Sheppey Group's recommendations to the Core Group, it was asked to prepare an operational policy for the team which included details of service mission, aims and objectives. In doing this, the group was to consult informally prospective team members, users and carers. The group was also asked to identify training needs for team members.

The Core Group considered other tasks that were required for implementation and these were allocated to three groups — the Training Group, the Management Group and the Sheppey Group. A project timetable and terms of reference for the groups were defined.

In order to ensure continuity and communication, the Training Group included members of the Core Group and the Sheppey Group as well as training specialists. Its tasks were to review the training needs as defined by Sheppey Group and to examine the extent to which they could be met through existing training programmes run by the two authorities, including Kent County Council's Care Managers and Team Leaders courses, care assistant training and NVQ proposals. From this, they developed a training plan which was presented to the Core Group.

The Management Group had the following tasks:

• To prepare a proposal for the pooling of resources to create a system of joint care management, to be submitted to the Area Management Team, the District Management Team (SSD), the District Management Board (Health Authority) and the FHSA.

- To arrange consultation with GPs through the Family Health Services Authority.
- To consult the Community Health Council, Age Concern and any other voluntary organizations, formally.
- To define education/training needs of senior managers, members of the County Council and District Health Authority.
- To set a timetable for implementation.

The importance of consultation is worth emphasizing. It was acknowledged by members of the various working groups that the future success of the project was contingent on broadening consultation with stakeholders. A GP facilitator, funded by the FHSA, assumed responsibility for liaising and consulting with GP colleagues about the project. The approach to public consultation drew on experience gained from piloting single-agency care management. Public meetings were held at two venues in the district. Direct care staff took responsibility for personally inviting service users and carers to attend and for ensuring that their needs for information, transport and escorts were met. A prerequisite for consulting people is the preparation of information about the proposed service that actually reflects their different interests. The success of such events is contingent on both good organization and the commitment of resources — especially the time, energy and thought of appropriate personnel.

Once past the initial stage of defining the project's aims, the responsibilities of the Core Group were relatively easy to identify. These included defining and responding to the work of the other project groups. Members of the Core Group also assumed responsibility for ensuring their agency and colleagues were kept abreast of developments. This was sucessfully achieved, and there were no signs of organizational resistance to the proposed changes.

A feature of this project was that the Core Group empowered other groups to take on tasks that they were best equipped by their knowledge and experience to fulfil. Further, the power to determine membership of these groups was also partly devolved and this may have contributed to their efficiency and commitment.

It was recognized that the groups would have to work in 'relay', with recommendations from one group being passed on to the others. The project consultants played an important role in making sure this happened. Consultants wrote reports about each meeting which were quickly circulated to group members for comment and revision; these reports were then immediately forwarded to any other group or individual who needed to be aware of, think about or act on their contents. In this respect the consultants had a crucial role in ensuring that the project structure worked.

Conclusions

This approach to project development worked well. A structure evolved that met the emerging aims of the project. The project was managed by a well constituted group, which empowered other groups to carry out the work that they could do effectively. Most crucially, the people who worked closest to the client were given power to define the shape of the new service. The project was a good example of interagency service development which harnessed power effectively. This included power based on status, knowledge, connections and time. This structure was strengthened by a clear definition of tasks, responsibilities and communication systems.

Training for community care

The Joint Training Project identified a number of tasks for training arising from *Caring for People*. The first, as already indicated, is that of building bridges in terms of understanding work roles, statutory requirements of each agency, organizational practices and models of service provision. Equally important is that of identifying common values, knowledge and skills across professions and work settings, and creating a shared philosophy of care. In order to achieve this, a strategy for training should be developed, based on the shared values and goals of the agencies involved. As the Medway case study illustrates, an essential step is to determine local arrangements for the delivery of services and ensure that training grows out of these arrangements. In this way training will both be relevant to local needs and meet the requirements of staff. The task, in other words, is to integrate training and staff development into the planning and management of services. Obviously, if the service is to be a joint service, then the training must also be joint.

Kingsley and Smith (1989) consider that there should be two main elements in a training strategy: 'one directed towards communicating the organization's goals, policies and values and encouraging a wider ownership and understanding of them; and a second stream of training focused on developing the practical capacities of staff in the organization to achieve those goals'.

The project groups addressed the issue of developing a training strategy in a number of ways. For example, in one project which involved senior and middle managers in the development of a joint planning system, the framework for training comprised three elements:

- an issues-based approach, where training was designed to tackle issues as they arose (rather than a pre-existing training programme);
- seminars on the process of change management;
- what was described as a management research approach — involving participants in developing and piloting schemes and ideas as a tool of management development.

The last element is important in that training can often become a substitute for management and be instituted in order to solve organizational problems; having a distinct focus on management development may prevent this from happening.

The projects approached the task of identifying training needs in different ways: some did quite detailed work on defining training to meet the specific skills they thought would be required; others defined clusters or areas of training needs which seemed to focus more on raising awareness and setting the context for staff. Practitioners contemplating care management services typically did not want over-elaborate syllabi, but rather a clear framework from managers and an understanding of how the system was intended to operate — particularly the use of information technology and budget management, and initial interdisciplinary team building to create trust and establish how decisions would be made. Beyond that, they felt that the implementation of *Caring for People* was a relatively straightforward task of building on common sense and good practice.

However, a reliance on good sense and professional practice may underestimate the changes in attitude required if services are to achieve one of the central elements of the philosophy of *Caring for People* — the move from a supply-led service (users get what is there) to one which is based on people's needs, as they perceive them. This entails a profound shift in the way services are planned and delivered. Such a change will not be learnt in the classroom but will require 'hands on' experience of innovative and different ways of working. It also means reflecting on that experience in the light of the values and principles that should appropriately guide community care services. It will therefore require training throughout a worker's career — an initial 'blitz' at the beginning will no longer be sufficient to support a complex and evolving service.

The major conclusion of this project was that *the best way to learn about working together is by doing it*. Taking an active part in a project with an agreed joint agenda to develop a joint system involved participants in learning about each others' tasks, roles and skills *and* how they could collaborate in a shared model of care. External facilitation proved a valuable tool in ensuring the effectiveness of this approach. An important ingredient here was an explicit focus on personal and organizational learning: people can only learn by doing if they have the opportunity to reflect on the experience. These are hardly new revelations, but they are too often forgotten or ignored in the turbulence that characterizes services at times of change.

The groups were very positive about the benefits of joint project work. In their experience, it could achieve attitudinal change, encourage creative thinking and be 'good news' for consumers. When users and carers or their representatives were involved in the process, it could help ensure that services were more user-centred (and often more cost-effective). In the process, it could make organizations and their staff more responsive and better able to communicate with each other. However, joint work needs clear commitment and direction from the senior management of all agencies and a recognition that it takes time and resources — there are no short cuts. It also requires a belief in the benefits for consumers of collaboration between agencies and disciplines.

Hardy et al. (1992) cautioned, on the basis of a study of jointly managed schemes in four counties, that such schemes were inherently fragile and vulnerable to organizational pressures that threatened their sustained development. Joint schemes were often seen as peripheral, an administrative inconvenience or a threat to the *status quo*, and may rely too much on 'mutual trust and altruism'. Follow-up of the work in the sites of the Joint Training Project confirmed the truth of this observation in at least one of the projects, at Blaydon (Peck, 1992); however, others — including the Medway Project — have survived, and indeed thrived.

In analysing the reasons for success and failure of the schemes they studied, Hardy and his colleagues (1992) emphasized the importance of clear objectives, commitment of all parties, sound management arrangements and opportunities for organizational learning. In the project evaluated by Peck (1992), a joint care management service for elderly people based on a General Practice, these factors were not sufficiently evident. Thus, the project was unclear about whether it was intending to provide improved services to existing clients or to identify and offer services to new referrals only. As a consequence, a half of all referrals were deemed 'inappropriate' by the care manager or assessment team before an assessment visit had even been undertaken. The total number taken on by the scheme was only 10 out of 28 referrals in nine months. It was not surprising, therefore, that both the originators and the referrers felt somewhat disillusioned. By contrast, in the Medway Project, the service itself took very much longer to get going; but by the time it did, most of the ambiguities had been cleared up. In particular, the agreement eventually reached on the principle of 'one door' of access meant that all referrals, including referrals of existing clients, came into the joint scheme — even if assessment concluded that a multidisciplinary service was not required. This was a much clearer arrangement.

Commitment and shared ownership were also found lacking in the Blaydon Project. Peck reports that one of the social services managers predicted that when the final review meeting took place there would be scant attendance from the health service. This prediction proved all too true, and the belief of the social services staff that the priorities of their health service colleagues lay elsewhere was apparently confirmed. On the other hand, as Peck observes, belief in others' lack of commitment can become a self-fulfilling prophesy, particularly if it is used as an excuse for being less than fully efficient in passing on information, giving notice of meetings and sending minutes. Rather than analysing these difficulties and learning from them, it seems that both agencies drifted apart. Those present at the review concluded that 'continued pressure on the practitioners to prolong the scheme beyond the pilot stage would not be warranted'. One can almost sense the feeling of relief.

Perhaps because there had been a much longer history of interagency cooperation in Medway, both among managers and practitioners, but also because the importance of shared ownership involving a shared commitment of resources had been emphasized from the beginning, these problems did not arise. Further, the considerable amount of attention given by a group of senior staff (the Management Group) to working out joint management arrangements for the project resulted in a strong and resilient structure which has provided a model for extension throughout the district.

At the time of writing, some three months after the full legal implementation of the NHS and Community Care Act, it is by no means clear that many health authorities and local authorities are willing to make a commitment to the kind of interagency working piloted both in the Joint Training Project and in a further series of initiatives, the *Caring for People* Development Programme (Carpenter, 1993). However, as Hardy et al. (1992) conclude, with the key ingredients of clarity of purpose, commitment and shared ownership, robust and coherent management arrangements and opportunities for organizational learning, survival and success are achievable.

Acknowledgements

Thanks are due to Jennie Williams, Steve Onyett and Helen Smith of the

Centre for the Applied Psychology of Social Care at the University of Kent with whom I worked on this project, and to colleagues from Newcastle University, the King's Fund College and LBTC: Training for Care.

References

Audit Commission (1986) *Making a Reality of Community Care.* London: HMSO.

Beckhard R, Harris R (1987) *Organisational Transitions: Managing Complex Change.* Reading, Mass: Addison-Wesley.

Carpenter J, Onyett S, Smith H, Williams J, Peck E (1991a) *'Caring for People' Joint Training Project.* Bristol: National Health Service Training Directorate.

Carpenter J, Onyett S, Williams J (1991b) *'Caring for People' Joint Training Project, Medway Site Report.* Canterbury: Centre for the Applied Psychology of Social Care, University of Kent at Canterbury.

Carpenter J (1993) *'Caring for People' Development Programme. Lessons from the Projects.* Bristol: National Health Service Training Directorate.

Department of Health (1989) *Caring for People: Community Care in the Next Decade and Beyond*, Cmd. 849. London: HMSO.

Department of Health (1990) *Caring for People: Community Care in the Next Decade and Beyond. Policy Guidance.* London: HMSO.

Department of Health, Social Services Inspectorate (1991) *Care Management and Assessment: Practitioners' Guide.* London: HMSO.

Hardy B, Wistow G, Turrell A (1992) *Innovations in Community Care Management.* Aldershot: Gower.

Kingsley S, Smith H (1989) *Values for Change: Principles and Approaches in Designing a Local Training Strategy.* London: King's Fund Centre.

Peck E (1992) *The Blaydon Joint Care Management Project.* Newcastle: University of Newcastle, Centre for Health Services Management.

7 Clinicians as managers: Convergence or collision?

Anna Lorbiecki

Introduction

During the past few years clinicians[1] have been encouraged to become more actively involved in the management of their hospital units as a means of implementing the recent NHS reforms stemming from the Griffiths Report (1983) and the White Paper *Working for Patients* (Department of Health, 1989a). This represents a possible *convergence* between the different ways in which the medical body and managers organize themselves. However, in view of the significant differences in the perspectives of the medical profession and managers there is always the danger that closer relationships will lead to some sort of *collision* of interests.

This chapter examines this dilemma in the following way. First I review the external changes and legislation which have placed greater emphasis on clinicians playing an active part in management. Then I look at the clinicians' response to this by analysing (a) collective/organizational reactions, and (b) individual experiences of their changing role. Finally I use this information to draw conclusions about the central question of convergence or collision.

Review of NHS management initiatives: 1948–1989

The NHS is a large and complex system. When looking at the recent changes in clinicians' roles it is important to understand the background of relevant legislation as this places such changes in the broader context. The management of a hospital unit has always proved controversial because it has to address the twin problems of providing free universal health care (i.e. free at the point of delivery, though paid for through taxation), while staying within budgetary limitations.

---

[1] This is the term generally used in the health services to refer to hospital consultants.

Over the past 40 years various attempts have been made to gain greater integration between the provision of health care (a medical concern) and cost (normally, a management issue).

In 1948, when the NHS was established, hospitals were organized on the basis of tripartite management, with doctors, nurses and administrators sharing managerial responsibility. Professional autonomy during this time was high, particularly among hospital consultants. This tradition of medical autonomy, however, was challenged in 1954 by the Bradbeer Committee who concluded that, to be efficient, hospitals needed one officer to be in charge of policy implementation, a chief executive (Moon and Kendall, 1993).

In 1967 the first 'Cogwheel' report (Ministry of Health, 1967) recommended that hospital medical work be reorganized in a way that encouraged doctors to manage their work more systematically, and for them to become more aware of the interconnections between the different parts of the service. Under this 'Cogwheel system', doctors from different specialities came together in divisions, and the representatives from these divisions formed a medical executive committee for the hospital as a whole (Ham and Hunter, 1988).

In 1974 the NHS was again reorganized to enhance clinicians' central role in the management of the services. Consensus management was introduced, whereby groups of administrators, nurses and doctors worked together in teams to reach unanimous decisions. Under the veneer of consensus management, however, lay very diferent patterns of organization for medical and managerial groups of staff. Brazell (1987) examined these patterns and noted that they were based on two different principles, each of which resulted in different ways of making decisions. For clinicians, decision-making was grounded in principles of autonomy and self-regulation resulting in structural arrangements which were collegial, individual and client-centred. Management, or rather administration as it was called in the NHS, was based on hierarchical control and coordination, accompanied by bureaucratic procedures.

It has been argued, however, that 'even under *normal conditions* there is a constant tension between the principles of governed, hierarchical control and coordination, and autonomy and self-regulation' (Kouzes and Mico, 1979, p. 460; my emphasis). These different guiding principles produced different criteria for measuring success. Clinicians were concerned with the quality of patient care and professional standards, whereas administrators were preoccupied with cost efficiency and effectiveness.

By the mid-1970s, however, conditions within the NHS were far from normal and many hospitals were operating in a state of financial crisis, which was to worsen in the 1980s. During this period the country witnessed a decline in national prosperity matched by pressures from: patients with higher demands for up to date, quality care; escalating costs of advanced medical technology (as a means of replacing obsolete methods of treatment); and an ageing population. One response to these economic pressures, as in other parts of the public sector which were facing similar problems, was the introduction of new management structures and principles (Davidson, 1987).

During the 1980s a number of managerial reforms were introduced into the health service, with the Griffiths report (1983) and the White Paper *Working for Patients* (Department of Health, 1989a) as centrepieces. Griffiths' judgement was not that the NHS was badly managed, but rather that it was not managed at all. This was a direct attack on consensus management, which characterized the NHS at that time. Instead of shared managerial responsibility it was recommended that a clearly defined management structure be established within the NHS, with a single general manager, acting as a chief executive, being solely responsible for the decisions previously delegated to consensus teams. There was also an implicit assumption that private sector management was superior to that which existed within the NHS. By offering attractive reward packages and good promotion prospects, it was envisaged that non-NHS managers would be drawn into the health service, bringing with them managerial skills which would enhance the efficiency of the service. This strategy, however, did not prove particularly successful as the majority of the general management posts were filled by internal candidates, many of whom had previously been administrators.

Pettigrew et al. (1992) argue, however, that the creation of this management structure, which included the appointment of regional, district and unit general managers, and the introduction of private sector style management practice, served to raise the status and the power of the previous administrative function. The establishment of these new posts was to prove significant because it created a viable career path for people who were interested in becoming managers in the health service. In 1991 the majority of general managers had been drawn from the ex-administrative pool. Although they had the same kind of health care background as the pre-Griffiths administrators of 1983, they were a different breed from their previous counterparts. These new managers had more powerfully defined roles, had received more formal education, and had, through their professional development, a firmer grasp of managerial principles. A management presence had been introduced into the health service.

As well as introducing formal management practices into the NHS, the Griffiths report emphasized the need to involve clinicians more closely in the managerial process, with a particular emphasis on the management of resources. The problem of dealing with resource pressures was not, however, a new concept for clinicians. They had been involved in this type of activity since the 1970s when clinical budgeting was implemented. Under this scheme clinicians were required to draw up a plan of objectives for clinical activity that incorporated detailed costing of the resources needed to reach the specified level of activity. Under the Griffiths proposal of 1983, this was replaced by management budgeting (MB). Although the essence of management budgeting was broadly similar to clinical budgeting, emphasis was placed on 'managing' resources. In 1986 fresh impetus was placed on involving clinicians in managing resources and the DHSS renamed the MB initiative as 'resource management'. The focus this time was on achieving *measurable* improvements in patient care through the better use of resources.

The shift in emphasis to better patient care and a wider choice of services reflects the spirit of the 1989 White Paper *Working for Patients*. The proposals contained within this reform sought fundamentally to change the organization of the NHS and thereby alter the attitudes and behaviour of those who worked within it. These proposals included the creation of the internal market; the extension of the resource management initiative; improving the quality of patient care through medical audit; and the introduction of Trust status. Each of these components sought to redefine the relationships between clinicians and managers, and as Harrison et al. (1989a) argue, these provisions, taken together, 'were designed, in part, to redraw the boundaries between management and medicine in favour of strengthening the former' (p. 7).

The separation between the purchase of health care and its provision created an internal market for the flow of resources which were attached to patient movement. This situation was intended to induce competitive behaviour on the part of purchasers and providers (Harrison et al., 1989b). As Burgoyne and Lorbiecki (1993) argue, the establishment of the internal market linked clinicians and managers and wove them into an economically controlled and structured network. Units would have to be internally reorganized in readiness for the new market environment. Local negotiations would have to take place between clinicians and managers on where and how contracts were to be handled (Harrison et al., 1992). Since clinicians and managers would each play an active part in drawing up contract specifications, closer working relationships would become imperative.

Working with Patients also included the proposal to extend the resource management initiative. This had initially been introduced at six pilot sites in 1987 (Arrow Park, Freeman Hospital, Guy's Hospital, The Royal Infirmary, Pilgrim Hospital and the Royal Hampshire County Hospital). Each of these hospitals embarked upon a rigorous costing exercise of all their clinical activities, using computerized information technology. Resource management was introduced to ensure that decisions on the allocation of internal resources, for clinical activities, were made on the basis of accurate information. Part of this strategy, however, was to make clinicians more aware of the costs of their activities and to persuade them to take a more active and responsive role in managing resources.

Brunel University was commissioned to evaluate the costs and benefits of resource management at these pilot sites. The results of that study showed that the introduction of resource management, among other health service initiatives (particularly the contracting of services for an internal market), was serving as a catalyst for fundamental cultural change (Buxton et al., 1991). The authors of that study also noted that clinicians' concerns about involvement in management had diminished and that clearly defined reporting structures were being established. The clinical directorate model (which will be explained in more detail later) emerged as the most favoured form of decentralized responsibility. Under this model a measure of managerial and budgetary responsibility was devolved to senior consultants who were also encouraged to manage their departments. By 1991, 130 hospitals were part of the formal extension of the resource management initiative and others were taking independent action towards embracing it.

Two years later, Pollitt (1993) analysed clinicians' reactions to the extension of the resource management initiative. He maintained that, contrary to historical portrayal, which depicted all clinicians as shunning responsibility for the management of resources, a minority of them were interested in participating in this activity. They were prepared to be actively involved if it could be proved that it enhanced the quality of patient care. Problems arose, however, due to the 'popular suspicion' that management would use the results from resource management to justify cost-cutting exercises, and the quality of patient care would become of only secondary importance.

Under the conditions set for the internal market, contractually agreed services were to be monitored by quality assurance procedures. This was to be achieved by the introduction of medical audit, which was to be used regularly to review professional standards of medical care. Medical audit is 'the systematic, critical analysis of the quality of medical care, including the procedures for diagnosis and treatment, the use of resources, and the resulting outcome and quality of life for the patient' (Department of Health, 1989b). Up until this point medical standards had been regulated by the medical profession itself, albeit on an *ad hoc* and voluntary basis. Under the proposals contained in *Working for Patients*, medical audit would no longer be voluntary and could take place in one of two forms: either by self-regulation, in which case clinicians would review their own work, individually or collectively; or through an external agency which could be brought in to manage it for them. Whichever option was chosen, medical audit was to be operational within the next two years.

However, as Pollitt (1993) explains, the idea of an external agent responsible for local medical audit created a wave of panic amongst the medical profession. They perceived the option of external regulation as more threatening than the compulsory review of their work because they were afraid that their freedom (clinical autonomy) to determine the content of their work would be restricted. Rather than lose their autonomy, clinicians accepted the principle of medical audit, with the proviso that it be regulated by the medical profession.

However, in bowing to the pressures to accept medical audit, the medical profession allowed a window of opportunity to be opened for management to exercise some control over the way in which decisions on medical care are reached. Under the terms of *Working for Patients*, managers have the power to initiate independent audits if they doubt the quality or cost-effectiveness of a given service. Managers are legitimately concerned with the quality and price of medical care because they are ultimately responsible for the provision of contractually agreed services for the internal market. Medical audit, therefore, contains the possibility of management constraining local medical monopoly over the choice of care to be offered to individual patients.

Initial responses from clinicians

One of the aims of the latest wave of NHS reforms was to encourage clinicians to take a more active role in managerial processes so as to break down the barriers that existed between them and managers. Although clinicians were encouraged to apply for the newly created general manager posts, as a means of gaining their commitment to management, this strategy was not very successful. Stewart and Dopson (1988) reported the number of clinical appointments as: 1 out of 14 regional general managers, 15 out of 191 district general managers and 110 out of 599 unit general manager posts. By 1991, some 6 years later, only 58 (out of approximately 120 clinicians appointed) remained in district and unit general management posts. Four major factors were given for clinicians' return to medical practice: insufficient remuneration, work overload, role conflict between their medical and managerial responsibilities, and peer group pressure (Millar, 1991).

Although clinicians' response to taking up general management appointments was disappointing, a different form of managerial involvement was emerging. In 1989 the Institute of Health Services Management was commissioned to conduct a survey on the models of clinical management being used in hospitals around the United Kingdom. The results of their survey (Disken et al., 1990) showed that the pattern of management within acute hospitals had, over the short space of ten years, undergone fundamental changes, with the consensus model of management being replaced by more hierarchical clinical management structures. Ham and Hunter (1988) argue that the adoption of clinical management structures was a response to the severe financial crises that many hospitals were experiencing in the 1980s.

They point to the particular example of Guy's Hospital, which encountered such crippling financial problems in 1984 that immediate action had to be taken to rectify the situation. This took the form of a cutback in services and a closure of beds. As a result of these measures, clinicians at Guy's lost confidence in their local management and proposed a new arrangement in which they would play a key managerial role. To help them find a solution to their problem these clinicians drew upon the experiences at the Johns Hopkins Hospital in Baltimore, which had an organizational structure which consisted of a management board and 14 clinical directorates each headed by a senior clinician. This model was adopted by Guy's and other hospitals subsequently and came to be known as the 'Clinical Directorate' model. This model of clinical management is significant because it altered working relationships in four crucial areas: between the lead consultants and their consultant colleagues; between lead consultants and the core staff attached to their speciality; between unit general managers and lead consultants; and finally between unit general managers and core staff.

It is important to note that clinical management originated at a time when consensus management was still the normal mode of operation within hospitals. Although clinical management changed the nature of clinical decision-making from collective to individual responsibility, normally under the aegis of a clinical director, the results of such decision-making still remained within the medical profession.

Clinical management within the NHS's new management structure, however, altered the nature of interpersonal relationships between clinicians and managers by bringing clinicians under direct managerial control. Senior consultants at the top of the clinical management hierarchy now report directly *to* unit general managers, or in the case of NHS Trusts to chief executives. This new reporting structure means that senior consultants (appointed to clinical management posts) are now subject to control from both managers and medics.

The effect on clinicians of their involvement in clinical management will now be examined in the light of a research enquiry conducted by myself and colleagues at Lancaster University on a national 'Consultants into Management' initiative.

Outline of the Lancaster study

In 1989 the Department of Health launched an initiative to fund 360 senior hospital consultants on regional management development programmes, which included attendance on a 3–4 week business school course as a major component. Each of these consultants were, or were hoping to become, involved in formal management roles, mainly as a clinical director or in other related roles. These programmes ran between 1990 and 1993 and were designed to provide hospital consultants with the necessary skills and knowledge to play an active part in implementing the changes that were taking place in the health service during that time.

The data reported in this study[2] were collected as part of a two-stage national evaluation of the overall effect of the initiative on the consultants which was also used to make recommendations on the development of best practice in management development for consultants. In order to evaluate these programmes it was first necessary to identify the managerial roles that were being expected of hospital consultants so as to assess the appropriateness of the management development provision, and to make recommendations for the future. Given that clinicians' involvement in management affected managers, as well as the medical profession, a research methodology was developed that would encapsulate a number of perspectives. This is known as 'stakeholder analysis' (Easterby-Smith, 1986) because it focuses on the views and experiences of different people with legitimate concerns in what is happening.

At a national level, the stakeholders included senior managers within the NHS Executive and members of the National Health Service Training Directorate/Department of Health Steering Committee responsible for the 'Clinicians into Management' initiative. At a regional level, they included regional general managers and the coordinators of the management development programmes. Local stakeholders included hospital consultants who were participating in the management development programmes, their unit general managers or chief executives and their consultant colleagues. In gathering data from such a wide range of viewpoints, a detailed picture emerged of consultants' roles in management and how these fitted into the strategic plans of the NHS.

Data were gathered from a sample of 90 consultants (a quarter of the total population) who took part in the management development programmes, and from a further 80 'significant others' who worked closely with the individuals concerned. This sample was selected to ensure that the full range of variation among the population of

[2] This chapter draws on data collected for an evaluation study commissioned by the National Health Services Training Division. I wish to acknowledge the contributions of my colleagues, Robin Snell and John Burgoyne, in the collection and primary analysis of this data.

participating consultants in terms of speciality mix, age, gender, prior managerial involvement, ethnic origin, current and anticipated managerial responsibilities was properly represented. Surgeons, physicians, anaesthetists, pathologists, psychiatrists, paediatricians and geriatricians were all included in the sample. Data were gathered in two stages.

In 1991, in-depth semi-structured interviews, lasting approximately one and half hours, were conducted with a sample of 25 clinicians. In addition, a further 25 interviews were conducted with 'significant others'. These were either unit general managers or clinical colleagues, who were asked to comment on the effect of the management development programme on the clinician concerned. The majority of these interviews took place at the hospitals where the consultants or general managers worked. The focus at this stage of the research was on:

- the consultants' current range of managerial involvement, in terms of role, responsibilities and activities;
- the reasons why they had been chosen to participate in the management development programmes;
- their experiences of the management development programme itself and how this related to their work;
- their general views on consultants' involvement in management.

In 1992 a further 65 participating clinicians and 55 'significant others' were surveyed by questionnaire to determine:

- the extent to which the consultants' managerial capability had been developed;
- the effect this had on the service provided in terms of patient care and quality;
- whether there had been an increase in managerial awareness within the clinical body as a whole;
- other outcomes of strategic significance.

Details of the evaluation of the regional management development programmes are discussed elsewhere (Lorbiecki et al., 1991, 1992).

For the purposes of this chapter, findings from the above research study have been examined to determine the extent to which consultants are becoming involved in management, what effect this might have on the ways in which clinicians organize and manage themselves, and the consequences of these changes on clinicians. While it is not claimed that the data obtained from the research sample are totally representative of hospital consultants as a whole, it does provide a good coverage of those clinicians who are at the early stages of becoming involved in management.

Survey findings

As one of the objectives of the 'Clinicians into Management' initiative was to foster managerial interest among clinicians who were reluctant to participate in management, we asked clinicians in our study why they had become involved in management. In analysing the views expressed by our sample of 90 consultants, a pattern of consistent motivating factors emerged. Management was regarded as something new, exciting and potentially challenging. It provided an opportunity for clinicians to be more influential over the quality of care offered to a larger patient population; and it held the prospect of widening career options. This latter finding is particularly significant because it challenges a claim made by Harrison et al. (1992) that the recent changes within the NHS had not changed clinicians' career patterns.

Widening clinicians' career options

Clinicians tend to achieve consultant status at an age which leaves them with a further 20 or 30 years of work ahead of them. An important watershed is reached about five years into their consultancy posts, at which time they begin to consider career options. (Five years' performance as a consultant is deemed necessary for them to be regarded as competent and credible; less time spent as a consultant is interpreted as failure.) Up until the latest reforms, the career options open to consultants, unlike managers, have been limited. These have been to:

- stay in the same post;
- move into research at a teaching hospital;
- move sideways to a bigger hospital; or
- concentrate more effort into committee work, medical politics etc.

Clinical management offers three further career options for consultants:

- move into a clinical director type post for a fixed period of time, with a view to returning to clinical practice;
- move into a part-time clinical director post for an unspecified period, while retaining a substantial clinical workload;
- move to a clinical director type post, probably initially part-time, with a view to developing a career towards full-time clinical directing, medical director or general manager or chief executive.

Part of the strategy of the NHS reforms has been to involve more clinicians in management. It would appear from our findings, however, that such participation will for the majority of consultants, at least within their immediate career horizons, be via a clinical, rather than general, management route. Involvement in general management, however, cannot be ruled out. It is feasible that some clinicians will move in this direction, later in their careers, using the experience gained in clinical management as a stepping stone.

Consultants' experiences of clinical management will be examined next so as to assess the scope of their managerial involvement. This has been achieved by analysing the day-to-day role responsibilities and demands made on clinical managers.

Clinical management roles

In gathering data from consultants and managers on how they saw clinical management developing, both now and in the future, we constructed a composite picture of twelve emerging roles. These are explained briefly and illustrated, where appropriate, with representative quotations.

Leadership

Clinical directors are being expected to take both a clinical and a managerial lead for their directorates. This necessitates participation in overall unit strategy and the ability to present sound arguments for their choice of direction. An example of clinical leadership is provided by a consultant who headed a directorate team and who 'persuaded a fairly intransigent unit general manager that each director needed to be represented on the Hospital Management Board'.

Understanding organizational complexity

Clinical directors are having to understand the structures and systems of the NHS and how these are being changed by the reforms and Trust status. At the time of the study, few clinicians were being exposed to the organization of the health service as a whole and they had little knowledge of underlying administrative and managerial systems.

Understanding and managing change

The rate of change within the NHS has been enormous, with individuals operating under tumultuous conditions. Clinical directors need to be equipped both to handle the changes they themselves experience and to handle sensitively others' defensive reactions to these changes. One manager spoke of a consultant's 'better knowledge base on motivation [which] has allowed him to better understand the other staff in the unit and he has used this to implement changes with full commitment'.

Collaborating in unit strategy

There is a need for clinical directors to collaborate with other senior members, both medical and managerial, on the general direction of their unit. They are involved in setting and implementing objectives for the unit, which requires an awareness of the unit's systems and procedures and knowledge of how resources are allocated. In setting strategic objectives they need to be aware of how these could affect other clinical directorates, as well as their own. An example was provided by one consultant who collaborated by using 'the deeper involvement of other consultants in planning, decision, and executive phases of my plans'.

Constructive team membership

As members of medical speciality teams, senior management teams etc., another role is called for — that of participant rather than leader. Team membership, however, can expose clinicians to unfamiliar medical specialisms or managerial functions. This requires good interpersonal skills and an appreciation of the different interests of a range of professional groups. One consultant spoke of a situation where 'redeployment was carried out without any problems by getting everyone to look at a staffing problem and guiding them to come up with their own solution'.

Team building

During the creation of a clinical directorate, specific attention needs to be paid towards the interests of different staff, particularly non-clinical (e.g. nurses and business managers) who may feel anxious about changes in authority structures. This requires an understanding of how individuals are differently motivated and a concern to find areas of common ground so that a cooperative working team can be established. It also requires a readiness to encourage participation and to grant access to management information, as illustrated by a consultant:

'I have been able to provide an alternative to the traditional role models by dismantling the rigid boundaries and introversion of disciplines by utilising the idea of "transferable skills" of each discipline to areas where they can support the cohesion of the directorate and corporate objectives more effectively.'

Negotiating

As Trust status brings with it the potential for local collective bargaining arrangements, any changes necessitate involvement with trade unions. This requires not only a knowledge of employment legislation and local practices, but also a readiness to accept the legitimacy of negotiating with trade unions before seeking to introduce changes which could affect individuals' employment rights. A consultant commented:

'Recently I was involved in disciplining a subordinate. One colleague was determined upon a predetermined outcome (i.e. dismissal) during the proceedings. I felt increasingly that this was unjust. Six months ago I would have given in for the sake of peace, but this time I stood my ground and persuaded the other person present to accept my view.'

Finance

Clinical directors may become budget-holders, which requires knowledge and understanding of the accounting and finance procedures used within the health service. They are involved in drawing up contracts for the internal market, which requires an understanding of how clinical activity is costed by local resource management systems. A general manager remarked about a consultant:

'He shows deeper than normal (for a consultant) understanding of the overall complexities of the range of figures produced each month. As a result he has put forward ideas involving clinical changes, ward clerks' duties, the way medical records should be processed and advice on the management of certain drugs.'

Providing a central lead on information technology

Clinical directors need to be familiar with information technology as they can be called upon to assist with decisions about their purchase. Where a unit adopts a central information technology strategy, they need to be able to establish and declare their precise computing needs. They may also have to take the lead in managing the introduction of computer systems in their directorates. A consultant told us:

'I am much more interested in information and information technology. I now have a greater understanding of clinical management information and have implemented my own computer-based Directorate system.'

Employee relations

Clinical directors can be required to manage a large number of staff — as many as 150 per directorate. This has implications for managing people and, in particular, the management of their clinical colleagues. A unit general manager said about a consultant:

'He is more understanding of their needs, wants and feelings and probably more patient and more confident to listen and help which has greatly improved their acceptance of him in his management role.'

However, as another consultant remarked:

'Relationships have deteriorated. My involvement at Business School caused suspicion amongst some colleagues. Was I abandoning clinical medicine for management?'

Quality assurance

As providers, under the internal market system, clinical directors are responsible for ensuring quality of patient care, through medical audit. This has implications for managing other clinicians within their directorate on the way in which their standards of work will be monitored. Under the conditions set for a competitive, internal market, patients would need to be valued as 'customers' as well as patients. A number of written comments on the questionnaire indicated how different consultants are taking this on board: 'Interested in quality'; 'Viewing patients as customers'; 'Implementing a monitoring system for waiting lists'; 'Encouraged me to become the medical audit lead for our district'.

Managing levels of clinical activity

Under business and job plans, clinical directors are required to reach agreement with purchasers and unit general managers/chief executives on activity levels and case mix; both of which require monitoring by information systems. A consultant stated: 'In meeting with our purchaser I have pursued a negotiation for a new project to the point of clear agreement'.

Analysis of clinical management roles

In analysing the elements of the roles set out above, it appears that clinical management displays a number of characteristics which are consistent with conventional management practice. Broadly speaking these roles can be clustered into three traditional areas of management — functional management, strategic management and human resources management. In the case of clinician management each of these areas contains the following range of tasks:

- *Functional management*, which includes finance, information technology, quality assurance and managing levels of clinical activity.
- *Strategic management*, which involves understanding organizational complexity and collaborating in unit strategy. This would also include an element of leadership in the sense of providing a vision on plans for the future.
- *Human resources management*, where clinicians would be concerned with employee relations, leading others, understanding and managing change, participating in and building good team relationships, negotiating on patterns and standards of work.

Our findings on the above range of clinical management activity are consistent with the clinical manager roles identified by Fitzgerald and Sturt (1992) through their analysis of a sample of clinical directors' job descriptions. As these authors commented, however, these emerging clinical management roles have implications for the selection and development of clinical managers. From our study we were able to ascertain that unit general managers had played an active role in the recruitment of clinical directors and were now included as a legitimate member on their appointment panels. Furthermore, lead consultants, from our sample, were keen to see evidence of management awareness and experience being demonstrated by those senior registrars seeking to pursue consultancy posts. The inclusion of management criteria and assessment in clinical appointments is important because it signals that managerial activity and responsibility are becoming a normal and expected part of a consultant's work.

Although managerial responsibility is becoming an important feature of consultants' day-to-day work patterns, they are exposed to little management development during the course of their formal professional training (Tietjen, 1991). The management development received by the majority of the consultants canvassed in our study occurred later in their careers, was often fragmentary and consisted of short, one-off events. The regional development programmes in which the clinicians participated represent an attempt to rectify the shortfall in provision by offering substantial and continuous development in management theory and practice.

A positive impression of management was formed by most of the consultants attending the business school courses, although they did query the appropriateness of applying private sector management practices to the NHS. Management was perceived to be different from administration, and while complex it was not difficult to learn the basics. Active involvement in, and learning about, management through the management development programme was gradually eroding the 'in-built hatred between doctors and managers'. Clinicians had acquired 'business language skills' which enabled them to communicate and negotiate better in a management world. As a result, working relationships between clinicians and managers generally improved, providing positive feedback on both sides. Clinicians were motivated and excited by the prospect of being involved in management as typified by one consultant who remarked: 'The programme has enhanced my appreciation of the importance of management, and in particular the importance of doctors becoming involved with the management of the health services'.

A number of conclusions can be drawn from the above analysis of clinicians' individual experiences of clinical management. Clinical management contains a number of roles and tasks which would normally be found in conventional management. It is attractive because it widens consultants' career options and provides them with the opportunity to influence unit strategy and thereby influence the provision of health care for a larger patient population. Exposure to management development opportunities has increased consultants' understanding of and commitment to management ideology. Being involved in management has improved working relationships between clinicians and managers.

Convergence or collision?

It would appear that the formal creation of a management structure, and the emergence of a clinical management one, provides both managers and clinicians with clearly defined *managerial* career paths. Within these structures, both senior managers and clinical directors are responsible for discrete bodies of staff, and are personally responsible for decisions made within their areas. The rise of these managerial structures suggests a more hierarchical model for the health service as a whole and a *convergence* in the style by which clinicians and managers organize and manage themselves. As clinical management begins to straddle the service and management domains, clinical directors will have to satisfy both managerial and clinical objectives.

The reasons why clinicians are taking a greater part in management are complex. Harrison et al. (1992) suggest that clinicians are motivated to become involved in management, when managers are perceived to be powerful. As management was only just developing when general management posts were introduced into the NHS, it is possible, therefore, that clinicians were not drawn to these posts because management was seen to be weak. There is, however, another side to this picture and this is provided by clinicians' involvement in clinical management. In this instance it could be argued that clinicians initially became involved in management precisely because it was weak. Where managers were seen to be ineffective in dealing with a financial crisis, as at Guy's Hospital, clinicians become involved because they thought the health provision was at risk. Once in clinical management, however, consultants are motivated to stay and others to join, because they are enjoying the experience, can exert more influence, and are able to maintain the balance of power between themselves and managers, thereby safeguarding their interests of clinical autonomy and self-regulation.

Clinical autonomy and self-regulation are guiding principles for the medical profession. Johnson and Boss (1991) maintain that since clinicians' work is highly personal and closely involved with matters of life and death, they have traditionally been given high levels of functional autonomy. In order to reduce stress, arising from a critical work environment, standardized operating procedures, routines and prescribed ways of behaviour have evolved, which have an important stabilizing effect. Interventions which seek to change clinical practice impinge upon clinical autonomy. This in turn disturbs clinicians' sense of security, strengthening resistance to such changes. However, the creation of the internal market in the NHS, with contractually agreed prices and assured levels of quality, produces a situation where clinical practice, and hence clinical autonomy, can be challenged.

Clinical autonomy could be perceived to be under threat by clinical management because clinical directors are directly involved with managers in deciding on the unit's strategy for the provision of health care for its total patient population. This involves making collaborative decisions on the allocation of resources for each clinical speciality, taking into account the type of contracts required for the internal market. In making decisions, choices have to be made on whether funds for a particular area should be increased or decreased, bearing budget limitations in mind. In making choices there is an implicit requirement for clinical directors to make value judgements on different areas of clinical activity which satisfy the internal market: whether, for example, it is better to invest in new technology for cancer treatment or to provide additional funds to shorten waiting lists for hip replacements.

In making choices on the health care to be made available, clinicians are faced with a range of conflicting dilemmas: ethical obligations to their individual patients; the varying needs of other patients within the total patient population; the success of their unit within the internal market; and the needs of their clinical colleagues. It is these dilemmas which could lead to a *collision* of interests within the health service. Tension has always existed in the health service, although this has usually been between clinicians and managers as they tussle with issues surrounding the quality and cost of medical provision. However, as responsibility for quality and cost has been devolved to clinical management, a new friction point has been created between clinical managers and their consultant peers. In acting as the interface between managers and consultants, it could well be clinical managers (rather than managers) who have to challenge consultants, in the interests of an internal market, on the content of their medical work. Collision of interests which has traditionally been an issue between clinicians and managers, may also be a source of in-built tension between clinical directors and their consultant colleagues, thereby creating discord among factions of the medical profession.

References

Brazell H (1987) Doctors as managers. *Management Education and Development*; **18**: 95–102.

Burgoyne JG, Lorbiecki A (1993) Clinicians into management: the experience in context. *Health Services Management Research*; **6**: 248–259.

Buxton M, Packwood T, Keen J (1991) *Final Report of the Brunel University Evaluation of Resource Management*. Uxbridge, Middx: Health Economics Research Group, Brunel University (research report 10).

Davidson N (1987) *A Question of Care: The Changing Face of the NHS*. London: Michael Joseph.

Department of Health (1989a) *Working for Patients*, Cmd. 555. London: HMSO.

Department of Health (1989b) *Medical Audit — Working for Patients Working Paper*. London: DoH.

Disken S, Dixon M, Halpern S, Shocket G (1990) *Models of Clinical Management*. London: Institute of Health Service Management.

Easterby-Smith M (1986) *Evaluation of Management Education, Training and Development*. Aldershot: Gower.

Fitzgerald L, Sturt J (1992) Clinicians into management: On the change agenda or not? *Health Services Management Research*; **5**: 137–146.

Griffiths R (1983) *NHS Management Inquiry*. London: DHSS.

Ham C, Hunter DJ (1988) *Managing Clinical Activity in the NHS*. London: King's Fund Institute.

Harrison S, Hunter DJ, Johnston I, Wistow G (1989a) *Competing for*

Health: A Commentary on the NHS Review. Nuffield Institute for Health Service Studies.

Harrison S, Hunter DJ, Marnoch G, Pollitt C (1989b) General management and medical autonomy in the national health service. *Health Services Management Research*; **2**: 38–46.

Harrison S, Hunter DJ, Marnoch G, Pollitt C (1992) *Just Managing: Power and Culture in the National Health Service*. London: Macmillan.

Johnson JA, Boss RW (1991) Management development and change in a demanding health care environment. *Journal of Management Development*; **10**: 5–10.

Kouzes JM, Mico PR (1979) Domain theory: an introduction to organisational behaviour in human service organisations. *Journal of Applied Behavioural Science*; **15**: 449–469.

Lorbiecki A, Snell R, Burgoyne J (1991) *Report of the Mid-stream Evaluation of the First Wave Management Development Scheme for Hospital Consultants*. Bristol: NHS Training Directorate.

Lorbiecki A, Snell R, Burgoyne J (1992) *Final Report of the National Evaluation of the First Wave Management Development Initiative for Hospital Consultants*. Bristol: NHS Training Directorate.

Millar B (1991) Clinicians as managers: medics make their minds up. *Health Service Journal*, February 1991.

Ministry of Health (1967) *Report of the Joint Working Party on the Organisation of Medical Work in Hospitals* (the first Cogwheel report). London: HMSO.

Moon G, Kendall I (1993) The National Health Service. In: Farnham D, Sylvia H (Eds), *Managing the New Public Services*. London: Macmillan, 172–187.

Pettigrew A, Ferlie E, McKee L (1992) *Shaping Strategic Change*. Beverly Hills: Sage.

Pollitt C (1993) The politics of medical quality: auditing doctors in the UK and USA. *Health Services Management Research*; **6**: 24–34.

Stewart R, Dopson S (1988) Griffiths in theory and practice: a research assessment. *Journal of Health Administration Education*; **6**: 503–514.

Tietjen C (1991) Management development in the NHS. *Personnel Management*; May: 52–54.

8 General practitioners and community pharmacists: Interprofessional relations in health centres

Geoffrey Harding and Kevin Taylor

Introduction

Traditionally, a pharmacist's activities have been predominantly concerned with dispensing prescribed medication, with approximately 3000 prescriptions dispensed per month in the average pharmacy in the UK (*Pharmaceutical Journal*, 1988). Nowadays, as most prescribed medication requires no formulation by the pharmacist and with the increasing use of prepackaged (original-pack) medicines, the nature of the pharmacist's professional role has changed and continues to develop. The services offered by pharmacists additional to their dispensing activities have become known as the 'extended role'. The 'extended role', outlined in the Nuffield Inquiry into pharmacy (Nuffield Foundation, 1986) and subsequent government Green and White Papers on primary health care (DHSS, 1986a,b, 1988) has many components, including advising clients on minor ailments, recommending treatments, 'counselling' on correct use of medication and various health promotion activities. Many aspects of this extended role depend on the pharmacist having an active input into the delivery of primary health care.

The efficient delivery of health services to the public relies on cooperation between members of the health care team. Several factors have been suggested as inhibiting effective collaboration and cooperation, including differences in the status, prestige and power of team members (Bond et al., 1987). Poor communication between team members and a failure to appreciate each other's roles have also been highlighted as factors undermining the potential of a team approach to health care (DHSS, 1986a).

It may be suggested that centralization of health services will

107

promote and enhance the concept of the primary health care team. Health centres provide a structure for such centralization and cooperation. They provide a base for central team members such as general practitioners, practice nurses, midwives and health visitors, and may include additional health professionals such as dentists, opticians, chiropodists and pharmacists.

The concept of an integrated health centre was first formulated in the Dawson Report of 1920 (Ministry of Health Consultative Council and Allied Services, 1920), which defined a health centre as 'an institution wherein are brought various medical services, both preventative and curative, so as to form one organization'.

Plans for the National Health Service in the UK originally provided for a national network of health centres, which it was hoped would bring together health professionals and provide local health authority services, particularly preventative services. However, by 1958 only ten such centres had been built because attracting the participation of general practitioners proved difficult (Ashworth, 1959). By this time groups of general practitioners were forming group practices to which local authority health workers were 'attached', ending the isolation of general practitioners from local authorities, one of the rationales for the establishment of health centres.

In the late 1960s there was renewed interest in health centres, such that in 1968 there were a total of 110 centres compared with 60 the year before (Brookes, 1974). This seems to have resulted from logistical difficulties in providing suitable premises for group practices and the need to provide health services to areas with new populations following large-scale rehousing and the building of housing estates.

In recent years there has been a steady increase in the number of health centres having integral pharmacies. Historically, the location of community pharmacies has tended to shadow general practitioners' surgeries, since pharmacies close to the surgery are likely to attract the greatest proportion of prescriptions for dispensing. The potential of an integral pharmacy within a health centre, however, extends beyond mere considerations of profit and client convenience; it also presents implications for the nature of interactions between medical practitioners, resident pharmacist(s) and other health workers.

Notwithstanding the factors inhibiting 'team' collaboration, it was suggested by the Nuffield Inquiry into pharmacy (Nuffield Foundation, 1986) that the provision of pharmaceutical services within health centres should encourage close links between pharmacists and the other health care professionals. This followed a recommendation in 1979 by the Royal Commission on the NHS that experiments be instigated into the employment of pharmacists in health centres. The concept of having pharmacists within the same premises as general practitioners is a romantic notion for pharmacists. For instance, in their submission to the Nuffield Inquiry, the Royal Pharmaceutical

Society of Great Britain stated that the introduction of pharmacists into health centres 'facilitated regular discussions with medical practitioners on prescribing patterns, information about medicines and the inclusion of pharmacists in practice discussion seminars'. The Company Chemists' Association stated to the same inquiry, that a health centre with a pharmacy provided a good example of the degree of interprofessional cooperation which can be achieved with 'doctors, dentists, nurses and pharmacists all together and working for the benefit of the patients'. A book on relationships between general practitioners and other health professionals, published in 1986, also romanticizes the notion that physical proximity equates with enhanced interprofessional relations: 'There are advantages in having a pharmacy next door to or even attached to a health centre so that pharmacists can discuss problems face-to-face with doctors and even attend their seminars' (Walton, 1986). The evidence to corroborate such assertions seems to have been predominantly anecdotal.

There are 9765 community pharmacies in England (*Pharmaceutical Journal*, 1993), of which fewer than 2% are located in health centres. Very little is known of the impact inclusion of a pharmacy in a health centre has on the interprofessional relations between pharmacists and general practitioners. For example, does the close physical proximity of general practitioners and pharmacists promote a collaboration and exchange of expertise? The potential benefits of pharmacists and general practitioners working together under the same roof may include the development of a synergistic relationship. With pharmacists' breadth of knowledge about drugs, therapeutic indications, costs, alternatives, etc., and pressure on general practitioners to maintain optimum prescribing cost-effectiveness, interprofessional collaboration would apparently benefit both professional groups: pharmacists would be able to enhance their profile by making a professional input towards general practitioners' cost-effective prescribing. However, collaboration might be considered a dilution of a professional knowledge base and consequently resisted.

In order to address these issues a study was conducted in 1988 of all (101) health centre pharmacies in England to evaluate the impact of close physical proximity on pharmacists' and general practitioners' interprofessional relations (Harding and Taylor, 1988a,b, 1989a,b, 1990). Since this study was completed there have been a number of reforms to the NHS which have had a particular effect on general practitioners. For instance, the government's White Paper *Working for Patients* (DHSS, 1989) proposed that general practitioners should work within a limited budget and prescribe cost-effectively. The effects of these developments are not represented in our data. One might speculate that these developments can only serve to promote collaboration between pharmacists, with their knowledge of drug costs, and fund-holding general practitioners acutely aware of their budgets.

Nonetheless, the study remains the only one of its kind and the data collected raise many issues concerning the complexity of such relations in this context.

Methodology of the study

The study was conducted in two phases. In phase one, questionnaires were sent to the managers (all pharmacists) of every English health centre pharmacy and to an equal number of managers of community pharmacies, comparable in terms of prescription turnover and location within the same Family Health Services Authority (FHSA). Usable questionnaires were returned by 93 (92%) of the health centre pharmacy managers and 90 (89%) of the community pharmacy managers.

In phase two of the study, a series of interviews was conducted with pharmacists and general practitioners using semi-structured interview schedules to ensure that each 'group' of participants was asked the same questions. Ten health centres with an integral pharmacy were chosen, one each from the Regional Heath Authorities in England which had one or more such health centres. Thirteen general practitioners, at least one from each health centre, were interviewed. The interview schedule included questions on the nature of pharmacists' queries to general practitioners, the general practitioners' attitudes to those queries, and the impact of pharmacists on general practitioners' selection of prescribed medication. The pharmacy manager of each health centre was also interviewed to characterize the pharmacists' perceptions of their relationship with prescribers, and questions were included relating to opportunities for informal contact, how they perceived their working relationships and procedures for dealing with prescription queries.

For comparative purposes the managers of ten community pharmacies and nine general practitioners working in health centres without pharmacies, located within the vicinity of the health centres containing pharmacies, were interviewed using a suitably modified interview schedule.

All interviews were tape-recorded and transcribed for analysis.

Findings of the study

Health centres with integral pharmacies are a relatively recent phenomenon: 70% of these pharmacies had opened since 1977. This trend appears to correspond to a growing recognition of the potential benefits of general practitioners and pharmacists practising within close proximity of each other. Eighty-one per cent of the pharmacies were situated within the fabric of the health centres (the remaining 19% of pharmacies categorized by the Department of Health as health centre pharmacies adjoined the centre in a separate building). More than two-thirds (68%) of these health centres were inaugurated with an integral pharmacy, and a further 16% incorporated one within a year of their opening.

Such close physical proximity seemed to encourage a comparatively higher frequency of GP-instigated consultations with health centre pharmacists compared with community pharmacists. Approximately one in ten (9.7%) health centre pharmacists reported being consulted by general practitioners 30 times per week or more, which was more than twice the number of community pharmacists (4%) who reported being consulted 30 times per week or more. Approximately half (53.8%) of the 93 health centre pharmacists surveyed were consulted fewer than ten times per week. This figure compared with nearly three-quarters (73.2%) of the community pharmacists surveyed who were consulted less than ten times a week.

One reason potentially inhibiting general practitioner/health centre pharmacist communication is organizational and structural considerations, such as the pharmacist having to negotiate access to general practitioners through reception staff. Of the ten health centre pharmacists interviewed, the majority (eight) reported that they usually contacted the general practitioner via the receptionist. Only two reported that they usually contacted general practitioners either face-to-face or by telephone. Indeed, only three health centre pharmacists reported having a direct telephone link with general practitioners. Pharmacist-instigated face-to-face communication was also made difficult by virtue of their having to arrange occasional cover of absence from the pharmacy.

By contrast, GP-initiated consultations with pharmacists were relatively unfettered. As one general practitioner commented: 'I go down and ask regularly when I've got a query. If I ever have a problem about drugs I always go down and ask them . . . I ring him far more often than he rings me'. Indeed, face-to-face contact with the pharmacist was considered routine for six of the thirteen general practitioners interviewed, whilst the others approached the pharmacist by telephone or a third party such as a pharmacy assistant.

The general practitioners' perceptions of pharmacists' influence on their prescribing was at variance with pharmacists' perceptions of their influence. Only one health centre pharmacist reported having any impact on long-term prescribing habits, while the remaining nine reported that they adopted a reactive, rather than proactive, role in relation to doctors' prescribing habits — waiting to be consulted about prescribed medication rather than initiating a consultation. Awareness of the general practitioner's prerogative to prescribe on the basis of clinical judgement inhibited one pharmacist to the extent that he felt he was not in a position to 'tell them (the prescribers) what to prescribe or to go along advising them'. Only by 'giving them a few drug price lists' would one pharmacist attempt to influence doctors' prescribing, while another believed that doctors were more influenced by pharmaceutical company representatives than himself: 'I think medical reps have more impact (on the selection and use of drugs). I've suggested generic preparations . . . I think the medical reps carry more weight there'.

In marked contrast, virtually all general practitioners reported making use of pharmacists as a resource for information on pharmaceutical matters, such as drug dosage and quantity (see Table 8.1). Moreover, eleven of the thirteen general practitioners interviewed reported that the health centre pharmacist had influenced, to some extent, their choice of prescribed medication: by recommending generic rather than proprietary products on the grounds of efficacy and cost; by restricting their prescribing because of the non-availability of products; by increasing their awareness of cost-efficient prescribing; and by promoting considerations of drug compatibility and availability.

All general practitioners 'considered the pharmacists' communications and queries were valid' and welcomed their intervention. This corresponds to previous findings reported from the USA by Haxby et al. (1988) who studied the advice given by five pharmacists to 33 'family physicians'. The physicians believed that 88% of these contacts were 'very useful' and 99% of the recommended actions were implemented. In this study, the pharmacists' role as a final check or 'safety net' for any potential errors made by prescribers was particularly appreciated by general practitioners. 'I find them very useful, I find it very comforting to have someone behind me making sure that I don't do something silly'; 'It's a check on whether you're doing right or wrong'; 'Pleased that checking process is there'. General practitioners' positive responses to pharmacists' drug-related queries

Table 8.1   General practitioners' consultative sources for drug dosage/quantity

Consultative source	GPs working in health centres with pharmacy ($n = 13$)	GPs working in health centres without pharmacy ($n = 9$)
Local pharmacist	0	5
Health centre pharmacist	11	0
Consultant specialist	3	0
Literature	1	4
Pharmaceutical representative	1	0
Hospital pharmacist	1	0

would appear to indicate that the pharmacists' contribution as a final check in the prescribing and dispensing process was welcomed, and that general practitioners appreciated that pharmacists are qualified to raise these queries. Only one general practitioner qualified his enthusiasm by pointing out that such queries were tedious for both parties.

Ready access to consultation with a pharmacist was also valued, as one general practitioner reported: 'I often have queries about problems of prescribing details and I wouldn't hesitate to ring up anytime to seek advice of the pharmacist'.

Health centre pharmacists' influence on general practitioners may reflect the fact that the pharmacists were less commercially oriented than their community pharmacist counterparts. Less than half (49%) of health centre pharmacies retailed non-medicine related merchandise, while this was obtainable from virtually all (97%) community pharmacies comprising the control group. Evidence of general practitioners' wariness in allowing community pharmacists to influence their prescribing for fear of receiving commercially oriented advice has recently been substantiated in a survey of 740 general practitioners' opinions on pharmacy (Spencer and Edwards, 1992). Twenty-seven per cent of general practitioners questioned by Spencer and Edwards indicated that they felt pharmacists were too influenced by commercial pressures to give unbiased advice. The fact that health centre pharmacies restricted their retailing function in favour of a non-commercial service ethos was appreciated by one general practitioner who commented: 'I think that health centre pharmacists are in one way in a privileged position in that none of their advice need be commercially orientated'.

However, whilst conceding that health centre pharmacists' advice may be less biased than that of their community counterparts, few general practitioners readily accepted that health centre pharmacists specifically would be directly receptive to the requirements of prescribers. Thus, while eight of the ten health centre pharmacists said that the quality and range of medical stock in the pharmacy were determined by what general practitioners prescribed, nine general practitioners considered that they had no influence on the pharmacy's stockholding. The remaining four said they probably did, but only indirectly, for example by the nature of their prescribing patterns.

Pharmacists were reported by general practitioners to intervene in the prescribing process, most often by querying dosage, strength and quantity of drugs prescribed (Table 8.2). These queries relate more to products than therapies. Health centre pharmacists' role as drug therapy experts, however, was not optimized by general practitioners (Table 8.3). These findings are corroborated by research conducted in Australia and the USA, indicating that physicians were more ready to accept product information rather than therapeutic information from pharmacists (Williamson and Kabat, 1971; Smith et al., 1975; Ortiz et al., 1989). The health centre pharmacist's role as 'drug expert' on matters other than dosage, strength or quantity, however, remained under-employed as general practitioners most often utilized a range of other consultative sources, most notably turning to consultant specialists on specific matters of drug therapy (Table 8.3).

Table 8.2 Frequency of common queries from the health centre pharmacists reported by general practitioners (n = 13) (adapted from Harding and Taylor, 1990)

Common queries	Reported frequency by general practitioners
Dosage	10
Product availability	5
Product strength	5
Drug interaction/incompatibility	2
Change to generic formulation	1

Table 8.3 General practitioners' consultative sources for drug therapy

Consultative source	GPs working in health centres with pharmacy (n = 13)	GPs working in health centres without pharmacy (n = 9)
Health centre pharmacist	5	0
Consultant specialist	6	3
Literature	2	6
Pharmaceutical company	1	0
Hospital pharmacist	3	2

General practitioners' and pharmacists' perceptions of each other's professional role define a framework within which each evaluates their interprofessional relationship. That is, their perception of the other's role incorporates the expectations of that role. A positive evaluation of one's interprofessional relationship therefore follows one's expectations being met. General practitioners who positively evaluate their professional relationship with pharmacists may do so on the basis of limited expectations of pharmacists' interprofessional role. Conversely, pharmacists who evaluate their professional relationship with general practitioners positively may do so also on the basis of limited expectations of general practitioners' interprofessional role. This may be represented diagrammatically as a matrix (Table 8.4).

Table 8.4 Matrix of expectations and evaluations of general practitioner/pharmacist interprofessional relations

	Positive evaluation	Negative evaluation
High expectation (extensive)	+/+	+/−
Low expectation (limited)	−/+	−/−

- *High expectations and a positive evaluation* (+/+) would be characterized by a 'meeting of professional minds' — an equitable dialogue in which knowledge is shared.

e.g. 'I often have queries about problems of prescribing details and I wouldn't hesitate to ring up any time to seek advice of the pharmacist . . . and he's most helpful in that respect.'

- *Low expectations and a positive evaluation* (−/+) would be characterized by reports which equated a satisfactory relationship with simply 'getting on' with a professional colleague.

e.g. For some health centre pharmacists a 'satisfactory relationship' with prescribers was defined exclusively in personal terms; i.e. 'getting on' agreeably with doctors and patients. By couching their response purely in terms of personal qualities, some pharmacists were unable to define their relationship more precisely: 'There's no reason why, it's just that we get on quite well'; 'We're on friendly terms'; 'It's a matter of relationships really . . . It's a good rapport between people'.

- *High expectations and a negative evaluation* (+/−) would be characterized by unrealized potential for interprofessional dialogue.

e.g. 'I feel it could be better, not from the point of view that we don't get on, but from the point of view that I think there should be more of a professional relationship . . . I would like to be more useful to them in cost-effective prescribing.'

- *Low expectations and a negative evaluation* (−/−) would be characterized by a perceived intention by other professionals to encroach on one's professional domain.

e.g. 'The pharmacist should give a brief, broad-based description of what drugs are doing, but shouldn't go into any detail'; 'I'm uneasy about the idea of pharmacists dispensing medical knowledge for two reasons — lack of knowledge and patient history. By no stretch of the imagination could the pharmacist be considered to be competent medically . . . in practice a lot of the advice patients seem to get from pharmacists is not good advice . . . pharmacist might be a very good pharmacist but I would feel uncomfortable about (him/her) giving advice on a cough.'

All general practitioners reported an appreciation of the pharmacist's pharmaceutical knowledge and accessibility and tended overall to evaluate their interprofessional relationship with pharmacists as positive. This stemmed largely from the pharmacists' role as a safety-net for any mistakes made by the prescriber, and to a lesser extent from an appreciation of a mutual exchange of professional and technical information; i.e. generally low expectations and positive evaluations. This contrasts with health centre pharmacists' evaluation of their relationship with general practitioners; i.e. generally high expectations and negative evaluations. General practitioners' perceptions of their relationship were therefore premised largely on the rather limited expectation that pharmacists' main function for general practitioners was to provide a professional screening service, albeit a highly skilled one: 'I would rely on her utterly to see that everything was all right because people (pharmacists) outside (of the health centre) would not know my habits as well'; 'I would expect this one (on-site pharmacist) to know my pattern of prescribing . . . to know what to expect of me if there were some glaring error or mistake'.

Conclusions

It is evident from the literature that general practitioners' perceptions of pharmacists currently owe much to recent developments in the pharmacist's role (Spencer and Edwards, 1992). One might reasonably expect pharmacists working in health centres to be at the forefront of such developments. There is, however, more to equitable interprofessional relations than establishing clear channels of communication. Evidence from this study indeed indicates that close physical proximity does not necessarily enhance interprofessional communication. While good interpersonal relations are important they are not a measure of interprofessional cooperation — they serve only as a medium for communication. It is the messages they convey that are of crucial importance. Interprofessional relations are also premised on other considerations such as an equitable and reciprocal interchange of information and skills. Pharmacists' extensive knowledge of drugs, drug therapy, drug costs, etc., are clearly significant, particularly for budget-holding general practices. Yet recent research has indicated that half of all general practitioners surveyed agreed with the statement 'All general practitioners should be allowed to dispense', and over a third agreed that 'Pharmacists should stick to dispensing and not venture into other areas of medicine' (Spencer and Edwards, 1992). These findings clearly have significant implications in terms of developing pharmacists' activities, particularly within health centres. Within health centres, extending the pharmacist's role may be perceived as territorial encroachment by general practitioners, just as dispensing doctors in rural areas may be perceived as invading the pharmacist's professional domain (Roberts, 1988).

Against a historical backcloth of antipathy between medical and pharmaceutical professions (Smith, 1980), health centre pharmacists have been pioneers in establishing bridges between the professions — especially in establishing good working relationships. However, much work remains to be done. Moreover, the health service is undergoing profound changes which impinge on general practitioners and pharmacists alike. Health policy increasingly emphasizes the importance of cost-effectiveness, quality assurance and the patient as consumer of health services. These changes herald a restructuring of the health service in which traditional professional boundaries may be redrawn in order to meet health policy objectives. In this respect the role of pharmacist as the prescriber's drugs 'expert' is apposite, in encouraging efficient, rational and cost-effective prescribing.

Research suggests that when doctors work in collaboration with pharmacists they prescribe more rationally and cheaply than those who do not; i.e. they are more critical in their choice of drugs and prescribe in smaller quantities (Van de Poel et al., 1991). The concept of the patient as consumer is another feature of the restructured health service which has implications for interprofessional relationships. The government's policy document *The Health of the Nation* (DHSS, 1992) stresses the importance of preventive measures in maintaining health. Health centres are thus increasingly adopting a proactive approach in promoting health, through screening programmes. In this sense, health centres are increasingly turning into health care centres which operate proactively in promoting as well as restoring health. Such health centres thus provide the infrastructure in which interprofessional relationships *could* be fully realized. If they are to achieve their full potential, however, new relationships between pharmacists and general practitioners must be forced.

Acknowledgement

The research upon which this chapter is based was supported by a grant from the Department of Health.

References

Ashworth HW (1959) The failure of health centres. *Journal of the Royal College of General Practitioners*; **9**: 357–364.
Bond J, Cartlidge AM, Gregson BA, Barton AG, Phillips PR, Armitage P, Brown AM, Reedy BLEC (1987) Interprofessional

collaboration in primary health care. *Journal of the Royal College of General Practitioners*; **37**: 158–161.

Brookes B (1974) The historical perspective in health centres. In: Wise ARJ (Ed.) *British Health Care and Technology*. London: Health and Social Service Journal/Hospital International.

Department of Health and Social Security (1986a) *Primary Health Care: An Agenda for Discussion*, Cmd. 9771. London: HMSO.

Department of Health and Social Security (1986b) *Neighbourhood Nursing: A Focus for Care (Cumberlege report)*. London HMSO.

Department of Health and Social Security (1988) *Promoting Better Health*, Cmd. 249. London: HMSO.

Department of Health (1989) *Working for Patients*, Cmd. 555. London: HMSO.

Department of Health and Social Security (1992) *The Health of the Nation*. London: HMSO.

Harding G, Taylor KMG (1988a) Pharmacies in health centres. *Journal of the Royal College of General Practitioners*; **38**: 566–567.

Harding G, Taylor KMG (1988b) Health centre pharmacies in England. *Pharmaceutical Journal*; **241**: 313–314.

Harding G, Taylor KMG (1989a) Pharmaceutical services and interprofessional communication in health centre pharmacies. *Pharmaceutical Journal*; **242**: 21–22.

Harding G, Taylor KMG (1989b) The interface between pharmacists and general practitioners in English health centres. *Pharmaceutical Journal*; **242**: 549–550.

Harding G, Taylor KMG (1990) Professional relationships between general practitioners and pharmacists in health centres. *British Journal of General Practice*; **40**: 464–466.

Haxby DG, Weart CW, Goodman BW (1988) Family practice physicians' perceptions of the usefulness of drug therapy recommendations from clinical pharmacists. *American Journal of Hospital Pharmacy*; **45**: 824–827.

Ministry of Health Consultative Council and Allied Services (1920) *Interim Report on the Future Provision of Medical and Allied Services*, Cmd. 693. London: HMSO.

Nuffield Foundation (1986) *Pharmacy: The Report of a Committee of Inquiry Appointed by the Nuffield Foundation*. London: Nuffield Foundation.

Ortiz M, Walker W-L, Thomas R (1989) Physicians — friend or foe? *Journal of Social and Administrative Pharmacy*; **6**: 59–68.

Pharmaceutical Journal (1988) 3000 average. **240**: 175.

Pharmaceutical Journal (1993) Professional allowance — Contractors in eight FHSAs will suffer the most. **250**: 413.

Roberts D (1988) Dispensing by the community pharmacist: an unstoppable decline? *Journal of the Royal College of General Practitioners*; **38**: 563–564.

Smith GH, Sorby DL, Sharp LJ (1975) Physicians' attitudes toward drug information resources. *American Journal of Hospital Pharmacy*; **32**: 19–25.

Smith MC (1980) The relation between pharmacy and medicine. In: Mapes R (Ed.), *Prescribing Practice and Drug Usage*. London: Croom Helm.

Spencer JA, Edwards C (1992) Pharmacy beyond the dispensary: the general practitioner's views. *British Medical Journal*; **304**: 1670–1672.

Van de Poel G, Bruijnzeels MA, Van der Does J, Lubsen J (1991) A way of achieving more rational drug prescribing? *International Journal of Pharmacy Practice*; **1**: 45–48.

Walton J (1986) Communication between doctors and members of other selected caring professions. In: Walton J, McLachlan G (Eds), *Partnership or Prejudice: Communication Between Doctors and Those in the Other Caring Professions*. London: Nuffield Provincial Hospitals Trust.

Williamson RE, Kabat HF (1971) Pharmacist–physician drug communications. *Journal of the American Pharmaceutical Association*; **NS11**: 164–167.

Part C

Education and Training for Working Together

Contributors to this section agree that interprofessional learning should offer possibilities for acquiring knowledge, skills and attitudes that professionals can take with them into their professional practice and post-basic education.

Whilst there are disputes over terminology, as Janet Gill and John Ling show, there is agreement that clear objectives for shared learning need to be set, and these need to focus on promoting increased understanding of other professionals' roles, enhancing teamwork, and acquiring knowledge, skills and attitudes relevant to practice. Development of communications skills is a primary aim. The need for thorough preparation of multiprofessional educational initiatives is also emphasized. Not only do students need to know what to expect from shared learning, but teachers and service managers require preparation for a multidisciplinary approach, and institutional structures may need to be adapted. Nils-Holger Areskog reports how this has been achieved in an ambitious project in interprofessional health care education in Sweden.

Existing interprofessional education projects vary from intensive introductory programmes which aim to set the scene for ongoing shared learning throughout courses to 'one-off' study days at strategic points. John Horder reviews developments in the UK, showing how initiatives have come from a variety of sources, while Peter Funnell discusses five broad approaches that have been adopted in different settings. Mary Thomas reports on work which developed and evaluated two different approaches to learning teamwork — one using printed material and the other a computer program.

Whichever approach is used, evaluation is essential. However, several authors point out that systematic evaluation of the benefits of interprofessional education is lacking. At present shared learning is often adopted as an 'act of faith', and there are dangers that it may create expectations in students which are not fulfilled when they enter practice. It could also be seen as a cheap way of papering over cracks in the present system, particularly the lack of resources and inadequate structural arrangements for cooperation.

Potential contradictions may arise between traditional professional identities and multidisciplinary learning and working. Challenging the fragmentation of knowledge and practice and the uniqueness of professional roles may have positive aspects, but can also lead to undermining of professional self-esteem and confidence.

All these issues need to be taken into consideration when planning and delivering interprofessional education, and until further evaluation has been undertaken it should not be seen as a panacea. It has yet to be demonstrated that positive student experiences on courses lead to long-term carry-over into professional practice, and until this has been done it is impossible to answer the key question 'Does multiprofessional education work?'

9 Multiprofessional education at the undergraduate level

Nils-Holger Areskog

Introduction

The European 'Health for All' policy adopted by the member states of the World Health Organization (WHO) in 1984 identified multiprofessional health education (MPE) as one of the activities to be given priority in order to reach the policy goals. At the ministerial consultation on medical education in Europe in 1988, the ministers and delegations highlighted the statement that medical education should seek to provide opportunities to train for multidisciplinary collaboration in health care. In addition, further interprofessional learning opportunities should be developed. A technical report *Learning Together to Work Together for Health* has been published by WHO (1988).

The need for multiprofessional health education in undergraduate studies has been identified in an editorial in *Medical Education* in 1988 by Areskog (1988).

At the European Health Community meeting in Strasbourg in 1989, experts stressed particularly the development of curricula for all health professionals, not only medical personnel. Areas of development identified were problem-oriented training, the need for structured links between pre- and postgraduate education, training in technology assessment, training in the management and economics of health care, the development of new concepts in the patient–doctor relationship, and the importance of ethical and legal considerations. In a recently distributed WHO Bulletin, *Changing Medical Education and Medical Practice* (Boelen, 1993), the notion of a 'five star doctor', including fundamental areas of expertise, is identified. One of these is efficient working in teams both within and across the health sector and other social and economic sectors, in order to respond to the needs of communities. There is also a need for broader cooperation between different health professions in order to improve communication both with health care consumers and with political and administrative

125

decision-makers at the societal level.

Undergraduate students already need to acquire knowledge and skills which allow flexibility in their future occupational function. Their education should stimulate them to develop their personalities, imaginativeness and empathy. At the same time the ability to analyse different situations and problems critically should be emphasized. It is also necessary for students to attain greater knowledge and understanding of the structure and total resources of health and social care in order to be able to use these effectively in the care and nursing of patients. Their education should give the students positive attitudes and tools for life-long learning in order to update knowledge and skills following advances in research and development in health care.

At the undergraduate level the development of team-work with health and social workers should be developed as part of the occupational role.

'Prevention' is a natural area for multiprofessional co-working, being unburdened by traditional occupational roles and limits. Undergraduate education should, more than hitherto, emphasize prevention in order to increase understanding of the relationships between illness, health and environmental factors, and to stimulate students towards active cooperation in health education.

Hypothesis of undergraduate multiprofessional education

It is assumed that the use of multiprofessional education (MPE) from the first days of the programme will influence attitudes in a positive direction towards future team-work and diminish the risk that students become trapped in a conventional professional role. MPE throughout the curriculum ensures continuity and a gradual progression from simple to more complex and difficult problems and skills. MPE helps learners and teachers to acquire the habit of using a multiprofessional teaching and learning approach. It will also prepare students for future multiprofessional programmes in post-basic, postgraduate and continuing education. MPE will create positive attitudes to and skills for participation in future multiprofessional research.

Some goals of undergraduate MPE

- The overall goal of undergraduate MPE is to prepare the minds of students for future life-long willing cooperation between different health care occupations.
- By using a common introductory curricular base (care), the students acquire basic knowledge and skills essential for continuing

education and their future professional roles.

- Use of MPE from the outset also develops a frame of common reference for performance within the health care delivery sector.
- Through attending recurrent common seminars, clinical sessions and theme days, students build up a common fund of knowledge and skills to further develop common values and attitudinal systems.
- In working sessions and group arrangements between two or more health care training courses, ways of working in future occupational situations are developed and opportunities for team-work training are given.
- All training courses and professions in health schools (faculties) should be involved, focusing upon the synergistic and specifically beneficial effects of MPE.

Some reasons for undergraduate MPE

- Through learning together in order to work together, coordinated action is facilitated around commonly agreed goals, with awareness and respect of other health professions.
- By sharing skills, experiences and attitudes, undergraduate students or professionals in continuing education gain insight into similarities and dissimilarities between the different health professions. An increased respect and mutual understanding of each other is thus facilitated.
- Through acquiring a broader mass of knowledge and skills it is easier to find solutions to complex problems and new competencies are acquired.
- Harmful corporatism may be prevented.
- Communication between different professionals and between professionals and patients/clients is improved. Education and practical work in multiprofessional teams may also promote multidisciplinary research in previously neglected areas.
- By introducing a common introductory MPE at the undergraduate level there is a possibility of developing common educational methods such as problem-based learning (PBL), and common frames of reference with common basic knowledge and skills essential for future education and professional work.
- MPE favours co-working, team training and mutual respect and understanding between the health education programmes and professions involved. During specific periods of education at different levels, students or workers with different educational backgrounds learn and train together with interaction as an important goal. Areas where MPE has been practised are, for example, a common introduction to health education, primary

health care, care of the elderly, chronic diseases and drug abuse.

Some advantages, difficulties and constraints of undergraduate MPE are summarized in Figs 9.1 and 9.2.

Undergraduate MPE in Europe

The European Health Committee of the Council of Europe recently conducted a survey (European Health Committee, 1993) which showed that MPE at the undergraduate level is still not widespread in Europe.

In 1977 the Paris-Nord University at Bobigny, France, introduced a 'common core' during the first year at the university for health-related education. Initially it was mostly theoretical and lecture-based, but in 1984 a two-year multiprofessional programme was implemented with both theoretical and practical elements.

In 1986 the University of Linköping, Sweden, introduced a full

---

- Develops ability to share knowledge and skills

- Promotes the concept of team-work to develop mutual respect and understanding

- Permits the introduction/integration of new areas of knowledge and skills in health care

- Assists teachers, learners and service staff to communicate more easily

- Allows the utilization of various competencies of each student in the team

- Promotes multiprofessional research, often in new or previously neglected areas, to ensure that all the pertinent aspects of a problem are considered

- Requires and promotes interdepartmental and interdisciplinary understanding and cooperation within institutions responsible for education and health care delivery

- Permits collective consideration of the allocation, utilization and assessment of educational and service resources according to ascertained needs

- Helps to ensure consistency and avoid contradiction or conflict in the curriculum design

---

Fig. 9.1   Some advantages of undergraduate MPE

introductory programme of joint education in the Faculty of Health Sciences. This 10-week programme involves six different professions, namely nurses, laboratory technologists, occupational therapists, physiotherapists, doctors and supervisors of social services in community care. A more detailed description of this programme is given elsewhere (Areskog, 1992).

In 1992 a similar type of multiprofessional study period was introduced in Tromsoe, Norway. Other centres that have reported undergraduate MPE include Dublin (Ireland), Cardiff (Wales), Malmoe Dental Health School (Sweden), Amsterdam, Utrecht and Maastricht (the Netherlands).

The Linköping model

In 1981 the Linköping Commission on Integrated Health Care Education proposed a trial project in the Health University of Ostergotland

---

- Uneasiness or resentment of teachers caused by the presence of students/health workers with different levels of education

- Students or teachers unwilling to experiment with different methods of learning and teaching

- Lack of skilled or experienced teachers for MPE system

- Difficulty in preparing a common core curriculum

- Unsuitable or inadequate methods of assessing the specific competencies for functioning as a member of a team

- Lack of learning and teaching material

- Overloaded service personnel unable to cope with field training needs of student teams

- Difficulty in implementing planned activities in the community

- Poor educational facilities, insufficient identification of training needs

- Fear of health professionals losing their identity and speciality

- Teachers feel that planning, consultation and evaluation make undue demands on their time

- Insufficient opportunities for on-the-job training

- Inadequate intersectoral training support

Fig. 9.2   Some difficulties and constraints of MPE

(Regional Health University, 1981). The directives for the commission from the Ministry of Education included early patient contact for students and coordination as far as possible between preclinical and clinical studies. Later, integration between traditional preclinical disciplines, with more emphasis on primary health care in community medicine,was included. There were also directives on integration between the different health care programmes. After criticisms from some authorities and professional organizations, the proposed initial study period was shortened, but fundamentally the ideology of undergraduate MPE was accepted and introduced in the autumn of 1986. These plans were in line with WHO targets for the 'Health for All by the Year 2000' programme. The Faculty of Health Sciences has at present more than 1200 undergraduate students in six different courses of between 2.5 to 5.5 years duration. Every six months 180–200 new students enter the MPE programme. Common objectives for all students are:

- an holistic approach to health and disease;
- an education with the patient in the centre and close contact with primary health care (PHC) and preventive work;
- an education with team training between different health education programmes and occupations;
- an emphasis on some previously neglected research areas in PHC, occupational medicine, geriatrics and care research.

In order to create flexibility and adaptiveness to future social changes in occupational roles, MPE and multiprofessional research are intended to develop new thinking, new roles and competencies, new responsibilities and areas of interest within health care and its delivery. Disciplines such as health economics, health information, evaluation of medical technologies, care sociology, social anthropology, ethics, service management, communication and information transfer are important. A common educational strategy for all programmes is problem-based learning in small groups with faculty teachers or health care professionals as tutors.

During the introductory common study period (10 weeks), tutors and lecturers come from all the above-mentioned disciplines and from primary health care, hospitals and the Faculty of Health Sciences, with representatives from all the health care programmes involved. Since the introduction of the programme, experience has been gained with more than 4000 students. During the introductory common study period the curricular content is dominated by behavioural and social sciences and science theory, focusing on wide problem areas, including Humans at Different Ages and in Different Societies, Human Development, Life Styles, and Handicap.

The introductory study period focuses not only upon acquisition of knowledge but also upon attitudes. Thus the students should, for example, develop opinions about health and disease, know about health development in Sweden during the last century, identify possibilities for disease prevention and health promotion, take into consideration the epidemiological situation of the community studied, understand the importance of psychosocial factors for the human life cycle, and identify ethical problems within health and sickness care.

The skills the students are taught include how to use problem-based learning, searching for information in a scientific library, evaluating a scientific paper, interpreting information from simple epidemiological data, interpreting a simple group process, and tolerating individual human differences.

Study setting (see Appendix)

A 'basic group' for problem-based learning consisting of 6–7 students representing all six educational programmes forms the nucleus for the study setting. Three to four 'basic groups' constitute a 'big group' for seminars. There are a small number of introductory lectures for all students together. However, the emphasis is on training in work and study methods. Some field studies in primary health care and/or the hospital setting are also performed. Not more than 15 hours per week are scheduled for lectures, seminars and tutor sessions in order to allow students time for learning individually and in groups. After the 10-week study period there is a common structured written examination evaluating knowledge, skills and attitudes.

Continuing undergraduate MPE

After the introductory period the students enter their specific curricular programmes but have intermittent multiprofessional sessions, seminars and theme days. They also have early practical training, including cardiopulmonary resuscitation.

During clinical training there are common sessions between two or three education programmes, highlighting patient care from different aspects both in primary and in hospital care. Examples of team-work studies are cardiac rehabilitation after myocardial infarction, with doctor, nurse, physiotherapist and occupational therapist involved, and diabetes care and information with doctors, nurses and nutritionists involved.

The team aspect is also highlighted in the field of cancer care and elderly care. A 2-week team training period in the PHC setting is planned at the final stage of courses for medical, nursing, physiotherapy and occupational therapy students in order to promote a smooth transition from the student role to the professional role.

How to implement undergraduate MPE

Political level

One prerequisite for MPE is to have a positive political will with legal, organizational and monetary incentives in order to create good conditions and a good study environment. Thus MPE and a team approach should be an established part of government policy. At the regional and community levels it is necessary to have active involvement of the primary health care system and the population of the community in order to identify the expectations and needs of the population regarding the current epidemiological and health situations in the community.

Institutional level

When undergraduate MPE and student health teams are introduced, the educational institutions need to assist governments and communities to understand MPE and the team approach. Further, the institutions need to undertake special preparation in health care delivery settings if the scheme is to function optimally. Therefore educational institutions have to plan for implementation of MPE in close collaboration with health care delivery institutions and personnel. Education has to be competency-based, with common educational objectives and joint educational planning between different health care programmes. MPE can be arranged in both hospital and primary health care settings; however, the latter is preferable in order to develop a more community oriented undergraduate curriculum than hitherto.

Educational principles and structures

MPE is optimized by using a problem-solving approach. PBL with small groups of students representing different health programmes is a good educational tool for MPE and team training. Students need to interact in small groups both among themselves and between patients and students. Common learning resources should be used, and it is necessary that library and educational tools reflect the needs of all the health care programmes involved. MPE also favours co-working with other than the educational sector in the society, such as socio-economic, social and communication sectors.

Teacher education and training

An absolute prerequisite is adequate teacher training for both MPE and team action. This should involve teachers from all participating disciplines and professions. Attitudinal change in favour of MPE and team work is an important goal that will also improve communication skills. The planning stage for MPE is an excellent training opportunity for teachers and professionals from different health occupations.

In conclusion, educational structures have to be adapted in order to promote educational integration both between disciplines and between professions in order to facilitate coordination and collaboration both within and across educational institutions and health care delivery institutions.

Guidelines for planning and implementing undergraduate MPE

The first essential is a planning committee with representatives from the different programmes involved. This group should produce documents for agreement around the MPE collaboration, including teacher and overhead costs, library costs, etc.

After agreement on the external formal and financial problems, a curriculum group should be constituted with representatives from all programmes involved, and preferably also consultants from a faculty which already has experience within the field. The task of this group is to work out a common core curriculum content for MPE to be included in the new curricula of the different courses.

A series of meetings should be arranged with staff from the different faculties involved in order to anchor and spread the new ideas and get feedback from teachers and students.

It is recommended that pilot studies should be arranged during the planning period with limited curricular content in order to check how the ideas function in practice. Examples of such pilot studies are theoretical and clinical group sessions in primary health care or in hospital care settings; field studies, with two or more programmes involved; or common theme days; or clinical sessions. If professional teams are established in, for example, primary health care or elderly care or within cardiac rehabilitation or diabetes care, they can be trained to interact with students from the different programmes involved.

Student and tutor evaluations should be administered after the MPE study period, and there can be a common final written examination. Evaluation by questionnaires to students and teachers can also be performed.

Comments and conclusions

At Linköping University, feedback on the introductory study period has on the whole been very positive and encouraging from both students and teachers. Students have requested more MPE in their specific curricula during the following terms.

The new medical programme at Linköping is currently under evaluation, but the other health care courses have already been evaluated (Bredange, 1991). The attitudes of teachers have been positive and they have shown a strong loyalty to the ideas of the Faculty of Health Sciences. Students feel that this kind of teaching furthers their skills in thinking critically and analytically, taking responsibility and working in a team.

On the whole, students have been more positive than teachers about undergraduate MPE. One reason for this is that teachers have very little previous practical experience of MPE, but consider it essential for future professional work.

It has proved difficult to introduce MPE successfully in countries and in situations where the level of education expected from students differs widely from profession to profession. It has also proved difficult to persuade established teachers from different health professions to meet together to discuss and agree upon a common curriculum. This difficulty extends to reaching agreement on both implementation and on final joint assessments (examinations).

Professional organizations have often been sceptical about MPE, fearing dilution of the specific knowledge possessed by their own professions. This has commonly resulted in fence-building around their own educational territory.

The most favourable situation for introducing undergraduate MPE includes students with about the same level of educational background, an educational method which places more emphasis on problem-based learning in small tutor groups than on lectures, a faculty planning group which contains representatives of all the professions involved and a willingness of primary care and hospital authorities to provide good training facilities.

Relatively few countries in Europe have implemented undergraduate MPE, but the examples given show that it is feasible and appreciated by both students and teachers. So far there are no follow-up studies of the long-term effects on professional outcomes. Research should be encouraged to find out the positive and negative aspects of MPE both during undergraduate education and later at the professional stage. The working hypotheses are that MPE induces positive attitudes towards interprofessional co-working and team-work in both PHC and hospital settings and that the demands involved in planning MPE are well compensated by the development of positive attitudes among students.

References

Areskog NH (1988) The need for multiprofessional health education in undergraduate studies. *Medical Education*; **22**: 251–252.

Areskog NH (1992) The new medical education at the Faculty of Health Sciences, Linköping University — A challenge for both students and teachers. *Scand J Soc Med*; **2**: 1–4.

Boelen C (1993) *The Five Star Doctor: Changing Medical Education and Medical Practice*, Bulletin 3, WHO/EDH/NL.

Bredange G (1991) *Faculty of Health Sciences from the Nursing Perspective*. Final report of an evaluation of the shorter health education courses at the Faculty of Health Sciences (in Swedish).

European Health Committee (1993) *Multiprofessional Education for Health Personnel: the 1990/1992 Coordinated Medical Research Programme*. European Health Committee, Council of Europe, CDSP (93) 10.

Regional Health University (1981) *Proposal for a Trial Project in Ostergotland (LIV)*. Report from the Linköping Commission on Integrated Health Care Education.

World Health Organization (1988) *Learning Together to Work Together for Health* (Technical Report Series 769). Geneva: WHO.

Appendix — Notes for students entering MPE

Objectives

The objectives are related to the cases/problems/situations that are studied during the different topics of the course. All topics are reflected upon from the perspectives of the individual, the group and the society. The intention is that small groups should work with all of the objectives, though not in connection with every case. Owing to the scope of the subject areas and the organization of the study period, no attempts will be made to harmonize the work of the groups. The depth of learning has to be related to the duration of the course. The objectives include knowledge, attitudes and skills.

Knowledge and attitudes

You should be able to:

- appreciate different perceptions of the concepts of health and illness
- elucidate factors that have influenced people's health from the 19th century to the present day

- identify possibilities for preventive and health-promoting measures
- understand developments during the human life-cycle, with emphasis on psychosocial factors
- explain how individuals and groups are governed in their behaviour by norms and values
- explain how differences due to culture and language affect health and illness
- understand the legislative framework of health care and social welfare services
- elucidate the economic consequences of ill-health for the individual and for society
- identify ethical problems
- evaluate various ways of looking at learning and knowledge.

Skills

You should be able to:

- apply PBL to your own studies
- seek information on your own in a scientific library
- assess a simple scientific publication on the basis of given criteria
- interpret information obtained from simple epidemiological surveys
- collect and process data and write and present a field study report
- interpret a simple group process and give and take criticism
- tolerate individual differences between people
- observe and meet people and carry on a conversation about a situation.

Working and study methods

Small groups

Six to seven students form a small group. Problem-based learning in integrated groups is the basic method of working. The studies have their starting-point in cases taken from the respective topics. All of the small groups work with all four of the topics, though not concurrently. Each small group has a teacher who acts as a tutor. The guidelines for the studies are given in the objectives. The group meets twice or three times a week, for about 90 minutes, according to a schedule.

Large groups

Three or four small groups together make up a large group, which engages in such activities as seminars, discussions and information meetings.

Training in skills

The small groups receive training in skills concerned with the scientific way of working. Guidance on the use of a library is offered at several points. Communication skills are taught in small groups by means of various exercises which are videotaped, analysed and discussed.

Seminars

Scientific attitude and oral presentation are taught in seminars. These are held in large groups and bring each topic to a conclusion. Students lead the seminar and each small group has about 45 minutes at its disposal. The group initiates questions on the basis of the knowledge gained, discusses methods of seeking information, the use of resources, experiences of the group's work, etc. The small group may also form a panel to be a resource within a given topic. The small group should stimulate the students in other groups to be active. The tutors of the small groups participate.

Lectures

Some of the lectures are common for all students and are held in Linköping, while others will be held at both study locations (Linköping and Norrköping). The areas are scientific theory (3 h), epidemiology (2 h), pedagogics (4 h), ethics and views of man (4 h), economics (3 h), holistic view of health (4 h) and medical anthropology (2 h).

Resource faculty sessions

There are resource faculty sessions within the following areas: prevention, epidemiology and vital statistics, legislation, social psychology, ethics and views of man, the concept of health, immigrant studies, statistics, economics and pedagogics. Each session will last about 2 hours and there will be 2–4 of them during the course. Information about resource faculty leaders and times of sessions will be displayed on the noticeboard. Students' questions should be presented three working days before the sessions. If no questions are presented there will be no session.

Field studies

Each small group will do a theoretical and empirical study of the inter-action between the environment and health as part of the training in scientific working methods. Guidance will be given by the tutor.

The students themselves must make the necessary contacts. The field study should be completed in five weeks and presented as a typewritten report, which has to be approved by the group's tutor.

The field study report will be presented at a seminar. Each small group has two hours at its disposal. For every report there will be an opponent group, responsible for the organization of the seminar.

Self-directed study

Scheduled time is limited to an average of 15 hours per week in order to give time for individual studies.

Assessment

Compulsory course items

The compulsory parts of the course are: Scheduled small and large group meetings, seminars, training in communication skills and the field study. Students are expected to take an active part in the work of their group. Information about the results of the completed compulsory sections is given at the end of the course.

In order to sit the end-of-term examination, completed compulsory sections are required. Compulsory parts of the course must be taken later in cases of absence.

Continuous assessment

Small groups: Everyone in a small group — students and tutor — evaluates himself or herself and the work of the group, at each meeting. The evaluation is done of the basis of the ability:

- to work according to the 'seven-jump' method
- to take responsibility for one's own and the group's work and learning

- to be active and prepared
- to give and take feedback and to remedy any shortcomings.

A special assessment form is used by each student and the tutor in a more comprehensive assessment half-way through the course.

Training in skills: The exercises in communication are evaluated both by the group members and the tutor. The videotaped sections are observed and interpreted.

Seminars: Both the seminar participants and the tutor evaluate subject content, information sources, oral presentation, initiating and dealing with questions and the distribution of the workload within the group.

Field studies: The report is passed/rejected by the tutor. Opposition to and defence of the study are evaluated in the seminar group according to the guidelines above.

Examinations

To sit the end-of-term examination, the compulsory parts have to be completed satisfactorily. The end-of-term examination covers integrated knowledge, skills and attitudes of the students' specific study programme during the whole term. Details can be found in the local syllabus and curriculum for the respective study programmes.

10 Interprofessional education for primary health and community care: Present state and future needs

John Horder

We have no accurate knowledge of the present state of inter-professional education for primary health and community care in the United Kingdom. This *was* known about six years ago, because a survey covering England, Wales and Scotland (but not Northern Ireland) had just been completed. The results of a new survey now being undertaken will not be available before this book is published.

This chapter will therefore (1) summarize the most important findings of six years ago; (2) trace relevant developments at the national level since then; and (3) propose what is needed now if an old idea is to influence present realities.

The national survey of 1988

The survey was commissioned by the Centre for the Advancement of Interprofessional Education in Primary Health and Community Care. It was carried out by post by the Institute of Community Studies, London. For its purpose the term 'interprofessional education' was taken to include any activity which fulfilled each of the following criteria:

- Its primary objective was education.
- It involved participants from two or more of the selected professional groups.
- The participants were *learning together* within a multidisciplinary context.

The professional groups included were general practitioners, social workers, district nurses, health visitors and community midwives.

In addition, students and trainees in each of the five groups were included. Activities involving medical students, student nurses or student midwives were also accepted as valid. It was not possible to include other professions, because resources were limited. The same reason explains the omission of Northern Ireland.

The target groups were people likely to have organized or taught in interprofessional activities. This was seen as a way of obtaining wider coverage and more comprehensive detail than an approach to practitioners from the selected professions. The target groups were:

Directors of nurse education
Heads of midwifery services
Course organizers in district nursing
Course organizers in health visiting } in colleges,
Course organizers in social work   universities and
Training officers in social work departments polytechnics
Undergraduate deans of medical schools
Regional advisers in general practice
General practice tutors.

Also included were heads of education centres, professional bodies and other organizations which might be involved in the education and training of primary health care professionals.

In all, 1518 questionnaires were sent out, with a response rate of 75%. The level of response varied by profession, being highest from nursing, midwifery and health visiting. It also varied between regions, the highest response coming from South West England at 83%. Even higher was the response from the education centres and professional bodies — 87% of which replied.

There were in all 695 valid examples of interprofessional education, involving a total of 466 individual organizing agencies. The level of participation by five selected professions was:

Health visitors   88%
District nurses   73%
Social workers   46%
General practitioners   37%
Community midwives   32%

Ninety-six per cent of initiatives involved either nurses or health visitors (a result which cannot be attributed to either the survey methods or the response rate from these groups). Six per cent of initiatives involved all five professional groups, another 12% four groups, 35% three and 45% two groups. The actual combination of professions is shown in Table 10.1.

Groups other than the five selected professions took part in the initiatives studied; for example, hospital nurses, hospital doctors, hospital midwives, school nurses, community psychiatric nurses. There was frequent involvement of both police and teachers relating to the considerable number of initiatives on child abuse.

The educational context

Interprofessional education took place most commonly as part of continuing education and professional development programmes for qualified staff. However, there was also considerable activity within the context of initial pre-qualification training and in post-qualifying or vocational training (see Table 10.2).

Table 10.1   How the professions combined in initiatives

Combination of professions	Percentage of initiatives
DN and HV	20
DN, HV and MW	11
DN, HV and SW	11
HV and SW	8
DN, HV and GP	7
DN, HV, SW and GP	7
DN, HV, MW, SW and GP	6
HV and MW	6

DN = district nurses, GP = general practitioners, HV = health visitors, MV = community midwives, SW = social workers.

Table 10.2   The educational context

Category of training	Percentage of initiatives
Undergraduate training (e.g. MB ChB; MB BS)	1
Initial professional training (e.g. RGN, CQSW)	8
Post-qualifying/vocational training (e.g. district nurse/health visiting certificate; general practice vocational training scheme)	18
Continuing education/professional development (i.e. educational activities for qualified practitioners)	83
Degree/diploma course (i.e. courses leading to a degree or diploma other than those in the first three categories listed above)	1
Other	1

Objectives

Respondents were given a choice of four objectives: (1) to increase knowledge of any topic; (2) to develop practical skills; (3) to increase understanding of the roles/views of other professions; (4) to promote teamwork/cooperation between professions. They were asked to rank them. The relative importance of each objective was some indication of why the initiative was organized on a multidisciplinary basis — whether it was merely for convenience or specifically to promote teamwork and develop understanding between professions.

In 53% of initiatives, respondents ranked 'promoting teamwork' and/or 'increasing understanding of the roles and views of other professionals' as the two most important objectives of the activity. In 64% of initiatives involving GPs, one or both of these aims were ranked highest.

Linking this to the educational context, over 80% of initiatives organized as part of initial professional training and/or post-qualifying/vocational training rated these objectives highest. This contrasts sharply with 47% of those in the continuing education/professional development category and with 33% of those which were part of degree/diploma courses.

Analysis of objectives in relation to subject reveals that initiatives on certain topics were more frequently organized with interprofessional aims. Sixty-five per cent of those on child abuse came into this category (see Table 10.3).

One in ten initiatives actually centred on teamwork and professional roles, but 92% had interprofessional aims which were clearly reflected in the subject matter.

Table 10.3 Subjects occurring most frequently in interprofessional education

Subjects	Percentage of initiatives
Child/family abuse	15
Teamwork/professional roles	10
Multiple subjects	8
General medical (including heart disease, diabetes)	7
Terminal care/dying/bereavement	7
Education and training	5
Management issues	5
Childbirth	4
Child health	4
Elderly	4
AIDS	4
Mental health/mental handicap	40

Educational methods

The various educational methods used in interprofessional education and the incidence of their use were as shown in Table 10.4. Most activities involved at least two methods. Of those with interprofessional aims, however, 7% used formal methods only.

This invites the question of how effective this method of learning can be in promoting teamwork and developing understanding between professions. It could be argued that these objectives can only be achieved where interaction between the various professional groups takes place in a learning situation, whether this be through discussion, group-work or specifically experiential methods.

Tables 10.5 and 10.6 show how the duration of courses was distributed, and their frequencies. In addition, 18% of initiatives took place as one or more sessions of an established course, leading to a qualification of higher degree or diploma.

In summary, while 39% of initiatives took place only once in a year, 67% took place five times or more in a year. In two-thirds of initiatives participation was optional.

Respondents indicated that the IPE activity described would either probably or definitely be repeated or continued in 86% of instances.

Table 10.7 shows the geographical distribution of initiatives. Approximately the same distribution was reflected in the number of agencies organizing activities within each region.

Developments in the UK since 1988

This section will focus on developments at national level since 1988. A small, personal selection from a very wide and diffuse field offers descriptions in some detail. The omission of many other important activities is inevitable — and regretted.

There has been exceptional intervention by government during the

Table 10.4 Educational methods used

Method used	Percentage of initiatives
Group work/discussion	86
Formal input (e.g. lecture or video)	73
Experiential methods (role-play etc.)	14
Individual study/project work	4
Visits (domiciliary or to agencies)	2
Exhibitions	1
Presentations/demonstrations	1
Tutorials	1

Table 10.5   Course durations

Duration	Percentage of initiatives
1 day (6 hours) or less	53
2–4 days	28
1 week (5 days)	6
6–19 days	7
4 weeks (20 days) or more*	5

* Of the initiatives in this category, 22 lasted between 4 and 8 weeks; ten lasted 12 weeks or more.

Table 10.6   Frequency of occurrence of interprofessional educational activities

Frequency	Percentage of initiatives
Once/one-off	29
Once a year	10
2–5 times a year	18
More than 5 times a year	7

last six years, affecting every part of the health and social services, whether through statements of policy or Acts of Parliament. Some of these have a direct bearing on the need for interprofessional collaboration and education for it.

During the same period a number of small organizations have been started at national level, each of which has some concern with interprofessional collaboration and therefore with shared learning. Their purposes are not identical, but they overlap with each other. Their joint contributions bear on interprofessional education through publications, conferences, experiments in education and through research.

Government interventions

Background

The demise of communism and the end of the cold war have coincided with a period of government characterized by an exceptional parliamentary majority, determined leadership and a marked political and economic ideology. This seeks to shift the balance between collaboration and competition towards the latter, in order to increase efficiency and value for money. It favours the market in contrast to government planning and regulation, in order to give increased influence

Table 10.7   Geographical distribution by NHS region

Location of activity by NHS region	Number of initiatives
Northern	39 (6%)
Yorkshire	35 (5%)
Trent	46 (7%)
East Anglia	19 (3%)
North West Thames	59 (8%)
North East Thames	43 (6%)
South East Thames	37 (5%)
South West Thames	21 (3%)
Wessex	39 (6%)
Oxford	31 (5%)
South Western	73 (11%)
West Midlands	52 (8%)
Mersey	28 (4%)
North Western	67 (10%)
Wales	59 (9%)
Scotland	40 (6%)
More than one region	7 (1%)

to 'consumers' — in the present context, those who use health and social services. With the same intention, decision-making is devolved to increasingly local levels. Thus power and control over resources is being transferred to those who manage services at regional, district and even more local levels. There is a new focus on setting clear objectives and checking that they have been achieved — in other words, on effectiveness as well as on efficiency.

Unfortunately a second influence — economic recession of unusual depth — has contaminated these changes in ideology, so that efficiency has had to change into a dominant concern with economies and cuts in services, largely unwanted even by government, since they undermine the intended changes.

The first reorganization affecting interprofessional relationships and arising from this fundamental shift in belief was the introduction of general management early in the 1980s. This was based on a further belief that effective and efficient organization was more often found in industry and commerce than in the health and social services, as they had developed by that time.

Also relevant was the introduction of the 'internal market' in 1990, whereby, for example, health service districts became purchasers of care, with a prime duty to assess the needs of their populations and then to make contracts with providers, such as hospitals, which had to compete for payments in respect of the particular services they offered.

Out of a multitude of changes in health and social services, two more must be selected for their potential relevance to interprofessional education. The first is the transfer of responsibility for 'community care' to local government — i.e. to the social services instead of the health service (1993). This particularly affects the increasing numbers of elderly people, in addition to those mentally ill or with learning difficulties. Closely related has been the more gradual policy of transferring as much care as possible out of institutions into the world where people live and work. This is an older trend, starting with the care of the mentally ill.

If those are the most important and relevant changes in the organization and work of health and social services, other fundamental changes have been introduced in education which are directly relevant to the traditions, status and training of all professional groups.

The first change brings the initial training of nurses and other groups before qualification into the university system. Similarly, polytechnics have been renamed and reorganized as universities. This change could in theory make interprofessional education in initial education easier to organize.

The introduction of 'National Vocational Qualifications' (1986–92) is a more fundamental change. This is the name given to a wide-ranging approach to training for jobs (Hevey, 1992). It concentrates on learning the specific competences required to achieve specific tasks and it offers a new set of qualifications when these competences can be shown to have been acquired by an individual worker. The system has been introduced first in relation to jobs requiring limited competences but, succeeding at this level, the system now moves upwards towards the tasks and competences hitherto carried out or achieved by social workers and nurses. Whether it will be further developed towards the training of doctors is undecided.

Relevance

All these changes have a bearing on interprofessional education. Managers, now introduced into all levels of the services, may or may not appreciate the importance of any form of training or retraining for the many sorts of professional for whom they are responsible. There are known reasons for anxiety here at the present time, especially when most managers are overwhelmed in coping with urgent and multiple problems in service organization resulting from changes in policy.

The relevance of the internal market is that post-qualification or post-registration and training has to be purchased in the same way as care has to be purchased. But money is limited and will always be so. Service needs are likely to attract a higher priority than education unless education is protected.

Transfer of care to the community makes collaboration between professionals more difficult because of the more scattered context in which they work. It makes the need for interprofessional education greater, but does not make it easier to organize. Meanwhile, transfer of control to local government is now revealing the pressing needs of elderly people (or the mentally ill) for coordinated and simultaneous health and social care. Their problems are usually multiple, involving both fields and indeed others such as housing.

The competences required at the lowest levels of National Vocational Qualifications related to health and social care are specified in terms relating to the needs of clients; for example (terminal care) 'enable clients to maintain and improve their mobility' or again (a core competence) 'enable clients to make use of available services and information'. This approach is most welcome. The practical task-oriented character of competences seems likely to appeal to managers. But at higher levels it provides an alternative to traditional qualifications controlled by professions and related to education which may be of a more basic, reflective nature. The higher the level, the more important it is to maintain the balance between theory and practice, between intellectual and attitudinal development, on the one hand, and practical skills on the other.

Interprofessional training assumes the existence of separate professions in some form, not necessarily the existing forms. The new approach may sometimes cut across professional boundaries by creating new roles out of new groups of competences. These new roles could be both more appropriate than existing ones and relate to lower levels of remuneration. The attraction to government and to managers concerned for economy is obvious. There is a further attraction for those who see value in reducing the power of traditional professions.

To predict the combined effect of all these influences on the development of interprofessional education in the longer term is difficult. The present effect is on balance negative, if only because of the turbulence, conflict, stress and anxiety caused by multiple changes introduced hurriedly and usually without prior experiment. There is clear evidence of a raised level of perceived stress, for instance in general practitioners (Hannay et al., 1992; Myerson, 1993; Sutherland and Cooper, 1992). There is also evidence that anxiety does not favour collaboration, but rather throws people back on themselves (Woodhouse and Pengelly, 1991).

For both professionals and managers time is more precious than usual and any form of continuing education is liable to be seen as a low priority for the use of time. Shortage of money resulting from the recent economic recession is one more barrier to progress.

But despite these discouraging influences, there is considerable evidence of increased activity, usually attributable to the initiatives of individuals.

New organizations at national level

Prior to 1988, interprofessional education had been the theme of seminars and conferences intermittently since 1966 (Thwaites, 1993). Particularly notable had been the work of a standing group representing the professions of social work, district nursing, general medical practice and health visiting which organized a conference in Nottingham in 1979, the proceedings of which were subsequently published (England, 1980).

The Centre for the Advancement of Interprofessional Education originated from a small conference in north London in 1984. It was formally established with a council in 1987. This was the first time that an *independent* organization with a *continuing* concern for promoting interprofessional education had been formed. Its role is to form links between people and organizations sharing this concern, to collect and disseminate information, to encourage and commission research, and to act as advocate at a national level. It organizes conferences and seminars, publishes a Bulletin, a bibliography and the products of research. It does not itself organize courses of training. It is now a Charitable Trust which has received support from the National Health Service Executive, charitable foundations and individuals, not least those who subscribe to it as members.

In the same year a Scottish organization INTERACT began to organize regular conferences for a variety of health care professionals in which were discussed issues affecting all of them in their working environment.

Also in the same year, the Michael Sieff Foundation was created to foster development and innovation in the care of abused and neglected children. It has held eight annual conferences at Cumberland Lodge, Windsor — for example (1992) about child protection in residential care. Concern was expressed about the increasing emphasis on cost-led rather than needs-led services. This was limiting time for therapy and building up problems for the future. A framework for managing allegations of abuse was accepted. The need for residential care to be given a higher profile, with proper recruitment and management of staff, was stressed.

The Marylebone Centre Trust started in 1988 and began to organize experimental courses which drew in participants from further afield than London. This centre launched the *Journal of Interprofessional Care* in 1991, aimed at present at organizers of education and teachers rather than at students or practitioners.

In 1990 the Health Care Professions Educational Forum originally brought together formal representatives of nursing and professions allied to medicine, in order to discuss issues of shared concern arising from government-inspired changes. It now includes social workers, but not doctors.

The Continuing Care at Home association (CONCAH), launched in 1991, is concerned particularly with collaboration in the care of chronic diseases.

The Standing Conference on Public Health (SCOPH) was launched in 1991. One of its first four aims is that of 'promoting multidisciplinary education and training in matters relating to health professionals'. The membership list confirms that it interprets 'public health' in the broad sense displayed in the government document *Health of the Nation*.

The Alliance for Primary Care and its associated Commission, launched in 1992 under the influence of the Prince of Wales when acting as president of the Royal College of General Practitioners, brings together a group of well-established and influential organizations — the Royal Colleges of General Practice, Nursing, and Midwifery, the General Medical Services Committee (British Medical Association), the National Association of Health Authorities and Trusts, the Carers Association. The National Centre for the Advancement of Interprofessional Education is represented on both bodies.

The Alliance was set up to press the needs of primary care with the government and to voice the shared concerns of the organizations which are engaged in this major part of the health service; they have formal representation in the meetings. The inclusion of the Carers Association is particularly significant.

The Commission is concerned with interprofessional education and team development. Its membership, drawn from a similar range of professions, is informal, based on the known interests and enthusiasms of those invited to join it. It is in the process of setting up six Prince of Wales Fellowships, each lasting three years. The Fellows will work in local areas in different parts of the country, helping to develop teamwork for the benefit of particular client-groups (e.g. the physically disabled and the mentally ill). They are required to produce reports which could have a relevance beyond the area in which they have worked.

This proliferation of new organizations must indicate a general trend. Although they overlap, none have identical aims or programmes. They inevitably compete with each other for the available financial support. There seems to be no single point of reference within the Department of Health to which they can relate.

Local initiatives with more than local significance

New Masters programmes

Storrie (1992) has reviewed Masters' programmes with an inter-professional focus. She found 21 programmes, compared with the single one recognized in 1987. They all fulfilled the three criteria for interprofessional education used in the national survey reported above. Apart from this they show a range of emphases, balancing interprofessional and multidisciplinary approaches on the one hand, with deepening knowledge of a particular client-group or system of care delivery and management on the other. The educational institutions organizing these courses were spread across England and Scotland, but not Wales or Northern Ireland. Most were based in single-discipline academic departments. The only courses jointly organized by medical and social work departments were at Southampton; the only ones jointly organized by nursing and social work were at Hull. But multidisciplinary content and staffing was the norm in all courses.

All but one of the 21 programmes could be grouped into four categories — those with a particular focus on a client-group (one), on care delivery (four), on planning, organization and management of services (three) and on interprofessional working (two).

The professional groups represented were medicine, nursing, social work, housing, planning, police, clergy, youth and community work, and pharmacy. All sought to attract as wide a mix as possible, but no programme claimed to have achieved a balanced intake. Nurses were most heavily represented, doctors rarely.

A large national initiative: the Health Education Authority's programme

This is the largest concerted initiative in the UK hitherto in interprofessional education for primary health care. It is a multi-professional, multidisciplinary and multiagency initiative. Its central purpose is to provide workshops (protected time, usually two and a half days residential) for primary health care teams which will enhance their activity as a team in disease prevention and promotion. The first pilot workshop was held in Yorkshire in 1987. Since then there have been around 300 workshops spread over the UK and involving over 8000 individuals. They were at first organized with the help of the Health Education Authority by planning teams organized by either District Health Authorities, Family Health Service Authorities or the GP Postgraduate Training structure.

The evaluation of the first 18 workshops (involving 521 primary health care professionals, representing 122 primary health care teams) reported that the majority of the plans and strategies developed by the teams related to coronary heart disease. They were valued by those attending:

- as an occasion for viewing and reflecting on current activities and developing new plans;
- for enhancing communication, teamwork and practice organization and helping to clarify roles and responsibilities in primary health care;
- for increasing awareness of their potential for multidisciplinary and multiprofessional approaches;
- for the emphasis the workshop had placed on the value of each member of the team;
- for the emphasis on the need for ongoing evaluation of activities.

A second evaluation report examines the diffusion of the primary health care team workshop strategy through the development of local organizing teams (LOTs) (multiagency planning groups at FHSA/district level) to organize and run the workshops, including preparatory work and follow-up and wider dissemination. The members of LOTs experience in this way a workshop process which they recommend to primary health care teams.

This large and successful initiative is still spreading (Spratley, 1989, 1990; Lambert, 1993).

The National Joint Training Project 'Caring for People'

In 1989 the government announced a policy to improve community health and social care. This would involve 'a shift of services designed to meet people's needs and a joint approach to service delivery between health and social services' (DHSS, 1989).

Seven separate sites were selected to provide a range of settings, populations and political affiliations. The task at each site was to carry out a multiprofessional review of the new 'caring for people' policy and to translate national policy into local practice. In the course of the task, consideration was to be given to the organizational requirements and training needed in order to establish effective working.

By the end of the project all sites were positive about the benefits of joint training. They were also clear as to factors which influenced whether joint training was a success or a failure. As a result of their experience one site concluded that 'most training strategies emphasize courses — this is clearly a mistake, most individual learning develops through participation in projects'. This conclusion was echoed by other sites; e.g. 'staff can be taught knowledge through courses, reading and other training materials, but understanding of the information only comes through working it in practice . . .'. The main conclusion of the report was that the best way to learn about working together is by doing it (Carpenter et al., 1991).

The Joint Practice Teaching Initiative

Since 1988, considerable efforts have been made by the English National Board for Nursing, Midwifery and Health Visiting and the Central Council for the Education and Training of Social Workers towards shared learning and credit transfer. Both bodies have a tradition of supervising students in practice, nursing longer than social work. Both instituted a formal training or guidelines for practice teaching within their own boundaries in 1989. In the same year the Central Council was given money over three years by the Department of Health to develop joint teaching for social work practice teachers, clinical supervisors in community nursing and field-work education supervisors in occupational therapy. The experiment was launched in 1990 and pilot projects were soon approved in Coventry, Exeter, London South Bank, Wales, Lancashire and Dundee (other projects were submitted later). A core module and curriculum for the joint training of three sorts of teachers was agreed by the three validating bodies. The overall aim (Brown, 1993) was 'to help practice teachers to come to grips with the attitudes, areas of knowledge and working practices of their professional neighbours'. Some of the projects have prospered, some have withdrawn.

Experience in the first three years of work has been evaluated by Brown (1993) and Weinstein (1993). Important lessons have emerged which are widely relevant about why some projects have succeeded and some have failed. Both authors stress the linkages between these projects and the wider patterns of joint working between service agencies and between educational establishments.

Brown identified three key issues:

- The practical relevance of the project to the priorities and concerns of the local service authorities. 'Educational establishments have some way to go in appreciating the pressing concerns of service authorities, both in the sense that authorities are experiencing very rapid changes . . . and that the changes have a very radical impact on traditional professional care roles.'

- 'A clear vision of where training is going and a practical grasp of how to get there — shared by partners in the training strategy.' The vision needs leadership which can bring together and hold together a group of enthusiasts. Shared commitments to collaborative work have to apply to internal relations within educational

establishments, whether departments or schools; these are sometimes surprisingly difficult. If key individuals, leaders, take on
other responsibilities, projects go 'off the boil'.

● 'Clarification about objectives and the identification of concrete outcomes for joint work.' A project associated with
the development of a jointly validated qualifying curriculum for community nurses and social workers seems to have
moved far by concentrating on that concrete outcome, while
the vaguer aim of developing a practice learning centre has
not kept pace. The tightly defined development, although
more ambitious, has been achieved more quickly and completely.

Weinstein's study parallels Brown's observations by recommending
market research to determine the specifications required to meet
needs and to ensure that the purchasers of training are committed to
and willing to pay for joint programmes. The joint practice teaching
initiative revealed the problem created by trying to combine two or
more existing courses:

'A useful analogy would be to imagine two companies trying to collaborate to produce a new product by using their existing plant and
machinery. The emphasis is on the product, ensuring that it still retains
the hallmarks of the two companies. Sufficient thought is not given
as to whether anyone will want or be able to afford the new product.'

Like Brown, she points to the essential role of enthusiastic project
leaders — 'the champions of change'; but growing pressures on such
individuals and the costing of their time by managers indicate that,
unless joint training becomes a mainstream activity, joint training
projects are unlikely to survive their champions or their available
money: 'While there is considerable government encouragement for
such initiatives, there is no framework for incorporating them into
mainstream professional education . . .'.

Learning together in daily practice

The few large educational initiatives described in this section stand
out from the mass of smaller ones analysed in the 1988 national
survey. But that survey only analysed organized courses. What
have not been mentioned in this chapter are the ongoing activities
in continuing education which take place, for example, in some
primary care teams attached to group practices or working in
health centres. By no means all are associated with the work of
the Health Education Authority already described. An exceptional,

long established example is described by Marsh and Kaim Kaudle (1976), but in general the extent and nature of this activity is undocumented.

Its gradual development in an inner-city practice was experienced by the author. Attachment of district nurses, health visitors, a midwife and a social worker required an extension of the practice premises. Communication between professionals can take place without shared premises, but it is far easier within them. People can meet to talk in corridors or over coffee. Other professionals are no longer 'them', but individuals familiar by face, name and ways of working. Case notes can be shared. But this much scarcely amounts to interprofessional education. What really counted was the discussion of shared 'cases' — especially cases which were puzzling, worrying or defeating. Regular attendance at twice-weekly case discussions over lunch, always in the same group, provided a time and a place in which the most reticent could say: 'I don't know the answer' or 'I have made a mistake'. It takes time and familiarity before people can risk their opinions, forget their dignity, reveal their anxieties or their failures. It also requires the sort of facilitation which draws people out and avoids all criticism.

Here is an ongoing educational activity, indistinguishable from the development of practice and service. Its strength is in its immediate relevance and its concentration on the shared problems which people find most difficult to deal with. Paradoxically, such discussions can be particularly helpful when problems seem or prove insoluble.

International developments

The European Network for Development of Multiprofessional Education in Health Sciences was formed in 1987. Its primary goal is to assist educational institutions, organizations and persons to focus upon multiprofessional education and research in health care. It has held annual conferences since then, in Finland, France, Poland, Portugal, Sweden and the United Kingdom.

At the annual conference in Kraków, Poland, in September 1993, the Swedish president, Professor Nils-Holger Areskog, made a confidential report on the Council of Europe's recent working group which he chaired. This has surveyed the present state of interprofessional education in European countries. Its report has recently been approved by the Council's Committee of Ministers. It is very much in line with the ideas of those who seek to promote interprofessional education in the UK (Council of Europe, 1993).

The aim is to improve collaboration by increasing awareness of other professions, respect for them and mutual understanding; by preventing tribalism, by proposing common objectives and shared values; by providing a common framework of knowledge, the breadth of which will bring new ways of solving patients' and clients' problems. To achieve these aims, interprofessional education needs to be introduced early in basic curricula and to continue thereafter. The experience of learning must reflect the way in which different professionals should later work together. For this, group work and shared projects are essential; simultaneous attendance at the same lecture is not enough.

The report makes clear that the UK has considerably more activity than other European countries in multiprofessional education after qualification. The Scandinavian countries have achieved more at the basic stage of education.

The notable example at that stage is at Linköping University's Faculty of Health Sciences where all students, whatever their future career, start their education with the same course, entitled 'Man and Society'. Under this title there are three themes: Man in Development, Lifestyle, Handicap. The aim is to contribute to understanding of the different factors which interfere with the health of man — especially the interplay between health and environment. This introduction lasts for ten weeks. The learning is almost entirely problem-based. At the end of this period the paths of students start to diverge, but they are brought together again at various stages of their courses (Areskog and Erikkson, 1991; Chapter 9 this volume).

The University of Tromso in Norway is now adopting a similar approach with a common introductory course of six weeks under the title 'The Tasks and Challenges of the Health Care System'. Later in their training students will return from time to time to multiprofessional group learning.

These Scandinavian initiatives were preceded by a pioneer experiment at the University of Paris-Nord (Bobigny). The first multiprofessional course (1977) was mainly lecture-based and theoretical. This was developed in 1984 into a 2-year course for orientation towards various health professions, in which an increased proportion of practical work, small group interaction and projects strengthened a claim to be the first *inter*professional course in Europe at the undergraduate level.

In this respect one might regret the consistent use of the term 'multiprofessional' in the Council of Europe report. It does not so clearly imply, either by derivation or by usage in the United Kingdom, the essential interaction in both learning and practice as does the term 'interprofessional'.

What is needed to advance interprofessional education and training?

What follows is a personal and tentative view, but one which takes into account the responses of 80 members of the National Centre for the Advancement of Interprofessional Education to an enquiry; these were received at the end of 1992. They were ably collated by Professor Hugh Barr.

The evidence reported above about the recent increase in the number of Masters courses suggests that a new national survey will show a general increase in educational initiatives in the last few years. If so, they will have been based on two beliefs: first, that collaboration between professions benefits patients and clients, while failures in collaboration can cause harm; and second, that collaboration is increased if members of different professions learn together as well as separately. The first belief is supported by a volume of day-to-day experience that harm arises from failure to inform, failure to explain, contradictory advice given to a patient by different people, gaps in responsibility and from the 'collusion of anonymity' (Balint, 1954). Waste arises through reduplication of effort. Failures in communication and collaboration account for a significant percentage of successful service cases against doctors (Neale, 1993). For all these reasons, formal experimental proof of effectiveness seems unnecessary (although it is available — e.g. Knaus et al. (1986) — about teamwork in relation to mortality in intensive care units). But this may not be true for the second belief.

A literature search does reveal objective evidence that shared learning or learning about the work of other professions can effect change in knowledge, attitudes or behaviour. This is additional to much more copious subjective evidence of satisfaction from students at the end of a learning experience.

As an example at the basic pre-qualification level, the study by Mazur et al. (1979), involving students from six professions, included objective tests before and after an 8-week period of shared learning. There was a control group. Measured positive changes were shown in behaviour conducive to teamwork and in the images which each discipline held of colleagues in other disciplines. Ninety-three per cent of the students stated after the experience that they now wanted to work in a team. The course, repeated over three years, demonstrated that learning is indeed needed if people are either to function well as team members or to teach others to do so. This training must be task-oriented.

As a second example, Beloff et al. (1970) were able to show relevant attitude changes in third- and fourth-year medical students in a controlled experiment. The changes were greater if reinforced a year later.

An example at the post-qualification level has recently been provided by Shaw (1994), studying three joint training courses about people with learning difficulties. Assessment before and after the courses showed that 75% of the participants had increased their awareness of organizations other than their own. Forty per cent attached increased value to the work of another profession. They also showed changes in their perception of the role of other professions.

Despite these and other examples, the volume of objective evidence is small. So too is the degree of positive change achieved. It is not achieved easily. There are examples of failure (e.g. Lewis and Resnick, 1966). Negative attitudes to other professions occasionally increase (McMichael and Irvine, 1984).

Further rigorous studies are unquestionably needed in this difficult but fundamental area, particularly studies which last long enough to see whether positive changes are sustained. They are needed because any large expansion in shared learning will incur costs in money, time and effort when there is stern competition for all these resources. (The support provided hitherto by departments of government and charitable trusts has been on a scale appropriate only to an experimental stage, except in the area of child abuse.)

The existing evidence does go some way towards answering the need for advice about the causes of success and failure in interprofessional education. This need was expressed by respondents to the CAIPE members' enquiry, mentioned above. Two principles are repeatedly mentioned:

- The best way to learn about working together is by doing it. Didactic teaching has a very limited place. Most emphasis should be on group discussion of cases or situations and on group involvement in a shared project with a shared purpose related to patient care.
- Teachers themselves need interdisciplinary training so that they can act as role models. But they, too, need the understanding and support of administrators and managers so that they can devote the necessary time and get funding.

Belief in the value of interprofessional education has led in the UK to the many initiatives in post-qualification and continuing education described earlier in this chapter. But much of the effort has to be directed to breaking down barriers already formed. Some of these have been created by the uniprofessional education and training which are traditional before qualification.

A measure of shared learning from the start, as at Linköping (Areskog and Eriksson, 1991), might be expected to prevent narrow vision, defensiveness and the tendency to stereotype other groups in ways which diminish them. But there is a dilemma. Experience has shown that students need to have acquired the basic skills of their own discipline before they can contribute usefully and feel secure enough to engage in interdisciplinary discussion (Mazur et al., 1979). Further experiments need to be evaluated.

Initiatives in pre-qualification shared learning, especially those involving medical students, are few and small. They are not easy to organize. More experimental models are needed.

Initiatives after qualification, although relatively frequent in this country, are subject to the difficulties which afflict the continuing education of all professional groups, except doctors. Nurses, social workers and members of professions allied to medicine all report that they usually have to pay themselves for any course organized away from their place of work and that it is difficult to secure release from service duties for this purpose. The situation varies from district to district and even between smaller units, but the general impression of difficulty is now inescapable. The minimum need is that those who allocate funds and manage service programmes should recognize the urgent educational need of professional workers merely to understand the changes which they are experiencing in such profusion and depth.

The last five years have brought exceptional turbulence and insecurity to all engaged in health and social services, including the managers. Turbulence and insecurity inhibit collaboration (Woodhouse and Pengelly, 1991; Horder, 1992a,b). Competition — the inevitable enemy of collaboration — is being promoted. The pressures of rapid change, combined with the effects of economic recession, have compelled that priority be given to the urgencies of the service. That education and training have not always been neglected is a credit to those who have realized its importance. But in this respect the national picture will prove to be one of great variation.

Who then is responsible?

It is clear from the 1988 national survey that many far-sighted individuals have assumed responsibility for local experiments all over the United Kingdom, even if in many cases their duration is measured in hours rather than days or weeks. They have achieved much, against difficulties which have been increasing.

But the initiatives of enthusiasts cannot be maintained for long or become generalized without support from policy-makers and without essential funding.

A succession of government documents and Acts of Parliament have advocated or assumed collaboration between professions. Some of the documents have advocated interprofessional training. The Centre for the Advancement of Interprofessional Education has received financial support from governmental sources among others (as have other organizations in the same field). But present government policy devolves responsibility, including responsibility for funding education. For example, Working Paper 10, the supplement to *Working for Patients* (Department of Health, 1989), particularly concerned with education and training, devolves responsibility to Regional Health Authorities. But there is now no encouragement to regions to ensure a consistent educational policy in their districts nor to reserve money for education; on the contrary, both have been further devolved. Moreover, Regional Health Authorities are now to be reorganized and to become outposts of the National Health Service Management Executive. Where will educational policy now be determined? Will funding be protected in future?

Responsibility for policy and funding for education and training after qualification seems at present to lie with purchasers, i.e. District or Family Health Service Authorities (now to be amalgamated) and fund-holding practices. For social work, a similar responsibility lies with local authorities. But it is the 'providers' (e.g. Trusts in the health service) which must compete for contracts to provide education as well as services — if *they choose* to do so. Do those who manage Trusts all understand why education and training matter? Will they express their understanding in their allocation of resources?

Acknowledgements

I am grateful to Professor Hugh Barr and Mrs Jenny Weinstein for helpful advice; and to Dr Ian Shaw for permission to quote from his PhD thesis.

References

Areskog N-H, Eriksson B (1991) *How to Educate Health Professionals for the Future.* Linköping, Sweden: Faculty of Health Sciences (workshop report).

Balint M (1954) *The Doctor, His Patient and the Illness.* London: Pitman.

Beloff J, Korper M, Weinerman E (1970) Medical student response to a programme for teaching comprehensive care. *Journal of Medical Education*; **45**: 1047–1059.

Brown S (1993) *Practice Makes Perfect: A Review of Issues and Lessons from the Joint Practice Teaching Initiative.* London: Central Council for the Education and Training of Social Workers.

Carpenter J, Onyett S, Smith H, Williams J, Peck E, Jones N, Crosbie

D (1991) *Caring for People Joint Training Project*. Bristol: NHS Training Directorate.

Council of Europe (1993) *Multiprofessional Education for Health Personnel*. Strasbourg: European Health Committee.

Department of Health (1989) *Education and Training: Working for Patients*. Working Paper 10. London: HMSO.

Department of Health and Social Security (1989) *Caring for People*. London: HMSO.

England H (Ed.) (1980) Education for cooperation in health and social work (occasional paper 14). London: Royal College of General Practitioners.

Hannay D, Usherwood T, Platts M (1992) Workload of general practitioners before and after the new contract. *British Medical Journal*; **304**: 615–618.

Hevey D (1992) The potential of national vocational qualifications to make multidisciplinary training a reality. *Journal of Interprofessional Care*; **6**: 215–221.

Horder JP (1992a) A national survey that needs to be repeated. *Journal of Interprofessional Care*; **6**: 65–71.

Horder JP (1992b) Interprofessional education. *Medical Education*; **26**: 427–428.

Knaus WA, Draper EA, Wagner DP, Zimmerman JE (1986) An evaluation of outcome from intensive care in major medical centers. *Annals of Internal Medicine*; **104**: 410–418.

Lambert D (1993) *Multidisciplinary Workshops for Primary Health Care Teams* (in press).

Lewis C, Resnick B (1966) Relative orientations of students of medicine and nursing to ambulatory care. *Journal of Medical Education*; **41**: 162–166.

Marsh G, Kaim Kaudle P (1976) *Team Care in Medical Practice*. London: Croom Helm.

Mazur H, Beeston JJ, Yerxa EJ (1979) Clinical Interdisciplinary Health Team Care; An Educational Experiment. *Journal of Medical Education*; **54**: 703–713.

McMichael P, Irvine R (Eds) (1984) *Finding a Way: A Course in Interprofessional Relationships*. Edinburgh: Moray House.

Myerson S (1993) The effects of policy change on family doctors. *Management in Medicine*; **7**:(2), 7–26.

Neale G (1993) Clinical analysis of 100 medico-legal cases. *British Medical Journal*; **307**: 1483–1487.

Shakespeare H, Tucker W, Northover J (1989) *Report of a National Survey of Interprofessional Education in Primary Health Care*. London: NHS Executive Personnel Development Division.

Shaw I (1994) *Evaluating Interprofessional Training*. Aldershot: Avebury.

Spratley J (1989) *Disease Prevention and Health Promotion in*

Primary Care. (*Team workshops organized by the Health Education Authority*) — *Evaluation Report*. London: Health Education Authority.

Spratley J (1990) *Joint Planning for the Development and Management of Disease Prevention and Health Promotion Strategies in Primary Health Care (Health Education Authority workshop programme for the development of local organising teams) – Evaluation report.* London: Health Education Authority.

Storrie J (1992) Mastering interprofessionalism: an enquiry into the development of Masters programmes with an interprofessional focus. *Journal of Interprofessional Care*; **6**: 253–259.

Sutherland VJ, Cooper CL (1992) Job stress, satisfaction and mental health among GPs, before and after introduction of the new contract. *British Medical Journal*; **304**: 1545–1548.

Thwaites M (1993) Interprofessional education and training: a brief history. *CAIPE Bulletin 6*: 2–3.

Weinstein J (1993) *Barriers to Implementing Successful Interprofessional Training Programmes, in the Context of the Mixed Economy of Welfare and the Changing Roles in Relationships of the Caring Professions: An Action Research Study*. MSc dissertation, University of the South Bank.

Woodhouse D, Pengelly P (1991) *Anxiety and the Dynamics of Collaboration*. Aberdeen: Aberdeen University Press.

11 Exploring the value of interprofessional shared learning

Peter Funnell

Introduction

From the mid-1970s there has been a surge of interest in, and critical study of, interprofessional shared learning in health care and related areas of social welfare. In this context, shared learning is identified as a means of promoting effective learning outcomes and securing value-added from structured learning interactions:

'A shared learning interaction brings together learners who would not otherwise meet in a structured learning context, and does so with the intention of enhancing learning outcomes. Usually such interactions are designed in recognition, or as a consequence, of contemporary occupational and employment behaviours which promote a holistic and non-fragmented quality response to market or service demands rather than one based on individual or occupational group specialization.' (Funnell, 1990, p. 151)

The current development of interest in interprofessional shared learning may be tracked to the 1974 enquiry into the tragic death of Maria Colwell, and to the painful recognition that insufficient attention had been given to interprofessional cooperation or the embedding of such cooperation into the pre- and post-qualificatory training of health and social welfare professionals. Subsequent enquiries in the field of child protection reinforce this view. Thus the Kimberley Carlile report recommended:

'. . . that employing Authorities take on board the need to ensure staff have adequate knowledge of the subject and of the importance of interagency cooperation possibly by shared learning.' (London Borough of Greenwich, 1987)

Similar views were also expressed in the report of the enquiry into child abuse in Cleveland (DHSS, 1988a) and the DHSS document

Working Together (DHSS, 1988b). Analysing the training implications of these findings, the Training Advisory Group on the Sexual Abuse of Children (TAGSAC) argued that there was a need for interagency cooperation:

> 'This has long been understood yet professionals and agencies continue to function in isolation or even at war with each other. The training implications of this failure . . . demand special recognition and a greater emphasis upon multidisciplinary interagency training. No single profession or group should be selected out as having the priority in training needs. This is one area in which all professions must work and train together.' (TAGSAC, 1988, p. 4)

The perceived significance of 'learning together' to facilitate 'working together' has been recognized and promulgated across a wide range of primary, secondary and community care provision (e.g. Royal College of General Practitioners, 1979; Council for the Education and Training of Health Visitors, 1983; Stevenson, 1985). Reviews of education and training practice in this area have revealed a significant number of essentially localized and uncoordinated examples of interprofessional shared learning (United Kingdom National Standing Conference of Health Visitor Training Centres, 1987; Shakespeare et al., 1989). In addition, representative and collective bodies have formed, most prominently perhaps the Centre for the Advancement of Interprofessional Education, a UK-wide centre now located at the London School of Economics, and INTERACT operating specifically in Scotland.

In all cases the development of teaching and learning strategies to facilitate interprofessional shared learning, and the creation of national networks to promote and encourage it, have been based upon a set of assumptions about its value. However, evidence suggests that such assumptions may themselves be problematic. Indeed, underpinning such assumptions of value is often a failure, or unwillingness, to acknowledge that at the heart of discussion about shared learning lies a contradiction between professionalism, and professional autonomy in particular, and the pluralism which forms the ideological bedrock of shared learning. This tension begs a number of critical questions. If professionalism implies a unique body of knowledge (with barriers to access to that knowledge and its application through formal training), can it fully embrace the openness associated with shared learning? If professionalism predicates status and hierarchy, can an approach to teaching and learning which requires participants of perceived equal status engaging in a process of sharing with mutual respect actually succeed? Ultimately can shared learning make any sufficient contribution to service provision or should its value be judged more accurately by other indices, whether educational (at the level of the individual) or political (at the more global levels of policy and organizational behaviour). Put simply, can interprofessional shared learning have value in a context where policy and organizational boundaries can act as constraints on 'working together', and where professionalism is dominant?

Responses to these questions need to go beyond concerns about teaching and learning strategies to confront and question the new market-orientated social reformist ideology of UK health and social welfare in the 1990s, and the place interprofessional shared learning has taken in representing that ideology. Not surprisingly, such reflection rarely appears in governmental or other official discussions of interprofessional shared learning. Indeed, it is occasionally presented as a universal panacea to a wide range of social problems and organizational and professional failures. As such it offers a low-cost but highly visible solution which directs attention away from the structure and purpose of health and social welfare by implicitly 'blaming the providers', whether they be the professional workers themselves or their teachers. Yet by directing attention towards the need for an educational solution to greater service coordination, it also diverts discussion from the appropriateness or not of existing professional and organizational boundaries, the relative powerlessness of the consumers of health and social welfare services, as well as from critical review of the adequacy of total resourcing and the prioritization of such resources across service areas.

Within this context this chapter suggests that interprofessional shared learning may well provide a valuable means of enhancing learning for individuals. However, such value is not axiomatic, nor is it a panacea for the perceived structural problems facing health and social welfare (e.g. Loney et al., 1985; Wicks, 1987). Indeed, in an educational context its use can be counterproductive. Given this, it becomes critical to establish the learning contexts which are best served by interprofessional shared learning, and the teaching and learning strategies which best exploit its potential.

The value of interprofessional shared learning

There is a common-sense attractiveness to the view that enhanced service delivery will result if those who must work together learn together. Despite this there is still little empirical evidence to support this view or to demonstrate that anything other than short-term benefit will accrue from shared learning interactions. A review of the literature suggests four major, often unstated, expected outcomes associated with shared learning.

The first identifies shared learning as a means of enhancing understanding of the roles and perceptions of other professionals, irrespective of the subject matter being considered. However, in practice the degree of success in terms of learners' enhanced understanding of the role and perception of others will depend on the willingness of such others to share. An individual's willingness publicly to disclose his or her role to other professionals will be influenced both by personal motivation and belief system, and by feelings of role security. Clearly the more secure an individual feels in a particular role the more likely is that individual to share with others without fear or threat. Conversely, an individual experiencing role insecurity, whether through role confusion or lack of a clear professional identity, may find the sharing of this problematic. Equally, the examination of the professional role of others, with their attendant conflicts and ambiguities, may do no more than reinforce such insecurity. Further, the sharing by other professionals of stereotypical role postures underpinned by negative attitudes may be counterproductive and reinforce both historical role conflicts and individual insecurity.

Given the human and political sensitivity of work in health and social welfare, an initial reticence to seek out and share perspectives which fall outside relatively safe organizational boundaries or uniprofessional theory and practice is understandable. That such organizational and professional barriers, acquired through previous professional socialization and operational experience, exist in other occupational arenas demonstrates the necessity of carefully assessing the means by which any form of shared learning is delivered.

The second expected outcome is the promotion of future teamwork and cooperation between professional groups. In practice this is difficult to demonstrate. Given that professional practice is determined by a constellation of factors, it is difficult to isolate one factor from others as generating a drive towards a particular form of behaviour. There is evidence to suggest that those who have completed a period of shared learning are enthusiastic about changing their professional practice, although follow-up research shows that such enthusiasm diminishes over time (David and Smith, 1987). Whilst such evidence must be treated with caution, it does suggest the need for subsequent practical reinforcement in the workplace of the products of shared learning.

This does, however, re-emphasize the contradiction noted earlier between notions of teamwork and the uniqueness of insight and contribution expected of a professional. If an individual professional perceives teamwork as reducing the salience of his or her contribution, then such teamwork may be resisted. Shared learning may influence behaviour, but fuller research is required before we can be precise about the extent to which it does and the duration of that change without reinforcement. Barriers to reinforcement may occur through legal, professional or organizational constraints. Interestingly the existence of such constraints begs important questions about the lack of coherence in the policy and practice of health and social welfare, and certainly challenges any notion of interprofessional shared learning as a panacea.

The third expected outcome identifies shared learning as contributing to the development of the learner's knowledge of agreed subject areas. The assumption that the learner's knowledge-base is enhanced through structured interaction with other professionals masks the methodological problem of teasing out one factor influencing learning from others. Learners are likely to learn more effectively when offered a range of learning methods, when they have some control over the style and content of the subject matter, and when they perceive purpose to that learning. Whether shared learning, over and beyond these, is itself capable of facilitating increased knowledge has not been substantiated. Put simply, it should not be assumed that knowing about others requires shared learning. Nor should it be assumed that shared listening, say to a didactic presentation, has any particular value. Even where the taught subject matter concerns interactional processes, it should not be assumed that a shared learning forum is required or necessarily desirable. Indeed, if incorrectly managed a shared learning experience of other professionals' attitudes and values may in practice constrain attempts to create 'professional relativism' or a recognition that all views of social reality are partial.

The fourth expected outcome identifies shared learning as enhancing the acquisition and development of practical skills. As contemporary vocational education and training focuses increasingly on competency and skills acquisition, shared learning may well be seen as a useful and relatively cost-effective means of delivering these. Again, however, the picture is complex as many factors influence the process of skills acquisition and development. For example, old and new skills may be in conflict or interfere one with another both in operational practice and in the formal learning context. New skills may be debased if they are perceived to be in the domain of occupational groups with lesser status. Success in a shared learning context is likely to depend on the teaching methods employed and the management of the learning experience.

Questioning the value of shared learning does not imply that it has no value. Rather it seeks to caution that judgements about value follow careful assessment. As with other forms of group learning, there is no reason to assume that the value associated with shared learning is discreet to any particular area of occupational activity (Jacques, 1992). Indeed, shared learning may have a degree of universal value in contexts where an understanding of the role and purpose of others is relevant to subsequent successful task completion. However, the means by which it is delivered must take cognizance of the particular needs and expectations of learners and the context within which learning is undertaken. Curriculum planners using shared learning need rather to structure interactions and content in such a way that they offer relevant and stimulating learning opportunities. Equally, the products of shared learning and the enthusiasm it generates amongst learners need to be acknowledged and supported after the interaction if such learning is to be transferred into practical action. This requires a set of organizational, managerial and professional commitments to shared learning which acknowledge its democratizing potential and possible impact on established work practices. This in turn requires the explicit and visible commitment of service and professional leaders at all levels recognizing that, whilst it is through the empowering of individuals that organizations change, it is through the leadership qualities of individuals that the culture for change is created.

Exploiting the value of interprofessional shared learning

It is through effective curriculum design and focused teaching, learning and assessment strategies that the value of interprofessional shared learning can be exploited. Recognizing the contribution of Kolb (1984), Boyd (1988) and Schon (1988), and the emerging specific literature associated with interprofessional shared learning, it is possible to distinguish five broad approaches designed to take advantage of the value of interprofessional shared learning.

The first recognizes that shared learning is more likely to generate value where learners are united by a common, and commonly perceived, task with clear end-products. Curriculum designers will need to produce contexts in which learners perceive the content and mode of learning as relevant. Such an approach delivered by interprofessional shared learning may have the effect of reducing professional isolation and problems of role ambiguity and insecurity, whilst offering opportunities for enhanced teamwork. It will also contribute to the extension of learning from the more conventional 'learning about' to a deeper form of 'learning to be' (Jacques, 1992).

The second acknowledges that effective interprofessional shared learning is most likely to occur where learners perceive themselves as equals. Damaging perceptions of self-worth, overt sexism or racism, or negative perceptions of occupational and group standing may all work against feelings of equality. This suggests that shared learning requires careful initial planning and the provision of group and individual support from those managing the interaction. An important aspect of this initial planning may be the creation of learning groups of individuals who perceive themselves as equal irrespective of their particular position in their own organization. Such an arrangement has the potential for facilitating peer bonding and encouraging sharing. Clearly any group can isolate an individual, whilst some individuals are skilled at using groups as tools by which to dilute or avoid responsibility. Clearly this is not the intention of shared learning, and the construction of feedback targets for learners, and rotation of leadership and reporting roles are possible solutions should this occur. However, such methods may impose a degree of control which contradicts learner self-determination. In practice solutions to such issues are likely to be specific to particular learning contexts, and the preferred learning styles of participants.

The third approach recognizes that shared learning demands the use of experiential teaching methods. Such methods, with their emphasis on learner experience, independence and openness, may be new and potentially intimidating to learners, particularly those whose educational experience has been in a traditional didactic mode. A rationale for shared learning needs to be made clear to learners, together with opportunities for them to evaluate, critically comment upon, and ultimately change, the mode of learning.

In terms of the fourth approach, Loxley (1980) offers four factors to promote effective outcomes from shared learning interactions: attraction (to include the status or prestige of deliverers, the learner's rationale for attending the shared learning interaction, and its content); support (to include the level of physical and emotional comfort available to the learner); breaking barriers (in particular to include techniques which de-role learners and promote interaction); and the creation of working groups which are task-centred and facilitated through shared exercises and common concerns. A similar checklist has been identified by Funnell et al. (1992) who identify the importance of balanced group membership; the professional status of participants; clarification of previous experience; the significance of representation from lead agencies; clarification of expected outcomes; and the importance of pre-event information and teaching styles. Together, these and similar approaches available in the literature offer a useful initial basis for consideration by curriculum designers. However, again in practice the means by which the curriculum is ultimately designed and delivered will be unique to each learning interaction.

The fifth approach acknowledges that the deliverers of shared learning should themselves have experience of learning, and preferably working, in this way. At a minimum this is likely to promote enhanced empathy with learners and sensitivity to potential professional and other pressures associated with sharing.

Conclusion

Interprofessional shared learning is a dynamic teaching and learning method which confronts the traditional fragmentation of knowledge into academic, vocational or professional specialisms. It encourages sharing based on mutual respect and a recognition of the contribution a number of professionals are likely to play in any example of service provision. As such it challenges the uniqueness of the professional role and can act to blur organizational boundaries. It is, therefore, not surprising that it has developed most strongly in the more generic areas of primary health care, child protection and community care. The message of the recent report of the Department of Health and Social Services Inspectorate is clear:

> '. . . the focus of services needs to shift from being agency (supply) driven to one which is user and carer centred. Agencies will therefore need to integrate their approach and shared training is a vehicle for this.' (DoH/SSI, 1991, S1.12)

However, despite these attractions shared learning is no panacea, nor the sole resolution to the structural 'fault lines' which might be identified in current UK systems of health and social welfare. There is sufficient evidence, including that presented elsewhere in this volume, to suggest that interprofessional shared learning has value. What educationalists and professional practitioners must ensure, however, is that it does not become a sacred cow slaughtered at the altar of political expediency during the next moral panic created by service inadequacies whose origins lie elsewhere.

References

Boyd D (1988) *Developing Student Autonomy in Learning*. London: Kogan Page.

Council for the Education and Training of Health Visitors et al. (1983) *Statement on the Development of Interprofessional Education and Training for Members of the Primary Health Care Teams*. London: CETHV.

David R, Smith B (1987) Preparing for collaborative working. *British Journal of Special Education*; **14**: 19–23.

Department of Health and Social Security (1988a) *Report of the Inquiry into Child Abuse in Cleveland 1987*. London: HMSO.

Department of Health and Social Security (1988b) *Working Together: A Guide to Arrangements for Interagency Cooperation for the Protection of Children from Abuse*. London: HMSO.

Department of Health and Social Services Inspectorate (1991) *Training for Community Care: A Joint Approach*. London: HMSO.

Funnell P (1990) Maximising the value of shared learning interactions. In: Farmer B, et al. (Eds), *Making Learning Systems Work* (Aspects of Educational and Training Technology XXIII). London: Kogan Page.

Funnell P, Gill J, Ling J (1992) Competence through interprofessional shared learning. In: Saunders D, Race P (Eds), *Developing and Measuring Competence* (Aspects of Education and Training Technology XXV). London: Kogan Page.

Jacques D (1992) *Learning in Groups*. London: Kogan Page.

Kolb DA (1984) *Experiential Learning — Experience as the Source of Learning and Development*. New Jersey: Prentice Hall.

London Borough of Greenwich (1987) *A Child in Mind: Protection of Children in a Responsible Society*. (Report of the Commission of Inquiry into the circumstances of the death of Kimberley Carlile). London Borough of Greenwich.

Loney M, Boswell D, Clarke J (1985) *Social Policy and Social Welfare*. Milton Keynes: Open University Press.

Loxley A (1980) A study of multidisciplinary in-service training in the interests of health care. *Social Work Service*; 24 Sept. 1980.

Royal College of General Practitioners (1979) *Education for Cooperation in Health and Social Work* (Occasional Paper 14). London: RCGP.

Schon D (1988) *Educating the Reflective Practitioner: Towards a New Design for Teaching and Learning in the Professions*. London: Jossey-Bass.

Shakespeare H, et al. (1989) *Report of a National Survey on Interprofessional Education in Primary Health Care*. London: Institute of Health Studies for CAIPE.

Stevenson O (1985) Education for community care. *British Medical Journal*; **290**: 1966–1968.

Training Advisory Group on the Sexual Abuse of Children (1988) *Post Cleveland: The Implications for Training*. London: National Childrens Bureau.

United Kingdom National Standing Conference of Health Visitor Training Centres (1987) *The Experience of Shared Learning Between Health Visitors and Other Students*. London: UKCC.

Wicks M (1987) *A Future for All*. Middlesex: Penguin.

12 Interprofessional shared learning: A curriculum for collaboration

Janet Gill and John Ling

Introduction

Interprofessional shared learning (IPSL) is a concept which is both widely promulgated and propagated but appears to carry a variety of meanings. The term appears in a range of situations and contexts but particularly those areas associated with health, social welfare and education. The precise meaning of the expression, or the expectations that accompany its use, are seldom made explicit. This unfortunately creates a communication problem since it is not always clear just what is or is not being described. This lack of precision, however, does not appear to daunt the large number of individuals and authorities who recommend its adoption. To the protagonist, interprofessional shared learning is seen as both desirable and beneficial; it sounds right and feels good.

Recourse to the literature reveals the extent to which interprofessional shared learning is being investigated and recommended as a highly desirable strategy for dealing with complex health and social issues. Recent guidelines (Department of Health and Social Security, 1988) on *Working Together* strongly advocate that different professional groups should introduce training programmes that involve IPSL activities. The Butler–Sloss report into the Cleveland Affair (Secretary of State for Social Services, 1988) strongly advised that there should be greater collaboration in the various health and welfare agencies involved in the delivery of care, and that IPSL be adopted as a means of achieving this. Likewise the English National Board for Nursing, Midwifery and Health Visiting has shown its support for such initiatives by validating post-registration courses involved in the training of community health workers (health visitors, occupational health and district nurses) whose course contains a substantial core element of shared learning. The implementation of 'community care' across health and social services has spawned a number of joint initiatives to promote effective joint working, most of which include recommendations for the joint training of health and social service personnel (Carpenter et al., 1991; Social Services Inspectorate, 1991).

In 1987 the Centre for Advancement of Inter-Professional Education in Primary Health and Community Care (CAIPE) was formed. Its aim is to 'create a national network which supports, stimulates and provides an exchange for ideas between many people who are offering educational initiatives jointly to more than one professional group engaged in the front line of primary health and community care'. A survey carried out by CAIPE in 1988 revealed that there were over 400 different places in the country involved in some kind of IPSL activity.

The interest being shown in IPSL has taken on an international dimension with the formation of the European Network for Development of Multi-Professional Education in Health Services (EMPE). At their 1992 annual conference in Tampere, Finland, distinguished academic speakers presented a variety of papers on the challenges of multiprofessional training for management and education in health care.

In other instances the development of IPSL has taken on a more formal approach. For example, at the University of the South Bank a master of science award in interprofessional health and welfare studies is offered to people involved in the caring professions, be they in public, voluntary or private sectors.

The semantic debate

Clearly there appears to be considerable evidence for arguing that IPSL is rapidly being adopted as a valued and worthwhile activity for promoting greater cooperation across professional boundaries. But as stated earlier, at the very heart of the issue there exists a semantic debate. What exactly do individuals mean when they advocate IPSL? It appears that some authors use several different words on a synonymous or interchangeable basis while others use very specific terms that apply only to precise situations. Consequently it becomes imperative to explore the meanings of the terms used before being able to examine the issues that underpin IPSL. Terms encountered include:

- *Interdisciplinary* — A situation where members of different professional backgrounds meet to explore areas of common interest and misunderstandings (Lloyd et al., 1973). Alternatively it is perceived as 'first and foremost a scientific category related mainly to research, a group which can be further subdivided into cross disciplinary and structural disciplinary' (Kocklemans, 1979).

- *Multidisciplinary* — Activities which solve problems outside the scope of the traditional and established disciplines by decomposing them into subgroups, which are then solved by purely disciplinary solutions (Jurkovich, 1984).

- *Crossdisciplinary* — This is based on the belief that 'no single social discipline can claim validity for the formulations developed within its own traditional cross disciplinary exchange' (Kocklemans, 1979).

- *Transdisciplinary* — Scientific work done by a group of scientists each trained in one or more different disciplines with the intention of systematically pursuing the problem of how negative side-effects of specialization can be overcome so as to make education and research more socially relevant (Kocklemans, 1979).

- *Interprofessional* — This involves shared training which aims to help professionals to work together more effectively in the interests of their clients and patients by enhancing cooperation (Michaud, 1970).

- *Intraprofessional* — A term reserved for those situations in which a professional group is subdivided into smaller sections each with specific areas of specialism. The dynamics at work are similar to those seen in interprofessional activities with a notable difference that in intraprofessional shared learning there already exists a basic learned commonality of perspective.

Euphemistic terms

In addition to the foregoing terms which have definitions and particular meanings, many writers display a tendency to use more general educational terms in a euphemistic sense. Included in this category are words such as 'common core', 'team teaching' and 'block timetabling'. The inference to be drawn is that, whilst these terms clearly have their own specific meaning, each could in a different context imply sharing, collectiveness and commonality, all part of a vague concept associated in many people's minds with IPSL. Following an exploration of the literature with regard to the nomenclature and the various meanings, it becomes apparent that the terms used appear to be based on different understandings of the nature of knowledge. From this perspective the terms are of much more significance than the immediate semantics and provide a valuable insight into a whole arena of educational thought. In summary, it was possible to identify four distinct categories in which the aforementioned terms were used either individually or collectively in various combinations. These were as follows.

Positivistic reductionism

A number of authors argue a case in which they claim that the positivistic reductionist approach which has served admirably for centuries is now bankrupt. The fragmentation of knowledge is ultimately limiting, and the only way forward is to reverse the trend of reductionism, and replace it with a philosophy that emphasizes integration — a view eloquently advanced by Capra (1982).

Holistic approaches

This position is a logical extension from positivistic reductionism, but the thrust of the argument focuses not so much on reductionism as making a case for replacing it with wholes. The notion of holistic care currently permeates contemporary models of health care provision, viewing each person as an integrated whole requiring a range of interventions designed to meet all activities of daily living. The implications for educationalists with responsibilities for curriculum development in the field of health care provision would suggest that they concern themselves with issues of classification and framing — ideas dominant amongst educational sociologists in the mid-1970s (Bernstein, 1971).

Common body of knowledge

Despite the continuing growth of subject and discipline specialism there exists an almost paradoxical increase in the number of professions who share a considerable body of common knowledge. This is not only true for the physical and social sciences but especially so for those involved in health and social welfare provision. Many syllabi determined by the various professional and vocational validating bodies contain large elements of common core curricula; e.g. psychology, sociology, health education, research and social policy. It is therefore argued that a case exists for IPSL. One such initiative currently taking place is the integration of three previously discrete training programmes (i.e. Occupational Health Nursing, District Nursing and Health Visitor training) into one basic course consisting of a large common core curriculum topped up by individual professional studies.

Economic benefits

If ever there was any doubt, today little remains regarding the necessity for educational activities to be economically viable undertakings. Income generation, short course provision, cost-effective measures and high staff/student ratios are all examples of economic forces at work in much current further and higher education. Against this background IPSL can be seen as making a significant contribution especially with respect to economies of scale. Why, it is asked, should one lecturer teach 20 students for one hour followed by the same lecture to another group, followed by the same lecture to yet another group, when the one lecture can be given to 60 students at one sitting? Ignoring for a moment the educational desirability or otherwise, this strategy clearly has much to recommend it from an accountant's standpoint.

Does IPSL work?

Given the growth of interest in IPSL and the array of influential authorities who advocate its adoption, one could be forgiven for believing that it was a highly successful strategy. There is no denying that it has an immediate common sense utility value which, all things being equal, might contribute in part to the beliefs that people hold about its use and effectiveness.

Closer scrutiny, however, reveals IPSL to be a very complex activity, and as such it is highly unlikely to fulfil everybody's expectations. Such a claim is not intended to decry shared learning as an educational process, but rather to question what appear to be accepted and self-evident assumptions about its value. If shared learning does offer enhanced learning then it seems right and proper that we should explore and understand the way in which this happens.

As part of this process it was decided to take advantage of a new curriculum initiative taking place at Suffolk College involving IPSL, and to research students' perceptions concerning their experiences.

Aims of research

This chapter reports the findings of research undertaken during 1991–92 which aimed to investigate the phenomenon of interprofessional shared learning as it applied to students on the DipHE Professional Studies (Health Visiting, District Nursing and Occupational Health Nursing) at Suffolk College. The researchers' major reasons for interest in the ideas of this particular group of students were that they shared a common nursing background (which may or may not have implications for their commitment to IPSL) and that they were joining a new course which was predicated on IPSL both philosophically and structurally. In addition, a study of shared learning within a profession at a post-qualifying divergent stage could provide insights which would enable understanding of how shared learning operates to be refined and developed.

Objectives

This chapter focuses on the findings with respect to the following objectives:

- to discover students' perceptions about the idea (concept) of shared learning and its anticipated value and anticipated barriers;
- to identify events or processes during the programme that enhanced or detracted from the experience of IPSL;
- to identify productive and counterproductive strategies related to the whole programme.

Before detailing the research methods used we will provide some background information about the course the students were undertaking.

Background information about the course

Rationale

In 1991, staff at Suffolk College decided to develop a new programme of study which would unify previous courses for the training of health visitors, district nurses and occupational health nurses into a combined 'Diploma HE Professional Studies' whilst retaining the specialist learning required for separate UKCC professional qualifications. The impetus for this initiative came from four sources:

- *National recommendation* — The unification of existing nursing specialisms as recommended by a range of professional bodies and reports, including the Cumberlege Report (Cumberlege, 1986), was influential, as also was the need to upgrade all post-registration courses to DipHE or degree level.
- *Local need* — The current dynamic context of primary health care provision revealed the need for community practitioners who could meet the changing demands of consumers and the health service by being both specialist, and aware of their interdependent roles and futures. Reduction of sponsorship locally for district nurse and health visitor training meant that joint training was

essential to maintain viable numbers.
- *College strategy* — The college is in the process of modularizing its higher education provision, and the Diploma was planned to meet the college mission to offer increased access and variable pathways. In addition, the course enabled rationalization of resources.
- *Course team beliefs* — The course team beliefs included a commitment to primary health care provided by health professionals with a common basic understanding incorporating holistic views of client care, and who were able to think critically, to practise with skill, to evaluate their work and to recognize both the independence and interdependence of their roles. Training of such professionals requires both commonalities and specialisms in content, and by learning together skills can be shared, barriers can be broken down and a flexible team approach developed.

Structure

The curriculum was designed with four main contexts:

- Common foundation studies were for all students in mixed professional learning groups covering those areas of competence and comprehension which are shared equally by all.
- Professional specialisms separated the students into learning groups according to professional orientation.
- Placement learning experiences were also within the specialist professional choice.
- Integrating studies used joint working teams drawn from the three professional groups to present seminars on issues of mutual concern.

Research method

Throughout this chapter we have used the term 'interprofessional', whereas definitionally we believe it would be more accurate in this instance to have used the term 'intraprofessional' as the students came from a shared background (see foregoing definitions). However, we decided to use the term 'interprofessional' as one which would be more familiar to our respondents.

The research was conducted by a series of four different questionnaires inviting individual responses. The questionnaires were timed to be completed at appropriate points within the course. The first questionnaire was sent to students prior to their starting the course, with an explanatory letter inviting their cooperation. The second questionnaire was distributed and returned after the students had completed an induction period. The third questionnaire was timed to coincide with the end of the common foundation studies and after completion of the integrating studies, which was at the end of the second term. The final questionnaire was given on completion of the course. It was not possible to pilot these questionnaires on a student group of similar composition as this was the first intake of students to a course of this kind. However, questionnaires were piloted by health professionals, students and staff, to ascertain ambiguity in the framing of the questions, which could then be rectified. A research steering group was also helpful for guidance and critical appraisal. Each of the questionnaires was different although there were some questions which were asked on more than one occasion. Both closed and open questions were used, and although this study is primarily qualitative, use of the Likert scale was introduced in one question. In our reporting we have used quantitative data only in respect of the distribution of responses; the overall strategy remains based on students' subjective comments on their experiences.

It is not our purpose in this chapter to reflect on the research method, but it is important to note that there was a substantial drop in the number of students completing the questionnaires between the start and the end of the course (see Table 12.1). As far as we are aware, the dropout rate had nothing to do with the concept of the course; some students left the course as part of normal wastage, but some failed to return the available questionnaires — most notably amongst occupational health nurses whose course was structured to end differently from the other two specialisms.

Findings

Expectations

Prior to admission all the students except one were aware that the course they were joining was a Diploma in Professional Studies predicated upon shared learning across traditional professional boundaries.

Table 12.1 Student cohort

	District nurses	Health visitors	Occupational health nurses	Total
Before joining	15	23	23	61
Final paper	12	17	9	38

For 3% of the students this factor was influential in their decision to study at this college, but for 77% the shared learning was attractive but not critical in their decision. The remaining 20% felt that this was either a matter of no concern (10%), not relevant (8%) or expected to be a hindrance (2%) in their professional training.

The high proportion of applicants indicating that the shared learning component within the course was taken into account in their application could be interpreted as a commitment to IPSL.

Understanding of IPSL

On first arrival in college, students were invited to state what they understood by the term IPSL. The responses were grouped in seven categories. In total, 70 replies were received from 54 students who completed the questionnaire. Of the replies, 56% identified IPSL as 'learning the same knowledge alongside other professionals'; 24% of the replies identified it as 'learning interactively from other professionals'. The remaining five categories each attracted a very small number of responses. Students' perception that learning the same knowledge alongside other professionals was a defining characteristic of IPSL could be interpreted as a recognition of the economic benefits of shared learning, or alternatively that students already identified a shared knowledge-base between their specialisms. No-one noted that shared learning necessarily involves interaction with the possibility of a mutual development of knowledge. This perception offers a paradigm of continuing learning which could be transferred to the workplace to enhance their abilities to work together.

Value of IPSL

The theme of increased knowledge was also reflected in the students' perceptions regarding the value of interprofessional shared learning, since 31% of responses indicated that the value of shared learning would be increased stimulation and knowledge. Unfortunately it was not made clear how this increase in knowledge would be achieved. Other perceived benefits included improved working relationships (26%) and understanding others' roles (25%). These concepts, whilst laudable in their own right, represent a rather simplistic analysis of the many and varied dynamics at work. However, it is only fair to comment that these views were expressed during the first week of the course, and it would be surprising if a more sophisticated level of analysis were used.

It is interesting to note that at the end of the course students were again invited to suggest what they understood as the value of shared learning. A total of 54 responses were received, of which 48% suggested that the value of shared learning was in understanding others' roles; 19% of respondents thought it would improve working relationships; and 9% thought the value could increase stimulation and knowledge. Improved communications, understanding organizational structures and sharing of attitudes were the other three reasons stated. Seven per cent of the responses indicated that there had been no value in the shared learning within the programme. The changes from the original perceptions are marked, with more emphasis being placed on understanding each others' roles, and only a few referring to increased stimulation and knowledge. The comparison between the two sets of responses seems to indicate that what has developed between the beginning and the ending of the course is a greater sense of active learning. The fact that some responses at the end of the course indicated that there had been no value in shared learning needs analysis in respect of the concept, its implementation, and course management implications.

Barriers to shared learning

Students produced the same number of responses in respect of barriers to shared learning as they had in respect of the value of shared learning. The barriers were classified into five categories: the largest number of replies (34%) concerned the structure and management of the course, and 33% noted adversely the size of the group. Whilst the former could be specific to this particular course experience, it could be argued, in respect of size, that students have identified a key component of effective IPSL.

Previous work (Funnell et al., 1992) noted that IPSL was not just a case of students being located in a situation to learn together, but that attention needed to be given to planning and course management of interaction between students, with a focus that addressed the processes. The students' identification of the size of the group as problematic can also be seen as part of the management of learning. Even with only three professional groups represented, the class size of more than 60 students was clearly seen as unsatisfactory, without addressing the cross-professional boundaries. The size of the group may also have wider applicability in that the difficulties noted may challenge the economic rationale for IPSL. The other three categories which the students identified were insufficient shared knowledge or activities, a lack of personal contact, and not enough sharing of understanding about roles. These views are congruent with previously mentioned perceptions that size, focus and overall management are crucial in determining the effectiveness or not of IPSL. A lack of shared knowledge or activities (24% of replies) could be interpreted as further evidence for claiming that skilled and sensitive management is a fundamental prerequisite and that benefits do not automatically occur simply by bringing large numbers of different, professional groups together. Sharing in both a physical and a psychological sense must happen if improved communications and understanding of others' roles is to take place. The importance attached to personal contact is a feature of shared learning that was identified in previous research (Funnell et al., 1992).

Student perceptions at the end of the course reflected similar concerns to those at the beginning: these include size of group, management of the course, including the pivotal roles of the course tutors, and lack of personal contact. Notwithstanding the barriers identified, 85% of the respondents indicated a belief in a common purpose for the three professional specialities. Health promotion, interpersonal skills and communication were identified as areas of overlap. Sixty-six per cent of the respondents thought that learning together would help them to achieve their learning objectives. Four broad categories of explanations were offered: most popular was learning from others' experience; then understanding professional colleagues; gaining a broader perspective; and lastly, developing communication skills. However, 13% dissented from this viewpoint, indicating that they could not identify any areas of overlap in knowledge and skills. Reference to opinions expressed on the initial questionnaire shows that 80% thought that shared learning was important. However, by the end of the first week of the course, only 67% thought that there were advantages, while 33% could see no advantage at all. This could suggest that large numbers, together with initial difficulties in starting a new course, had caused doubts to appear.

Specific course modules

The mid-term opinion questionnaire was conducted at the end of the common foundation inputs and after integrating module work had been presented, some six months into the course. At this time students were asked about the shared learning that had been intrinsic to the common foundation programme. Seventy per cent of the respondents thought that sharing the common foundation modules with students from other professional groups had been beneficial, whereas 30% had not thought so. These percentages reflect those of the first week's students' responses in answer to a question about their perceived value of shared learning. This raises questions as to whether students were predisposed in attitudes towards shared learning, rather than actually experiencing any benefit. The principal reason given for the benefits of the common foundation programme was the gain in knowledge regarding the roles of other professionals. Those who failed to note benefit attributed this to group size being too large, and that there were alternative ways to learn about the roles of other professionals. A similar question about the integrating module reveals a different picture, with 96% of respondents believing that the process of sharing this module was beneficial because groups were smaller, there was increased communication and interaction and learning occurred about each other's roles and differing perspectives. This echoes previous work (Funnell et al., 1992) that identified interactive learning as being productive in gaining value from shared learning.

Preparation for working together

The end-of-course questionnaire asked if the shared learning experiences and opportunities had prepared students for working together. None of the students thought they had been prepared 'very well' and none thought 'not at all'. Sixty-six per cent thought they had been prepared 'a little' and 34% thought themselves to be adequately prepared. When questioned about where their learning experiences and opportunities occurred, 82% identified the college as the principal place of learning and only 7.5% thought the placement experience was paramount. Another 7.5% thought learning had been equal in both settings and 2.5% noted 'not in either'.

Responses to another question seeking to identify where particular features of working together had been learned are reproduced in full in Table 12.2. One of the surprising outcomes is that a third of the responses indicated that most aspects of working together were learned in the placement setting. This is at variance with student responses to a previous item on this final questionnaire in which they identified shared learning experiences as occurring predominantly in college. This discrepancy could be interpreted by a number of differing explanations; for instance, that the students shared a number of learning experiences in college which were not concerned with the particular aspects specified in the table. Alternatively, it could be postulated that shared learning was a formal teaching method within the college setting, whereas students in placement were not working with peers in a collaborative way, and therefore they interpreted shared learning experiences and opportunities as being predominantly college-based. The variables in Table 12.2 are concerned with collaborative working practices which may well have been 'caught' by placement experience, but which were not part of the taught college course. The questions asked in the table are about aspects of working together, which may have seemed more appropriately learned in placement. Yet again the relationship between shared learning and working together is both crucial and complex. Another interpretation could be that the aspects specified

Table 12.2 Learning to work together in various locations*

Which part of the programme especially helped you learn about:	Specialist module	Placement experience	Common foundation	Integrated module	None
(a) Aspects of cooperation and liaison with other professional groups	11	16	16	26	1
(b) The activities/tasks of other professionals	6	15	12	28	3
(c) Making contact with other professionals	12	27	7	13	4
(d) The roles of other professionals in the management of client care	10	19	9	22	3
(e) The roles of other professionals in joint planning of care	10	22	5	13	8
(f) The value of interprofessional cooperation	11	18	10	21	3
(g) Problems that might be encountered in interprofessional cooperation	14	21	8	15	7
(h) Strategies to avoid or reduce problems in interprofessional cooperation	14	16	6	10	11
(i) Cooperating with other professionals in the strategic planning of services	15	24	3	8	8
(j) How to access input from other professionals	15	24	2	6	8
TOTAL SCORES (616)	118	202	78	162	56
PERCENTAGE OF TOTAL SCORES (100%)	19%	33%	13%	26%	9%

*Students were invited to identify those areas of the programme where they had learnt about specific aspects of working together.

in the table are more detailed and acted as a prompt to inspect and reflect more fully on the shared learning process that had taken place. Nine per cent of the responses declare that neither experiences gained in placement nor in college contributed to students learning about working together. This must raise questions about the expectations of shared learning — a programme which was set up with a specific purpose to facilitate working together using a structure of shared learning to encourage this still leaves 9% responses showing that some students thought that some aspects of working together had not been addressed anywhere in the programme. It is also of interest that the common foundation programme only accounts for 13% of the responses on this table. Again, as the course was structured to focus much of the shared learning in this part of the programme (in fact, in terms of time, this was the largest component) more questions are raised both about the process and content of this element of the course. This needs to be compared with the 70% responses indicating that the common foundation programme had been beneficial. When students were invited to make additional comments, a total of 30 different responses were collected. Thirteen of these comments could be categorized as features of the course management.

Discussion

Curriculum management

The 'F' factor

Prior to commencement all students except one were aware that the course was multidisciplinary; whilst only a few stated that this was influential in their choosing to seek admission to the programme, a large majority declared that shared learning was an attractive factor. Using the modern idiom we have dubbed this the 'F' (fanciability) factor. As discussed earlier in this chapter, IPSL is seen by many as the most appropriate strategy to adopt in the management of many of today's complex health and social welfare issues, despite there being little awareness of precisely what constitutes IPSL. Therefore it could be argued that the findings support the generally held view that a course based on IPSL principles possesses more appeal than a con-ventional/non-IPSL programme.

The sustaining power of the F factor is, however, thrown into doubt by the disclosure that, at the end of the first week, only two-thirds thought there were advantages associated with IPSL and the rest could see no value whatsoever. The significance of the low value assigned to IPSL is exacerbated by the students' perceptions that shared learning was largely restricted to 'learning some knowledge alongside others'.

However, by the end of the course, when asked about the extent to which IPSL had prepared them for working together, 34% thought 'adequately' and 66% thought 'a little'. From this it would appear that IPSL does have an attraction which waxes and wanes over a given period of time. However, many programmes using an IPSL approach are run over a relatively short period (one, two or three days). It is difficult to extrapolate from the study the true impact that the F factor has on recruitment to these courses.

Previous work (Funnell et al., 1992) found that courses run with an IPSL strategy will usually attract a number of participants labelled 'content only members'. The term refers to those individuals who attend such courses but who have no interest in the process of IPSL, and are simply interested in the acquisition of knowledge on the given topic. No quantitative data have been obtained on this phenomenon, but organizers of educational programmes should recognize that not all participants are motivated by the F factor of IPSL.

Size of the group

Students, prior to joining the course, gave no evidence of thought about the size of the group. However, by the end of week one (and as a recurring theme in subsequent questionnaires) size was identified as being a substantial barrier to effective shared learning. The large numbers in the group appeared to preclude opportunities for personal contact and establishing the rapport required to explore each other's roles. Learning to work together needs to be based on an active understanding of what other people do in their work, and training events need to address this. Current educational pressures mean that ways of increasing the size of the learning group are often being sought but, if shared learning is to have an impact on working together, consideration needs to be given to the optimum size of the group. The evidence from this cohort of students is that the integrating module (size 8–10 students) was felt to be the appropriate size for shared learning from each other to take place, whereas other components of the course in larger groups were not.

Group membership

The authors anticipated that students' shared common professional identity at the point of entry to the course would assist the process of shared learning. Yet many barriers were identified, and at the end of the course 7% of responses indicated that there had been no value in shared learning, and 13% of respondents could not identify any areas of overlap in knowledge and skills. It is possible to speculate that students on a training course leading to a professional qualification are learning the roles of their intended profession, and moving away from the shared status of nursing with which they all started. The need to espouse the new role may well lead them to accentuate their differences both from what they were before, and from the others on different routes sharing the course. The course was designed with a focus on commonalities as well as different professional routes, but it seems that unless shared learning is seen as essential and integral to each professional qualification, shared learning may continue to be seen as problematic, marginalized or irrelevant by some. Working together competencies may need to be specified and assessment methods devised so that interprofessional working is seen as intrinsic to professionalism. Greater clarity about the contribution that shared learning could make would then be possible.

Interactive learning

Whilst most students identified IPSL as learning alongside others, another group perceived the interactive possibilities of IPSL in learning from other professionals. We think that shared learning has potential, when interactive, to develop knowledge across boundaries and to encourage students to become active participants in their own learning. Arguably this is an essential part of being professional workers responsible for their own continuing learning. What is not known is whether exposure in college to interactive shared learning as a process for developing knowledge is transferred to the workplace either during the course or subsequently. Interactive processes require that students are able to talk with each other without having to raise their voices, are able to establish eye contact, feel sufficiently confident both to express their opinions and to explore uncertainties in front of others from different professional backgrounds. These conditions, however, are seriously compromised by large groups which preclude such intimacies.

Placement experience

A basic belief embodied in IPSL is that, through the process of sharing with others, there will not only be an increase in knowledge, but that this knowledge will facilitate and enable individuals to work effectively with individuals from other professions. A key component in this process is the contribution made by placing individuals in the actual work situation. Here the learner is exposed to powerful influential forces described in Bandura's work on social learning theory (Bandura, 1977). Role models provide the learner both consciously and unconsciously with a range of behaviours about the very nature of 'how it is'. Stripped of the theory and book knowledge learners are confronted with the challenges of working together with individuals from other professional groups, who may operate with strict demarcation practices. Work situations which contradict what is taught in theory or where there is a reluctance to change outmoded practice places the student under considerable stress. This phenomenon was recognized by Argyris and Schon (1974) who believed that it was fundamentally wrong to attempt to change the work practices of established/senior professionals via students or recently qualified professionals. In an attempt to explore students' perceptions about learning to work together, course members were asked to identify those specific areas of the programme that facilitated the process. Surprisingly only 33% identified placement experiences as being the most important factor, a result which undoubtedly poses more questions than it answers. Fifty-eight per cent of the responses highlighted college-based learning as especially helpful. These were distributed, with the integrating module receiving 26% of the responses, the specialist module 19%, and the common foundation programme rating 13% of the responses. The remaining 9% responses indicated that learning about the features itemized had not taken place at all. If the results are valid, then the implications at the very least warrant sober reflection on why and how this should be. Time is clearly a factor; with a college/placement ratio of at least 2:1, students have a much greater opportunity to get to know one another and form meaningful relationships in the college setting. Additionally, being 'on placement' carried with it notions of transience and non-permanency, not to mention novice status, which may affect the student's learning. Similarly these factors may affect the practice supervisor. It could be argued that the role of the practice supervisor as teacher is underdeveloped, and that the experience of working together with other professionals may be limited so that the role model that students need may be lacking. Equally it could be hypothesized that the practice supervisor might unconsciously believe that, because of the complex nature of interprofessional collaboration, there is insufficient time to explore all the issues involved and therefore may not make an overt attempt to raise them, nor provide an adequate role model.

It could, however, be argued that there is a genuine dichotomy between ideology and practice. Most, if not all, students are aware of the 'credibility gap' (i.e. the difference between what is taught in the classroom and what actually happens in clinical practice). Some authorities recognize this phenomenon to the point of actually teaching safe ways to cut corners. Working together may be one such ideology which in reality may not exist, or be of such an intangible nature as to render it unachievable. If this is the case, then exponents of IPSL could be guilty of raising false expectations, a serious state of affairs with practical and ethical dimensions.

Development of a typology

The preceding discussion about aspects of curriculum management and clinical placement illustrates the complexity surrounding the implementation of shared learning initiatives. We would postulate that for effective outcomes all of these aspects need to point in the same direction; that is, shared learning should encompass learning to share with other professionals in order to work together for the benefit of users in working environments which demonstrate cooperation. For educators proposing to use shared learning, the results of this study and our previous work would seem to suggest a tentative typology for interprofessional shared learning to refine some of the semantic ambiguity alluded to in our introduction. It seems that there are at least three components in shared learning:

- the interactive experience of learning with different significant others (process);
- knowledge about the work, roles and responsibilities of different significant others;
- knowledge focused on the skills and strategies for collaboration.

We have identified five differing models which are loosely categorized as IPSL which are permutations of the three components identified above (see Fig. 12.1).

The traditional model

This is the model where professionals learn separately about the roles and responsibilities of other professionals as part of training to work together. The IPSL is in the content of the learning — the shared knowledge about each other's work — but with no direct contact with each other in the learning environment. This was the usual pattern of professional training in the past.

The reformed model (parallel)

Parts of the Diploma in Professional Studies on which the current research was based illustrate the parallel model, where students from a similar base moving into different positions within the same larger category (community health services) share the learning process. The shared content of learning may not be explicitly concerned with roles, responsibilities, negotiations across boundaries and other aspects of learning to share, but the common purposes will be addressed. Heavy reliance is placed on learning from the interactive processes.

The overt content of the learning event is undeveloped in respect of collaboration. Health education is an example, where all three professional groups need the information but each will incorporate this knowledge into their own work separately.

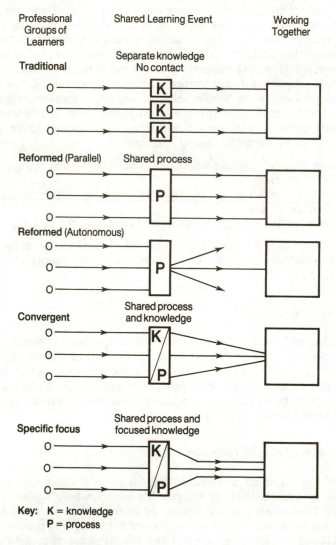

Fig. 12.1 Typology of IPSL

The reformed model (autonomous)

Another reformed model where the focus is on the process of shared learning, but the content of what is learned is not necessarily directed towards shared working, is the autonomous model. This is where learners come from a range of different backgrounds, share a learning event, have the stimulus of the others' contributions, and may or may not use this shared learning to enhance their working together. The common foundation social sciences would be an example of this.

The convergent model

Both the process and the content of learning in this model are directed towards enhancing the abilities of professionals to work together across boundaries as a result of this shared learning experience. In the Diploma in Professional Studies this strategy was characterized by the integrating module, where students in mixed groups chose and shared topics to which each would bring particular knowledge/perspectives that were relevant. The supposed outcome is that students learn about each other, how to collaborate and what issues are shared concerns through the process of preparing presentations together rather than there being overt tuition about learning to share.

The specific focus model

This was the characteristic model of our previous research, where professionals with wide remits attended learning events about a specific issue (in our case, child protection). Most of the professionals had responsibilities that were much broader than child protection, but they came together to focus on this one aspect of work where professional interdependence is unquestioned. The knowledge and the processes of the learning event were geared towards effective working together, and skills and strategies were taught and developed to enhance this. Workers in health and social service departments are concerned with effective joint working (Ormiston and Haggard, 1993) which specific training can address.

The typology has arisen from our research and is offered as an instrument for further investigation of interprofessional shared learning.

Conclusions

This chapter set out to give an account of an educational experience of interprofessional shared learning as perceived by students from a nursing background in post-qualification training. Ever conscious of the limitation of self-reporting, our findings include some interesting insights and points for further debate, and yet we cannot claim any definitive conclusions as to the value of IPSL. There are disparities in outcomes which are confusing, and the variables identified are multi-faceted and too numerous to offer clarity. We can confirm that IPSL is not the panacea for the education of health professionals, and it may even be stated that IPSL promises more than it delivers. We hope that the development of the typology may be a step to enlighten further debate.

It is also to be hoped that in the ensuing discussion and polemic concerning IPSL the needs of the professions' clients will not be sacrificed on the grounds of educational fashion or lost in a battle of ideology between various educational pressure groups. We believe that 'the benefits from the educational process are often synergistic and not specific to a single educational effort' (Simmons, 1975).

References

Argyris C, Schon D (1974) *Reflective Practitioner: Theory in Practice, Increasing Professional Effectiveness*. London: Jossey-Bass.

Bandura A (1977) *Social Learning Theory*. Hemel Hempstead: Prentice Hall.

Bernstein B (1971) On the classification and framing of educational knowledge. In: Young MFD (Ed.), *Knowledge and Control*. London: Collier–Macmillan.

Capra F (1982) *The Turning Point*. London: Wildwood House.

Carpenter J, Onyett S, Peck E, Smith H, Williams J (1991) *Joint Training Project Report*. Bristol: NHS Training Directorate.

Cumberlege J (1986) *Neighbourhood Nursing: A Focus for Care*. Report of the Community Nursing Review. London: DHSS/HMSO.

Department of Health and Social Security (1988) *Working Together*. London: HMSO.

Funnell P, Gill J, Ling J (1992) *Developing and Measuring Competence*. London: Kogan Page.

Jurkovich RP (1984) *Problems in Interdisciplinary Studies*. Cobham, Surrey: Garner Publishing.

Kocklemans JJ (Ed.) (1979) *Interdisciplinarity and Higher Education*. Pennsylvania: State University Press.

Lloyd G, Borland M, Thwaites M, Waddicor P (1973) An interdisciplinary workshop. *Journal of the Royal College of General Practitioners*; **23**: 463.

Michaud G (1970) *Problems of Teaching Research in University*. Paris: Ceri Centre of Education Research and Innovation (OECD).

Ormiston H, Haggard L (1993) *A Long Road*. Sutton, Surrey: Community Care.

Secretary of State for Social Services (1988) *Report of the Enquiry into Child Abuse in Cleveland*. London: HMSO.

Simmons J (1975) Making health education work. *American Journal of Public Health*; **65**.

Social Services Inspectorate (1991) *Training for Community Care — a Joint Approach*. London: Department of Health.

13 Learning to be a better team-player: Initiatives in continuing education in primary health care

Mary Thomas

Introduction

Pereira-Gray (1987) states:

> '. . . that the various health care professionals should unite their efforts to provide the best possible service for the patient is bland, true and self evident. It is however quite extraordinarily difficult to achieve in practice.'

Much research into team-working problems has focused on what *prevents* collaborative working. It is frequently concluded that education has a part to play in solving team problems.

Educational initiatives for team learning range from single study days for vocational trainees, to in-depth programmes for established practitioners. Some have used discussion formats; others have used strategies that involve interviewing simulated patients.

At what career point is it most useful to introduce these initiatives? What should be the main educational strategies adopted to enhance collaborative working? Should we continue to develop courses in an *ad hoc* manner, mainly for professionals who are already motivated towards enhancing their own team-working skills? Should professionals learn about team-working away from their own team members, in the hope that they will be able to act as change agents on return to their clinical practice? Or should we look for some fundamental principles that will inform the nature of learning to be a better team-player, so that educationalists, facilitators of courses as well managers and providers will know best how to enhance team-working skills? Based on principles of adult learning, of small group dynamics and founded in experience of developing problem-based learning materials, I propose a new dynamic framework. Within this, we can analyse existing initiatives and design even more effective team-learning opportunities.

Barriers also exist to developing effective team-learning. I will refer to texts that detail educational initiatives. However, the main thrust of this chapter is based on new insights obtained while designing two quite separate educational programmes for collaborative learning.

Recent educational initiatives

While the past focus has largely been on undergraduate joint learning initiatives, Argyris and Schon (1974) proposed that the aim should not be to change a profession through its students alone. Indeed, a WHO Study Group (1988) concluded that, for maximum effect, formal multiprofessional collaboration needs to be introduced early in basic or undergraduate education programmes and continued throughout the curriculum in post-basic, postgraduate and continuing education.

Thomson (1983) reflects on the perversity that competition regulates students' entry to institutions, as well as their progress towards success, while collaborative learning is little valued. Should a collaborative style of learning be imposed on a previously competitive one?

Ling et al. (1990) question whether it is possible to use collaborative learning to increase knowledge:

'The real value of shared learning lies in providing a forum that gives professionals the opportunity to participate in applying their knowledge to real life situations.'

Salkind and Norrell (1980) described an early initiative in primary care. The St Bartholomew's and Hackney Vocational Training Scheme chose discussion group techniques and developed a 'long term group' — GP trainees, a health visitor, a social worker, a receptionist and a district nursing sister. The group ran for two years and the participants demonstrated significant gains in professional motivation and interprofessional understanding. GPs, rather than GP trainees, would have made the project even more interesting — and closer to the composition of the primary care team in action.

A variety of other educational initiatives have been undertaken. For example, Brooks et al. (1981) described the organization of a course developed in Manchester. Trainee GPs, student health visitors and student district nurses met for one annual study day, composed of lectures and small group discussions. England (1984) described another initiative from the University of Sussex: running annually since 1977, it involved one and a half study days for trainee health visitors, trainee social workers and general practitioner trainees.

Pearson et al. (1985), in the Burford Nursing Development Unit, piloted an innovative workshop format for established professionals. They used simulated interviews, with actors portraying patients. The Exeter Group (Jones, 1986) has continued to develop study days for GP trainees, district nurse students and health visitor students.

Runciman (1989) reports a collaborative research project which examined, through video, slides and questionnaires, the scope and content of health assessment of old people at home. Her findings support arguments for developing team-work through shared learning. Bowling (1981) comments that very brief periods of shared learning in vocational or post-basic education probably have little impact. Meanwhile, Mangham (1988) challenges:

> '. . . the position of researchers and observers, scholars and writers who pay flying visits to organizations, distribute a few questionnaires or conduct a couple of interviews as being as ludicrous as the anthropologist who spends a couple of weeks with a particular tribe and seeks to reveal all.'

Perhaps these words of caution are true for designers of educational programmes as well.

Some newer educational initiatives

In the late 1980s and early 90s, two new multiprofessional learning initiatives were designed specifically for primary care health care professionals by researchers based in Scotland. The *print programme* was based on written text to support multiprofessional learning sessions. It resulted from a collaboration between the Scottish National Board for Nursing and Midwifery, the Centre for Medical Education at the University of Dundee, and the Scottish Postgraduate Medical Education Council. The *computing programme* uses a computer program to trigger multiprofessional discussion. It was developed in collaboration between the Centre for Medical Education at the University of Dundee, the Department of Education at the University of Glasgow, and the Cancer Relief Macmillan Fund.

The print programme had an action research focus. A series of educational triggers and patient management challenges were created, alongside a model of team functioning (Thomas, 1992). Each trigger consisted of a visual image of a patient (e.g. a man with cancer), supported by key statements from each professional in the team. These statements reflected a real issue in practice. The aim was to stimulate discussion in the team about how the participants dealt with such an issue.

Each patient management challenge presented a series of problems in different contexts (e.g. cancer care, psychological care, care of the chronically ill, prevention). Based on critical incidents described by individuals or groups, the patient management challenges enabled individuals to reflect on how they currently functioned in a team and how they would prefer to function.

The print programme was designed to be used by a multi-professional group who either already worked together in close collaboration or had the potential to do so. After the programme, participants' new learning, whether it was attitude change towards colleagues or patients or an altered conceptual framework of disease and health within families, would initiate the process of appropriate change in clinical practice.

The computing programme, a quite separate initiative called 'Unite the team!', promoted multiprofessional collaboration in the area of palliative cancer care (i.e. patients with advanced cancer). The computing challenge was designed to discover how different professionals perceive and assess the problems of specific patients, families or colleagues. The specific patient and family problems used were based on critical incidents in palliative care.

This problem-based strategy enabled the team members to reflect on the similarities and differences of their assessment strategies. Each team could also decide how well-coordinated their responses were in the clinical situation; i.e. how well they understood each other's assessment criteria. The programme let each of two teams test how closely they could predict how the other team had assessed the same situation.

The print and computing programmes were both designed to provide joint continuing education in a team-work context to experienced health care practitioners from different disciplines. The professionals were already working in physical proximity in varying degrees of collaboration around patients and families. The phrase 'intact team' denotes that these were not teams artificially created to undergo a learning experience away from their current work environment. Intact teams already work from the same base or have the same population to manage: they are not an arbitrary mixture of individuals who will subsequently return to their own different teams.

Health care professionals have large demands on their time and limited preparation for collaborative functioning. These features of their working practice increased the challenge of designing both educational programmes.

There are too many variables simply to compare and contrast the design, development and use of the print and computing programmes. However, some of the key issues identified in both programmes might influence the success of other educational initiatives designed to enhance collaborative working. On this basis I will attempt to provide a new framework for future designs.

A model to analyse educational initiatives in teams

A framework for thinking about groups in psychoanalysis was developed by Cohn (1969). This was used by Bramley (1979) to reflect on peer group learning in higher education. I have developed and expanded their work in conjunction with the development of the print and computing programmes. It is now possible to conceptualize, with relative ease, the multiple variables of team-work: individual, task, environment, power, leadership, stereotyping, educational preparation and expectations. The model can incorporate the 'process' elements of a group (in our case a health care team) as part of the dynamic of what, in the original framework, is described as 'balancing'.

In Figs 13.1 and 13.2 the components of Cohn's original framework can be seen. In a group, 'balance' of these components is not always easily achieved and 'collapse' can occur. Just think of a learning group where the individual (*I*) needs or the group (*We*) needs are not acknowledged as important. The task function of the group will soon fail; i.e. it will not be engaging, active or creative. Alternatively, if you ignore the expectations individuals have of a group (*Auspices*) or fail to consider the physical and psychological environment of the group (*Globe*) the lack of balance will reduce the success of the task.

The fundamental principle of adult learning, used in the development of both programmes, stresses the importance of the individuals accepting responsibility for their own learning (Knowles, 1970). However, when learning occurs in groups, both the educationalist designer of the programmes as well as the person who may act as facilitator must understand and be able to utilize the concepts that Cohn originally proposed.

My modification to Cohn's idea conceptualizes not one but three Globes or Worlds. Each reflects a different context of group interaction. As Fig. 13.3 illustrates, globe A reflects the world of team as described in the literature, globe B reflects the world of team in the educational programme and globe C reflects the real world of team in clinical practice. Within this framework the 'auspices' are the expectations individuals have of team-working.

The detailed design and development of the print and computing programmes are described elsewhere (Thomas, 1992). Here I propose a template for multiprofessional learning which can be used:

- to analyse existing team-work educational initiatives;
- to inform the development of new programmes or research strategies;
- to help individuals reflect on their own team-work skills.

Past research into team-work in primary care has revealed aspects of Cohn's model: namely, the Auspices, Globe, I, We, It and the balancing function. Many of the early studies, for example, looked at role function or issues of territoriality (Challela, 1979 and Navarro, 1977) which could be considered as 'We' components of Cohn's structure, while Gilmore et al.'s study (1974) of the nursing team in general practice began to address the leadership role or balancing function.

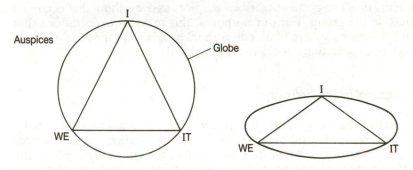

Fig. 13.1 A diagram to show Ruth Cohn's Theme Centred Interaction (TCI)

Fig. 13.2 Cohn's TCI – A collapsed system

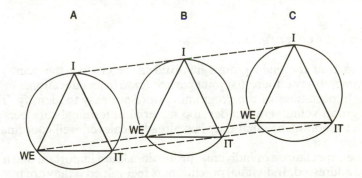

Fig. 13.3 A diagram using Cohn's TCI to reflect the links between the World of Team in the Literature (A), the World of Team in the Educational Programme (B) and the Real World of Team in Clinical Practice (C)

My aim is to identify which different parts of Cohn's framework can be used in teams when the print and computing programmes are being used. If these are clarified in each of our educational initiatives then the task will be to achieve fidelity or *design for the best fit* between the three Globes or Worlds. In essence we are aiming to design educational initiatives that will promote reflective thinking and the real world of team functioning.

The various elements in Cohn's framework will now be examined more closely.

Auspices

Cohn (1969) originally described auspices as everything that occurred outside the group. For our purposes, this includes expectations that individuals may have of an educational programme for team-work as well as expectations of team-working itself.

Auspices in the literature

Research has suggested that the world of team is influenced by our expectations and preparation for team-working. Lack of formal preparation for collaborative working may significantly reduce the effectiveness of the practitioner attempting to work as part of a multiprofessional team (Hunt, 1983). Research reveals little about how different professions and professionals view the prospect of multiprofessional learning. Yet, when patterns of attendance at multiprofessional courses are analysed, some practitioners seem reluctant to take part.

Auspices in the print programme

For each of the eight groups involved in developing the print programme, this was their first joint participation in an educational initiative. Expectations of the programme were not easy to identify. That one group volunteered to develop material in terminal care perhaps reflected confidence that they had already achieved well coordinated terminal care.

The expectations of individual professionals are important and need to be addressed. Individual practitioners feel valued if they are treated as equals. It was not, therefore, assumed that the GP would necessarily be the coordinator of the team or the selector of individuals to be part of the study. The way that individuals are invited to take part in an initiative can be quite crucial.

Bramley (1979) described how students' expectations of the organization offering the educational programme will either add to or detract from its credibility. For example, one senior nurse manager commented that any programme from a centre of medical education might really have as its purpose a strategy to keep the nurses in line. There is a need to understand the sensitivity of each different professional involved in the team.

Auspices in the computing programme

The groups involved in developing the computing programme already had a continuing commitment to the development of multiprofessional learning through study days and programmes. The hospice teams already had strong conceptions of themselves as good teams. Invitations to team members were made through one or more contacts in each organization rather than by individual letters being sent to each potential participant. These coordinators were neither senior managers nor necessarily the most powerful people in their respective groups: their training responsibility gave them an insight into who might be interested in the project and how best to approach them.

In general, members of the computer development groups had positive expectations of the programme. These may have been enhanced by their knowledge and previous experience of the educational institutions and the cancer charity involved in the design. Participants' only reservations before using the programme were some degree of anxiety about computer use and questions about the gaming element.

Globe

Cohn (1969) described the globe as encompassing the psychological and physical elements in a group. In primary care teams the physical environment of the health centre influences how accessible people are to one another. In addition, team members bring particular psychological feelings to the group at different times. For example, unresolved conflict may leave residual feelings of frustration within the team.

Globe in the literature

Physical proximity, providing different professions with the opportunity to work together, has been encouraged by the development of health centres. Increasing personal contact will help replace stereotypes of other professions with more realistic perceptions (Bruce, 1980).

Globe in the print programme

The physical and psychological factors in each of the eight teams involved in developing the print programme showed up when the groups started trying to solve the patient management challenges together. Some behaviour seemed incongruous. For example, four of the eight teams failed to meet on a regular basis to discuss patient issues other than in pairs. Also, meetings of three or more professionals were held in quite different venues from their normal routine. This may be of importance when looking at the impact on interaction in the team. Four teams met on neutral territory (e.g. a staff room or teaching area). Two teams met in the health visitor's room. The remaining two met in the consulting room of the GP.

Attempts were made to arrange seating in a horseshoe or circle but desks often became barriers. One GP refused to move from his position behind his desk.

In another setting, some members of the group commented that they had no obvious leader but their seating arrangements seemed to indicate otherwise. The GPs were sitting at one side of the room with a table in front of them, while the other members of the team were seated around the edge of the room.

Psychological factors are difficult for the researcher and team members to explore in group settings, especially when the agenda is not to reveal these, as in a T-group. Brief studies may not give enough time to build the level of trust needed for psychological issues to be addressed. Fundamental to observation or reflection by the researcher as facilitator is what Bramley (1979) calls 'listening with the third ear'. It was possible to record notes about the group climate which did provide additional information about the process of interaction.

These groups met on several occasions, and developed a climate of trust. This may be one result of regular meetings in any working team.

Time, precious to busy professionals, proved to be critical. This study required special periods of time allocated to it. In an example of speaking on behalf of and perhaps pre-empting another professional, a senior nurse manager thought a particular health visitor would not have the time to be involved. In general, however, each team was able to allocate a minimum of one hour, at weekly to monthly intervals. The meetings tended to be over lunch, though one group met immediately after the GP's surgery. District nurses often found it difficult to attend, reflecting the reduced control which some professionals have over their own work.

Globe in the computing programme

The computing challenge raised slightly different physical and psychological issues. There was less diffidence about being involved. All teams were motivated and expressed interest in the project, knowing that they were part of a developmental programme. One significant feature was the gaming element, involving competition and scores. This extra psychological dimension was taken either seriously or humorously. The workshop format formed the basis for only one meeting, rather than a series of meetings, as in the print programme. The individuals in the computer teams knew each other well. Ice-breaking exercises were more to do with introducing the facilitator (researcher) and the programme to the group.

The workshop took some time and it was particularly difficult to run if any of the participants was late arriving or had to leave early.

Psychological tensions arose in response to the computing programme rather than resulting from interactions between professionals. For example, participants were asked to generate five criteria for assessing a particular patient problem. Some would have preferred to select five from an existing list. Anxiety was also expressed about using a keyboard for the first time and disagreements with the feedback on screen occurred.

Because tensions seemed to be created, this game became known as a challenge. Mixed-discipline groups were used to make up each team around the computer. This avoided setting up professionals in opposition to one another. In addition, care was taken with the feedback language on screen.

Although the computing programme was designed around one specific context of care (i.e. palliative care), it could be used by a larger variety of professionals than the print programme, including social workers, chaplains, volunteer coordinators as well as doctors and nurses.

I

As Cohn suggested (1969), the individual psychological unit, the I, must maintain its sense of uniqueness in the group. In team-working, this can be very difficult and may become associated with the feeling of uniqueness associated with the professional role. Thus the individual feeling may link itself with 'I am a general practitioner' or 'I am a health visitor'.

I and the literature

None of the literature in the health care field on multiprofessional learning reflects on the I needs, other than as they relate to a professional role. The literature places the patient as central to care but it seems to ignore the I needs of the practitioner, just as much of western thinking has tended to remove the centrality of the consciousness of I from observations of our world. In providing some characteristics of the good team member, Mangham (1988) impinges on this area. Tannenbaum and Davis (1983) also note that individual perceptions may need to change.

I and the print programme

The main aim of the print programme was, through the challenge of problem-solving, to trigger each individual's personal perception of their world of team. The programme was also intended to create a climate where the individual had the opportunity to reflect on his or her attitude towards the team and to renegotiate practices.

Any change in behaviour over the period of the meetings could have had two causes: a direct result of increased familiarity between the professionals or an enhanced feeling of safety with the facilitator and the educational initiative.

Certainly, the team where individuals showed the most inhibitions in interacting, continued to do so in spite of the programme. This suggests that fundamental issues of team-work remained unaddressed. Other behaviours suggested some insecurity. For example one professional kept his coat on during the meeting, and one individual talked excessively. It is perhaps an indication of the group's maturity that members felt safe to express the individual I in these ways. It is tempting to guess how such behaviour might translate into interaction with patients as well as discussions about patient needs. Does the dominant talker really listen? Is the person behind the desk reluctant to accept new ideas? Does anxiety prevent the silent members asserting themselves? Are they thus devolving responsibility to others? The print programme was limited, however, and such issues did not become the focus of discussion.

The print programme did recognize the importance of the variety of ways in which different professionals may meet patient and family problems. This required the development of separate points of entry to the patient management challenge.

For example, the GP may meet the patient at the surgery: the district nurse is unlikely to make contact with a patient unless a referral is made. In fact, the team model that supported the patient management challenges was a construct based more on professional roles than on an analysis of individuals in groups. This increased individuals' difficulty in identifying how they fitted into the model and may have inhibited revelations about self.

In Cohn's framework, the individual should interact appropriately to the benefit of the group and ultimately the task. Therefore, individual issues must be addressed in team-working and learning.

I and the computing programme

In the computing challenge it was impossible for one person to interact with the program. In a patient and family scenario each practitioner identified the criteria used in assessing a patient. For the groups, each containing a range of professions, to reach a consensus each member had to explain his or her personal criteria. This did allow individuals to reflect on their own perceptions of assessing a patient's needs. However, used once only, the challenge may have had limitations in meeting the I needs in the group.

The task was common to every member of the group but, in leaderless groups, a very dominant group member could inhibit exploration of other individuals' criteria.

We

The concept of We means, for Cohn, the group relatedness, or the feeling of belonging. For team-working in health care this may be a professional-group relatedness as well as an interprofessional one.

We and the literature

Team-building literature objectifies the We of teams by describing how to build the We feeling in others (i.e. how to be a team leader). Little is written about how to be part of a team. Tannenbaum and Davis (1983) described in some detail elements that may need to change both I and We needs. For example, it is possible to move away from viewing an individual with reference to his or her job description and towards viewing an individual as a whole person.

We and the print programme

In the print programme, each team was already considered to be a good working team. Members were mostly confident in the amount of We feeling they had.

This confidence was indicated in several ways, such as their use of humour, and the way they addressed one another. They could also move quickly from the paper challenge to interacting around real clinical situations. Groups that were mature and met regularly seemed more able to do this. Such groups also tended to show evidence of anticipatory planning rather than crisis management. In some challenges, they were confident in deciding that certain paper situations would have been pre-empted in their practice. Alongside this feeling of We came a sense of the enhanced value attributed to the Other, with an ability to challenge freely different perceptions expressed by other professionals.

Significant change was measured when option choices in the problem material were analysed. The factor which influenced responses to perceptions about team was not the individual or the profession to which that individual belonged, but the team or group of which they were part. This was found to influence significantly how the individuals responded both before and after the educational programme, when asked about their perception of the team (Thomas, 1992).

We and the computing programme

In the computing challenge, practitioners experienced a We situation as multiprofessional groups interacted around a computer. Participants could examine their own attitudes to knowledge and decide which components of this knowledge were most valuable.

Each team was required to predict how the other team thought, using the other team's assessment criteria and trying to rate each scenario as the other team had. Each team was multiprofessional. If uniprofessional groups had been used then stereotypes might possibly have played more of a part in predicting the responses of the other team.

The challenge was: 'How well do you really know the other team?' One method was to note who was in the group and who was likely to be the most influential in persuading the group of its thinking. Trying to think like the other team caused the most amusement: 'This is too much fun to be education', was one comment.

Although this point is not directly addressed here, the computer may be viewed as an extra member of the group. It can supply information or store the group's expertise. The effect of poorly constructed on-screen feedback did become apparent. For example, an over-enthusiastic response (written by the programmer) of 'That was disastrous' made one team member particularly angry. Humour does not translate without a paralanguage (the way in which something is said). Instead of becoming part of the We in this situation, the computer became something the group needed to challenge, affecting the nature of team-learning. In addition to an element of competition with the other team, a feeling of competition with the computer may also develop. At the least, this distracts the participants from the main task.

Within the We component of the computing programme, it was anticipated that individual professionals would explore their proprietorial attitude to knowledge. In fact, this was observed, as different professionals debated the additional information they would need to complete their assessment. In one team discussion, a member explored a new concept: the GP reviewed maladaptive and adaptive coping for stress in family carers. He had not used the concept previously but it had underpinned the social worker's assessment criteria. This level of debate must have enhanced the practitioners' understanding of one another.

There are some limitations to the use of the computing programme. The team around a computer may differ from the group that interacts in the clinical setting. Nevertheless, the participants for each workshop did come from the same work setting and had the potential to work together. Thus, these professionals will probably approach their world of team more closely and became more able to reflect on attitudes and to review practices.

It

'It' is the topic addressed by the group or the theme of its action. Bramley (1979) expands this idea in the learning group, suggesting that the theme needs to be active (see below). The main theme for health care teams is that of managing patient and family problems. In the world of educational initiatives for team-working, the theme is the course content.

It and the literature

Within the literature on multiprofessional learning in continuing education, the theme or It has been the main focus for discussion. Courses in multiprofessional learning are described by Brooks et al. (1981), England (1984), Pearson et al. (1985) and Jones (1986). Lectures, small group discussions and simulated interview technique are all discussed.

It and the print programme

Cohn's essential idea was that the It or themes need to be active or engaging. No lists were to be made of 'the problems of team-work' for example. Instead, the It should provide an opportunity actively to engage with the 'world of team'. The print programme does this through patient management challenges or paper and pencil triggers.

Four different contexts of care were chosen. In the triggers and through the patient management challenges, the active theme was: 'What type of team are you in now and what sort of team would you prefer to be in?' Individuals decided how to respond and how they thought their closest colleagues in different professions would respond.

The problem-based focus let individuals enter the programme at a point relevant to their own practice. The challenges and triggers were based on critical incidents generated by experienced practitioners. They were written in a minimalist fashion (i.e. without excessive contextual data that might cause the participants to distance themselves from the programme).

The theme was not only active but designed to be flexible. Individuals working alone would still be able to interact with the material. Feedback to participants was given in terms of a team model, a coordination–integration continuum which enabled individuals to decide how they might prefer to function.

The strategy seemed to comply with the requirement for an active theme. It would have been useful also to have challenged the teams initially to produce their own critical incident and reflect upon it. They could then have used this to decide the type of team they were in and the type of team they would prefer to be part of.

It and the computing programme

In the computing programme only one context of care was used, namely, palliative cancer care. However, the active nature of this programme was revealed as two direct challenges for the participants:

- 'What assessment criteria do you use as an individual and as a team in this aspect of care?'
- 'How well can you predict how the other team would assess the same situation?'

A simple statistical technique made feedback available numerically and as verbal comments written on-screen. The main purpose was to trigger reflection on the congruence of assessment strategies among different professional groups. Where disparities existed, discussion and renegotiation could go on to influence clinical practice.

Scenarios with a minimalist approach were generated from critical incidents provided by experienced practitioners. One series directly addressed stress in professionals, whereas others were patient and family focused.

The fact that one comment suggested that too much fun was occurring may indicate the degree of engagement for some participants. However, some found the lack of a menu-driven program, (i.e. one where concrete directions for the workshop were on-screen) made engagement more difficult. The nature of this single intervention triggered direct queries from participants, asking 'What will I get out of this?'

The experiential nature of the learning contrasted with many other uses of computers; for example, accessing knowledge on a database or multimedia system. For some participants there did seem to be a conflict, in that they had expectations that the computer would provide the answers to team-work problems.

The balancing function

Bramley (1979) has explored the balancing component of Cohn's theme-centred interaction. In small-group teaching in higher education she describes the tutor's function as twofold. The tutor first structures the globe so far as is possible. He or she ensures its stability, which is essential if the triangle is to remain stable. This means consistency of time, location and furniture.

Second, once students feel safe, the tutor will concentrate either on the individual or the group as a whole or on the theme, according to whichever requires concern at any given moment. Once the second function is established, the globe recedes: intensive work proceeds more rapidly.

The balancing function and the literature

The balancing function is not directly noted in the literature. There is evidence of collapsed systems or non-functioning groups in studies of team-work cited in Bruce (1980), Gilmore et al. (1974), Pritchard (1978) and Dingwall and McIntosh (1977). Collapsed systems (see Fig. 13.2) may occur when there is a lack of balance among the Auspices, Globe, I, We and It components.

The balancing function and the print programme

In the print programme (where the programme was not being used by individuals in isolation), the balancing function was achieved, in part, by the group itself. The group moves from individual reflection to group perception, to the challenge on paper. This balancing will depend on preparation by participants and on the learning climate created. Facilitation or leadership may be a natural process, present in a mature group as a sort of rotating leadership. In addition, the I and We components have already been addressed and have been allowed to be expressed. For such a group, the task and its influence on the rest of the model is significant.

The success of the balancing function in a new educational initiative may reflect how well each individual facilitator achieves a non-proprietorial attitude towards each issue. This suggests that facilitation should be provided objectively, perhaps by someone outside the group, using the educational material.

The balancing function and the computing programme

The computing programme needs to be facilitated by someone who is at ease with the computing programme and the objectives of the workshop. Part of this workshop involves leaderless groups operating around computers. Maintaining a balanced system depends on the resources present in each of the groups. However, 'listening with the third ear' is perhaps the best description of the facilitator's role.

Educational programme development

What is the 'best fit' for each of the components Auspices, Globe, I, We, It and the balancing function? What preparation must precede educational initiatives developed to promote collaborative learning?

Individual practitioners should feel that their specific needs have been addressed. Any programme must be perceived as having positive benefit for their own practice, for the quality of patient care they can provide, and for the quality of their interprofessional collaboration. The success of any initiative will depend on its status and its reputation (including who is running the study day or who sponsored the resource material). In addition, success requires preparation of facilitators and the appropriate preparation of participants.

Individual participants in multiprofessional learning need to be prepared to interact in a process, taking responsibility for their own learning and taking risks. This is illustrated in a comment from a participant in the computing challenge: 'I suddenly realized how quickly I backed down in the discussion and was not prepared for the challenge.'

For the Globe component, the right climate, both physical and psychological, requires adequate time be allocated to any multiprofessional learning initiative. A programme with inbuilt flexibility that allows participants to meet more than once is best.

When dealing with issues in intact (existing) teams, it is important to encourage reflection.

For the I component, the educational programme should recognize the need for individuals to express themselves and to be given confidence to reflect on their roles in the team. Empowering individuals does not solely depend on imparting knowledge; it involves giving professionals a climate that will enable them safely to explore the issues around team-work.

Educational programmes may need to be written for an egalitarian team (i.e. a team of equals) although we know that this is not the real World of Team. This lets the team address the problem of status differences or stereotyping in their own team.

For the We component, it can be assumed that no educational initiative will tap into the exact We feeling in every clinical situation. In fact, this may not be desirable if a We feeling is absent or the climate is demotivating. There is probably an advantage in developing a task that maximizes the We feeling; for example, through using a gaming approach, or strategies to reduce tension.

The opportunity for an individual to be in a team and to obtain feedback about how their team is operating can motivate, even if this team was only established for one session. The more frequently the educational initiative allows different professionals to meet, the greater the likelihood of developing the We feeling.

Educational material should be designed to allow attitudes to be explored safely. However, the associated facilitator will influence how problems in the We area are addressed. When the facilitator role is filled by someone from outside the team, awareness of individual and group interaction may be heightened.

For the It component, elements of a programme (for example, a series of problem-based challenges) can trigger engagement. This also enables professionals to interact both as I and as We. They obtain feedback on the ways in which different professionals are meeting the challenges of patient care, as individuals and as members of a team. The It is really encouraging the practitioners to reflect on how they might change.

Envisioning Cohn's framework as a three-dimensional globe, the danger of system collapse exists if the I, We or It components are not balanced within the Globe and the Auspices. This balancing function captures the process element of any group activity: it may be the most significant aspect of a multiprofessional learning programme.

The balancing function hinges on facilitation. It may emerge from within the group or from outside. There are great advantages to a system which gives control of the learning initiatives to the group itself — as long as they have sufficiently mature systems for facilitation of their own group processes (i.e. they are aware of group processes and have negotiated a facilitator from within). If not, potential for change may be compromised. Existing patterns of functioning are unchallenged, through unequal power differentials or a lack of awareness of stereotyped patterns of behaviour.

Summary

I have addressed some of the challenges in designing educational programmes for established practitioners in primary health care teams. Successful group interaction can be conceptualized in a model of interaction that encompasses the nature of the physical and psychological factors influencing a team, as well as the tasks they have to perform. This model can become almost a checklist, a means of identifying how well a new educational programme addresses the multiple variables that contribute towards team functioning.

Two educational programmes with which I was involved were the first to be analysed using the extensions of Cohn's model. Not only must the I, We, It, Globe and Auspices be considered in each situation, but they must also be balanced. Collapsed globes may occur because of failure in educational design or inappropriate facilitation. Collapse will also be less likely to provide the best climate for the participants to focus on their World of Team.

If the educational design has taken into consideration the preparation of its target group, if it is flexible and problem-based, if it focuses on real patient, family and team issues, then with appropriate facilitation it should be able to meet the unique needs of each team.

For every team, whatever the issues that need to be addressed, the balance of the World of Team in the educational programme is informed by the World of Team in the literature and is essential to the success of achieving balance in the real World of Team in clinical practice.

Becoming a better team player

If we seek educational strategies that will result in sustainable change in collaborative working in teams, then short-term results are not enough. Processes need to be developed that working teams can continue to use. This will require challenging existing attitudes and being able to confront real problems. Such a process needs skilled facilitation.

If we achieve my suggested fidelity between educational programmes and the real worlds of the teams, we may also need to reappraise our own approach. How should we design educational programmes for collaborative learning? How best do we aid collaborative learning initiatives?

The following template for educators, facilitators and team members may be of help.

Thomas's template for multiprofessional learning

For every pair, try to move from the left towards the right.

- Avoid the individual's expectations of collaboration.
  - Incorporate the individual's expectations of collaboration into the educational programme.

- Learn about collaborative working as individuals.
  - Learn about collaborative working with your own team.

- Focus on the individual professional role in team-working.
  - Value the individual, personal role in team-learning.

- Perceive positive group feelings as essential in education programmes about team-work.
  - Be able to accept confrontation, in addition to valuing feelings of group relatedness.

- Learn through subject-centred discussion groups.
  - Actively learn through problem-based educational strategies.

- Use teacher-centred strategies that are of short duration and enhance mainly knowledge about health care teams.
  - Use student-centred strategies that are facilitated to become incorporated into the real practice of health care teams.

References

Argyris C, Schon DA (1974) *Theory into Practice: Increasing Professional Effectiveness*. San Francisco: Jossey-Bass.

Bowling A (1981) *Delegation in General Practice*. London: Tavistock.

Bramley W (1979) *Group Tutoring: Concepts and Case Studies*. London: Kogan Page.

Brooks D, Hendry A, Parsonage A (1981) Towards the reality of the primary health care team: an educational approach. *Journal of the Royal College of General Practitioners*; **36**: 285–286.

Bruce N (1980) *Team-work for Preventive Care*. Chichester: John Wiley.

Challela M (1979) The interdisciplinary team: a role definition for nursing. *Image*; **11**: 9–15.

Cohn R (1969) The theme-centred interactional method. *Group Process* (formerly *Journal of Group Psychoanalysis and Process*); **2**: (2), 19–35.

Dingwall R, McIntosh J (Eds) (1978) Team-work in theory and practice. In: *Readings in the Sociology of Nursing*. Edinburgh: Churchill Livingstone.

England H (1984) Working relationships: a workshop for increasing mutual understanding in social work, general practice and health visiting. *Trainee (Update)*; 100–104.

Gilmore G, Bruce N, Hunt M (1974) *The Work of the Nursing Team in General Practice*. London: CETHV.

Hunt M (1983) Possibilities and problems of interdisciplinary teamwork. In: Clark J, Henderson J (Eds), *Community Health*. Harmondsworth: Longman.

Jones RVH (1986) *Working Together, Learning Together*. London: Royal College of General Practitioners (occasional paper 33).

Knowles M (1970). *The Modern Practice of Adult Education: Andragogy versus Pedagogy*. Falet, Chicago, Illinois: Association Press.

Ling J, Funnell P, Gill J (1990) Nurse Education. Issues–shared learning. *Nursing Times*; **86** (1): 65–6.

Mangham IL (1988) *Power and Performance in Organisations*. Oxford: Blackwell.

Navarro V (1977) *Medicine Under Capitalism*. London: Croom Helm.

Pearson A, Morris P, Whitehouse C (1985) Groups: a new approach to interdisciplinary teaching. *Journal of the Royal College of General Practitioners*; **35**: 381–383.

Pereira-Gray DJ (1987) *Preface to Working Together, Learning Together*. London: Royal College of General Practitioners (occasional paper 38).

Pritchard P (1978) *Manual of Primary Care: Its Nature and Organisation*. Oxford: Oxford University Press.

Runciman P (1989) Health assessment of the elderly at home: the case for shared learning. *Journal of Advanced Nursing*; Feb. 14.

Salkind MR, Norell JS (1980) Teaching about the primary health care team: an experiment in vocational training. *Journal of the Royal College of General Practitioners*; **30**: 158–160.

Tannenbaum R, Davis SA (1983) Values, man and organisations. In: French, Bell, Zawacki (Eds), *Organisational Development Theory in Practice and Research*. Texas: Business Publications Inc.

Thomas ML (1992) *Multiprofessional Learning in Continuing Education*. Unpublished MEd thesis, University of Dundee.

Thomson D (1983) Competition and Collaboration in Higher Education for Health Care. *Nurse Education Today*; **7**: 21–23.

WHO Study Group (1988) *Learning Together to Work Together for Health.* Geneva: WHO (Technical Report Series 769).

Part D

Underlying Issues Examined

Interprofessional working is a goal that is not easy to achieve. There are numerous barriers to the changes needed to ensure optimum team-working, ranging from clashes of personality to occupational structures. This section addresses many of the issues which have been found to be, or have the potential to be, causes of friction between different occupational groups. Some of the causes of friction can be overcome while others are more intractable, arising from practices embedded in the structures of our society. However, if active consideration is given to including the user or patient in interprofessional decision-making, there is potential to overcome the barriers and divisions between occupations.

Stephen Ackroyd focuses on organizational issues, and in particular on the adoption of inappropriate forms of management in the NHS which have compounded the problems of morale currently being experienced in nursing. Ackroyd outlines the changing structure of the NHS and considers the introduction of general management, arguing that the new management introduces the notion of rationing which is antithetical to the nurses and their training. Nurses are a pivotal occupational group in the delivery of health care and in debates regarding interprofessional working. Yet nursing is an occupational group which is overshadowed by the medical profession.

The domination of health care by the medical profession is a theme taken up in the chapter by Kevin Kendrick. The medical model of care, not surprisingly perhaps, dominates in the hospital yet nurses bear some responsibility for the continuing dominance of the medical profession and its model of health care.

Christine Henry examines the need for 'ethical appraisals' to take place in health care organizations and considers the findings from a case study in one health authority management audit.

The centrality of ethics to professional practice is discussed by Kevin Kendrick who takes a close look at the UK Central Council's code of professional conduct for nurses. Kendrick poses a number of questions regarding codes of conduct, arguing that there are many dilemmas between the paper prescriptions and the reality of nursing practice.

The potential for overlap and conflict between management and professional activities is the focus of Julie Dockrell and Gail Wilson's chapter. They point out that the management of interprofessional working is especially important with regard to the care of older

people who may require the attentions of a number of different professionals and service managers. Dockrell and Wilson express concern at the introduction of inappropriate private sector models of
management into human service agencies. They argue that each service may require different management strategies in order to deal
with the changing demands made on their service. The dynamics of
interprofessional working relationships are discussed using findings
from research into the manager–user interface.

Following on a growing number of initiatives, there have been
attempts to increase the choice and control by women regarding the
care they receive. Jane Sandall discusses the changing relationships
between midwives and obstetricians and their relationships with
women. Sandall is cautious about the professionalizing strategy
of midwives and discusses the implications of this strategy with
reference to 'continuity of care' schemes currently being introduced
in the UK.

The need to take account of the perspectives of women as participants in their own care is emphasized in Sandall's chapter, and
June Greenwell returns to this topic arguing that health care is not
sufficiently user-oriented. If health, rather than illness, becomes the
focus of health care, then the idea of who the health professional is
changes to envelop a wide diversity of occupational roles such as the
leisure service manager. Through using a wider ideal of health, questions arise about the setting of standards and the assessment of outcomes for users and carers. Greenwell outlines a number of changes
both inside and outside the health service which have the potential
to fundamentally affect interprofessional working relationships. In
particular the increasing, and recently accepted, importance of alternative medicine in health care will affect the relationship between the
public/patient and the health care professional.

The need to include the patient in the evaluation of effectiveness
of health care is reiterated by Eileen McLeod. In the discussions of
interprofessional working and team-working there is, by definition,
an exclusion of the patient. Professionals working together, making
decisions together, can mean that assumptions regarding patients'
needs are made. Based on research regarding the way in which social
work referrals are made in hospitals, McLeod argues that the system
of interprofessional working acts to ratio the help given to patients
rather than acting as a gateway to improving patient care.

The relationships between nurses and doctors which have developed
over this century are discussed by Lesley Mackay. From research in
Scotland and England, Mackay reflects on the managed performances
of doctors and nurses in the delivery of health care and the way in
which they can act to disadvantage the patient.

What emerges strongly from this section is the centrality of the
patient and the user in health care. The patient has not been of

primary importance in the delivery of health care. The professional groups need to think about the ways in which the needs of the patients and carers can be addressed. In focusing on a goal beyond narrow occupational self-interest and professional exclusion, the barriers between the different professions may come to be seen as potentially surmountable.

14 Nurses, management and morale: A diagnosis of decline in the NHS hospital service

Stephen Ackroyd

Introduction

Much of the recent research that bears on the experience of hospital nurses, the front line troops of the hospital service, has consistently revealed a good deal of distress and dissatisfaction (Mackay, 1988, 1989, 1990; Hockey, 1987; Francis et al., 1993). Although wastage from the profession has subsided from the very high levels recorded in recent years as the most recent recession has deepened, there remains considerable concern about the loss of trained personnel from the nursing profession. At the very least, it is clear that nursing is passing through a period of upheaval and change. Some research of my own supports this conclusion, indicating that the effect of change may be very damaging: not only is morale amongst nurses low, but it is also probably symptomatic of fundamental changes in their outlook and behaviour. There is every indication that the traditionally strong professional ethics of the nurse are being re-evaluated and, possibly, discarded by significant numbers of the profession (Ackroyd, 1993a). The question is now not whether a change in the outlook and behaviour of nurses is occurring, but how rapidly it is moving and with what consequences.

In this chapter, a case will be made that the problems of nurses in the NHS hospitals today have a great deal to do with current policies towards the provision of hospital services. These are having a considerable effect on the role of the nurse and more generally on the effectiveness of the service. Even without such policy developments as the introduction of general management, nursing would be under considerable pressure from such things as the increasing number of treatments available (not to mention their generally increased technical sophistication) and the increasing interest in health care and its quality on the part of the general public. In these circumstances,

222

the adoption of inappropriate forms of management can be seen to make the problems of the nurse — which are not at all insoluble in themselves — a great deal worse.

It is undeniable that there are some key processes of change acting on the NHS, which have been in motion for some time, and which have effects that are not entirely good. However, these could, relatively easily, be identified, understood and, where necessary, checked. But it is not clear that the adoption of the directive 'general management' now being rapidly introduced in realization of the Griffiths reforms will have the desired effects. So far, such obvious objectives as reducing the costs of care, increasing effectiveness in delivery, improving the experience of treatment for patients, and, last but not least, improving the quality of work experience for professional staff, are not being achieved. As this chapter is being written, the daily papers are reporting that the waiting lists for NHS surgery have topped one million people for the first time. Indeed, it is by no means clear that general management can solve the problems that the hospital service now faces. Put simply, the adoption of directive 'general management' following the Griffiths Report (1983), which has been consolidated in the years since, is based on the misconception that there needs to be fundamental changes in the direction of a market basis for health care provision.

Historical structure of the NHS hospital service

The hospital service within the NHS always was an unorthodox structure. This is because the organization was not carefully designed. Existing hospitals were simply grouped together under the control of local councils — as a result of a political deal with the doctors made by the Labour government — in the aftermath of the Second World War (Klein, 1989). Certainly, writers and analysts who have examined the NHS hospitals since the war have found that they were, organizationally speaking, very unusual. Davies and Francis, for example, writing in 1976, argued that the NHS hospital was neither a classic bureaucracy nor a professional organization: it combined aspects of both. Moreover, there were distinct aspects of political coordination present as well. Although the NHS hospitals were soon taken out of the control of local councils, the hospital boards and health authorities which were set up instead were recognizably political structures. The analysis advanced by Davies and Francis (1976) was that there were elements of three types of hierarchy in NHS hospitals: clinical–professional, administrative–bureaucratic and political. As such, these organizations were fascinating objects for the organizational analyst:

they simply did not fit the prescriptions of organization theory. It was a puzzle how such organizations worked at all, never mind effectively. The results of research into such questions were to show the ways in which there was practical accommodation between these different organizational hierarchies. In practice the bureaucratic organization accommodated itself to professional authority by various mechanisms and professional authority deferred to political power on a regular basis. By virtue of there being informal and cooperative relations in the interstices of formal hierarchies, elements of different hierarchies coexisted, and the organization continued to function effectively. There was what might be called a continuous 'politics of accommodation', in which practical rules of conduct regulated relationships between different occupational groups. Indeed, for some writers (e.g. Anthony and Reed, 1990; Ackroyd, 1992) the development of informal and regulative relationships of this kind was the key to the practical efficiency of public services, and the basis on which the management of hospitals could and should be developed. In short, the basis of the efficient working of the hospital service was the cooperation of different professional groups, which involved a good deal of self-management.

Whilst practical self-management in the delivery of care was the basis for the functioning of the NHS hospitals, this worked inside the tripartite formal structure that has been described. There was not, however, equality between the political, the administrative–bureaucratic and clinical–professional spheres. Although there was, supposedly, local political control of the NHS, the consultants, as the dominant group within the clinical–professional hierarchy, had a decisive influence on events. They had themselves significant representation on the hospital boards and health authorities, and so could shape policy and influence critical decisions. Administration was also quite highly developed from the early days of the NHS hospital service, but was even more firmly subordinated to the clinical hierarchy. It had mainly record-keeping and servicing functions. Administrators exercised rather little authority. In short, hospitals were clinically rather than administratively or politically directed. The doctors' clinical authority and prestige — informally at least — was the lynch-pin of the system. But the key role of the nurses in making the system work, in delivering the majority of patient care, and in many other organizing activities, was also very important. Because of the centrality of the health workers in the arrangement, this pattern of organization has been described by Klein (1989) as being basically a 'producer's cooperative'. It has been argued elsewhere that this was a distinctive form of management as well (see Ackroyd, 1992), since the producers of hospital treatment (the doctors and nurses) effectively coordinated and directed the organizations in which they worked.

It ought to be acknowledged more fully that the practical activity of the nurses, and, in particular, their organizational skills, were extremely important to the delivery of hospital care and to hospital organization. Their activity had several aspects, the most obvious of which was their clinical role. But this extended into and included many organizational and managerial activities. By converting the clinical decisions of doctors into what we might call 'regimes of care', which include the organization of all activities on wards, nurses managed the practical delivery of hospital care without external direction. Nurses did more than simply extend clinical aspects of doctoring. In particular, they provided coordination — arranging the movements of patients, ensuring supplies of material to the wards and managing the cooperation of other health professionals. More than any other group, they orchestrated the activity of the hospital. Hence, a good deal of practical management of personnel and material was necessarily a part of the traditional nursing role. Although such activities were subordinated to clinical matters in their perceived importance by nurses, for whom their role has always been, first and foremost, a clinical activity, their practical organizational skill was an extremely important contribution to hospital organization. The loss of these functions with the development of specialized management has been fateful for nurses.

The importance of the nurses in securing control of the hospital service with the clinicians can hardly be exaggerated. That the nurses secured such a central position within the NHS hospitals was entirely predictable. A cooperative division of labour between doctors and nurses long predated the NHS. Gamarnikow (1978) sees the development of nursing as a replication of the paternalistic relations of the Victorian family in the world of work. Between around 1870, when the largely female profession of nursing was first established, and 1948, when the National Health Service was legally constituted, the doctors and nurses had evolved a stable pattern for working together (Abel-Smith, 1960). The doctors were always the senior partners in health care provision, of course. As today, it is they who stipulated the curative elements of any treatment, leaving the nurse to put a package of care — of which the drugs or treatment were just one element — into practical effect. Working in close cooperation with the doctors, however, was no doubt responsible for the nurses adopting many of the patterns of behaviour and conduct already developed by the doctors. The nurses adopted a similar graded hierarchy; for example, strong professional ethics and similar arrangements for licensing practitioners. This practical partnership was effective, and for decades was the basis of the successful production of hospital care. With some justification, nurses and many other observers see every reason to try to retain many features of this tried and tested division of labour.

But things are changing: the work and conditions of the nurse are no longer simply the product of tradition and of behaving according to ingrained standards acquired during training. For reasons yet to be considered, nurses are having to respond to new demands. No less than three significant kinds of new demand are being made. In addition to new technical demands for new treatments and procedures, there are two other sources of change affecting traditional regimes of care. On the one hand there is the public, in the shape of patients and their relatives, who are becoming more vocal in their requests; on the other hand there are the new managers, who are insisting that nurses respond to managerial directives as well as traditional definitions of hospital care. The managers have been eroding traditional organizational functions of nurses and eroding their autonomy. The result is that only a minority of nurses today regard their work as a vocation as they used to do (Mackay, 1990; Francis et al., 1993). Morale has taken a nose-dive, and wastage from the profession is high. A good part of the diagnosis of these symptoms must feature changes in management and organization, and the reallocation to administrators of the organizing tasks that were historically part of the role of the nurse.

Despite their organizational unorthodoxy, the NHS hospitals were remarkable organizations. Throughout the 1950s, 60s and 70s, the service delivered — and still does — a high level of medical services to millions of people. It has an enviable record of clinical success and public satisfaction. Paradoxically, however, high levels of performance have not in any way reduced the task that confronts the service. Surprising though it may seem, the provision of health care does not reduce appetites for health and health care; on the contrary, it is one of the factors that causes them to increase. In the circumstances, local political control was, increasingly ineffective in rationing provision and keeping costs down. The public demanded more and more. In response, doctors innovated more and more treatments. The consequence of these developments was that costs greatly increased and constantly threatened to spiral out of control. As will be argued, a key outcome of these processes was the partial disassembly of the producer's cooperative type of management.

The main reason for this was that increasing costs produced, little by little, almost exclusive subsidy of health services by the central state; and, along with that, the exertion of central control on costs. Inevitably, of course, growth in administration also contributed to increased costs, and so exacerbated rather than reduced the underlying problem. In the 1970s and 80s, administrative development was evident, adding greatly to overheads. But this development was not merely the expansion of traditional administrative services which, as I have argued, were essentially support services for clinical initiatives.

It also involved the extension of administrative authority and control into new areas of hospital organization — many of which were traditionally the responsibility of the clinical hierarchy of doctors and nurses. As a result, the producer's cooperative form of management was increasingly challenged by what we should recognize as a centrally directed form of administration developed to extend control over expenditure. In this emergent management system, the administrative cadre forms a link between the central government and local structures. The administrative cadre is the means by which local control of budgets is established and enforced. In this arrangement the administrative cadre becomes much stronger, extending new forms of control which, among other things, encroach on the traditional organizational autonomy of the clinical hierarchy.

This, then, was the NHS hospital system at the close of the period which can be characterized as that of its greatest success, and which, for the sake of argument, can be identified as the end of the 1970s:

- Hospitals were still nominally in the control of local health authorities with political control, but were also increasingly subject to administrative direction emanating from the central state.
- A centrally directed and growing administrative cadre was increasingly developing accountancy-based limits on expenditure with the aim of curbing costs.
- Administrative overheads and the costs of an increasing range of treatments and clinical services were rapidly growing. Medical services were stretched by provision not only of standard treatments and procedures, but of many innovatory treatments as well. A good number of these were of questionable value and/or had a very small number of potential beneficiaries, whilst reducing the availability of resources for routine treatments. Waiting lists as well as costs were increasing. Some routine medical procedures were often not readily available in some localities.
- The general public was becoming increasingly restive about the services provided to them and increasingly concerned to have a say about the availability of services and their quality.

The combination of these factors would lead to a relative decline in the efficiency and effectiveness of the NHS hospital service over the next decades, despite the increasing resources devoted to it. The government's solution to these problems was the introduction of general management emerging from the Griffiths reforms (1983). It is an aim of the remainder of this chapter to question the likelihood of success for these changes and possible alternatives to them.

Organizational problems of the NHS in the last decade

An elementary but useful kind of analysis of organizations, stake-holder analysis, may be used to consider the forces acting on the NHS hospitals in recent times, and to consider the question of the likely effect of the introduction of general management. Stakeholder analysis lists the parties in and around organizations that have an interest in them. It also considers the characteristic orientation of stakeholders towards the organization and the powers and resources available to them to achieve their ends. Finally, stakeholder analysis considers the shifts in internal alliances that particular dispositions of power and resources are likely to bring about.

The major external stakeholders in the NHS at the time of the Griffiths reforms in the early 1980s were just two: the central government, and the general public. The primary interest of the former was in limiting costs (and had much more of an interest in this than political structures in the locality) and only secondarily accepting the need for an adequate level of service. Hence, there was pressure from the government to limit costs, and a growing realization that local political control was often quite ineffective. On the other hand, the interests of the general public were pulling in a quite opposite direction — towards the improvement of basic care and constant pressure for the provision of highly specialized treatments. Most importantly, however, alliances of internal stakeholders (the doctors, nurses and administrators) with external stakeholders changed the pattern of relationships between occupational groups in the hospital service profoundly, as we shall see. Only the nurses as an occupational group had an unequivocal interest in retaining the status quo, and would continue to attempt to hold the delivery of care together in its traditional pattern. By contrast with this, the aspirations of the other internal stakeholders would all have an impact on the terms and conditions under which nurses work.

The disposition of external stakeholders in the NHS has produced a new configuration of internal alliances among major occupational groups. On the one hand there is the consumer–provider relation-ship, and the impact that increased consumerism has had on the provision of treatment. This has seen dramatic growth in the scale and range of provision. On the other hand there is the government–administrator relationship, and the impact of increasing demands for control of costs by the government. This in turn has caused admin-istration to grow in scale and influence. The meshing of these two processes has been less than beneficial. This is because, embedded in these relationships, there are alternative and partly incompatible principles on which the organization of the NHS hospitals can be based.

Development of the consumer–provider relationship

Perhaps the most obvious aspect is that the relationship between the hospital doctors and the public is a reciprocal relationship. By reducing the costs for patients of medical treatment to around zero, the advent of the NHS brought about a very close correspondence of interest between the doctors and the patients. As a result, the doctors have been willing providers of more and more forms of treatment. The public have been avid, and sometimes gullible or credulous, consumers. Quite clearly, the NHS has not inhibited research and development, and there are many examples of treatments initiated in the NHS that are acknowledged to be the best in the world. But a consequence of this arrangement has inevitably been to draw resources — both of expertise and money — from other areas of work. The organization of the NHS has been sufficiently dynamic to allow the emergence of centres of excellence but, equally, the supply of routine treatments — the unglamourous 'haemorrhoids and hips' — have been neglected to some extent because so much skilled manpower and resources are used for more exotic procedures. It is precisely in the area of routine treatments — which can greatly improve the quality of life for many people — where waiting lists are longest. Thus, a less fully acknowledged aspect of the diversification that increased demand has called forth, is the variation in the standard of service available. In brief, there are some marked differences in the effectiveness of hospitals, units and individual doctors that are not known to the public. Certainly, the new consumer orientation of the medical profession has not involved the complete sovereignty of the consumer. The doctors are still very powerful in limiting information and rationing forms of provision. More pertinently, it is they who are gradually engineering the extension of private treatment, and dictating the directions of this growth.

Clearly also, however, the consumer–provider relationship has been strongly influenced by changes in the attitudes of consumers. Public service workers everywhere are finding that they have to take notice of what the public wants much more than in the past. Failure to do so can lead to the withdrawal of consent and to anger and aggression. In other public services, similar effects can be observed. The police present themselves as a 'service' like education, and, in turn, schools have to compete for pupils. The shifts here have been more than cosmetic. Indeed, changes in the attitudes of consumers of the health service have, among other things, helped to fuel a great deal of innovation. The extension of provision has been associated with a steady erosion of the distance between providers of care and consumers. It is no longer possible for doctors to hide, quite so completely, behind their magisterial authority. Doctors (or very often nurses as their proxies) have to explain many things that they did not formerly. We may describe changed attitudes as interacting with provision to produce a democratization of the relations of health care provision. These changes have profoundly altered the conditions of demand for health services.

Development of the government–administration relationship

As has already been stated, the administrative function in the NHS hospitals was always well-developed in some of its aspects. Having carried out organizational research within NHS hospitals in the 1970s and 80s, I can report at first hand that the record-keeping functions of administration were extensive. However, many records were kept that had no valuable managerial purpose. Often the justification for such records was the need to make returns to central government, particularly the Department of Health. But there was much detail kept that had no such use or indeed other conceivable function. Record-keeping was just something that had always been done. At no time has there been any serious attempt to reduce the size of the administrative cadre necessary for traditional administration, and there has been growth in the size of the administrative cadre with central government's growing interest in reducing costs. By 1974, the NHS had absorbed most of the remaining functions of the local authority medical officers of health, and no less than four tiers of administration were extant in hospital provision. By this time, too, direct management from Whitehall of regional health authorities had been established, which in turn subordinated two other levels of administrative control in the shape of area authorities and the districts. In 1982, as a prelude to the introduction of general management in hospitals, the area health authorities, as the middle tier of administration, were abolished, with regions controlling the activities of a larger number of smaller authorities. However, there was little or no reduction of the administrative overhead or of the numbers of administrative staff employed. The administrative hierarchy was not, in fact, reduced by many of the government reforms, despite a recurrent rhetorical appeal to the need for economy and the desirability of autonomous and decentralized management. As Pollitt (1993) suggests of the White Paper of 1989:

> 'The overall effect of these changes was to introduce a clear and effective chain of management command running from districts through regions to the Chief Executive (an office introduced by Griffiths in 1983) and from there to the Secretary of State.'

The development of centrally directed management gradually and inevitably changed the character and functions of hospital administration. It moved away from a role that was supportive of the clinical hierarchy, towards more directive activities based on the authority of central government. In this change, NHS administrators have combined their traditional record-keeping functions with an interest in controlling expenditure. As they have developed this function, they have gradually set limits and controls on the initiatives of hospital doctors and made incursions into the traditional organizational autonomy of nurses. Accounting practices that were, at best, a small part of record-keeping historically, have grown in importance to become a central feature of administration, and basis for decision-making (Coombs and Green, 1989; Nanaphiet, 1992). The new outlook of the administrative–managerial cadre has inevitably shaped the style of new management that has developed in the NHS. It is now mainly orientated towards control of operating costs. Its activity, far from being simply supportive of the activities of health professionals, now involves the exertion of control over them primarily through placing limits on budgets. But, in many ways, the new health service management is primitive and inappropriate — it employs book-keeping rather than accrual accounting or systems models, and is still excessively bureaucratic.

Examining the basis of the consumer–provider relationship in the NHS, it is clear that the basic organizational problem is that the service is the victim of its own success. It is the satisfactory nature of provision which, more than anything, has fuelled demand. In view of this it seems quite questionable whether the appropriate thing to do is to introduce quite different principles for the provision of care. The basis for provision to the present has been need — as defined mainly by the clinicians and, secondarily, by the public. Under general management, the proposal is for provision under an administered market. This arrangement attaches significant costs to provision by clinicians and so allocates the administrative–managerial group a key role setting limits on provision. It is they who decide the relative costs within which clinical provision and consumer choices can be made. It can be argued, however, that a more rational (and less costly) response would be to extend and augment existing relations of provision so that they can undertake any necessary rationing in conjunction with their clientele. What seems to be missed is that management in the administrative form now being developed displaces a system of self-management (and which, with some development, could continue to be viable). As it is, the new management has the effect of challenging the traditional vocational conception of the nurse as the basis for organizing hospital care.

Not only are current developments unnecessary from a more

adequate view of what management should be, but they also represent an enormous and permanent addition to costs. A parallel example may help to bring home these points. Only quite recently it was realized by managers in manufacturing that enormous savings could be made by abolishing that class of worker (inspectors) whose sole function was to check the quality of the output of other workers; and, by making sure each worker produced a quality product in the first place, jobs could be enlarged as well. The introduction of general management in the NHS seems to be an example of an opposite process. The capacity for efficient self-management is precisely what the nurses have amply demonstrated in their history. Overlaying this system of self-management with management by cost controllers is analogous to the introduction of a class of inspectors whose criteria of adequate service are quite different from those traditionally invoked. The main contribution of this development is to introduce a new basis for control and direction, one which cuts across existing processes, whilst greatly adding to costs. The paradox of the health service is that the health providers have been mostly providing a quality service, and which many from overseas admire, without significant external managerial intervention and direction. It is certainly difficult to see how the activities of 'management by book-keeping' can do very much to dramatically improve the quality or effectiveness of care. What is needed is the development of the consumer–provider relationship to include the management of all aspects of care. This proposal has been referred to elsewhere as 'participative management' (Ackroyd, 1992, 1993b). In essence, participative management involves developing existing managerial aspects of the consumer–provider relationship rather than the managerial aspects of the relationship between government and local administration.

Effects on the situation of the nurse

Many of the contemporary changes in the work of the nurse can be related to the processes set out above. The nurse has always been between the doctor and the public, a position that is becoming more and more uncomfortable with the emergence and development of health care consumerism. Increasingly also, the nurse has to face the attentions of the new managers, and this is having an even more dramatic effect on experience at work. This can be seen by considering the impact of the developments described above on the traditional role of the nurse.

As a work role, nursing has always had some remarkable features. High levels of satisfaction typically accompany periods of intense work. This in itself is not an unusual thing, especially amongst skilled and professional employees. To the casual observer, however, nursing is not a skilled job. There are, in fact, rather few aspects of the work in general nursing that would be automatically defined as being skilled. This is particularly true amongst unqualified nurses and nursing auxiliaries where there is a complete lack of content that would conventionally be defined as requiring skill. Even today, amongst higher graded staff, highly technical aspects of the work — the need to monitor medical technology or requirements for handling and administering drugs, for example — are often quite limited. But it would be wrong to conclude that nursing is an unskilled job. Even the lowest grades of nurse exhibit a lot of professional pride and identification with their work which is neither false nor misplaced. Surprising though it may seem, working hard, in what is conventionally regarded as a menial way — feeding, washing, dressing, cleaning, making beds, preparing for theatre, and dealing with difficult relatives, in succession, all day long — is consistent with a satisfying work experience. The problems of past and present are not that there is too much work to be done: the opposite is, in fact, often the case. The skill of the nurse is precisely that of being able to define and accomplish what needs to be done for the patients, to decide the order and priority of tasks according to their therapeutic benefits, and then to accomplish them. The vocational aspect of identification with the job has as an important ingredient this ability and willingness to manage the delivery of care. With good reason, all grades of nurse often do express high levels of job satisfaction (Ackroyd, 1993a).

Because self-management is a central aspect of the vocation of the nurse, many of the changes in work tasks that follow from the development of the consumer–provider relationship are being successfully accommodated by the profession. The need to know about new and complex treatments and procedures is, more often than not, a source of pride. Nurses have accepted new technologies and new regimes of care continuously in times gone by without very much difficulty, and continue to do so. It is remarkable that, in discussions of the introduction of new technology in the NHS it is intrusion of managerial information technology that is cited as the source of discontent and rejection and not the introduction of medical technology as such (Coombs and Green, 1989; McNulty and McLellan, 1990). By and large, the ability to deal with technology is generally recognized to enhance the standing of the profession. In addition, however, managing the practical aspects of care has always been central to the nursing role. It is part of the skill of the 'good nurse' (Mackay, 1989, 1992) to be able to handle practical matters like obstreperous patients and their families as part and parcel of competent performance. This also continues. Indeed, it was one of the shocking and revelatory accidental discoveries of a recent period of fieldwork to note just how many highly charged and emotional encounters there

are between patients and nurses on wards today. The problem for
the nurse in this situation is that she or he must often face trucu-
lence and argumentativeness without either much medical knowledge
or managerial authority. However, it was equally noteworthy that
such incidents of public anger as were witnessed were not treated
as particularly remarkable by nurses themselves, but were seen as
everyday matters to be taken in their stride. Handling such situations
can readily be seen as a necessary extension of the practical skills of
the job, as part of the professional expertise of trained nurses, and is
regarded as such by them.

The development of consumerism, however, has not led, as might
be expected, to the extension of the nurses' role in the management
of patients. Management of patients — in the sense not only of handling their needs and complaints, but also of controlling their movements in and out of the hospitals and through a sequence of procedures — was once almost the exclusive concern of the nursing hierarchy. The matron of a large hospital undertook a great deal of its
day-to-day management in this sense, as an extension of her position as senior nurse. This function has, undoubtedly, decayed under
the development of centrally directed administration and management. The Salmon Report (1966) advocated the extension of management by nurses on the traditional hierarchical model — and drew on
an implicit comparison with industrial line management. Salmon is
perhaps best regarded, with the benefit of hindsight, as the last attempt
by the nursing profession to retain significant degrees of executive
authority, even if the main target of their aspiration in this respect
was their own membership. Clearly, however, the atrophy of the
more diffused managerial powers of the nurses is not desirable. There
is every indication that the introduction of self-selected criteria of
quality and service would be quite acceptable to nurses, as would
the participation in broader management decision-making. The
truncated experiments with team-based management in the 1970s,
finally acknowledged to a degree by the White Paper *Working for
Patients* in 1989, might have been the basis for a significant extension
of producer-cooperative relations into a new model of management.
The flattening of nursing hierarchies that is evident today can only
encourage team-working which, if the analysis deployed here is
correct, always was the basis of the efficient and effective delivery
of care in NHS hospitals. This would have been a fully participative
style of management — involving all health professionals and the
public in decision-making — which evolved its own criteria for
rationing. Potentially, participative management along these lines is
both efficient and effective. However, the real failure to develop this
style of management resulted from the failure to interest significant
numbers of senior doctors in setting up and running such a system.
Failing in this, the massive extension of general management — which

means, in effect, the continued imposition of a bureaucratic form of control and direction — had a certain inevitability.

General management: a solution or a problem?

The new managerial structures that have been gradually introduced into the National Health Service over the last two decades are designed to deal with the problems of provision in the following way. First, it is suggested that the existing system of provision is inefficient and wasteful. Secondly, new procedures and relationships can be introduced that will tighten up on waste, save money, and thus allow new procedures and treatments to be paid for. The idea is that the same inputs to the system can be put together in different combinations so that more adequate provision is secured for the same outlay. But it is doubtful whether much saving can be made in this way. There is little evidence that hospitals are actually systematically inefficient, as is now taken to be self-evident. In the private sector, very similar patterns of autonomous working as are common in the public services are now being advocated and adopted.

It is certainly correct that there were sources of waste in the old structures. One thinks, for example, of such things as clinical procedures that offered little benefit or which were enormously costly. Methods for funding of new and experimental treatments and research is one of the most needed reforms of the NHS. Although constrained somewhat by the new consumerism in health care, doctors still have too much power in determining their level of clinical activity and in rationing provision. There are still too few checks on the inefficient surgeon or inept consultant, and the waste from under-used resources and technology is considerable. There is an enormous and largely unacknowledged problem of too much bureaucracy and too many accountants. But none of these sources of waste will actually be directly confronted by the new forms of management. The flaw in the argument for general management is that there is not the scope for the reduction in costs from configuring factors of provision in different ways: costs are, inevitably, likely to increase in response to public demand. The amounts of possible savings are, in any case, greatly outweighed by the costs of the new managers necessary to make them. The internal market, and the general management associated with it, is simply a costly way of limiting the overall level of public spending on health care, without appearing to be.

But, more importantly in the context of this exercise, there is a really destructive cost of general management that has been so far unacknowledged. This is the effect that many of its procedures and mechanisms have on nurse morale. Given the cost-limitation activities of managers, it is obvious that nurses and nursing will come in for a good deal of attention from them. Wages are, after all, the largest single cost to the NHS and nurses are the largest occupational group. Moreover, it is nurses who use the bulk of the consumables in treatment. In addition, they are professionally less well-organized than doctors, and have neither the professional power nor status of doctors with which to counter the authority of management. One way and another, nurses have come in for a good deal of attention from the new management.

The cost-saving controls exerted by new management fall disproportionately on nursing activities, and this had a considerable impact on nurses' experience of work in recent years. It is obvious why this is so. The point to note is that management is imposing the rationing of hospital care in ways which contradict the principles embedded in the vocational training of the nurse. Nurse training, and most of their practical experience, leads them to place the welfare of the patient first, and to organize and manage practical affairs in a way that directly supports therapeutic ends. Thus the practical activity of nursing has entailed considerable involvement in management, although they have not tended to think of it in these terms. As has been argued in the body of this chapter, nurses have been effective managers to such an extent that their activity has actually organized the working of hospitals. Despite this, the new management has successfully imposed a new definition of what counts as efficient management. This has forced nurses back on to a narrow, clinical definition of their competence; but still leaves them having to defend a concern about standards of care. From the point of view of the nurse, management is imposing a concern for things that are rather unimportant (how much things cost), neglecting or being ignorant of things that are very important (patient welfare) whilst effectively denying the legitimacy of objections to current practice based on alternative models of management.

In sum, there are many indications that directive general management is the source of the nurses' inability to respond positively in the current situation. What management requires of them cuts across and often contradicts precepts of their professional training. In fact it is not only or even mainly that managers have required new procedures from nurses, or that managerial decisions about such things as reduced manning levels, have made working life problematic. In essence, it is because general management has entailed active encroachment into the autonomy of the nurse. Imposed priorities, driven primarily by the desire to husband resources and to ration provision, have significantly disrupted the self-managed pattern of work organization that is the basis of the vocational character of nursing, without taking away responsibility for the quality of care. Managers need to take note of the consequences of this. It is a salient fact that morale can be shown to be lowest precisely in those areas of hospitals, and amongst those staff, that are functionally most important for the hospital organization (Ackroyd, 1993a).

References

Abel-Smith B (1960) *A History of the Nursing Profession*. London: Heinemann.

Ackroyd S (1992) Nurses and the prospects for participative management in the NHS. In: Soothill K et al. (Eds), *Themes and Perspectives in Nursing*. London: Chapman & Hall.

Ackroyd S (1993a) Towards an understanding of nurses' attachments to their work. *Journal of Advances in Health and Nursing Care*; **2**: (3), 23–46.

Ackroyd S (1993b) A case of arrested development? Some consequences of inadequate management in the British police. *International Journal of Public Sector Management*; **6**: (2), 4–15.

Anthony PD, Reed MI (1990) Management roles and relationships in a district health authority. *International Journal of Health Care*; **2**: (2), 20–31.

Coombs R, Green K (1989) Work, organisation and product change in the service sector: the case of the UK National Health Service. In: Wood S (Ed.), *The Transformation of Work?* London: Unwin Hyman.

Davies C, Francis A (1976) *Perceptions of Structure in NHS Hospitals*. Staffordshire: University of Keele (sociological review monograph 22).

Dawson S, et al (1992) Management, competition and professional practice: medicine and the market place. In: Whipp R, Bresnen M, Davies A (Eds), *The Challenge of Change* (Proceedings of the Employment Research Annual Conference, Cardiff).

Francis B, Peelo M, Soothill K (1993) NHS nursing: vocation, career or just a job? In: Soothill K et al. (Eds), *Themes and Perspectives in Nursing*. London: Chapman & Hall.

Gamarnikow E (1978) Sexual division of labour: the case of nursing. In: Kuhn A, Wolpe A (Eds), *Feminism and Materialism*. London: Routledge.

Griffiths R (1983) *NHS Management Enquiry*. London: DHSS.

Hockey J (1987) A picture of pressure. *Nursing Times*; **83**: (2), 26–27.

Klein R (1989) *The Politics of the National Health Service*, 2nd edn. London: Longman.

Mackay L (1988) No time to care. *Nursing Times*; **84**: (11), 33–34.

Mackay L (1989) *Nursing a Problem*. Milton Keynes: Open University Press.

Mackay L (1990) Nursing: just another job? In: Abbott P, Wallace C (Eds), *The Sociology of the Caring Professions*. Basingstoke: Falmar Press.

Mackay L (1992) Nursing and doctoring: where's the difference? In: Soothill K et al. (Eds), *Themes and Perspectives in Nursing*. London: Chapman & Hall.

McNulty D, McLellan F (1990) Nursing and the new technology. In: Abbott P, Wallace C (Eds), *The Sociology of the Caring Professions*. Basingstoke: Falmar Press.

Nanaphiet J (1992) Decision-making and accounting: resource allocation in the NHS. In: Gowler et al. (Eds), *Case Studies in Organisational Behaviour*, 2nd edn. London: Paul Chapman.

Pollitt C (1993) *Managerialism and the Public Services*, 2nd edn. Oxford: Basil Blackwell.

Salmon Report (1966) *Report of the Committee on Senior Nurse Staff Structure*. London: HMSO.

Strong P, Robinson J (1990) *The NHS: Under New Management*. London: Oxford University Press.

15 Nurses and doctors: A problem of partnership

Kevin Kendrick

Introduction

The nurse–doctor relationship is at the centre of health care practice and delivery. Traditionally, this association has involved the nurse giving prescribed care based upon the doctor's orders. Such convention has continued to fuel the image of the nurse as the doctor's handmaiden and servile helper. Recent innovations have been introduced to give nurses a greater sense of their role as responsible and autonomous practitioners; Project 2000, the higher award, and open access to higher education all indicate the dynamic educational developments which steer the nursing profession towards the millennium. These educational themes have been partnered by evolving ideas and unfolding roles in clinical nursing; primary nursing, nursing development units, clinical practice development nurses and the scope of professional practice all point towards the increasingly autonomous remit of the contemporary nurse.

Despite these broad attempts to 'professionalize' nursing, research indicates that doctors and members of the public continue to see nurses as subservient, passive and acquiescent (Mackay, 1989, 1993; Holloway, 1992). Nurses and doctors undoubtedly have key roles to play in the provision of health care, yet tremendous disparity exists between the two professions. Chadwick and Tadd (1992) comment upon this position:

> 'Characteristically the doctor has been portrayed as "all knowing" and powerful; the nurse as caring, unselfish, obedient and submissive; and the patient as helpless and utterly trusting.' (p.49)

A central reason to explain the professional inequality between doctors and nurses is the different power base which each group holds. Many complex factors have contributed to the evolution of this power-based scenario. Turner (1986) argues that the servile themes traditional to nursing has allowed doctors to prescribe and delegate the activities of care-giving. Given the influence which medicine holds in contemporary health care, an examination of its evolution and themes will provide a degree of insight to explain the professional dichotomy which continues to exist between doctors and nurses.

The evolution of the medical model

The medical model has been the principal method, approach and knowledge base underpinning western health care for the last 300 years. A strong influence upon the development of the medical model emerged during the Renaissance and its chief exponent was the philosopher, Renè Descartes.

The Renaissance was a period of great intellectual growth; the boundaries of knowledge were constantly challenged as innovative thinking and enquiry caused academics to question traditional propositions. Descartes was a central figure in many philosophical and mathematical debates, devoting much of his attention to investigating the relationship between the mind and the body. What emerged from this was a radical enquiry which confronted and challenged all conventions concerning mind–body discourse.

Prior to the Renaissance, the dominant mode of thinking was that all actions were controlled and ordained by divine will. Descartes contested these themes, believing that the mind could best be seen as an autonomous entity free from external influence. Such reasoning was based on the premise that the body was directly analogous with a machine because both had parts which could break and need repair. The final stage in Descartes' argument continued this theme and maintained that the body should be studied by reducing it into components and sections. Initially this took the form of splitting the body into systems but has progressed, with scientific advancement, to the point that we can now study at the submolecular level.

Descartes' philosophical view of the split between the mind and the body is known as 'Cartesian dualism'; it has been consistently challenged and questioned by philosophers during subsequent centuries, especially the philosophical behaviourists (e.g. Ryle, 1949). However, by attempting to give philosophical rigour and analysis to a conceptual split between mind and body, Descartes greatly influenced the method of scientific medical enquiry; he provided the impetus for ever-increasing specialization and treating parts of the body rather than the body as a whole.

Cartesian dualism placed the body firmly in the medical domain and gave licence to a reductionistic approach which rapidly gained ascendancy as the most scientifically acceptable method of discovering new knowledge. This mode of practice has contributed greatly to the way in which medical research has developed and is carried out. Humankind has benefited from this, and the efficacy of contemporary medical therapies and treatments certainly has its roots in the mechanistic ethos of Descartes' treatise. Medical specialists offer a breadth of knowledge and expertise which could never be found in the generic practitioner.

For example, oncology would never have existed if the pathology of cancer had not been reduced to the intricate physiology of the cell. Emerging from this is a strong argument in support of the essential themes which underpin the medical model; if medicine's main aim is to confront the disease process and do everything realistically possible to achieve a cure, then Descartes' exemplar provides a valid basis for such an endeavour.

Returning to the theme of nurses in relation to doctors, the dominant image consists of the nurse implementing care which the doctor has prescribed. To a degree, this process can be traced to the influence of the medical model upon nursing and the division of labour which subsequently emerged in the practice setting. Whilst the medical model can be accepted as the mode of operation for doctors, whether such an approach is suitable to nursing needs to be questioned.

The medical model and nursing practice

As noted above, the chief remit of the medical model is to address the pathological processes of disease; the success of which is the curing of the patient. However, when these themes become the basis for nursing practice it creates an atmosphere which can lead to the patient being seen as a condition rather than a person. This is especially true when a patient has a terminal illness. Many writers have argued that nurses who practise within the framework of the medical model reduce the patient to the status of a condition because this allows them somewhere to hide from reflection on their own mortality (Menzies, 1970; Thompson, 1979; McIntosh, 1977). This shift from the patient as a valued subject to devalued object is found in many of the ward-based activities operating when nursing care is influenced by the medical model. Pearson and Vaughan (1986) comment upon the relationship between the medical model and nursing:

'However, the biomedical model is reductionistic and dualistic in approach — it both reduces the human body to a set of related parts and it separates the mind from the body, and its common use in nursing is no longer appropriate. It is not geared to the needs of individuals and its dominant effect on health care has led to it being used in the interest of health professionals rather than those who seek, need or are directed to health care. Therefore, it can no longer be acknowledged as a possible choice when nursing teams are selecting a model for practice.' (p. 25)

Even today, when nursing models and individualized care are playing an increasingly prominent role, it is still common to find work organized according to tasks, routine and physical care-giving. This approach finds particular prominence in the organization of work in wards for care of the elderly. Kitson (1991) comments upon a lack of distinction between the medical and nursing frameworks by stating:

> 'When one considers the corresponding nursing care model, which could have served as the theoretical framework for the geriatric nursing care model, a major problem arises, namely that nursing does not have an operational model independent of the medical model.' (p. 23)

This failure to develop a framework which establishes those characteristics of nursing separate and distinct from medicine cannot be blamed solely on the dominant nature of the medical model. To use terms such as 'autonomous', 'responsible' and 'accountable' in relation to nursing practice seems quite facile when the medical model holds such influence over the approach used for the delivery of care. Nurses must accept a degree of culpability for the level of inertia which has allowed this position to continue and prosper. Kitson comments upon this professional indictment by stating:

> 'Nursing practice seemed content to follow in the wake of medical innovation and change. In consequence, nursing was unable to consider seriously the complexities involved in providing care. Nursing also failed to determine its essential components and failed to build a framework that would ensure the goal of care was achieved in the practice setting.' (p. 220)

Why has nursing allowed itself to have been so affected by the themes underpinning medicine? Further analysis is needed to identify those factors which have contributed to and continue to influence the biomedical model as a dominant influence upon nursing.

The power of stereotypes

Both doctors and nurses are involved in the business of caring. However, there are fundamental differences in the themes which inform the delivery of care by each group. Medicine intrinsically holds a male world view of objectivity and value-freedom. This approach involves a causal explanation of disease where care is predominantly associated with cure. Conversely, nursing is value-laden and traditionally associated with the nurturing aspects of maternalism. These different representations have contributed to an image of the passive and unquestioning nurse in compliance to the dominant and patriarchal doctor.

Biological determinism has played a key role in promoting the idea of nursing as women's work. Perhaps the earliest proponent of this notion was Florence Nightingale who equated the idea of being a good nurse to that of being a 'good' woman. Gamarnikow (1978) examined Nightingale's writing and clearly illustrates the emphasis which is placed upon female virtues as a basis for the moral aptitude required for nursing:

> 'Nightingale insisted on the existence of a close link between nursing and femininity, the latter being defined by a specific combination of moral qualities which differentiated men from women. The success of nursing reforms depended primarily, according to Nightingale, on cultivating the "feminine" character, rather than on training and education.' (p. 116)

The so-called 'feminine' traits to which Nightingale appeals are synonymous with the themes of domiciliary servitude and deference which have traditionally fettered women and men. In another seminal paper, Lewin (1977) presented a transactional analysis to describe a relation between the essence of nursing and the relationship between a mother and child:

> 'The identification of nursing with femaleness derives not only from its "unselfish service" component, but from the importance of physical nurturance, and a sort of material intimacy, which also enter into the image of nursing work. The close acquaintance of the nurse with the messy details of illness is not unlike the mother's necessary involvement with infantile body functions.' (p. 91)

The practice of nursing frequently involves caring for intimate aspects of the human condition. The aesthetically undesirable elements of dealing with faeces, urine, vomit and other physiological features are countered by the sense of bringing comfort to patients in need. Lewin draws an analogy between such essential activities and the role of the mother in caring for an infant. Both situations demand responsible actions but the key feature is the emphasis which is placed upon maternity, femaleness and being a woman. Such themes are seen as exclusively female because of the male world view which dominates society; this is mirrored by the disempowered standing which women have traditionally suffered in scenarios with men — within either the domestic or the clinical environment.

These stereotypical images of nursing being synonymous with motherhood and femaleness are supported by media representations which foster and promote the notion that nurses' work is subservient to that of doctors. Mackay (1989) comments upon this tendency by stating:

> 'Greater respect is bestowed on doctors because they can "cure"

people. Doctors can postpone death, therefore they command both authority and respect. Stereotypes in the mass media appear to enhance the status of doctors at the expense of nurses. Nurses are presented in the media as being less helpful and less empathetic to the needs of patients and doctors. Yet when the reality of nurses' work is considered, the stereotype is revealed for what it is: a put down of nurses and of women.' (p. 46)

The very essence of stereotypical imagery can create a labelling scenario which seldom reflects reality. Walsh (1991, p. 105) asks us to view stereotypical images of doctors and nurses with a critical gaze; failure to do so can lead to conflict: 'The reader should always beware stereotyping and those who would reduce medical–nursing relationships to a state of trench warfare!' Of course, nurses and doctors are as susceptible to the power of stereotyping as anybody else and this can mirror itself in the interprofessional relationships which exist between the two groups.

It may be argued that the clinical environment resembles a microcosm of the wider society; there are issues of status, class and a multitude of mechanisms implemented to try and maintain or jockey for power. Doctors enjoy more status because their work is prescriptive and nurses are traditionally trained to fulfil an unquestioning and compliant role (Bradshaw, 1984). Moreover, Braito and Caston (1983) argue that the majority of doctors come from higher socio-economic groups than their nursing counterparts, with all the associated factors of better educational qualifications and prestige. These complex issues display themselves in various ways at the clinical interface.

Power, rules and hierarchies

Interprofessional relationships between doctors and nurses have always been highly influenced by hierarchical considerations. This has intrinsic links with the cultural ethos of the British class system; nurses who have trained abroad are not constrained by this rigid framework and are able to address their relationship with doctors on a basis of much greater parity. Mackay (1993) comments upon this by stating:

'These overseas nurses may show none of the deference and acquiescence of the British trained nurse. They are not part of the class and status system. Because of that, these nurses are treated differently, enjoying a more equal relationship with the medical profession; and they treat doctors differently, as equals. These nurses can be particularly scathing about home grown nurses' refusal to question doctors' decisions or to take responsibility.' (p. 122)

Mackay goes on to make the interesting observation that such nurses do not perceive any disparity between themselves and doctors and that any conflict is more likely to occur with their British-trained nursing colleagues.

However, the vast majority of nurses and doctors have gained their professional qualifications in this country and comply with the hidden rules and agendas involved with that process. The process of learning to be a doctor or nurse is fraught with covert pressure to ascertain quickly the distinct cultural features which both professions have. Melia (1987) describes how student nurses quickly discover how being in hospital depersonalizes patients and that scant regard is paid to privacy or interpersonal space. This is at stark variance to the ideal which learners are taught in lectures prior to going into clinical areas. Eventually, continued exposure to situations which threaten patient's dignity or individuality leads to desensitization and the student nurse may no longer view such themes as essential to becoming accepted by one's peers. Thomson et al. (1988) reflect these themes in the following statement:

'The process of becoming a nurse is in some ways similar to that of becoming a patient. The loss of a certain amount of identity, taking on a generalised role and behaving accordingly, are experiences common to nurses and patients. The student has a uniform, the patient nightwear; decisions about day-to-day living have been taken from the person and placed in the hands of the organisation, for example, mealtimes, off-duty for the nurse, waking and sleeping times for the patient. New nurses often feel that they are in a rigid hierarchy which relies upon rank and punitive measures rather than rationality and reason.' (p. 24)

Conversely, Adshead and Dickenson (1993) argue that medical students see themselves as scientists with a clear clinical mandate to use these skills to diagnose, treat and cure disease. This level of objectivity is absent in student nurses who value more highly the elements of caring as opposed to curing. However, not only do medical students view their work as having more intrinsic value than nursing, but they also have negative role models who propagate the view that nurses are essentially there as a pair of 'helping hands'. These two disparate levels of initiation set the tone for future relationships which doctors and nurses experience in their clinical work; it is a scenario borne out by tradition and is a prominent feature in the status quo of ward-based reality. Mackay (1993, p. 65) argues that the difficult relationships which many students and junior doctors experience with their senior colleagues is based upon a circular process of accepting that dominant and brusque attitudes become more acceptable with increased seniority — this ethos is passed down the medical 'pecking order' and is an important part of the hidden agenda. Moreover, Mackay also comments that a similar process occurs in the relationships between doctors and nurses: 'The same circular process, of course, is to be found regarding nurses' experiences in their dealings with members of the medical profession. No wonder it is difficult to effect change.'

Early writers such as French and Raven (1959) used the term 'expert social power' to describe the level of knowledge which a professional may have, and how this can influence a position of private acceptance in either individuals or groups. This theme is further reinforced by Penner (1978, p. 85), who argues that professionals are perceived as having a strong knowledge base and, therefore, 'an expert has social power because they are perceived as correct'. Although the term 'professional' may be used in relation to both doctors and nurses, we have already seen that factors such as gender and class, and differences between the value which doctors and nurses hold towards each other's work, influence the perception of power at the clinical interface. Johnstone (1989) highlights this discrepancy between what nurses do and what doctors think they should and are capable of doing by stating:

> 'For example, some doctors apparently believe that nurses are incapable of sound rational thought, and are incapable of grasping the essence of sound moral thinking. These doctors are loath to accept that nurses have any independent moral responsibility when caring for patients. As these doctors are invariably in positions of power, they are more than able to ensure that a nursing perspective on patient care, and related moral issues, are effectively constrained.' (p. 1)

However, it would be inaccurate to suggest that doctors hold complete power in relationships with nurses.

Despite massive differences in pay, the position of sister is analogous with that of a medical consultant; each heads a team and each is vicariously responsible for the care which is given to patients by members of those teams. On this basis alone, the relationship between the sister and consultant must be both amicable and supportive. This relationship allows the sister to hold considerable influence regarding any problems involving the attitude or practices of junior doctors, as Mackay (1993, p. 66) states: '. . . life can, and will be, made pretty uncomfortable for any doctor who repeatedly rides roughshod over the more senior ward nurses'.

However, despite this level of authority, the reality is that, with regards to diagnosis and treatment, nurses are powerless and must await the legal prerequisite of 'doctors' orders' before implementing the care associated with such orders. Once again, the cure-oriented aspects of clinical medicine seem to hold more intrinsic worth than that of nursing's care-based elements. This is a theme which continues to influence the 'hidden agenda' in nurse/doctor relationships. While this perception is allowed to continue there is little chance of an enacted sense of parity between doctors and nurses. Adshead and Dickenson (1993) reflect these sentiments in the following:

> 'If nursing is defined as being about caring, and medicine about curing,

medicine will continue to be seen as more important. If the role of the female paradigm profession of nursing is seen as caring, the old stereotype of the nurse as the doctor's "helpmeet" will be revived. Caring is likely to be seen as less important than curing because we fear death and wrongly attribute to medicine the power to cure us of mortality.' (p. 167)

This inherent disparity between medicine and nursing is being challenged by innovations in both nurse education and practice.

Towards change

Nurse educators and theorists are striving to influence a paradigmal shift which will bring nursing to a position of professional equality with doctors. While life in the ivory towers of academia is versed in the rhetoric of accountable and autonomous practice, the reality for most nurses remains one of a subservience to doctors (Bridges, 1990). It is facile to use the language of professional rhetoric when the levels of morale and self-belief are so low among nurses (Barry et al., 1992). Moreover, a number of reports and papers comment on the high level of nurse wastage and poor esteem within the NHS, arguing that a fundamental shift in roles and attitude is needed if professional autonomy is to be achieved (e.g. Price Waterhouse, 1988; Martin and MacKean, 1988; Waite et al., 1989; Beardshaw and Robinson, 1990).

Arthurs (1992) argues that the schism between theoretical discourse and practical realities has increased the levels of uncertainty among clinical nurses. To read and hear of the revolutionary developments in education can lead the practitioner to a state of abject confusion. After all, how can all the talk about increased standing and autonomy have any real substance when the subjective reality is often one of poor self-esteem, low staffing levels and, by necessity, a system of care based upon task allocation.

Organizational research has drawn a clear correlation between the levels of involvement in the decision-making process and feelings of control. In terms of logical sequence, this increased sense of autonomy is clearly aligned with improved satisfaction and feelings of well-being (Herzberg et al., 1959). Applying these themes to nursing, professional standing and worth contribute greatly to the overall sense of fulfilment (Hayward et al., 1991). Arthurs (1992) argued that the premise on which increased autonomy can be achieved must involve a fundamental shift in the way practising nurses see themselves.

Given the evidence which has been presented in this chapter, it is difficult to envisage a defined pathway by which nurses can improve poor confidence and a lack of belief in their own value; this is mirrored and supported by research findings which reveal that seven out of ten nurses feel abused and denigrated by processes inherent to the

NHS (Cole, 1992) Furthermore, a study by Melhuish et al. (1993) revealed that only 30% of nurses felt they could influence doctors and only 9% thought they could influence general management. The findings of research give a clear indication that nurses feel impotent and unable to either voice or enact the themes of autonomous practice and professional choice. Given the inherent barriers and difficulties which restrict nurses' professional growth, it is hard to envisage a solution to the unequal standing which exists between doctors and nurses. However, Melhuish et al. (1993) give a pertinent comment about the future development of nurses and their roles:

> 'While the high value accorded the nurse's role by patients might provide a buffer to some of the stresses that nurses face, this alone cannot sustain the profession as it seeks to establish its niche in the coming years. Nurses need to be positive about their role and pro-active in developing and explaining it. If nurses themselves lack a clear vision for the future then others cannot be expected to accord the profession due recognition.' (p. 335)

This inability to be proactive hardly mirrors the activities of the medical profession. Doctors have a strong reputation for solidarity which gives focus, strength and depth to their cause. As we have seen, there are many factors which allow medicine to enjoy this powerful position; likewise, there are reasons why nurses have failed to assume a similar standing — paradoxically, as the evidence of this chapter supports, medicine's empowerment is intrinsically linked to the disempowerment of nursing. If this situation is ever to change and autonomy becomes a subjective reality for practitioners, then a process of enablement must take place at the 'grass roots' — nobody can 'ring the changes' for nurses except nurses.

Enabling change

As mentioned at the start of this chapter, recent times have seen major developments in clinical nursing practice: primary nursing, nursing development units, clinical practice development nurses and the scope of professional practice all illustrate such innovations. Moreover, small groups and individual nurses form dynamic 'pockets' of excellence throughout the realm of practice. This theme is reflected by Holmes (1991) who argues:

> 'Clinical leaders will create an environment in which therapeutic relationships with patients and collaborative relationships with other health care professionals are possible. Effective application of the skills of leadership, therefore, expands the role of nurses, setting a standard for professional practice and helping to guide its development. This can only be of benefit both to patients and to the quality of the care they receive.' (p. 16)

Nurses are acting as change agents and the themes of accountable and responsible practice are being enacted and striven for — but not on a universal basis. The essential point is that professional autonomy is often achieved through a process of enlightenment; as Lynch (1993) states:

> 'Too often, feelings of helplessness and lack of opportunity are the result of restricted awareness. One must realise that power is not only a function of one's position but, more importantly, a state of mind.'
> (p. 181)

This process of increased awareness is analogous to the writings of Kuhn (1970), who used the term 'paradigm shift' to describe a passage of change in the tenets central to scientific research. The focus of this theory is based on the notion that dissatisfaction associated with working within a scientific framework may lead to an intellectual crisis which can, ultimately, only be resolved through redefining the terms of the project. However, Kuhn argues that the validity of the new terms must be recognized by the most powerful of the scientists before they gain acceptance and standing. What is interesting about Kuhn's theory is that the period of change or crisis may be recognized during its process, but it is only with reflection that the full impetus and extent of the changes become apparent.

There is an important difference between Kuhn's theory and what is happening in nursing; the most powerful members of the profession do not have to accept all the terms within the process — it is changing from the grass roots upwards and leading to increased levels of confidence. This will enable a gradual increase in practitioners' self-esteem. As Kuhn notes, paradigm changes are not fully noticed when in process, which means that doctors will not have heeded the gradual emergence of major changes in nursing. As Beardshaw and Robinson (1990, p. 25) state: 'The reaction of doctors to any transformation of the nursing role remains largely unknown, but it is unlikely to be wholly positive.' Doctors may have little wish to know of the changing themes which will influence autonomous and accountable practice within nursing, but eventually the process of change will be complete.

What will emerge from this is poignantly described by Lynch (1993):

> ' . . . political, economic, and personal forces are slowly toppling the rigid walls of the traditional hierarchy, opening new vistas for organisational restructuring and creating a different paradigm for management. The old hierarchy, in which power was centred in a few, is giving way to an organisational network with shared power. . . . Empowerment occurs as all within the network share the same vision, pool their energy and creativity, and move towards the same goal in a way that

is effective and meaningful.' (p. 183)

However, the different influencing factors, explored in this chapter, suggest that the relationship between doctors and nurses will always be open to a degree of conflict and antagonism. Such a suggestion may make Lynch's comments sound like well-meaning rhetoric, but developmental changes — collaborative care planning and case management — do give hope for the future. After all, a certain amount of conflict between doctors and nurses will inevitably occur, as it does among any professional groups which work closely together. This chapter has confronted some of the intrinsic elements involved in the nurse/doctor relationship; it has revealed that there are, indeed, many problems in this partnership but, as Mackay (1993) states: 'It is hard to please everyone: there are few perfect partners.'

References

Adshead G, Dickenson D (1993) Why do doctors and nurses disagree? In: Dickensen D, Johnson M (Eds), *Death, Dying and Bereavement*. London: Sage, 161–168.

Arthurs D (1992) Measuring the professonal self-concept of nurses: a critical review. *Journal of Advanced Nursing*; **17**: 712–719.

Barry J, Soothill K, Williams C (1992) Managing nurse wastage. In: Soothill K, Henry IC, Kendrick KD (Eds), *Themes and Perspectives in Nursing*. London: Chapman & Hall.

Beardshaw W, Robinson R (1990) *New for Old: Prospects for Nursing in the 1990s*. London: King's Fund.

Bradshaw PL (1984) A quaint philosophy. *Senior Nurse*; **1**: 35.

Braito R, Caston R (1983) Factors influencing job satisfaction in nursing practice. In: Chaska N (Ed.), *The Nursing Profession: A Time to Speak*. New York: McGraw-Hill.

Bridges JM (1990) Literature review on the images of the nurse and nursing in the media. *Journal of Advanced Nursing*; **15**: 850–854.

Chadwick R, Tadd W (1992) *Ethics and Nursing Practice: A Case Study Approach*. London: Macmillan.

Cole A (1992) High anxiety. *Nursing Times*; **88**: (12), 26–30.

French WL, Raven CA (1959) *The Basis of Social Power*. Michigan: University of Michigan Press.

Gamarnikow E (1978) The sexual division of labour: the case of nursing. In: Kuhn A, Wolpe A (Eds), *Feminism and Materialism: Women and Modes of Production*. London: Routledge & Kegan Paul.

Hayward AJ, Will VE, MacAskill S, Hastings GB (1991) *Retention Within the Nursing Profession in Scotland*. Glasgow: University of Strathclyde Department of Marketing.

Herzberg F, Mausner B, Synderman BB (1959) *The Motivation to Work*. New York: John Wiley.

Holmes S (1991) Clinical leadership: a role for the advanced practitioner? *Journal of Advances in Health and Nursing Care*; **1**: (3), 3–20.

Holloway J (1992) Media representation of the nurse. In: Soothill K, Henry IC, Kendrick KD (Eds), *Themes and Perspectives in Nursing*. London: Chapman & Hall.

Johnstone MJ (1989) *Bioethics: A Nursing Perspective*. Sydney: WB Saunders/Baillière Tindall.

Kitson AL (1991) *Therapeutic Nursing and the Hospitalised Elderly*. Harrow: Scutari Press.

Kuhn TS (1970) *The Structure of Scientific Revolutions*. Chicago: University of Chicago Press.

Lewin E (1977) Feminist ideology and the meaning of work: the case of nursing. *Catalyst*; (10–11), 78–103.

Lynch E (1993) Organisational networking: empowerment through politics. In: Marriner-Tomey A (Ed.), *Transformational Leadership in Nursing*. Chicago: Mosby–YearBook, 171–188.

Mackay L (1989) *Nursing a Problem*. Milton Keynes: Open University Press.

Mackay L (1993) *Conflicts in Care, Medicine and Nursing*. London: Chapman & Hall.

Martin JP, MacKean J (1988) *Can We Keep Nurses in the Health Service? A Study of Nurse Retention in Two Health Districts*. Southampton: Institute of Health Policy Study, University of Southampton.

McIntosh I (1977) *Communication and Awareness in a Cancer Ward*. London: Croom-Helm.

Melhuish E, Maguire B, Nolan M, Grant G (1993) The professional role of the nurse. *British Journal of Nursing*; **2**: 330–335.

Melia KM (1987) *Learning and Working: The Occupational Socialisation of Nurses*. London: Tavistock.

Menzies N (1970) *Communication and Stress: A Nursing Perspective*. London: Macmillan.

Pearson A, Vaughan B (1986) *Nursing Models for Practice*. London: Heinemann.

Penner L (1978) *Social Psychology: A Contemporary Approach*. Oxford: Oxford University Press.

Price Waterhouse (1988) *Nurse Retention and Recruitment: A Matter of Priority*. London: Price Waterhouse.

Ryle G (1948) *The Concept of Mind*. London: Hutchinson.

Thompson I (1979) *Dilemmas in Dying*. Edinburgh: Edinburgh University Press.

Thomson IE, Melia KM, Boyd KM (1988) *Nursing Ethics*. Edinburgh: Churchill Livingstone.

Turner BS (1986) *Medical Power and Social Knowledge*. London: Sage.

Waite R, Buchen J, Thomas J (1989) *Nurses In and Out of Work*. Brighton: Institute of Manpower Studies (report 170).

Walsh M (1991) *Models in Clinical Nursing: The Way Forward*. London: WB Saunders/Baillière Tindall.

16 Professional ethics and organizational change

Christine Henry

This chapter examines professional ethics within an organizational culture, and introduces what it means to be a professional. An introduction to the meaning of professional ethics is given which attempts to clarify how principles and shared values are inherent in the process of managing effective change. Some issues that arise from developing codes of professional practice and the charters are discussed. In particular, attention will be given to ethical practice and the use of an 'ethics and values audit' as a management tool for health care organizations. In brief, it is argued that there is scope for facilitation of good management practice in these times of organizational change.

What it means to be a professional

To understand the concept or nature of a profession or the ideology of professionalism, it is important to reflect on some sociological, ethical and political views. In addition, it seems increasingly important to recognize the implications in practice of the value placed on what it means to be a professional.

Characteristics of a professional group have been identified by a number of authors. Freidson (1970) suggests that the following traits are characteristics of a profession:

- Ownership of a recognized body of knowledge exclusive to that profession with development of new knowledge through research.
- Self-government through a body that sets and monitors its own standards of practice.
- Control of recruitment and training.
- Monopoly for practice in its own field of work with registration by the state.
- Conformity to moral and disciplinary codes of behaviour.

- Autonomy for practice which assumes greater accountability for individuals within that profession.
- A public ideology of service to a client group.

Gray and Pratt (1989) remark that issues of personal and professional accountability and ethical decision-making are linked to professionalism. The notion of accountability is central to professionalism and perhaps lies at the heart of practice, where the medical profession serves as a good example.

According to Gillett (1989), the Hippocratic Oath itself was initially concerned with the identification of a moral code of practice for a group of people who were prepared to commit themselves to certain norms and a set of values. The oath affirms certain standards and expectations of members of the medical profession with the professional body regulating and controlling standards of practice. A more recent expression of the parameters of practice is seen in the Declaration of Geneva (1968), where the expected norms for the profession are identified as a set of values to be shared by the members (Faulder, 1985, p. 131).

Today the oath is no longer formally taken but the medical profession nevertheless is bound by a duty to the principles and values implied within its dictum. Perhaps the most fundamental of these principles is that of beneficence (of which more later), from which other sets of values emerge and provide a framework for practice.

Evans (1991) remarks that the concept of a professional role in relation to moral conduct has contributed to the conflict which occurs when professional guidelines seem to be at odds with ordinary morality and/or the law. The recent case of Dr Cox, a consultant rheumatologist who was convicted of attempted murder for giving a chronically ill patient a lethal injection, highlights the issue (McKie, 1993). Dr Cox had gone beyond the legal boundaries of his professional role as a doctor and, whilst violating the law and his professional position, he nevertheless demonstrated his respect for the patient's autonomy in his desire to end her suffering. If we consider professional accountability as a central issue in practice, to whom or for what is the practitioner accountable? If the emphasis has within its context a maxim that the 'patient's best interest' is paramount, how is this measured or justified when such a principle is violated by controls from outside the profession? Was Dr Cox in fact guilty of murder?

The message from the General Medical Council, quoted in the *Guardian* (1992), was that a good doctor who takes action of this sort will not be regarded as reprehensible, and it is clear that despite the controversy surrounding the legal outcome of this case, the medical profession saw fit to support Dr Cox by his remaining on the Medical Register.

In the absence of any moral or indeed legal consensus, the professional is often placed in a position where it is difficult to maintain two conflicting sets of ethical prescriptions, one for the profession and one for the patient. It follows, therefore, that there is a growing need for professional ethics to be regarded as a pivot for professional decision-making, based on a greater understanding and identification of shared moral principles and values that will equip the practitioner to deal more appropriately with the dilemmas of today's health care practice.

The concept of autonomy is, in many ways, one which may only be approximated, in that we are all to one degree or another 'governed' by 'rules' which restrict our freedom and self-determination in both private and public domains. This has proliferated into a much greater awareness and desire for autonomy during 'illness', to an extent that increased autonomy for patients has strongly affected the autonomous position of the professional. However, as a moral agent, the professional must be able to act freely and make choices based on underlying moral principles. Wilcox and Ebbs (1992) remark that to 'profess' means that, within a particular community, vows are taken. Henry (1994) suggests that this not only emphasizes membership but concerns making a commitment to a 'mission' to follow rules of caring. In turn, the rules of caring involve moral values and principles, one of which is the principle of autonomy.

Evans (1991) points out that professional ethics should take account of intuition, convention and legalism, which may provide other parameters for professional decision-making but which may not serve as any moral guide for action and should not be solely relied upon.

Throughout the professional socialization process, the learning of roles, norms, values and beliefs occurs. The script that the professional has is learned, and if rigidly adhered to it may suggest direction and control from a person in another profession. Henry (1994) remarks that a professional may be rigidly locked into a sociologically defined role and could adhere to a script defined by someone else, especially if the other professional who directs has a stronger sense and image of their own professional autonomy. Nurses, in the past, have been 'other directed' by the medical profession. This narrowly defined perspective follows from a sociological view based on expectations and norms which may not allow for the wider and deeper adherence to moral principles and values.

Within an organization, a change from a custom or culture, as a process of claiming professional or self-emancipation, may be for better or worse. Henry (1994) gives the example of the nurse portrayed in the book and film *One Flew Over the Cuckoo's Nest* (Kelsey, 1973). The nurse rigidly keeps to the organizational norms and role, emphasizing not only the abuse of power and role but also the dire consequences for the psychiatric patient. The nurse clearly kept to her defined role and used her position and professional knowledge to influence the doctor's decisions regarding the patient's treatment and care. The psychiatrists depended on the nurse's judgement of the patient's behaviour and it became obvious that the disruptive behaviour of the main character was seen as a violation of the organization's accepted norms and values. It is interesting to note the degree to which the patient's autonomy was violated within such an environment, where the demonstration of any personal autonomy (self-emancipation) was identified as deviant behaviour and led to barbaric consequences with ECT and surgical intervention finally eliminating any capacity for self-determination. In this particular fictitious case the principle of *respect for persons*, and in turn *respect for personal autonomy*, was disregarded. Furthermore, two other major moral principles were not upheld. These are *non-maleficence*, the duty not to harm, and *beneficence*, the duty to do good. Beneficence is fundamental for health professionals in that it requires a positive action to 'do good'. In the above case direct harm was caused through the client's loss of self-determination.

Missions, charters and codes

The narrow view of professional ethics as a guide, or a set of prescriptive rules for the professional, is no longer tenable. It is much more than this and professional ethics with attending policies, charters and codes of conduct/practice need to be discussed within a wider moral frame of reference.

Professional ethics in its application to practice examines the ways in which individuals practice, as well as how codes of professional conduct are constructed. Furthermore, professional ethics has been identified as dealing with ethical issues related to power, role and the position of professionals within an organization. Professional ethics is clearly a branch of ethics in the sense that it aims to assess individual and professional behaviour and the quality of moral values. Professional ethics in the widest and deepest sense offers ways of enquiring into behaviour and may support moral justification for actions and the professional decisions taken. In everyday usage the term 'morals' is often used to mean the same as 'ethics', but whilst morals *concern* human conduct and values, ethics is the *study* of both. Ethical theory may help to solve moral dilemmas and principles are necessary for theory. Whilst missions, charters and codes cannot solve moral dilemmas, they do have other important functions. Missions, charters and codes are underpinned by moral principles.

The understanding of what is meant by moral principles is crucial and central to ethical practice, particularly if we intend to 'practice what we preach'. Principles are guidelines for human conduct, with a broad universal application. In other words they provide a focus for the way in which we should behave towards each other and are central to ethical theory. The principle of 'respect for persons' has, for example, important implications for the ways in which individuals perceive and behave towards others. Respect for persons is central to health care, and with that respect goes rights, responsibility, personal integrity, autonomy and value. The term 'person' is a value-laden term, like the moral term 'good' (Abelson, 1977; Henry, 1991). Used as a moral term, respect for persons becomes central to health care practice, as an important moral principle grounded in professional ethics. In practice, the professional, as a moral advocate, may have to make decisions on behalf of the client/patient. It is often necessary to adopt the role of an advocate on behalf of the very ill patient, the young infant or the severely mentally incapacitated person. Consequently, if respect for that person is not maintained as a guiding principle for the advocate, the individual may be greatly disadvantaged. Furthermore, denying personal status takes away rights and responsibilities. When individuals are not treated as persons, unethical and inhumane practices occur. Recent history provides many examples of individuals being treated as 'things' without rights or recognition, as behaviour during civil and world wars serves to show. Values are much more subjective and broader than principles; they do not necessarily have to be moral. Organizations may share values but these may militate against a moral principle. Values have a personal interpretation and may violate or support principles and/or professional practice.

The moral directives of the professional role have been seen to find their origins through oaths and declarations. More recent directives are issued through the medium of charters, codes and missions. If moral guidelines for practice emerge through identifying universal principles such as respect for persons, the pursuit of autonomy and accountability for action, the question raised is one which seeks to establish whether such principles underpin the development of these mission statements, charters and codes.

Mission statements

Mission statements may be seen as statements of intent. In the construction of a mission statement, ownership of the principles that underpin the statements must be a priority for the members of the organization to recognize their value. Continual evaluation is essential. A major criticism of a mission statement may be seen when it appears to be totally 'at odds' with what appears to be the accepted behaviour of the members of the organization, particularly those in higher management. However, mission statements, charters and codes may form part of the process towards *practising what we preach.*

Charters

Charters are statements that summarize good practice and identify standards from which professional practice may be measured. They reach a wide audience and are useful across all professional groups. The aim of any charter is to create ultimately a better service through defining national and local standards as parameters for practice. Charters are clear examples of ways in which standards can be explicitly identified. Within a charter there should be evidence of universal principles and values. However, difficulties arise in how charters are constructed and in the ways in which their implementation may occur. Construction of a charter through identification of standards and ways to improve those standards ought to be through research-based audits that capture the views of all the 'stakeholders' within the organization. If those attempting to maintain identified standards of practice do not identify with those expected to achieve them, the charter becomes meaningless.

The *Patient's Charter* (DoH, 1991) identifies rights and standards aimed at improving the delivery of health care services. Its origins were based on a view that it provided targets for health professionals to reach as a method of improving standards of practice at a defined optimum level. This charter also reaffirms the fundamental principles of the NHS. The patient's charter emphasizes efficiency through better management and a greater respect for and value of human resources within the NHS. Furthermore, the focus is on patient's rights to a specific level of service.

Codes

Codes are more closely linked to specific professions. Both charters and codes identify guidelines for the benefit of the professionals and the clients. However, a charter is not legally or professionally binding, whereas a code is at least enforceable by the profession and may be used to measure the appropriateness of action and behaviour, although not functional in solving a moral dilemma. Violating a code may lead to legal action although it is not in itself governed under legal statute. Codes are specific in their themes for guidance. In general terms they must be interpreted in the appropriate context (Heywood Jones, 1990). A code is relevant to real-life situations and it is essential that the practising professional understands his/her own code. The professions often have the benefit of respect from the public, who generally rely on the professionals' ability to make reasonable and sound judgements. Like charters, codes set guidelines for standards and identify principles that underpin practice. However, codes go further in that they provide professions with directives through professional regulation of the individual's professional conduct.

Mission statements, charters and especially codes of practice/conduct may evolve from moral principles implicit within professional ethics. This point is important in that it clearly sets charters and codes within an ethical framework. According to Passmore (1984), a code cannot automatically be justified because of its relation to a special class of persons. A code is necessary to protect and also warn the professional of abuse and misuse of his/her position. According to Passmore, professionals may be called upon to act in ways that may well be 'beyond the call of duty' and which may place them in conflict within the professional role. For example, Henry (1994) notes that professionals have privileged access to special knowledge through education and practice. This knowledge may be withheld (from patients or clients) with what the professional identifies as 'good reason' but which may be regarded as being unethical. In therapeutic practice and research, *both confidentiality and informed consent*, based on the special privilege of knowledge by the professional, are essential. Codes of moral conduct need to state explicit professional guidelines which direct and advise the individual in his/her practice. Whilst codes cannot solve moral dilemmas they do have other important functions which may help to raise levels of ethical awareness within the professional fields.

Professional ethics within an organizational framework

It has been suggested that the framework within which an organization functions is influenced by the behaviour and actions of the members within the organization. Ethical behaviour is fundamental to professional practice and is identified through professional standards and norms.

Professional ethics derives from the discipline of *ethics*. It considers not only the ways in which professionals practice but also how ethical practice is applied in and through codes of professional conduct and behaviour. Professional ethics encompasses principles and values central to and foundational upon *normative ethics* (to do with norms and prescribing ways in which to behave; generally concerned with rules and implies standards and values; how we ought to behave — see, for example, Norman (1983)).

Ethical issues arise within the parameters of professional ethics in areas of management and professional decision-making. Hence, professional ethics is involved at all levels within the organizational framework. Professionals adopt self-scrutiny through professional regulation. Organizations, particularly within the fields of health and education, pursue their professional autonomy through self-scrutiny, reflecting upon organizational behaviour and policy. In part, one way of achieving a mechanism for self-scrutiny would be through the development of charters and codes. However, before constructing guidelines it is necessary to identify shared principles and values which in turn may contribute to the setting of standards. In order to begin such a process and to avoid imposing principles, values and standards from a 'top down' approach, an evaluation of the views of the members of the organization would be of great value. Identifying the perception of the values and ethical practices of an organizations' members should provide a basis on which an ethical framework for practice could be introduced. One such approach may be achieved through an organizational research based 'ethics and values audit'.

Leaders working within organizations are constantly under pressure from social, economic and ideological forces. Health and educational organizations have to respond to these community and societal pressures where there is an increasing ethical concern for fair resource allocation and identification of priorities. Mission statements may reflect the ethics and values underpinning priorities chosen within the organization. The mission statement of a hospital or 'health care trust' will directly influence professional practice in a number of ways, especially if the mission statement is owned by the organization's members. The ethical practice ought to be collaboratively shared amongst professionals and would gain more effect if permeated through strong and equitable leadership. Shared principles of practice provide greater opportunity for achieving standards that will accomplish identified goals, whilst relationships within and outside the organization ought to be built on collaboration. When competition *is the only value* the corporate nature is disadvantaged (Henry et al., 1992).

Professional ethics has a diversity of application and should be supported by a theoretical foundation. This would involve ethical analysis within the context of the organizational structure and its community through focused research that involves empirical and normative enquiry. According to Wilcox and Ebbs (1992), colleges and universities have a responsibility to their clients (staff and students) to adhere to their legal and moral charters. Likewise, health care organizations are held accountable to the community for which they serve. In previous sections it has been stated that the professional is a moral agent and advocate. Members of professions form the central core of a 'health care' organization and therefore, collectively, the organization may be perceived as a moral agent. Principles and obligations are normative ways of understanding and giving direction to, and being supportive of, moral agency. It is therefore crucial for an organization to reflect consistency in its moral practice. The ethical concerns for health care organizations manifest themselves through decision-making, equity, fairness, honesty and trust. Professional ethics applied through an ethically driven system seek to identify and organize standards, ensure individual responsibility, whilst identifying shared principles and values for the support and delivery of the mission statement, charter or code.

The use of an ethics and values audit (EVA)

The Ethics and Values research-based Audit (EVA) carried out at the University of Central Lancashire in 1992 was the first of its kind in the UK. The aim was to carry out a survey of ethics and values to establish whether the organization lived up to the values held within its mission statement. The view was taken that all large organizations have problems putting values into practice.

The EVA project takes a research orientation in order to validate, as far as is possible, its findings. It presents the beginning of a process for managing change effectively and lays the foundation on which to build and develop charters, codes of practice and subsequently for setting standards. Part of the EVA's originality is that it is a 'practical course in ethics' for professionals within 'people' organizations. The *Education Guardian* in November 1992 announced 'A practical course in ethics' for its review of the EVA. Any organization, through its management profile, sets goals and norms which do not necessarily reflect or encourage moral or professional behaviour. The structure and processes within a profession, and the demands from outside the profession, influence individual behaviour and integrity. The EVA presents only the beginning of a process with an opportunity for maintaining professional integrity and corporate success. The emphasis is given to ethically driven strategies, in order to support the most valuable resource of any organization (i.e. its staff/clients). In giving direction for policy, charters, codes and professional practice and behaviour its aim is to enhance delivery and improve care for clients. Ethical practice in management is clearly linked to a number of psychological issues involving individual and professional well-being. The process of managing change is based on the principles of respect, integrity and the pursuit of quality. Furthermore, the valuable human resources are community members and stakeholders of the organization who influence and reflect the organization's success or failure.

Wilson (1993) suggests that the concept of the ethics and values audit is beginning to develop. In a review, Wilson remarks on the significance of the publication of the first EVA:

'In years to come, when many more organisations are conducting such audits, this is likely to be seen as the first serious attempt to quantify the profound effect ethics and values have on organisational behaviour and performance.' (p. 105)

Apps (1993) remarks that, although the EVA took place in an institution of higher education, it has much to offer nursing education and practice in times of change. Apps draws parallels with the health service and points out that mission statements, through setting ideals, all too easily 'result in dichotomies of idealism versus reality' (p.49). She mentions further that the audit examined something fundamental to the organization's stability; i.e. the facilitation of both staff and students' awareness of their own moral conduct and of the organization's culture.

The EVA findings were presented in three parts. Parts 1 and 3 deal with the findings, recommendations and some detail of what principles, values and ethical practice mean. Part 2 contains an explanation and analysis of methodology. The methods used by the research team included a questionnaire, a values identification grid (modification of Kelly's Repertory Grid), open-ended interviews and case studies.

The case studies emerged from an ethics 'hot-line' which provided an opportunity for staff and students to voice and identify feelings at grass-roots level, whilst preserving anonymity and confidentiality of the individuals who chose to participate in the study.

Part 1

This part of the EVA report examines the purpose and identifies the aims of the project. It raised the pivotal question: 'Can there be a highly moral corporate culture in any organization?', especially when in times of change it is faced with social, economic and political pressures? The EVA identified the mission statement, the Equal Opportunities Policy and the university's Charter for Management as focusing upon people. The main aim was a concern for identifying values that underpinned the mission statement, how these values were shared and demonstrated through the organization, and how staff and students both perceived the identified values and recognized their implementation through practice. Essentially it was important to establish a framework on which values could be identified and supported by moral principles. The outcome of the EVA involved producing a profile of principles and values of the university in order to develop ways in which to implement and enhance good practice. Part 1 outlines ten themes which identified issues concerned with: informal supportive networks; mutual respect and trust; peer group integrity; honesty and openness; interpersonal relationships; organizational decision-making processes; styles of management; management practice; use and abuse of power roles; and the provision of staff resources.

Wilson (1993) points out that the ethics and values of any organization are comprised of two distinct elements which focus on the stated goals expressed through the mission statement and codes and the values and beliefs of individual members of the organization. Wilson states that 'the process of an ethics audit is that it maps out how far values are shared between these two elements' (p. 104).

Part 1 of the report provides a detailed profile of the themes and values in the curriculum, a policy analysis, and recommendations. The recommendations were said not to be *prescriptions*, but '. . . represent an attempt to encourage a university's management style and culture in which recognition and respect for all members of its community is the paramount value' (p. 32).

Part 2

This part introduces the ways in which an ethical audit can be carried out. Six methods were used to collect data: a questionnaire; an interview technique; a values identification grid; case studies; analysis of policies; and a brief curriculum analysis. The desirability of having six methods for data collection seemed important for giving credibility to an 'in-house' research project. Out of a total of 1200 staff, 603 respondents participated in the study. Wilson (1993) notes that 'the whole ethics audit was a two-way process of information retrieval and dissemination' (p. 104). He mentions that the methods used in carrying out an ethical audit should go beyond conventional techniques such as attitude surveys, in order to collect the appropriate response from those most affected by the findings — i.e. senior managers. In addition, Wilson remarks on the process of the enquiry, suggesting that the methods used involve identification of missions and codes at one level moving towards an examination of the way in which 'organizational processes support and nurture the values of an organization' (p. 105). The Foreword of the EVA states that the ethical audit was only the beginning and it invited the organization to join in a process of ongoing participation.

Part 3

This part focuses on four major principles that are regarded as essential to ethical theory and which underpin the development of missions, charters, codes and standards for professional behaviour.

Autonomy is stated by Henry and Pashley (1990) to mean 'that we are able to control our lives and to some extent our own destiny'. Many influences affect our ability and capacity to be an autonomous agent, of which money, power and status are but a few. The EVA report suggests that in reality we can never have full or absolute freedom of choice even though autonomy is a distinctive mark of the person. The EVA report recognizes that autonomy, whilst being important, may conflict with the needs of the organization.

Non-maleficence means to do no harm and implies moral action rather than virtue. If this principle is not upheld, harm may result not only in restriction of liberty but also through injury to an individual's professional reputation.

Beneficence is central to health care organizations and means that one ought to give help to others whenever necessary. However, beneficence may conflict with autonomy. For example, if one acts in the best interest of the patient in order to avoid harm, the action may interfere with the patient's wishes, values or beliefs and the freedom of their individual choice(s).

The principle of *justice* is concerned with respect for persons and the interactions with individuals or groups. The EVA report points out that fairness is implicit and governs what is due and to whom. When justice is applied to the organization, it implies the importance of informed decision-making to effect and influence the ultimate welfare of staff and clients. It also relates to equal opportunities, embracing fairness, impartiality, merit, need, equality and equity.

Conclusions

Edel (1986) remarks that if ethics is a practical discipline it must include dealing with practical moral problems. Professional ethics is derived from normative ethics and may be applied to practical problems within an organizational framework. Wilcox and Ebbs (1992) have independently identified the four principles of 'autonomy', nonmaleficence', 'beneficence' and 'justice' as important principles for professionals within the organizational framework. It follows, therefore, that these principles are important for any 'people' organizations, particularly NHS organizations. The EVA is only the beginning of the journey towards a synthesis of empirical, conceptual and normative enquiry that will encourage the development of ethically driven systems that will improve quality within organizations.

Professional standards and codes are guidelines to generally accepted norms. In one sense they may help to direct and support ethical practice. However, charters and codes are often necessary when a culture is undergoing change. As Bellah et al. (1985) state, such changes may reflect a lack of consensus of values. Gilbert (1991) mentions that when relationships are skewed by 'disparities of power' it may be impossible to change them from within. He remarks that one particular way to change, where the disempowered can challenge the empowered, may be to form other relationships with a common purpose. This would involve both the establishment of a common purpose and shared values where elements of fairness and justice prevail, especially within a caring community and particularly a health care organization. Processes for managing change from inside the organizations are clearly essential, in order to meet and respond to the political, social and ideological demands from without. Not a quiet revolution, but an ethical one.

References

Abelson R (1977) *Persons: A Study in Philosophical Psychology*. London: Macmillan.

Apps J (1993) Nursing education and practice. *Journal of Advances in Health and Nursing Care*; **2**: 47.

Bellah et al. (1985) *Habits of the Heart: Individualism and Commitment to American Life*. Berkeley: Berkeley University Press.

Department of Health (1991) *The Patient's Charter*. London: HMSO.

Edel A (1986) Ethical theory and moral practice in terms of their relations. In: DeMarco JP, Fox RM (Eds), *New Directions in Ethics: The Challenge of Applied Ethics*. London: Routledge & Kegan Paul.

Evans M (1991) Professional ethics and reflective practice: a moral analysis. In: Gray G, Pratt R (Eds), *Towards a Discipline of Nursing*. Edinburgh: Churchill Livingstone, 309–334.

Fadiman C (1985) *The Faber Book of Anecdotes*. London: Faber & Faber, 325.

Faulder C (1985) *Whose Body Is It? The Troubling Issue of Informed Consent*. London: Virago.

Freidson E (1970) *Professional Dominance*. New York: Atherton.

Gilbert P (1991) *Human Relationships*. Oxford: Basil Blackwell, 155.

Gillett G (1989) *Reasonable Care*. Bristol: Bristol Press.

Gray G, Pratt R (1989) Accountability: the pivot of professionalism. In: *Issues in Australian Nursing 2*. Edinburgh: Churchill Livingstone.

Guardian (1992) BMA warns doctors on euthanasia law. 18 Nov.

Henry C (1991) The ethical boundaries of research practice with particular reference to the concept of the person. *Journal of Advances in Health and Nursing Care*; **1**: 1.

Henry C (1994) Professional ethics: health, nursing education and research. In: *Community Ethics and Health Care Research* (in press).

Henry C, Pashley G (1990) *Health Ethics*. Lancaster: Quay Publishers.

Henry C, Drew J, Anwar N, Campbell G, Benoit-Asselman D (1992) *EVA Project: Report of the Ethics and Values Audit*. University of Central Lancashire.

Heywood Jones L (1990) *The Nurses' Code*. Lancaster: Macmillan.

Kelsey K (1973) *One Flew Over the Cuckoo's Nest*. Pan Books.

McKie L (1993) Editorial comment. *Journal of Advances in Health and Nursing*; **2**: (3), 1–2.

Norman R (1983) *The Moral Philosophers: An Introduction to Ethics*. Oxford: Clarendon Press, 15.

Passmore J (1984) Academic ethics? *Journal of Applied Philosophy*; **1**: 63–67.

Wilcox JR, Ebbs SL (1992) *The Leadership Compass: Values and Ethics in Higher Education*. Washington, DC: George Washington University.

Wilson A (1993) Translating corporate values into business behaviour. In: *Business Ethics: A European Review*, **2**: No. 2.

17 Codes of professional conduct and the dilemmas of professional practice

Kevin Kendrick

Introduction

The image of the nurse as the doctor's handmaiden is being radically challenged by contemporary developments and themes. Over the past decade, progressive changes and policies have engendered a new impetus for nurse education, management and practice. Emerging from this climate of innovation are clear indications that the culture of nursing is being rigorously charged by the language of professionalism. Nurses have always been expected to place great emphasis upon delivering excellence in practice. However, the 'new' terms used to describe the duties and obligations implicit in this process strongly suggest individual ownership and responsibility for nursing actions. Nurses are told to exercise accountability, accept responsibility and operate from a position of professional autonomy. The principal agency for encouraging and overseeing the implementation of these themes is the United Kingdom Central Council for Nursing, Midwifery and Health Visiting (UKCC). Moreover, the chief mechanism by which the council provides guidelines for practice is through its *Code of Professional Conduct* (Young, 1989).

The existence of a code of conduct is frequently cited as a prerequisite to being accepted as a profession. Durkheim (1957) and Parsons (1951) are both early writers who acknowledged the importance of professional codes for preserving the best interests of clients over that of the practitioner. This notion is clearly indicated by the UKCC's code which asks that practitioners act to: '*safeguard and promote the interests of individual patients and clients*' (UKCC, 1992).

The code also encourages nurses, health visitors and midwives to act in a way that is beneficial to society's interests, justifies public belief and upholds the reputation of the professions. All of this illustrates that the themes of the code are important indicators for the acceptance of nursing as a profession.

In this chapter I will be concerned with how pragmatic the code is for helping practitioners to deal with the dilemmas that are an everyday part of professional life. There can be no doubt that the principles inherent to the code are designed to promote beneficial outcomes; but we have to analyse how far they can be used to provide a cogent structure for confronting and dealing with difficult situations. My intention is not to denounce, rebuff or rebuke the central role that the code has for setting professional 'guidelines'. However, we shall use the 'tools' of ethical analysis to consider the efficacy of these 'guidelines' for promoting accountable, responsible and autonomous practice. The essential premise of my argument is that professional codes must be seen as means to an end and not just as ends in themselves. Whilst a principle may be thought to have intrinsic value, it must be examined for its worth to become operational. Our line of enquiry will maintain that codes of professional conduct provide the stimulus and starting point for moral analysis — but in brief, they do not tell the whole story.

The foundation of duty

The historical dimensions of nursing are entrenched in the notion of duty; this tradition is succinctly entwined in the most central of nursing edicts, 'a duty of care'. Within contemporary nursing there remains a strong allegiance to this theme. Recent political developments have promoted the idea of health consumerism and the rights of the client — nurses are seen to have a duty to uphold and respect these rights. This approach is based on the intrinsic and inalienable relationship that exists between 'rights' and 'duties'. Broadly speaking, once a duty of care has been established, the client has a right to be cared for and the nurse must facilitate care-giving. The UKCC *Code* encourages high standards during professional endeavours and expects all practitioners to operate within its framework and guidelines. This is reflected in the following extract:

> 'The Council is the regulatory body responsible for the standards of these professions and it requires members of the professions to practise and conduct themselves within the standards and framework provided by the code.'

Statements of this nature serve to reinforce notions of duty, and the maxims within the code provide motivational guidelines for nursing actions. Basing actions upon duties, rules or motives has a long history in ethics and is known as *deontology*. Kendrick (1993) presents the following comment about this method of moral thinking: 'This school of ethical analysis maintains that being moral entails acting from a sense of moral duty, respecting others' rights and honouring one's obligations.' This interpretation clearly aligns itself with the themes of the professional code of conduct and the onus which it places upon registered practitioners.

The person most closely associated with deontology is the philosopher Immanuel Kant. He was a prolific writer on the notion that people have intrinsic worth and value. Furthermore, he argued that an essential part of being human is the ability to use reason in deliberating over the moral worth of an action. For Kant, this ability invariably found itself rooted in a sense of duty.

There are many attractive elements to Kantian ethics. In particular it places a great deal of emphasis on respect amongst persons and encourages a fervent sense of individual duty. Tschudin (1986, p. 32) summarizes these themes by stating: 'A right action is only so if it is done out of a sense of duty, and the only good thing without qualification is a person's good will: the will to do what one knows is right.'

Kant devised a complex moral theory, consisting of three formulations of what he called the 'categorical imperative'. Their precise interpretation and mutual relations are a matter of controversy. Kendrick (1993, p. 924) simplifies the different formulations as follows:

- An action is only moral if you are willing for it to be applied to everyone, yourself included, as a universal law.
- For an action to be moral it must never lead to people being seen just as 'means to an end' but always as 'ends' in their own right.
- In wishing to be moral, individuals must act as members of a community where everybody is seen as having intrinsic worth (ends in their own right).

The essence of the categorical imperative can be readily applied to the duty-based nature of nursing. Kant's first principle is a clear indication that all people have intrinsic worth and should attribute respect to each other. Most societies would agree that it is intrinsically wrong to steal another person's possessions. The implications of Kant's theory are that persons wishing to undertake such acts should be willing to accept the same being done to themselves. The first principle of the imperative asks us to consider that our actions, once undertaken, can then be perpetrated by everybody else — as if a universal law existed to validate the activity. Of course, this would also mean that the original perpetrator of an act of theft would have to accept somebody else quite validly stealing personal and treasured possessions. Expressed simply, the first principle is a moral edict that requires us to ask 'Would I like this act to be done either to myself or those close to me?'; if the answer is 'No' then Kant would have serious reservations about the moral worth of the motives underpinning the action. These themes are often introduced to the novice nurse who is asked to care from a basis of duty. Whilst this may initially seem like a simplistic formulation, it can act as a strong image for mental reinforcement and maintaining standards during the delivery of care. Moreover, it reflects the distinct and synonymous link between elements of duty and nursing.

The second of Kant's principles further emphasizes the notion of equal respect amongst persons and resolutely argues that individuals should never be seen or treated solely as means to an end. This does not mean that people cannot work together or help each other — the key theme is that this should involve some degree of mutual reciprocity. An example of this is the first-year student nurse who needs to attain the skills of giving an intramuscular injection. Obviously, to be able to perform this task safely and competently requires the cooperation of a willing patient. Whilst a patient may be used as a means to an end (the end being the nurse performing a skill competently) this does not echo the full essence of this part of the imperative. Giving a drug through the intramuscular route should result in some therapeutic worth for the patient; thus, the process has benefited the nurse through the acquisition of a skill and the patient through the beneficial effect of the injection. Kant did not object to individuals being used as a means to an end as long as they are also valued as ends in their own right.

The essence of the second principle in the imperative does not just apply to the nurse/patient relationship but extends to all interaction within the professional milieu. Not only are nurses required to respect patients as being of equal worth, but this must also govern the professional ethos in dealing with colleagues. This duty to enact the principle of respect for persons is a cogent thread throughout the UKCC *Code* but it finds particular relevance in two clauses:

Clause 6: 'Work in a collaborative and cooperative manner with health care professionals and others involved in providing care, and recognise their particular contributions within the care team.'

Clause 7: 'Recognise and respect the uniqueness and dignity of each patient and client, and respond to their need for care, irrespective of their ethnic origin, religious beliefs, personal attributes, the nature of their health problems or any other factor.'

We have repeatedly seen that respect is a central element in Kantian thinking and the word appears frequently throughout the UKCC *Code*. A strong emphasis upon respect emerges from the third and final part of the imperative; its essential message is that persons form a community where each member has equal worth as a moral decision-maker. As nurses, we meet colleagues or patients who may have very different values or beliefs to our own. Sometimes these differences are informed by cultural or religious diversity. Kantian ethics suggests that the key issue is to respect the freedom of other individuals to hold moral perspectives and to act upon them — this is part of what it means to treat others as ends. If this is applied to the professional setting it asks that all people have equal authority to express and defend their respective positions. Once again, we can say that this theme runs throughout the *Code*; however, another clause specifically supports this notion:

> Clause 5: 'Work in an open and cooperative manner with patients, clients and their families, foster their independence and recognise and respect their involvement in the planning and delivery of care.'

To this point we have seen that duty-based approaches to ethical thinking and analysis have a long history in moral theory. This has been supported with reference to deontology and the philosopher most closely associated with it, Immanuel Kant. Moreover, we have drawn clear links between the deontological approach and the duty-based themes that run throughout nursing. The *Code of Professional Conduct* provides a series of guidelines and principles that inform a practitioner's professional obligations and preserve the traditional emphasis on duty-based care-giving. However, whilst we may say that principles of duty provide indications that can help give directions about professional conduct, there are problems with such approaches that demand clarification and analysis.

Duties as ends in themselves

A glaring problem with duty-based approaches to morality, and Kantian ethics in particular, is that they tend to portray certain maxims as absolute, universal and all encompassing. This can be shown by referring to an imaginary figure whom we will call 'Mr X'. We can also convey that this person considers himself to have a strict and highly structured sense of personal morality; indeed, he is proud to be known as a 'person of principles'. One of the principles Mr X feels he has an absolute duty to uphold is never to tell a lie; he holds the fervent belief that the truth should always be preserved. One day, Mr X is taking a leisurely walk in the countryside when a young woman comes into sight looking very distraught and angst ridden. As the woman comes nearer to Mr X it becomes obvious that something is making her very frightened; as she passes Mr X she cries 'For goodness sake, if you see a man running this way with an axe don't tell him that you have seen me.' Mr X is quite perplexed by the woman's request, when suddenly he is confronted by an angry looking man wielding an axe and asking the whereabouts of the young woman. Given the strong allegiance which Mr X feels with the duty never to tell a lie, he advises that the woman was last seen crouching behind a bush down by the stream, and so, the man with the axe takes off in hot pursuit.

Kant would almost certainly reassure Mr X that his actions were of a solid moral nature. One of the most important elements in deontology is that duties and principles are upheld and abided by. According to this rationale, Mr X has maintained his moral integrity by not telling a lie. Moreover, having been truthful, he could not then be held accountable or responsible for the moral behaviour of others. The man with the axe may have had perfectly innocent intentions. For example, he may have disarmed the original man with the axe and be running after the woman to enquire of her safety and give reassurance. However, because there are so many possible variables and unknowns, the best course of action is always to follow one's sense of duty and principles. Of course, such thinking is fraught with inconsistencies and dangers.

Whilst the account of our fictional Mr X may seem a little extreme, it does raise an interesting issue about strict obedience to duty-based rules. The point may have been made that Mr X could not be held responsible for the actions of others but, if the young woman had been injured (or worse) by the man, does it not leave Mr X in a position of moral culpability? Furthermore, is this 'blame-worthiness' lessened by the fact Mr X stood by his principle and duty of never telling a lie? This highlights the inflexibility and limitations of basing morality on the notion of duty as a universal absolute.

Mr X was an abstract and fictional representation designed to highlight the rigidity of absolute duties. However, there are many examples from the real world which highlight an unquestioning bond to duty-based dictums; certain religions forbid their members from accepting whole-blood products during medical treatments. Moreover, members of the armed forces are required always to fulfil their duty to obey orders even if this involves life-threatening manoeuvres. There is much room for debate about whether or not a principle/duty can ever be thought to be ubiquitous and applied as a categorical tenet. Returning to our earlier example, most societies and individuals would accept that stealing was wrong. However, can we make it a definitive rule that stealing is always wrong no matter what the circumstances or consequences of standing by such a principle would be? Imagine yourself in the middle of a war zone; for the last seven days you have survived by drinking small amounts of water and eating mouldy cheese. These meagre supplies are fast diminishing and your malnutrition is bordering upon starvation. Suddenly you stumble across an orchard of apples and a bomb has blasted a hole in the surrounding wall. As a rule, you would normally never consider stealing — the apples do not belong to you, but how many of us would not take the fruit in this situation? The consequence of us not taking the apples would probably mean death by starvation. What would be the most moral option — to adhere to our duty never to steal or take the fruit and improve the chances of survival? This clearly illustrates that the consequences of breaking allegiance with strict rules and duties can sometimes prove far more beneficial than an unquestioning acceptance of them.

Within nursing we have certain rules which are perceived as absolute and principal amongst these is the duty of care. However, sometimes the maxims within a duty of care can be at variance with each other. Consider the following principles:

- a duty to do good (beneficence);
- a duty to do no harm (non-maleficence).

At first glance these principles seem closely related. However, further analysis does reveal distinct differences between the two themes. As nurses, we always try to ensure that our actions promote good and preserve the best interests of the patient. This leads us to an interesting and penetrating question: 'Can we say, with universal candour, that nursing actions always promote good results for patients?' It is very doubtful that any of us can say 'Yes' to this question; to a large extent this is because harm is an intrinsic part of some nursing actions. The simplest example of this is when we give an intramuscular injection; every time we introduce the syringe it causes pain which, even to a very small degree, can be equated with harm. Many other nursing interventions carry the same ethos; antibiotics can cause an irritating rash, aspirin can cause gastric erosion, diamorphine or other opiate derivatives can cause chronic constipation. Given the amount of harm which can result from some of our actions, we are led to ask if the principle of non-maleficence is appropriate and applicable as a universal tenet in nursing.

Presenting the absolute duty of 'a nurse will do no harm' is an impractical notion because it can never be totally enacted within the professional role. We have already seen some of the 'harm' which can be induced by nursing actions. This theme has been explored and analysed by Illich (1975) with particular reference to the medical profession. He used the phrase 'iatrogenesis' to describe the harmful results and illnesses that can result from the interventions of doctors. For example, Illich makes the following claims:

'It has been established that one out of every five patients admitted to a typical research hospital acquires an iatrogenic disease, sometimes trivial, usually requiring special treatment, and in one case in thirty leading to death. Half of these episodes resulted from complications of drug therapy; amazingly, one in ten came from diagnostic procedures. Despite good intentions and claims to public service, with a similar record of performance a military officer would be relieved of his command and a restaurant or amusement centre would be closed by police.' (p. 87)

Illich has been criticized for not placing enough emphasis on the amount of good which medicine achieves. This is a valid criticism and it leads us to the centre of the debate about absolute duties as all-encompassing principles. We can say with a degree of certainty that the primary intention of practitioners is to promote beneficence and to strive to achieve non-maleficence. However, to place these two themes in the language of absolute duties is no more than an exercise in rhetoric and cannot be upheld in the 'real' world of delivering care. The key issue is not to insist that health professionals abide unquestioningly by a duty to do good and a duty to do no harm — clearly the two duties are not always reconcilable as consummate themes. The essential worth of the two principles is found in balancing them both together, not viewing them as isolated absolutes. Returning to our intramuscular injection, whilst the initial result may be pain or harm, this is usually outweighed by the amount of good which results from the therapeutic worth of the injected drug. This serves to highlight that the balance between beneficence and non-maleficence can help practitioners to reflect on the worth of an action. The essential problem with this is that the consequences of an action cannot always be forecast — crystal ball gazing is a poor basis for moral analysis. Despite this drawback, trying to weigh the moral worth of an action against the harm which it may produce at least asks for a degree of questioning, reflection and analysis; this is surely more acceptable than a passive acceptance of absolute, but conflicting, duties.

Practitioners at the 'cutting edge' of health care delivery have always had an intuitive awareness of the precarious balance between beneficence and non-maleficence. The power relationship between doctors and nurses has usually resulted in the nurse handing issues of a moral nature over to the doctor, who then tries to deal with them through the value-free objectivity of a 'clinical decision'. Contemporary practice challenges such themes, and 'team-work' and parity in the decision-making process demands input from all interested parties. However, perhaps the balance between beneficence and non-maleficence becomes particularly prevalent in the difficult dilemma of breaking the news to a patient that an illness will result in death.

In such situations, nurses can find themselves faced with many conflicting demands. Autocratic doctors may argue that it is their professional responsibility to give such news to a dying patient or, conversely, the patient's relatives may take the categorical stance that their loved one must be spared the news of a dreadful prognosis at all costs. However, despite these conflicting themes, if a patient asks a nurse, 'Am I going to die?', then the balance between beneficence and non-maleficence becomes of paramount importance. A mixture of professional experience, the interpretation of the patient's cues and the inferences the nurse makes from these all help to indicate the most appropriate way to proceed.

Such themes feature strongly in trying to discern the balance between beneficence and non-maleficence and identifying the most appropriate way to proceed. In the final analysis there are no definitive answers; the truth is that the person is going to die and there are no absolute principles which can guarantee that we give such information in a non-harmful way. Truth is perfect whilst the human condition is imperfect; reconciling the two is always a fraught process. Hebblethwaite (1991) supports this notion by stating: 'There is a recognition that "the truth" will almost inevitably be painful and almost nothing can make it painless, but we must be careful not to underestimate anyone's inner resources' (p. 85).

In this section I have tried to present an argument which highlights the inadequacies of duty-based principles as moral panaceas which can be applied and invoked for all ethical 'ills'. Emerging from this is a clear theme that duties or rules can rarely stand as absolute and isolated 'ends'. Duties, whatever their nature, remain rhetorical unless they give clear and non-conflicting directions for the pathways of practice.

We have seen that the duties of beneficence and non-maleficence must have value as means to an end if they are to have meaning and essence for practitioners. This can be said with equal efficacy about the principles embodied in the UKCC *Code*. In essence, they provide the starting point for discussion, analysis and professional discernment, but they are not categorical absolutes. Chadwick and Tadd (1992, p. 14) pursue this line of enquiry and comment: 'A code of conduct or ethics should perhaps be seen, not as the last word on ethics, but as a stimulus to moral thinking.' With this in mind, I will now concentrate on the themes of accountable, responsible and autonomous practice in the light of the UKCC's *Code*. A chapter of this nature could not possibly cover every aspect emerging from the professional code in relation to practice; but I do hope to raise some issues which highlight the code's essence for considering difficult dilemmas.

The code in practice

The UKCC *Code of Professional Conduct* places a great deal of emphasis on accountable practice:

> 'As a registered nurse, midwife or health visitor, you are personally accountable for your practice and, in the exercise of your professional accountability, must: . . .'

This statement serves as an introduction to the 16 clauses within the code; moreover, the word 'responsibility' occurs throughout these directives and has particular relevance and impact in the second clause:

> Clause 2:   'Ensure that no action or omission on your part, or within your sphere of responsibility, is detrimental to the interests, condition or safety of patients or clients.'

As a general theme, considerable confusion surrounds the notions of accountability and responsibility. Sometimes people use the terms synonymously or interchangeably and a lack of lucidity envelopes both themes. Such a position can leave practitioners in a bewildered state and demands that clarity is achieved before the terms can be competently interpreted and applied. Pearson and Vaughan (1986) recognize the difficulties which emerge from both words and differentiate between them in the following way:

> 'While the two ideas are inextricably linked, there is a clear difference between them. Accountability implies that a situation has been assessed, a plan been made and carried out, and the results evaluated. Responsibility refers to the task or "charge". Thus nurses can be offered the "charge" or responsibility for carrying out a particular action. In agreeing to accept the responsibility for that action, they become accountable for fulfilling it.' (p. 49)

Accountable practice finds its central essence in the nurse/patient relationship; however, whilst this may be the focal point of care-giving, accountability also extends to the nurse's employing organization and beyond, ultimately, to the UKCC. Applying this to the professional setting demands that practitioners must be able to give an explanation and rationale for their actions. Kendrick (1992) gives the following example to illustrate how practitioners are answerable for their professional activities:

> 'If you are given and accept the task of helping a patient/client with restricted mobility to exercise, then you are responsible for implementing and completing that task. At the same time, you become answerable to the client and other ruling bodies which safeguard, maintain and oversee standards of care. If the client were to fall while exercising, you might have to answer to your employers — you would attempt to show that despite the client's fall, you carried

out your responsibility competently and carefully.' (p. 38)

The call for practitioners to practise in an accountable and responsible manner clearly supports contemporary notions surrounding professional autonomy. However, considerable confusion surrounds the pragmatic implications of autonomy since its literal meaning of 'self-government' can be a cause of potential conflict when two parties, at variance with each other, are both trying to express self-determination. Such altercations are common in the professional arena; it may be a point of contention between a nurse and patient or, conversely, it may be a professional disagreement between members of the health care team. Beauchamp and Childress (1982) present the following interpretation of what the essence of autonomy involves:

> 'The autonomous person determines his or her course of action in accordance with a plan chosen by himself or herself. Such a person deliberates and chooses plans and is capable of acting on the basis of such deliberations, just as a truly independent government is capable of controlling its territories and policies.' (p. 59)

Nobody can be autonomous in the literal sense of true 'self-government' because such an idea would involve isolation. Society exists because of human interaction; if we tried to operate as autonomous but solitary agents then life would be intolerable. What is required is a common acceptance that each person has intrinsic worth and value underpinned by the notions of respect and inherent equality. It is inevitable that the expression of autonomy will sometimes lead to contrary perspectives; what is essential is that all parties, be they colleagues or patients, have equal licence to hold, express and defend their respective positions. The UKCC *Code* exists to give guidelines for such practice.

I shall now present some vignettes to illustrate how the themes of accountable, responsible and autonomous practice are encouraged by the code.

'Freedom to speak out'

Nurses who feel there is a need to speak out or 'blow the whistle' on poor standards of care will read with interest Clause 11 of the UKCC *Code*. This states that nurses should 'report to an appropriate person or authority, having due regard to the physical, psychological and social effects on patients and clients, any circumstances in the environment of care which could jeopardize standards of practice'. The following scenario highlights the dilemma faced by 'Ansell', a newly qualified staff nurse working in an acute mental health setting. He is concerned about staffing shortages and the effect this is having on standards of care:

'I realize that I've only been qualified for three months but things just don't feel right. Because our staffing levels are low it means that patients are being sedated and left unobserved for long periods — surely that isn't what caring is about. The situation is particularly bad at weekends and night-time; the number of violent incidents involving disturbed patients has definitely increased during these periods. Anyway, I went to see the Unit Manager about my fears and tried to argue that better staffing levels would cut back on the need for sedation and give us the chance to implement other therapies. The manager told me that staffing levels were commensurate with units of similar size throughout the country and that they managed okay. What really got to me was that he said more experience would teach me to manage my time better and cut down on the need I felt to have more staff around. But what really put the icing on the cake was when he said "If you can't take the heat, stay out of the kitchen". I felt abused, disillusioned and inadequate.'

It has been argued throughout this chapter that principles, by themselves, can only be the starting point for further analysis. Ansell has interpreted the themes of Clause 11 in a literal sense; the problem is that it gives no guidance to nurses who feel that those in 'appropriate authority' are not responding as they should. In the case of Ansell, he has been made to feel, as many whistleblowers do, that his own inadequacies are in some way contributing to the problem. Clause 11 encourages accountable practice through the exposure of factors which hinder safe and competent standards. Unfortunately, the consequences of applying literal principles can sometimes be detrimental towards the nurse who has felt 'duty-bound' to take action.

'Declining to give care'

Most nurses have experienced times when they have been asked to do something which may be beyond their level of competence and knowledge. This can be a disturbing event because it demands that we acknowledge our limitations and decline to undertake that given action. However, Clause 4 of the UKCC *Code* puts an obligation upon practitioners to acknowledge limitations in competence: 'Acknowledge any limitations in your knowledge and competence and decline any duties or responsibilities unless able to perform them in a safe and skilled manner'.

Let us consider these themes in the following scenario which highlights a dilemma faced by a first-year nurse undertaking a BA degree in nursing studies. Prior to commencing the degree course, Charlotte has worked as an enrolled nurse in an ophthalmic unit and undergraduate study gives her the opportunity to convert to first-level registration and obtain a degree. During her first clinical placement, on a ward for care of the elderly, Charlotte experiences an incident where she has to refuse to perform a procedure asked of her by a senior staff nurse:

> 'The unit is very busy and a high percentage of the patients are doubly incontinent. Our house officer had asked that one of our elderly female patients be catheterised because her urinary incontinence seriously threatened her pressure areas. I felt uneasy about this because maybe catheterisation wasn't the best way of dealing with the problem; anyway, the real issue was that Janet, the senior staff nurse, asked me to perform the catheterisation. She knew that I was a qualified EN and asked could I do the "job" because she, the staff nurse, had to do the medicines. It's been years since I've performed a catheterisation because I've spent my time in ophthalmics — I had to tell Janet that I felt unable to perform the task. The staff nurse accepted what I had to say but I felt very uneasy having to assert myself — I shouldn't have been asked to do it in the first place.'

Charlotte is completely justified in taking the position she has. She is clearly supported by Clause 4. However, the senior staff nurse should certainly be made aware of Clauses 12 and 14 which both deal with the competencies, workloads and pressures of colleagues. By asking Charlotte to deal with a catheterization she has compromised the position of a student which could have led to dire consequences. In practice, of course, it is always hard to take steps to refuse a request from a senior staff member — it can seem as if we are admitting failure. However, lack of experience or training is never a failure; the real failure would have been Charlotte attempting to do something potentially dangerous which she is not competent to perform.

Conclusions

We have examined the philosophical themes which underpin duty-based approaches towards moral thinking. Emerging from this is a clear relation between duty-based edicts and the UKCC *Code of Professional Conduct*. The essential value of such codes is that they provide a clear 'window' through which professional dilemmas may be viewed. However, merely 'viewing' a dilemma has little impact upon it and further analysis is needed to address all aspects of a difficult situation. I suggest that ethical analysis can provide the necessary 'tools' to help achieve such an endeavour. A chapter of this nature does not have the scope to cover all aspects of the *Code* in relation to the professional setting. As Chadwick and Tadd (1992, p. 15) state: 'Ethical practice depends on nurses using their capacity for moral reasoning and autonomous decision-making to think about the Code of Conduct and its application in specific cases.'

Acknowledgement

Grateful thanks are given to Professor Ruth Chadwick, University of Central Lancashire, for her help and advice during the preparation and writing of this chapter.

References

Beauchamp TL, Childress JF (1982) *Principles of Bio-medical Ethics*. Oxford: Oxford University Press.

Chadwick RF, Tadd W (1992) *Ethics and Nursing Practice: A Case Study Approach*. Basingstoke: Macmillan Press.

Durkheim E (1957) *Professional Ethics and Civic Morals*. London: Routledge & Kegan Paul.

Hebblethwaite M (1991) Shall we pretend it isn't happening? *Journal of Advances in Health and Nursing Care;* **1**: 2.

Illich I (1975) *Medical Nemesis: The Expropriation of Health*. London: Calder & Boyers.

Kendrick KD (1992) *Accountability and Research Based Practice*. Didsbury: Open College Press.

Kendrick KD (1993) Ethics and nursing practice. *British Journal of Nursing*; **2**: 18.

Parsons T (1951) *The Social System*. New York: The Free Press.

Pearson A, Vaughan B (1986) *Nursing Models for Practice*. London: Heinemann.

Tschudin V (1986) *Ethics in Nursing: The Caring Relationship*. London: Heinemann.

United Kingdom Central Council for Nursing, Midwifery and Health Visiting (1992) *Code of Professional Conduct for the Nurse, Midwife and Health Visitor*. London: UKCC.

Young P (1989) *Legal Problems in Nursing Practice*. London: Harper & Row.

18 Management issues in interprofessional work with older people

Julie Dockrell and Gail Wilson

Interprofessional relations are a key component in caring for elders. The multiple health and social care needs of frail elders (Bromley, 1990) make it essential for service managers to deal with other agencies in planning and delivery services. Thus, the context of providing services for this client group highlights many of the issues that are common in other branches of health and social care. This chapter concentrates on two aspects: first, the management of interprofessional activities, in terms of its impact on elderly service users; and second, the conflict between management models derived from private manufacturing industry and their application to this management of human service agencies.

The changing management context

Multiple needs at the level of individual users have a direct organizational effect. Interdisciplinary working is more likely to be the desirable norm (in terms of service provision). From the point of view of service managers, the needs of older people mean that they will be managing a mix of professionals. In the health services, occupational therapists, physiotherapists and a range of different nursing specialists may be grouped into one organizational unit. In social services or the voluntary sector, qualified social workers may work alongside occupational therapists, home care organizers and residential social workers. All may feel they have professional concerns which occasionally conflict (Wilson and Dockrell, 1994). Equally, staff within one service may be united by what they perceive as a threat from another service. The threat may even be seen as a takeover. For example, some of the therapeutic activities previously provided by psychologists are now more widely provided by nurse practitioners, social workers and care staff (Milne, 1993). Alternatively, professionals may feel that another group is directing so much work towards them that they can no longer fulfil their professional standards.

Recent legislation has emphasized the importance of inter-professional relations in service provision for elderly people. The NHS and Community Care Act 1990 requires local authorities to consult with users and voluntary and private sector agencies and to contract for care to the private sector. At the same time the introduction of care management has allowed social service departments to recruit unqualified staff to posts that would formerly have been confined to social workers. In community nursing there is a parallel move away from highly qualified and relatively expensive staff, such as health visitors (Strong and Robinson, 1990), towards nursing assistants. This tendency to rely on less qualified staff brings its own management problems. Professionals may find their skills devalued or their working practices subjected to enforced change. In the circumstances, interprofessional tensions and tensions between qualified and unqualified staff are to be expected. Sometimes these tensions will have to be contained within one organization, but equally they may exist between agencies. A traditionally lower proportion of qualified staff is likely to become an increasingly important issue as voluntary sector and private agencies take over more caring activity, such as nursing homes for frail elders, private domiciliary care and day care. In addition, staff in voluntary or private services often feel downgraded by qualified staff in the stage-funded agencies (Gutch and Young, 1988), even though the latter do not have a monopoly of professional qualifications.

The division between managers and professionals is not new (Scrivens, 1988; Normand, 1993; Palmer, 1993). In health and social services for older people this division can be seen as a distinction between professionals who deploy specialized skills, techniques or knowledge which they have learnt during some form of recognized training, and managers who maintain and develop service organizations. Management and professional activities can overlap in elder care, particularly in the lower rungs of the management hierarchy or in 'flat' organizations. The extent of the overlap varies, but is likely to be present for most first- and second-line managers. Since managers (or administrators or bureaucrats) are often placed in opposition to professionals, the overlap may cause conflict. In theory, professionals relate to individual users and should offer treatment or service regardless of cost or other 'non-professional' considerations (Rowbottom and Billis, 1987). In practice, professionals have always operated within limited resources and have rationed their services in various ways (Lipsky, 1980). The key issue, in the changes following the introduction of internal markets, is that the rationing process has now become very much clearer (Harrison et al., 1992; Le Grand, 1991). It is no longer easy to maintain the ideal of the professional motivated solely by user needs.

An increase of 25% is predicted in the numbers of people in the age groups where physical and mental frailty is most likely (the over-80s) between 1991 and 2001. This rise, combined with a slowing down in the growth of resources allocated to elder care (Griffiths, 1988), will make rationing decisions still more obvious. In authorities where budgets are devolved down to care managers, even front-line professionals have to budget and take decisions which they formerly referred upwards. Professionals who have become first- and second-level managers are therefore more likely than in the past to face conflicts of interest and feel under stress.

Management theory

The second important consideration in any discussion of management in health and social care is the absence of service-specific models of management and organizational behaviour. Government exhortation and much management training appears to assume that a management model developed for the private manufacturing sector can be straightforwardly applied to health and social care. In this model, outputs can be clearly identified and quantified and the sole customers are service recipients. Attempts by the government to set up internal markets at the same time as the charter initiatives (Harrison et al., 1992) have further reinforced the idea of a private-sector model.

Present government policy which treats management skills as transferable between private and public sectors, and between different branches of each, further reinforces the idea that a private manufacturing model is adequate. It is not surprising that the particular characteristics of public-sector management or the special needs of different groups of users can get lost in the urge to implement changes as fast and as efficiently as possible. For example, DoH management competencies produced in 1992 (DoH, 1992) made no mention of service users and treated management as if it occurred within a single organization. Competencies relating directly to user needs or to interagency relations were omitted. A more recent version (DoH, 1993) includes users (defined as customers/consumers) but still omits competencies which are related to interagency contacts. The model used is one of a single agency in which managers have a defined span of control.

The use of the term 'customer' is itself highly misleading. Very few elderly users of health and social services have enough money to pay for the services they need. Despite the rhetoric of choice in *Caring for People* (DoH, 1989), services cannot afford to hold spare capacity so that people can choose what they want when they want it. The 'customer' in the new internal market system is not the individual service user but the purchaser who places a contract for service. In health care this is increasingly the budget-holding general practitioner or the district health authority (sometimes jointly with the Family Health Service Authority). In social care the main purchaser is the local social services department. Users may be forced to share the cost on a means-tested basis but they do not become 'customers' in any way that gives them market power.

In reality there are service users at two main levels — individual and organizational. At the level of the individual customer, there can be a conflict of interests over whether the patient or client is the main user of service or whether the service is designed primarily to help the carer (when there is one) continue to care. At the organizational level, most service providers are aware that there are many other users of their services besides clients, patients or carers. Different sectors within a complex system of elder care use each other (Dockrell and Wilson, 1994). Thus hospital consultants in acute wards will be using long-stay wards or rehabilitation wards; these wards will be using nursing homes, residential homes or domiciliary services in order to keep up their rate of discharge; social services will be relying on district nursing services to help keep clients in their own homes where they would otherwise have to move into an institution; and so on. Increasingly since the NHS and Community Care Act 1990, statutory services are using voluntary and private residential providers.

A final consideration on the issue of who is the customer for human service agencies relates to the fact that even private-sector agencies are likely to be partly financed by government. Before April 1993, central government paid fees for low-income residents in private and voluntary residential and nursing homes. There was an automatic right to support after a means test. Since then the right to support has been removed and only those who are assessed as needing institutional care can be assisted with the costs. The money is now transferred to social service departments and is unlikely to keep pace with demand. Local authorities frequently contract with private domiciliary care agencies to provide a service that clients cannot afford to buy for themselves. These contributions from the state reflect the complex nature of the social production of welfare. (See Davies and Challis (1986) and Davies et al. (1990) for an elaboration of this concept.) Society is willing to help pay for older people, or to pass legislation setting up or regulating agencies who assist them. It follows that society, in the form of taxpayers, voters or politicians, will also have an impact on the delivery of health and social care. Managers may be able to ignore these wider customers or users in their day-to-day work, but their influence is always present (Wilson, 1993).

Research aims

While interprofessional cooperation in services for older people has been advocated for many years (DHSS, 1978; Acheson, 1981; Health Advisory Service, 1983; or see Allsop, 1984, pp. 110–120), little has been done in terms of investigating the processes by which managers deliver services or the impact of management activities on elderly service users. In the research reported below, the aim was to investigate aspects of the management of interprofessional relations as they affect users of services.

The data reported in this chapter comes from a broader-ranging investigation studying the manager–user interface.[1] The research was based on managers of elder care organizations who were following a day-release course.[2]

The study was an interdisciplinary project considering contacts between managers and service users. The project was designed to outline the role of the manager in relation to service users. Data were collected about all contacts with service users in a multidisciplinary framework. Our concern in this chapter is to highlight the information which relates to management issues in interprofessional work with older people.

Research methods

The participants

The analysis is based on diaries kept by 29 managers from 28 organizations. The sectors to which they belonged were as follows:

Social services	10
NHS	7
Voluntary sector	6
Other	6

As might be expected, there were major differences in management activities and environments between the sectors. In addition, within each sector participants frequently worked in different management environments, served different management functions and had differing professional allegiances. For example, 'social services' included field social workers, residential home managers, home care managers and day-centre managers. Although they worked for the same sector of public service they had varying professional backgrounds.

Social workers or those with a social-work related qualification

---

[1] The study was funded from the Department of Health NHMSE.
[2] The course — Certificate/MSc in Management of Community Care Services for Older People — is run at the London School of Economics and is accredited by the ENB.

predominated in the social services, and nursing staff in the health services. There were nurses in other sectors and some staff who saw themselves primarily as voluntary sector managers rather than as professionals. The following were the professional affiliations of the participants in the study:

Nurse	9
Non-residential social services	9
Residential	4
Other	7

The participants ranged from senior locality managers with responsibility for several services, to first-line care managers with no staff directly under their control. Management roles were often perceived in quite different ways. The managers from the NHS included community psychiatric nurses who saw their roles differently from district nurses and from hospital-based nurses. There were no general practitioners in this group. The managers from the voluntary sector were more similar to each other than to most managers in statutory services in that they all experienced a wide degree of autonomy, relatively flat hierarchies and managed small groups of volunteers or low-paid staff.

The procedure

The study used a range of methods to elicit managers' activities and contacts with service users and other professionals. The research activities and their intended purposes are shown in Table 18.1.

The project began by setting up workshops to consider who the service users were. In each workshop participants were divided into groups. Numbers in groups for each task ranged between four and six. Participants were divided into groups for the initial workshop setting out the context of the research and discussing the concept of service user. The first round of diaries developed this initial theme and asked managers to distinguish between users defined as clients, patients or carers, and users defined as other professionals or agencies.

The second and third stages of the diaries considered the effect of the participants' activities on users, defined as clients, patients and carers. The management activities identified were those which occurred both within the organization and activities which related to other organizations. In the second stage the aim was to consider the management of interprofessional activity within the organization as it affected users. The third stage asked managers to record cases where the actions of other professionals or other agencies' service had an impact on users.

Each round was followed by an interprofessional workshop which combined a consideration of the issues raised in the previous set of diaries with a focused discussion on the next round. Focus groups occurred at a number of stages in the study with the specific aim of addressing problems in practice.

Table 18.1 Research activities and purposes

Activity	Purpose
Workshops	To elicit problems in terminology and working practices
Diary study	To provide details of perceived working practices and management-based activities
Case studies	To provide detailed information of the ways in which management practice and interprofessional work directly impinged on services for a client
Focus groups	To resolve problems and inconsistency in data collection and interpretation

Research results

The first workshop highlighted the complexity of the process. All five groups produced the same results — service users were very widely defined (i.e. clients, patients, carers, other professionals in the same agency and other professionals in different agencies). In addition most managers felt under pressure from other agencies who used their services. As an example, both health and social service managers identified stresses arising from pressure by hospital consultants trying to speed up discharge of frail elders.

Discussion in the workshops indicated that management contacts with users could be divided into two categories, direct and indirect. Direct contacts were usually face-to-face or on the telephone, but sometimes they were written. Indirect contacts reached managers via their front-line staff and resulted in changes which influenced the service given to users; for example, supervision which resulted in new ways of servicing a difficult user, or training which provided the professionals with new competencies.

Direct contact with users arose because many managers were still providing a front-line service alongside their management function. As outlined above, managers could experience conflict between providing a front-line professional service as had been done before promotion, and managing the service. For example, first-line managers often carried a reduced case-load. In other cases, particularly for more senior managers, direct contact with users was likely to be limited to dealing with complaints or with special cases.

Indirect contact with users covered a wide range of service-related management activities which are described below. It is possible to argue that all management of an organization designed to deliver services is user-related. However, this did not appear to be the view of participating managers. Evaluation of the stages of the research showed that they found the focus on users both useful and refreshing. This report is therefore limited to the activities that they identified as affecting elderly service users.

Range of managerial activities

The range of activities reported by managers was very wide. They could be classified into four main types: information collection and communication; staff development and training; rationing and boundary setting; service planning and organization design. Each of these types of activity was influenced by issues relating to interprofessional and interagency activities. There was potential for overlap between the classifications, but many aspects of the four types of activity could be united under the heading of maintenance of service quality.

Span-of-control issues are a key feature in the management of interprofessional relationships. In most organizations that deliver elder care, managers have a reasonable degree of control over the range of professionals working for them. However, the management of interprofessional relationships across agencies raises greater problems. Relations with other agencies are part of the environment in which the agency has to operate. Most managers saw this aspect of their environment as hostile in organizational terms. The hostility, however, was caused by the introduction of competition via internal markets, financial constraints and the pressures of reorganization. The demands of users — defined as other agencies — frequently could not be met. The important issue for the management of interprofessional relations lies in the way such structural pressures towards poor interprofessional relations are dealt with. Diplomacy in dealing with other agencies combined with careful attention to building personal and professional contacts can minimize the impact on users.

Information collection and communication

The multiple needs of frail elders and fragmented systems of service delivery posed special problems of communication and data collection for managers at all levels. Professionals need to access resources both within their own organization and from agencies in order to meet the needs of elderly service users. In the first instance improvements or changes in service provision needed an understanding of user needs and also of the lines of accountability and control within their own organization. It was otherwise difficult to make any changes. The second major information need was for managers to be aware of the ways in which other organizations met user needs. This entailed a degree of communication between organizations which was often lacking. Managers could act as a guide to their service for professionals in outside agencies. Under the NHS and Community Care Act, local authorities must specify what needs they will meet; but the information may still not be fully accessible to users or to other professionals. In addition, forums for joint discussions and planning can enhance understanding across organizations. Such activities are, by necessity, time-consuming.

Managers also recognized the need to develop records and statistics-based information systems in a range of services. Statistics could also be used in a regular process of interagency service monitoring. Shortfalls were taken as a basis for negotiations to improve services. However, the project participants realized that negotiating skills were needed to ensure that interprofessional standards reflected good working practices rather than just paper results.

Advocacy on behalf of individual elder service users, or more generally as a way of combating ageism, was seen by many managers as part of their work. This attitude applied across professions and agencies. Some voluntary organizations were set up with advocacy as a principal aim. They constantly had to deal with health and social service professionals whose values differed from their own.

Staff development and training

Many managers chose interprofessional training as a key issue in developing services for users. It took place in a variety of contexts: formal, in terms of courses set up or materials prepared; or informal. Much informal training was done during staff supervision sessions or in other encounters between managers and staff. Such staff development was a key area in quality assurance. It needed time and expertise. Managers might have the necessary knowledge themselves, but they might also need to understand the needs of other professionals or non-professional staff in their own organizations and find appropriate training.

Interagency training was a very important component of some management activities. Private and voluntary agencies were increasingly requesting training from professionals in the state sector, but managers in specialist voluntary organizations such as the Alzheimer's society provided information and training to a very wide range of state and voluntary agencies.

Some training was directly related to raising the competence of staff within the service. Some was more clearly directed towards users' needs. For example, interprofessional training in how to handle violent patients led to the suggestion that aggressive users as well as their victims could be included in post-crisis support groups. This could be seen as a move towards user empowerment in a public-sector based management model, but would be irrelevant in a private-sector model where the user has no buying power.

Developing staff or deploying weaker staff or volunteers in less demanding work was another aspect of quality assurance. Staff whose work was below standard, or who were the subject of user complaints, had to be dealt with. However, in the public sector where staff rights were strong, or in voluntary organizations where the ethos of voluntarism made standard setting more difficult, there was no easy option of immediate dismissal. Managers who were not from the same profession could find that the interprofessional aspects of the situation were an additional cause of friction.

Rationing and boundary-setting

At the worst, staffing issues could be reduced to managing shortages and rationing services. Scarce resources meant that staff were often not available to cover for sickness or training. At best, managers were able to restructure services or to develop innovative ways of using staff so that users benefited even though resources were short. For example, new teams which were set up by redeploying existing staff could provide an innovative and enthusiastic approach at virtually no extra cost.

It was common for managers to report that shortages of staff had highlighted the need to set service boundaries. In some cases such boundaries were simple issues of professional competency. They might be defined by law, as for example, writing prescriptions, or they might be determined by professional training or accepted custom. For example, an elder who was known to be suffering from financial abuse was likely to be referred to a social worker. Boundaries were important because it was difficult to guarantee a standard of service if they were not clearly set. A user may find that she fell between services or that she was offered one or more services apparently without any clear reasons. Even if boundaries are set, users may still fail to get a service, but the reason is likely to be one of staff shortage rather than confusion over professional boundaries.

In other cases boundaries were renegotiated or fully defined for the first time. For example, in some local authorities only qualified nurses were allowed to give medication in residential homes, but in others care attendants or home care staff issued medicines. Clearly defined procedures were essential when staff who were not fully trained took on new work. This was another service-oriented management activity which needed negotiating skills.

Shortages of staff or equipment were dealt with in a variety of ways. The simplest was to blame other agencies or other professionals. Most managers recognized that this was not productive even though they sometimes found it inevitable. A more constructive approach which was more likely to be available to managers in the voluntary sector, but not confined to them, was to encourage users, including carers, to campaign for more resources. Managers were acting as advocates for service users either directly or indirectly.

Another approach to resource constraints was to modify existing systems to take account of shortages. Often the impact on users was negative. New assessment procedures which stressed professionally defined risks, rather than an interprofessional approach to user needs, were intended to target the most frail or to limit service claims. Changes to intake teams or faster throughput in hospital wards were another response to lack of resources. In one case, lack of occupational therapists led to very long waiting lists and caused social workers to stop referring clients for OT assessment until waiting times dropped.

Although it appears that front-line workers bore the main brunt of service shortages in their dealings with users, managers had a role in calming and diffusing user complaints about cuts in service or poor quality. Such managerial activity could either be one-off, as in the case of individual complaints, or it could be part of the service structure — for example, when user forums were established. In the latter case it was more likely to involve other professionals.

Aspects of service structure and service planning

Service structures were not static. Most managers were either involved in restructuring or could foresee that it would be likely in the near future. Organizations that were not changing internally were still having to cope with changing pressures from outside. For example, patient or resident mix was changing rapidly as a result of new policies following the NHS and Community Care Act 1990. In most cases, middle managers were not in charge of restructuring or respecification of job descriptions but had to implement policies decided at senior level. Multiple lines of accountability are common in services employing professionals (Owens and Glennerster, 1988). In such circumstances standards cannot be successfully set or changes in service specifications implemented without multidisciplinary negotiations.

Managers in the voluntary sector usually worked in flatter hierarchies than did those in health and social services. The difference in structure meant that they were often closer to users and had relatively little authority in comparison with middle managers in health and social services. They easily felt marginalized by mainstream health and social services. Voluntary-sector managers were also in the weak position of having to apply for funds from local government or health service. The change from grants to different forms of service contract meant that they needed data to support their applications.

Shortages of funds made service planning very difficult in many areas. New needs such as services for ethnic minority elders were very difficult to develop when cash was short. As a result, ethnic minority users depended for specialized services almost entirely on the voluntary sector. (See Bowling (1990) for examples of this problem.) Front-line staff or first-line managers could work hard to establish relations with voluntary groups but find their efforts wasted if backup from mainstream services was not forthcoming. There were cases where front-line staff built up trust and interest in ethnic minority communities only to find their line managers refusing to make necessary staff time available or failing to cooperate across agencies to provide premises.

Maintenance of service quality

The issue of service quality appeared in a wide range of activities. Managers might set their own quality goals or standards within their own organizations. However, in an interprofessional context they usually had to negotiate rather than simply set standards. This was sometimes true within agencies but still more so across agencies. For example, hospital discharge procedures which had to be set up under the NHS and Community Care Act involved agencies with different procedures and different views of quality.

The place of users in terms of quality assurance varied across organizations. Social services had complaints systems which allowed managers to address poor service in an interprofessional context. Some voluntary organizations had systems of quality control which regularly involved users but a more common approach was for users to be involved only sporadically in crisis situations.

Conclusions

Successful management of interprofessional relations needs to recognize two categories of user: professionals and non-professionals in other agencies; and clients, patients and care-givers. Managers need good communication skills and respect for users and other professionals. Communication takes time, and time is a resource. It was important that managers had time to explain to other professionals what their service could and could not offer. Users of all types needed help in order to negotiate the range of services on offer. Meetings needed to be regular and well attended, another time issue. Informal contacts were also very important. The collection of service data became a tool in interprofessional management for some.

It appeared from the data that managers thought of service planning and the development of services structures in terms of their own organizations. It could be argued that the ability to look beyond the confines of the organization and take a wider view of health and social care systems should be confined to higher-level managers. Private-sector management theory would suggest that such a strategic vision is the role of senior management. The White Paper *Caring for People* (1989), and subsequent legislation and official guidance, imply that such vision is essential but imply that it is confined to senior managers.

There are problems with this argument in public-sector organizations where interprofessional working is the norm. It has repeatedly been shown that agreements to cooperate or coordinate can be reached by high-level management but that there is a strong tendency for them to break down at service level. Hospital closure and the subsequent arrangements for former patients is a common example (Korman and Glennerster, 1990). The traditional private-sector based remedy is to strengthen lines of accountability. However, interprofessional and interagency cooperation cannot easily be accommodated in such a model. While some formal arrangements can be agreed at high level and then translated into cooperation between health and social services (for example in hospital discharge arrangements), much work remains outside a statutory framework. The day-to-day service needs of users, combined with the day-to-day aspects of service rationing, call for more flexible and possibly more temporary approaches. It follows that if users are not to suffer from resource constraints and gaps in service, first- and second-line managers need a wider vision of interprofessional relationships than they are expected to have at present by the NHS Training Directorate.

Shortages of staff or other resources were an issue for managers in terms of having to cut or request extensions to existing services. Others allowed more imaginative solutions which could involve changes in the way different professionals or grades of staff were deployed or negotiations with other agencies for changes in service mix and the shifting of service boundaries. However, managers who negotiate across service or professional boundaries were likely to find that they needed to deal with interprofessional rivalries, suspicion and intransigence. Managers reported far more negative than positive events under these heads.

The evidence from this research is that most managers can identify actions of managers in other agencies as threatening to their own service but that they do not always see their own actions (or do not choose to record such actions) in the same way. Damaging decisions were recorded in the diaries but nearly always as the decisions of others.

The models of management most commonly advocated in health and social care, by the NHS Training Directorate among others, assume that management skills are widely transferable and that they are exercised within a single organization. There may be exceptions at senior levels where a strategic vision is called for, but in general services organizations are compared to firms in private manufacturing industry and managers expected to function accordingly. Such models also assume measurable outputs and ignore the existence of diverse groups of professionals, who may have their own objectives and standards and their own lines of professional accountability.

The data collected in the present study highlight the dangers of making simple generalizations from private-sector management skills to public-sector management. Many first- and second-line managers were in a dual role both managing and providing services. They needed skills of reassurance and diplomacy as well as the ability to stand firm in the interests of users and staff. Managers needed to communicate, collaborate and negotiate between organizations and within organizations between different professions. The ability to see beyond the immediate confines of one agency was essential for managers at all levels.

References

Acheson D (1981) *Primary Health Care in Inner London: Report of a Study Group*. London: London Health Planning Consortium.

Allsop J (1984) *Health Policy and the National Health Service*. London: Longman.

Bowling B (1990) *Elderly People from Ethnic Minorities: A Report on Four Projects*. London: King's College Age Concern Institute of Gerontology.

Bromley DB (1990) *Behavioural Gerontology: Central issues in the Psychology of Ageing*. Chichester: John Wiley.

Davies B, Bebbington A, Charnley H (1990) *Resources, Needs and Outcomes*. Aldershot: Avebury.

Davies B, Challis D (1986) *Matching Resources to Needs in Community Care*. Aldershot: Gower.

Department of Health (1989) *Caring for People: Community Care in the Next Decade and Beyond*. London: HMSO.

Department of Health (1992) *Managers Working for Patients*. Swindon: National Health Service Training Directorate.

Department of Health (1993) *Managers Working for Patients*. Swindon: National Health Service Training Directorate.

Department of Health and Social Security (1978) *A Happier Old Age: A Discussion Document on Elderly People in Our Society*. London: HMSO.

Dockrell J, Wilson G (1994) Older people and their systems. In: Messer D, Meldrum C (Eds), *Psychology for Nurses*. London: Prentice Hall.

Griffiths, Sir R (1988) *Community Care: Agenda for Action*. London: HMSO.

Gutch R, Young K (1988) *Partners or Rivals? The changing relationship between Local Government and the Public Sector*. Luton: Local Government Training Board.

Harrison S, Hunter D, Marnoch G, Pollitt C (1992) *Just Managing: Power and Culture in the National Health Service*. Edinburgh: Macmillan.

Health Advisory Service (1983) *The Rising Tide: developing services for mental illness in old age*. London: HMSO.

Korman N, Glennerster H (1990) *Hospital Closure*. Milton Keynes: Open University Press.

Le Grand J (1991) Quasi-markets and Social Policy, *the Economic Journal*; **101**, (408), 1256–1267.

Lipsky (1980) *Street Level Bureaucrats: dilemmas of the individual in public services*. New York: Russel Sage Foundation.

Milne D (1993) *Psychology and Mental Health Nursing*. BPS Books.

Normand CEM (1993) Changing patterns of care: the challenge for health care professions and professionals. In: Malek M, Vaconi P (Eds), *Managerial Issues in Health Care Management*. Chichester: John Wiley.

Owens P, Glennerster H (1988) *The Nursing Management Function After Griffiths: Second Interim Report on a Study in the North-West Thames Region*. London: London School of Economics and Political Science/North West Thames Regional RHA.

Palmer S (1993) Z and the art of management. *Nursing Standard*; **7**: 5 May, 45–47.

Rowbottom R, Billis D (1987) *Organisational Design: The Work Levels Approach*. Aldershot: Gower.

Scrivens E (1988) Doctors and managers: never the twain shall meet? *British Medical Journal*; **296**: 1754–1755.

Strong P, Robinson J (1990) *The NHS Under New Management*. Milton Keynes: Open University.

Wilson G (1993) Users and providers: different perspectives on community care services. *Journal of Social Policy*; **22**: 4.

Wilson G, Dockrell J (1994) Elderly care. In: Carrier J, Owens P,

Horder J (Eds), *Interprofessional Issues in Health and Community Care*. London: Macmillan.

19 Choice, continuity and control? Recent developments in maternity care in Britain

Jane Sandall

Introduction

The control and management of birth is an important issue for any society. As Margaret Stacey noted: 'Reproduction is a crucial area which reveals starkly the relations between health care and the dominant social values' (1988, p. 259). Since the early 1970s there has been a lively debate about how much choice and control women want over the care they receive. This debate about the relationship between professionals and childbearing women and the impact on interprofessional relations are the central themes of this chapter.

The literature on the maternity services has had a recurrent theme of the need to have a more 'humanized service'. In the 1960s, there was enough concern to issue a policy statement called *Human Relations in Obstetrics* (Ministry of Health, 1961). The distress caused to a woman by seeing as many as 20 different professionals during her pregnancy and meeting a stranger for the birth has been documented by lay and professional groups for many years.

Continuity of care by the midwife had been seen as a desirable 'ideal' way to overcome these problems, but too difficult to achieve in practice (Select Committee, 1980, para. 292). The Maternity Services Advisory Committee (1982, para. 1.10) went further and recommended the use of midwives in a more independent capacity, and were aware of the 'numerous consumer complaints about the so-called impersonal nature of care in hospitals, where maternity services are now concentrated'.

Continuity of care has thus been advocated on three grounds. First, if women get to know and trust a few staff well, they are more likely to feel confident about expressing concerns and feel in more control of the reproductive process. Secondly, midwives are more likely to provide more sensitive care. Thirdly, the social support literature (Elbourne et al., 1989; Oakley et al., 1990) suggests beneficial effects on pregnancy and birth outcome.

What is continuity of care?

The aim of this chapter is to examine the schemes for continuity of care that are being set up by midwives in Britain in response to the most commonly expressed wish of pregnant women, which is that they be attended during their pregnancy, labour and postnatal period by a midwife who is not a stranger. *If continuity of care is the model for the future, then this has important implications for other professionals and supersedes the home/hospital, technological/natural birth debate.*

The notion of continuity of midwifery care started initially with several articles in the midwifery press by Caroline Flint in the early 1980s (1979, 1981), followed by a randomized trial at St Georges Hospital in 1983 (Flint et al., 1989). This resulted in greater maternal and midwife satisfaction, along with less intervention and morbidity in the experimental group and an estimated 20–25% reduction in cost.

In 1986 the Association of Radical Midwives (ARM) published *The Vision*, a draft proposal for the future of maternity services. This proposed that 70% of midwives would work in community-based group practices, giving continuity of care in conjunction with teams attached to consultant obstetricians. A Royal College of Midwives discussion document (RCM, 1987) proposed community-based midwife care including midwife-controlled beds, and recognized the fact that there is some doubt about the assumption that the safest place of delivery is a consultant unit. By 1989 the ARM, in a response to the White Paper *Working for Patients* (DoH, 1989) was proposing group practices of midwives, emphasizing the cost-effectiveness of care by midwives who would contract for services with the new purchasing authorities.

Many schemes propose that pregnant women should refer themselves initially to a team of midwives who give continuous care to a group of pregnant women within a defined geographical area, regardless of the pregnancy outcome. The midwives would give total care on their own responsibility if the woman is healthy and in association with an obstetrician if problems are identified. These schemes have had high media coverage, study days have been run and teams have been established in various ways in North London (Domadia, 1990), West London (Rosser, 1990), Oxford (Watson, 1990), Bloomsbury (Kroll, 1989), Guildford (Frohlich and Edwards, 1989) and the Rhondda (Russell, 1988). Although rigorous evaluation has been minimal, there has been government funding of a research study in

Aberdeen (RCM, 1991) and a DoH commissioned national survey of team midwifery (Wraight et al., 1993), which found that the reality of continuity of care is much more difficult to achieve than simply reorganizing midwives in teams (Flint, 1993).

The political and economic context

Enthusiasm within midwifery and by women themselves for continuity of care needs to be put into the economic and political context of health care in the 1980s and 90s. Governments have been concerned to keep health costs down, and one of the major ways of doing this has been through an increasing emphasis on cost-effectiveness (National Audit Office, 1990). This concern to contain costs has been noted in Canada (Romalis, 1985) and the USA (Annandale, 1989), where the state has been increasingly concerned to cut costs by using midwives, especially when recent research shows that the outcome in terms of satisfaction and infant and maternal morbidity appear to be no worse and might even be improved (Campbell and Macfarlane, 1987). Accompanying the concern with escalating costs were doubts about the adverse impact of high-technology obstetrics on perinatal and maternal morbidity (Chalmers et al., 1989).

Along with increased clinical evaluation and audit, economic assessments were beginning to show that the 'centralization of maternity units was not based on good evidence about the cost-effectiveness of the policy' (Mugford, 1990). I would suggest that the increasing emphasis on cost-effectiveness and evaluation of medical care since the early 1980s has focused government attention on maternity care, particularly as this is an area of medicine where consumer opinion and increasing litigation receive higher than average media attention (Ennif et al., 1971).

This has been demonstrated by a keen interest in the last five years from the British government, the midwifery profession and women's groups as to how routine maternity care should be organized. For example, following the National Audit Office and Committee of Public Accounts reports on the maternity services (NAO, 1990) and the strong interest by some members of parliament (e.g. Audrey Wise), the terms of reference of the backbench Health Committee of the House of Commons were:

'To enquire into maternity services to determine the extent to which resources and professional expertise are used to achieve the most appropriate and cost-effective care of pregnant women and delivery and care of newborn babies.' (House of Commons, 1992)

Where previous enquiries tended to focus on mortality (e.g. Select Committee, 1980), this time the Health Committee stressed that central to the enquiry was the management of normal pregnancy and birth.

In response the report of the Expert Maternity Group headed by Baroness Cumberlege, *Changing Childbirth* (DoH, 1993) has proposed for consultation a series of action points to be achieved by purchasers and providers. Specifically, within five years 75% of women should be cared for in labour by a midwife whom she has come to know in pregnancy. This would involve a woman having the option (along with the existing options) of booking her care with a community-based midwife who would provide total care in hospital or at home, depending on the woman's choice. Care would be provided either alone if there were no complications, or in partnership with an obstetrician if complications arose. This implies a significant shift to midwife-led community-based care and midwifery beds in maternity units within five years. *What impact will this have on interprofessional relations, and is this what women want?*

Women's views of maternity care

In drawing on sociological research on women's views, I attempt to explore if continuity of care is what women want, and examine the issues for the providers of care in making the relationship between a woman and her midwife paramount.

Although doubts were expressed about obstetric practice in the academic literature in the 1970s (e.g. Richards, 1975; Oakley, 1980; Macintyre, 1977a,b), it was the consumer organizations that played a key role in the debate around childbirth (e.g. Robinson, 1974), followed up by media and parliamentary interest that resulted in the government commissioning Ann Cartwright's (1979) survey of women's experiences of maternity care.

There is evidence of increasing interest by the government in gaining consumer views (Mason, 1989). *Working for Patients* (DoH, 1989) underlines the wider contribution of patients' views to assessing quality of care, although as Stacey pointed out in 1976, 'the term "consumer" is of limited value in understanding the status and role of the patient'.

There are theoretical and methodological difficulties in this type of research into consumer views of medical care, as Locker and Dunt (1978) identified. Reid and Garcia (1989, p. 137) and Mason (1989) discuss the specific difficulties of getting women's views at the time of birth. These views also change over time, and answers given depend on where they are being questioned, by whom and the form of question.

Interpretations of reported satisfaction are also difficult to interpret, as alternatives are difficult to envisage and service users tend to prefer the familiar (Porter and Macintyre, 1984).

Sociologists have used the medical dominance viewpoint to explain the hospitalization of birth and active management of labour (Cartwright, 1979; Tew, 1990), resulting in loss of control and alienation of women. The assumption that the increased use of technology was responsible for a decline in mortality rates had been questioned in general (McKeown, 1976), and specifically in obstetrics (Cochrane, 1971, p. 63; Tew, 1985; Chalmers and Richards, 1977).

The early feminist literature was polemical and intentionally political (Arms, 1975; Haire, 1972) and was critical of the medical model imposed on pregnancy and birth. On the other hand, the arguments of Shorter (1982), based on historical evidence of working class women, suggest that it was only because of the advances in nineteenth century medicine that women were able to liberate themselves from the hazards of pregnancy and childbirth, and it was this liberation that paved the way for the success of modern feminism. This highlights a need not to glamorize the past (see Macintyre, 1977a).

As Chalmers (1978) points out, obstetricians are particularly vulnerable to lay criticism and pregnant women are less willing to adopt the sick role (McKinlay, 1972). Thus there has been a focus in sociological research on the notion that women and obstetricians have 'competing ideologies of reproduction', where women see pregnancy and birth as a normal process over which they should exert active control and in which medical intervention should only occur in exceptional circumstances, and obstetricans see it as a potentially pathological event to be controlled and managed (Comaroff, 1977; Graham and Oakley, 1981; Nash and Nash, 1979).

This assumption that all women share the same view has been challenged by Nelson (1983), who argues that the major influences on the 'middle class model' of birth (the natural childbirth movement, feminism, consumerism, and 'back to nature' romanticism) have little appeal to working class women. Further, this model is predicated on the idea of choice, which has less appeal to women who have fewer opportunities to exercise choice in their daily lives. (For a more detailed discussion, see McNeil et al. (1990, p. 10).) Reid (1983, p. 87) also provides evidence of a distinctive working class perspective, for whom 'the birth was often dismissed as something to be got through, a necessary hurdle to motherhood'; as did McIntosh (1989), who found that working class women's expectations were 'utilitarian and negative', regarding the process as means to achieve an end. As previous research has shown, women tend to accept the service offered, in the assumption that it must be the best (Riley, 1977; Cartwright, 1979; Porter and Macintyre, 1984).

In contrast, a recent prospective study of 825 women (Green et al.,

1990) has challenged these findings, in that women of all social classes were likely to subscribe to the ideal of a drug-free labour. What was important was feeling in control, and the more interventions a woman had, the less in control she felt, but only when she believed they were unnecessary. All these studies have enabled women to speak for themselves and confirmed the sociological critique. Women have complained about impersonal care, lack of continuity of carer and long waiting times (Reid and McIlwaine, 1980), and also unnecessary use of interventions and lack of explanation in labour (Cartwright, 1979; Oakley, 1980). The MORI poll reported in *Changing Childbirth* (DoH, 1993) reported that 72% of women would like the option of a different type of care, 22% said they would like a home birth, and 44% said they would like a midwife-led domino delivery.

The conclusion to be drawn is that women have different views depending on their level of education, class and race (which is only just beginning to be explored — see Phoenix (1990)). One theme that does appear to come through consistently from all the studies of consumers' views is the lack of information, explanation and poor communication, bearing out Cartwright's conclusion that working class women, like middle class ones, want to be informed, but they are less successful in obtaining information. (See also Jacoby (1988) for a more detailed study.) Haug and Lavin (1983) have pointed out that having adequate knowledge is crucial to informed patient decision-making; *the key question is, how does the professional/patient relationship mediate this?*

Since the early 1970s concern has been expressed about short-comings in the nature of consultations concerned with reproduction (Doyal and Pennell, 1979). Shapiro et al. (1983) found women did not receive all the information they wanted from their obstetrician, yet there was an absence of conflict and a high level of satisfaction. It is suggested that the encounter is subtly manipulated by the obstetricians in a way which keeps issues off the agenda and women 'unaware that their interests have been set aside' (Shapiro et al., 1983, p. 145).

Sociological research in obstetrics has attributed much of women's passivity and inability to take an active role in decision-making to the high-status male providers controlling information flow and structuring the physical encounter (Oakley, 1980). Comoroff (1977) and Cartwright (1979) found that midwives had a different paradigm of pregnancy from doctors. Thus Annandale (1987) hypothesized that female midwives would enable women to be more in control of their birth. But in reality, the need to emphasize normality in order to prevent events transgressing obstetric norms tended to motivate midwives' practice behaviour and inhibit possibilities of patients' raising anxieties about complications, resulting in patients not being consulted about decisions made during labour.

Oleson (1990) asks if the increase in women doctors, achieving

Lorber's (1985) 'critical mass', will change the setting of care and rules for emotional labour; but surely the answer lies in the autonomy of the care-giver. As Kirkham (1989) concluded, one of the reasons why midwives fail to provide women with information during labour is that they themselves are unhappy with the policies they are required to implement.

One of the most important findings to emerge from theoretical and empirical approaches to the professional–patient relationship is that the nature of the relationship has a major influence on patient satisfaction, and that levels of patient satisfaction have been found to be directly associated with therapeutic outcomes and health status, but that structural constraints very often impinge on the social relationship that engenders this effect.

Issues raised by schemes for continuity of care

Emotional labour

The emotional complexity of caring in medical work has been recognized by Scheff (1978). Its relationship to power relations within an institution are raised in Hochschild's (1983) study of air stewardesses in the USA, a work which defines emotional labour as 'the induction or suppression of feeling in order to sustain an outward appearance of calm that produces in others a sense of being cared for in a convivial safe place'. Thus in this case, emotional labour is a commodity in the sense that it is directly appropriated to increase airline company profits.

Stacey (1981) reminds us that the emotional component of human service has been ignored by classical sociological theories. She explains this lack of understanding of 'people work' as the result of theories that emphasize the marketplace and the state; thus domestic labour is ignored, as is the range of work situations where loving and caring are involved. So, when its significance is underestimated, emotional labour skills used in the workplace are devalued and not rewarded financially (Hochschild, 1983). Also, even when valued by staff, emotional labour tasks take second place to medical ones, when subject to time and staff constraints (James, 1989). Without doubt the work of the midwife involves this kind of emotional labour; for example:

> 'Being a midwife is going to put you in danger of having your heart pierced — but that's okay, because when it does, a lot of love gets out that way. It will make you a better midwife.' (May Gaskin, 1978, p. 284)

The tendency to undervalue emotional labour could present

problems for midwives who propose that a major advance for continuity of care is the 'relationship' it engenders: firstly, by undervaluation
of these skills, and secondly, by associating emotional labour as a
'gendered' process. The latter term was used by Davies and Rosser
(1986, p. 105) to explain jobs which capitalize on the qualities and
capabilities a woman had gained by virtue of having lived life as a
woman. Such jobs are labelled as secondary and integrated into the
labour process through 'gendered' work roles. Thus it is extremely
important to remember that the sexual division of labour and its
relationship to tending tasks has a central place in any analysis of
the caring relationship (Ungerson, 1983).

What are the drawbacks of professionalism?

It is also important to remember that the concept of professional
'carries an ideological load' (Salvage, 1988), and within nursing and
midwifery the concept of professionalism is popular and has informed
strategic thinking. It has also been assumed that professionalization
is a desirable goal, but this may not be so. Thus for Salvage,
professionalism is as much about 'pursuing the narrow interests of
a particular group as it is about improving health care' (p. 100).
Oakley (1984), too, has argued that the current obsession for professional status may be counter-productive, at a time when there is
a lack of confidence in professions in general. Noting the increasing
assertiveness by 'consumers' of health care, she suggests that an
alliance with women would be more fruitful in gaining occupational
and consumer satisfaction, especially as the importance of social and
emotional support to maintain health is being formally recognized
(Oakley et al., 1990).

Lastly, one of the major effects that the pursuit of professional status
has had is to reinforce existing gender and class divisions within an
occupation. As Abel Smith (1960) and Heagerty (1990) suggest, the
search for professionalization by the lady nurses and midwives in the
1900s was more an expression of antipathy to those recruited from the
working class: 'The very fact every woman thought she could nurse
made it all the more necessary to exaggerate training requirements'
(Abel Smith, 1960, p. 62).

This antipathy towards midwives who either cannot pursue full-time
work (because of dependent children), or operate outside the norms
and practice independently, has continued today. For example, disciplinary control of independent midwives has continued (Drife, 1988;
Demilew, 1989), as have discrimination against women with children
attempting to train as midwives (Braun, 1990), downgrading of midwives returning to work part-time (Sandall, 1990), and a reluctance to
implement job sharing (McDowall, 1990). But professional strategies

have always relied on the single woman's or the man's career path (Davies and Rosser, 1986). For midwives setting up schemes for continuity of care, the issue of job sharing presents contradictions in a work organization pattern which may require rotating 12-hour shifts, being on call, and full-time commitment. Furthermore, job shares increase the number of midwives in the team, which is a contradiction to the established purpose of having a few midwives establishing a good relationship with each woman.

Relationships with obstetricians

Debate about the respective roles of midwives and medical staff is not a new phenomenon, and much discussion of maternity care in the twentieth century has focused on this issue. There is no dispute that obstetricians should be responsible for the care of women with complications, but there has been a lack of clarity as to where 'normal and abnormal' boundaries are drawn, with a tendency to regard the process as a trajectory with pathological potential (see Kitzinger et al., 1990, p. 152). Reading the literature on professions, one would expect a certain amount of opposition to midwives reasserting their control over the birth process, and indeed the proposals for continuity of care have been seen as a threat to the 'obstetric team' (Howie, 1987).

The early studies that looked at midwife/obstetrician relations in Britain found that, although midwives made a claim to be practitioners in their own right, this was rarely recognized in practice. Walker (1976) found that midwives strongly held the view that they must work as a team as the woman's needs were paramount; as a result midwives, like nurses (Stein, 1967), developed strategies to avoid overt conflict — which Kitzinger et al. (1990) call 'hierarchy maintenance work'. Robinson's national study (1985; see also Robinson et al., 1983) of the role of the midwife, which surveyed midwives, health visitors, GPs and obstetricians, also found that midwives were not exercising the degree of clinical responsibility for which they were qualified and that decision-making had been taken over by medical staff.

Kitzinger et al. (1990) found that increasing interpersonal contact between midwives and consultants (by cutting out the registrar) resulted in greater midwife autonomy, and better relationships with the consultants, but 'the power of the consultants to determine the protocols of the labour ward meant that their attitudes were crucial' as the system meant that consultants spent more time in the delivery suite on call (Kitzinger, 1990, p. 160). Annandale (1987) also found that midwives working in an American free-standing birth centre (which had an explicit philosophy of patient control and natural childbirth) were still constrained by the obstetric policies and protocols of the backup hospital. *Thus, consultant obstetrician support for innovations in maternity care still appears to be an essential element of a successful programme.*

General practitioners

There has been a long history of economic competition between midwives and GPs for their patients (Dingwall et al., 1988). The GP's role in maternity care has been declining throughout the twentieth century. In 1927, 85% of deliveries were under the care of the GP and this has fallen to less than 6% in England and Wales in 1988 (Smith and Jewell, 1991). The participation by the GP at the time of birth continues to decline, and many feel their skills are rusty and would support the midwife as the key professional present at 72% of births. GPs who are actively involved in intrapartum care are seeking an alliance with midwives in forming pressure groups such as the Association for Community Based Maternity Care, but not without some tension on both sides (*Midwifery Matters*, 1990, 1991). Robinson et al.'s (1983) survey found role duplication, and this was again highlighted in a Health Committee report (House of Commons, 1992). As a result, the *Changing Childbirth* report (DoH, 1993) has suggested that the current fee structure for maternity payments to GPs should be reviewed to provide a realistic fee for those who are involved in intrapartum care. *The outcome of this review will significantly affect the future role of midwives in community-based maternity care, for the financing of maternity care significantly affects the roles and responsibilities of the professionals involved.*

Discussion

The ideology of schemes for continuity of care reasserts control over the heart (in a metaphorical sense too) of the practice of midwifery. Thus midwives are claiming a discrete sphere of knowledge and expertise, legitimated by a desire for a more equal partnership with women in an area where medical care has been criticized.

Like the primary nursing model (White, 1985), it has a powerful appeal to all the interest groups within midwifery: to the generalists by emphasizing the primacy of the midwife/woman relationship, to the academic professionalizer by offering increased autonomy; and to government and managers (whose support is vital to implement change) (Stocking, 1984) by providing cost-effective care.

Current attempts to develop professional status are dependent on state mandate, funding and political expediency. The interest shown by the British government in the cost-effectiveness of midwife care and the alliance that midwives have forged with consumers may well enable this particular female professional project to be successful. But midwives need to remember that what a woman wants is a trusting, supportive relationship with one or two midwives who will be with her through her pregnancy, birth and the postnatal period, who will support her, be her advocate 'within the system' and enable her to be more assertive in making sure her needs are met. There is a danger that the ideology of continuity of care arising from a profession aiming to increase its autonomy and sphere of practice may lead us to lose sight of this ideal. Midwives should be aware of the issues involved in pursuing this particular path, and further evaluation of the experiences of women and midwives who are involved in this model of care needs to be done prior to the wholesale reorganization of the maternity services.

References

Abel Smith B (1960) *A History of the Nursing Profession*. London: Heinemann.

Annandale EC (1987) Dimensions of patient control in a free standing birth centre. *Social Science and Medicine*; **25**: 1235–1248.

Annandale EC (1989) The malpractice crisis and the doctor–patient relationship. *Sociology of Health and Illness*; **11**: (1), 1–23.

Arms S (1975) *Immaculate Deception*. New York: Bantam Books.

Association of Radical Midwives (1986) *The Vision: Proposals for the Future of the Maternity Services*. Ormskirk: ARM.

Braun J (1990) *Sex Discrimination Against Student Midwives*. Midirs information pack 15, December.

Campbell R, Macfarlane A (1987) *Where to be Born? The Debate and the Evidence*. Oxford: National Perinatal Epidemiology Unit.

Cartwright A (1979) *The Dignity of Labour? A Study of Childbearing and Induction*. London: Tavistock/Institute for Social Studies in Medical Care.

Chalmers I (1978) Implications of the current debate on obstetric practice. In: Kitzinger S, Davis J (Eds), *The Place of Birth*. Oxford: Oxford University Press.

Chalmers I, Richards M (1977) Intervention and causal inference in obstetric practice. In: Chard T, Richards M (Eds), *Benefits and Hazards of the New Obstetrics*. London: Spastics International Medical Publications.

Chalmers I, Enkin M, Keirse MJNC (1989) *Effective Care in Pregnancy and Childbirth*. Oxford: Oxford University Press.

Cochrane A (1971) *Effectiveness and Efficiency*. London: Nuffield Provincial Hospitals Trust.

Comoroff J (1977) Conflicting paradigms of pregnancy: managing ambiguity in antenatal encounters. In: Davis A, Horobin G (Eds), *Medical Encounters: The Experience of Illness and Treatment*. London: Croom Helm.

Davies C, Rosser J (1986) Gendered jobs in the health service: a problem for labour process analysis. In: Knights D, Willmott H (Eds), *Gender and Labour Process*. Aldershot: Gower.

Demilew J (1989) The struggle to practice: a sociological analysis of the crisis within the British midwifery profession. Unpublished MSc thesis, University of South Bank.

Department of Health (1989) *Working for Patients*. London: HMSO.

Department of Health (1993) *Changing Childbirth: Report of the Expert Maternity Group*. London: HMSO.

Dingwall R, Rafferty A, Webster C (1988) *An Introduction to the Social History of Nursing*. London: Routledge.

Domadia N (1990) The team concept in hospital midwifery. *Midwife, Health Visitor and Community Nurse*; **26**: 412–414.

Doyal L, Pennell I (1979) *The Political Economy of Health*. London: Pluto.

Drife JO (1988) Disciplining midwives: a better system is needed. *British Medical Journal*; **297**: 806–807.

Elbourne D, Oakley A, Chalmers I (1989) Social and psychological support during pregnancy. In: Chalmers I, Enkin M, Keirse MJNC (Eds), *Effective Care in Pregnancy and Childbirth*. Oxford: Oxford University Press.

Ennif M et al. (1991) Change in obstetric practice in response to fears of litigation in the British Isles. *Lancet*; **338**: 616–618.

Flint C (1979) A team of midwives: a continuing labour of love. *Nursing Mirror*; **149**: (20), 16–18.

Flint C (1981) Continuity of maternity care, parts 1–5. *Nursing Mirror*; issues 2–22 December.

Flint C (1993) *Midwifery Teams and Caseloads*. London: Butterworth.

Flint C, Poulengeris P, Grant A (1989) The 'know your midwife' scheme — a randomised controlled trial of continuity of care by a team of midwives. *Midwifery*; **5**: 11–16.

Frohlich J, Edwards S (1989) Team midwifery for everyone — building on the 'know your midwife' scheme. *Midwives Chronicle*; **102**: 66–70.

Gaskin IM (1978) *Spiritual Midwifery*. Summertown, USA: The Book Publishing Company.

Graham H, Oakley A (1981) Competing ideologies of reproduction: medical and maternal perspectives on pregnancy. In: Roberts H (Ed.), *Women, Health and Reproduction*. London: Routledge & Kegan Paul.

Green JM, Coupland VA, Kitzinger JV (1990) Expectations, experiences and psychological outcomes of childbirth: a prospective study of 825 women. *Birth*; **17**: (1), 15–24.

Haire D (1972) *The Cultural Warping of Childbirth*. New York: International Childbirth Association.

Haug M, Lavin B (1983) *Consumerism in Medicine: Challenging Physician Authority*. Beverly Hills: Sage.

Heagerty BV (1990) Class, gender and professionalization: the struggle for British midwifery, 1900–36. Unpublished DPhil thesis, Michigan State University (lodged RCM library).

Hochschild AR (1983) *The Managed Heart: Commercialisation of Human Feeling*. Berkeley: University of California Press.

House of Commons (1992) *Health Committee Second Report: Maternity Services*, vol. 1 (Chair N. Winterton). London: HMSO.

Howie PW (1987) The future role of midwives. *British Medical Journal*; **294**: 1502.

Jacoby A (1988) Mother's views about information and advice in pregnancy and childbirth: findings from a national study. *Midwifery*; **4**: 103–110.

James N (1989) Emotional labour: skill and work in the social regulation of feelings. *Sociological Review*; **37**: (1), 15–42.

Kirkham M (1989) Midwives and information-giving during labour. In: Robinson S, Thomson AM (Eds), *Midwives Research and Childbirth*, vol. 1. London: Chapman & Hall.

Kitzinger J, Green J, Coupland V (1990) Labour relations: midwives and doctors on the labour ward. In: Garcia J, Kilpatrick R, Richards M (Eds), *The Politics of Maternity Care: Services for Childbearing Women in Twentieth Century Britain*. Oxford: Clarendon Press.

Kroll D (1989) Team approach in Bloomsbury. *Midwives Chronicle*; **102**: 305.

Locker D, Dunt D (1978) Theoretical and methodological issues in sociological studies of consumer satisfaction with medical care. *Social Science and Medicine*; **12**: 283–292.

Lorber J (1985) More women physicians: will it mean more humane healthcare? *Social Policy*; **16**: 50–54.

Macintyre S (1977a) The myth of the golden age. *World Medicine*; **12**: (18), 17–22.

Macintyre S (1977b) The management of childbirth: a review of the sociological research issues. *Social Science and Medicine*; **11**: 477–484.

Macintyre S (1981) Communications between pregnant women and their medical and midwifery attendants. *Midwives Chronicle and Nursing Notes*; November: 387–394.

Mason V (1989) *Women's Experience of Maternity Care — A Survey Manual*. A manual produced by Social Survey Division of OPCS on behalf of the Department of Health, HMSO, London.

Maternity Services Advisory Committee (1982–85) *Maternity Care in Action* (Pt. I, 1982; Pt. II, 1984; Pt. III, 1985). London: HMSO.

McDowall J (1990) Working in tandem. *Nursing Times*; **86**: (28), 72–73.

McIntosh J (1989) Models of childbirth and social class: a study of 80 working class primigravidae. In: Robinson S, Thomson AM (Eds), *Midwives Research and Childbirth*, vol. 1. London: Chapman & Hall.

McKeown T (1976) *The Role of Medicine: Dream, Mirage or Nemesis*. London: Nuffield Provincial Hospitals Trust.

McKinlay JB (1972) The sick role: illness and pregnancy. *Social Science and Medicine*; **6**: 561–572.

McNeil M, Varcoe I, Yearley S (1990) *The New Reproductive Technologies*. Basingstoke: Macmillan.

Midwifery Matters (1990, 1991) Letters columns — issue 47 (1990) and issue 48 (1991).

Ministry of Health (1961) *Human Relations in Obstetrics* (Central Health Services Council, Standing Midwifery and Maternity Advisory Committee). London: HMSO.

Mugford M (1990) Economies of scale and low risk maternity care: what is the evidence? *Maternity Action*; **46**: 6–8.

Nash A, Nash JE (1979) Conflicting interpretations of childbirth. *Urban Life*; **7**: 493–513.

National Audit Office (1990) *The Maternity Services: Report by the Comptroller and Auditor General*, no. 297. London: HMSO.

Nelson M (1983) Working class women, middle class women, and models of childbirth. *Social Problems*; **30**: 284–297.

Oakley A (1980) *Women Confined: Towards a Sociology of Childbirth*. Oxford: Martin Robertson.

Oakley A (1984) The importance of being a nurse: what price professionalism? *Nursing Times*; 12 December.

Oakley A, Rajan L, Grant A (1990) Social support and pregnancy outcome. *British Journal of Obstetrics and Gynaecology*; **97**: 155–162.

Oleson V (1990) The neglected emotions: a challenge to medical sociology. Plenary Lecture, BSA Medical Sociology Conference (reported in *Medical Sociology News*, December 1990).

Phoenix A (1990) Black women and the maternity services. In: Garcia J, Kilpatrick R, Richards M (Eds), *The Politics of Maternity Care: Services for Childbearing Women in Twentieth Century Britain*. Oxford: Clarendon Press.

Porter M, Macintyre S (1984) What is, must be best: a research note on conservative or deferential responses to antenatal care provision. *Social Science and Medicine*; **19**: 1197–1200.

Reid M (1983) Review article: A feminist sociological imagination? Reading Ann Oakley. *Sociology of Health and Illness*; **5**: (1), 83–94.

Reid M, Garcia J (1989) Women's views of care during pregnancy and childbirth. In: Chalmers I, Enkin M, Keirse MJNC (Eds), *Effective*

Care in Pregnancy and Childbirth. Oxford: Oxford University Press.

Reid M, McIlwaine G (1980) Consumer opinion of a hospital antenatal clinic. *Social Science and Medicine*; **14A**: 363–368.

Richards M (1975) Innovation in medical practice: obstetricians and the induction of labour in Britain. *Social Science and Medicine*; **9**: 595–602.

Riley D (1977) *War in the Nursery: Theories of the Child and the Mother*. London: Virago.

Robinson J (1974) Consumer attitudes to maternity care. *Oxford Consumer*; May.

Robinson S (1985) Midwives, obstetricians and general practitioners: the need for role clarification. *Midwifery*; **1**: 102–113.

Robinson S, Golden J, Bradley S (1983) *A Study of the Role and Responsibilities of the Midwife*. London: King's College (NERU report 1).

Romalis S (1985) Struggle between providers and recipients: the case of birth practices. In: Oleson V (Eds), *Women, Health and Healing*. London: Tavistock.

Rosser J (1990) Team midwifery in Riverside: interview with Jane Duncan. Midirs information pack 14, August.

Royal College of Midwives (1987) *Report of the RCM on the Role and Education of the Future Midwife in the United Kingdom*. London: RCM.

Royal College of Midwives (1991) RCM Commission on legislation relating to midwives. *Midwives Chronicle*; **104**: 295–296.

Royal College of Obstetricians and Gynaecologists (1982) *Report of the RCOG Working Party on Antenatal and Intrapartum Care*. London: RCOG.

Russell C (1988) The 'know your midwife' scheme in the Rhondda. *Midwifery Matters*; (36), 14–15.

Salvage J (1988) Professionalization — or struggle for survival? A consideration of current proposals for the reform of nursing in the United Kindom. *Journal of Advanced Nursing*; **13**: 515–519.

Sandall J (1990) Do nurses with children want to return to work? *Senior Nurse*; **10**: (8), 9–11.

Scheff TJ (1978) Emotion work and distancing in medical settings. In: Gallagher EB (Ed.), *The Doctor–Patient Relationship in the Changing Health Scene*. US government publication.

Select Committee (1980) *Short Report of the Social Services Committee on Perinatal and Neonatal Mortality*. London: HMSO.

Shapiro MC, Najman JM, Chang A, Keeping JD, Morrison J, Western JS (1983) Information control and the exercise of power in the obstetrical encounter. *Social Science and Medicine*; **17**: 139–146.

Shorter E (1982) *A History of Women's Bodies*. London: Allen Lane.

Smith L, Jewell D (1991) Contributions of the general practitioner to hospital intrapartum care in maternity units in England & Wales in

1988. *British Medical Journal*; **302**: 13–116.

Stacey M (1976) The health service consumer: a sociological misconception. In: *Sociology of the National Health Service* (Sociological Review Monograph 22) Keele University.

Stacey M (1981) The division of labour revisited, or overcoming the two Adams. In: Abrams P, Deem R (Eds), *Practice and Progress: British Sociology 1950–1980*. London: Allen & Unwin.

Stacey M (1988) *The Sociology of Health and Healing*. London: Unwin Hyman.

Stein L (1967) The doctor/nurse game. *Archives of General Psychiatry*; **16**: 699–703.

Stocking B (1984) *Initiative and Inertia: Case Studies in the NHS*. London: Nuffield Provincial Hospitals Trust.

Tew M (1985) Place of birth and perinatal mortality. *Journal of the College of General Practitioners;* **35**: 390–394.

Tew M (1990) *Safer Childbirth? A Critical History of Maternity Care*. London: Chapman & Hall.

Ungerson C (1983) Women and caring: skills, tasks and taboos. In: Kuhn A, Wolpe AM (Eds), *Feminism and Materialism: Women and Modes of Production*. London: Routledge & Kegan Paul.

Walker JF (1976) Midwife or obstetric nurse? Some perceptions of midwives and obstetricians of the role of the midwife. *Journal of Advanced Nursing*; **1**: 129–138.

Watson P (1990) *Report on the Kidlington Midwifery Scheme*. Available from Institute of Nursing, Radcliffe Infirmary, Woodstock Road, Oxford OX2 6HE, England.

White R (1985) Political Regulators in British Nursing. In: White R (Ed.), *Political Issues in Nursing*, vol. 1. Chichester: John Wiley.

Wraight A, Ball J, Seccombe I, Stock J (1993) *Mapping Team Midwifery: A Report of the Department of Health*. Brighton: IMS (report series 242).

20 Patients and professionals

June Greenwell

Introduction

Two of the emerging themes in health care and health promotion are the need for professional staff to collaborate more effectively to achieve the maximum possible health gain, and the need to be more responsive to the 'consumers' of health care, the patients. In this chapter I shall argue that these two aspirations are inextricably linked. Both require individual professions to recognize that health service delivery and health promotion is the product of team-work, and both need patients to be partners within interprofessional health teams. Furthermore, these are not options for health professionals, since longstanding trends and current policies have already combined to alter the roles of both patients and professionals.

The role of a patient has been changing for some decades, and for reasons more fundamental than the reorganization of the NHS; but policy directives are accelerating change in organizations, and in the behaviour of practitioners. A particular incident linked to the Patient's Charter illustrates how changing the way the patients are viewed can have unexpected effects on interprofessional relations. A unit manager described to me an interprofessional conflict that he had needed to resolve:

> 'We are trying to promote better customer relations and put across a less condescending air . . . one of the quality standards is that if patients are delayed in clinics then somebody should regularly keep patients informed as to the reasons for the delay . . . a consultant was having a little bit of a tantrum and so he decided he wouldn't see his patients very quickly. So the nurse, and one has to admire her a bit, went out and said to the patients "I'm sorry for the delay, the consultant's having a tantrum". Which didn't enhance the relationship! But it brought the relationship issue to a head, and we have been able to resolve it since.'

Now this incident was not directly generated by patients, nor was the Patient's Charter created in order to influence interprofessional relations, but the existence of the charter meant that the nurse felt able to make a public statement that ignored normal interprofessional courtesies, and the relative status of herself and the consultant. It is an untypically blunt example of how a formal change in the status ascribed to patients leads to adjustments in the power balance between professions.

Looking from a wider perspective, there are four areas I want to discuss where there is a visible process of adjustment to interprofessional relations. The development of clinical directorates and the devolution of budgets to the ward level require modifications to team-working in hospital. The system of buying 'packages of care' for individuals in the community, together with the movement of services from hospitals to families, is meaning that both carers and users of services are becoming colleagues of professionals in providing care and treatment. The use of contracts for purchasing has increased the importance attached to monitoring and evaluating services, and measuring the outcome of treatment in order to inform and justify purchasing decisions. There is currently a much greater professional and political emphasis on health promotion than has existed for many decades, and this is also producing a cultural change in professional values.

These changes add up to a significant shift in both interprofessional and patient/professional relations, but it is not a consistent pattern of change. Health service users are an undifferentiated mass of individuals. Public attitudes to organized health care include suspicion, consumerism, and a readiness to trust implicitly the judgement of medical practitioners. Illman (1991) describes a study of patients registering with GPs in Reading, which showed that a majority registered with the nearest GP, and only 4% compared GPs' practices before choosing. An Australian study has shown that patients want to trust their doctor, do not want to make choices as to treatment, and prefer to leave health care decision-making to professionals (Lupton et al., 1991). The textbook health consumer, carefully selecting the best health care option from a range of options, may still be a theoretical concept.

Traditional patterns of patient/professional relations in health stem from a model of the ill person who places him or herself 'in the doctor's hands', a dependent individual cared for by a paternalistic individual. In contrast, health gain can only be achieved when individuals take responsibility for their own health in communities that have succeeded in creating healthy environments. In moving from a sickness service to a health service, professionals have to move from being paternalistic providers to become health facilitators. This is a demanding programme of change, particularly when it is only one aspect of a changing service.

As a consequence, it is easy for user involvement to appear as a luxury to be set aside for the present, or nothing more than a mechanical process of meaningless consultation to enable a managerial objective to be ticked on an evaluation sheet. If this is the result of health service change, then working practice in the new systems of service delivery will once more marginalize patients, and minimize the chance of achieving optimum health again. Furthermore, it will alienate an informed public who sometimes perceive themselves as being in the vanguard of health promotion, ahead of the health professionals.

Health promotion and health professionals

For those who work in health care it is easy to assume that interprofessional relations are controlled by either the professions themselves, or are adjusted in response to governmental or managerial initiatives. Both viewpoints ignore a far more basic, though slower, programme of change that stems from wider debates, and requires responses from government as much as from professions. The impact of alternative medicine is a clear example. The array of 'alternative' therapies that are now accepted and utilized by some health professionals have been developed and promoted almost entirely outside the formal health care services. Public support has sustained them, and encouraged a reassessment of their worth by health professionals. For significant sections of the public, the concept of a health professional has been widened to include the practitioners of alternative medicine — and the professions have been compelled to respond and adjust their concept of the health care 'team' accordingly. Alternative therapists may only be grudgingly tolerated by some health professionals, but their existence as an element in the provision of health treatments is recognized, and is an indicator of how public assessment of the value of treatment can compel a revision of professional attitudes. Professionals follow public attitudes as well as influencing them.

Growing sympathy for alternative medicine has another impact on attitudes to health care delivery; it has a subversive tendency, encouraging challenges to accepted authority. In part this is energized by a deep suspicion of modern pharmaceutical drugs. The organized and collective aspect of this attitude provides some of the opposition to immunization programmes, to the fluoridation of water supplies, and campaigns against lead contamination. The individualistic aspects of alternative medicine (e.g. therapies such as yoga and the Alexander technique) may be regarded sympathetically by health professionals accustomed to working with individual patients, while the campaigning arm of alternative medicine is more at ease with a collective political process that is alien to traditional systems of health care delivery. Professional health care staff are being urged to be responsive to patients at a time when 'patients' have an array of attitudes that negates any simplistic response to their definition of health needs.

The 'dominant ideology' of medicine has also been changed by a sharper focus on the patient's influence in prevention of illness. The realization in the late 1950s that patients' attitudes were significant determinants of the success or failure of epidemiological programmes led to a new conceptualization of the patient. Once acute physical conditions such as carcinomas were seen to be influenced by decisions taken when patients were healthy, the relationship of health professional and patient had to change. As Armstrong (1993, p. 64) puts it, 'The boundary between healthy person and patient became problematic'. An understanding that health service users are active players in determining their own health is now commonplace, established in the World Health Organization's policies (1981), and embedded in the targets set in the White Paper *Health of the Nation* (DoH, 1992); but the concept needs to move on so that it has a stronger influence on systems of professional accountability, and interprofessional team-work.

Once health is the focus of concern rather than medicine, the concept of a health professional changes. It has to encompass a far wider array of potential and actual colleagues than the traditional hospital or GP-based grouping of doctor, nurse and therapists. The employees of agencies who have a low visibility in traditional and hospital-dominated health care systems have to become health service partners, and these changes have to be reflected in the programmes of health institutions. With publication of the Green Paper *Health of the Nation* (DoH, 1991), and anticipating the subsequent White Paper, Ashton (1992) saw a new opportunity for the Family Health Service Authorities to be innovative in encouraging new alliances, and suggested that:

> '. . . the foreign ministry function of forming alliances for health in the local area, whether it be for accident prevention, or to facilitate the provision of exercise facilities, is now a clearly legitimated aspect of the work of health agencies in the UK.' (p. 3)

A concept of interprofessional health work that includes traffic police, sports hall managers, and the leisure officer of local councils, is far wider than the traditional one, requiring a radical move away from the predominantly self-contained world of the hospital, clinic or GP practice. Ashton's description of public health as part of a health service 'foreign ministry' suggests that networking with other agencies constitutes a distinctively different programme for health professionals. The carefully nuanced hierarchies of hospital or primary health care teams have to adjust to more egalitarian working relationships. Watkins (1987), a community physician, trenchantly depicts public health medicine as being:

'. . . as far as it is possible to be from the medical profession's dominant ideology with its individualistic approach to the illness of individuals and the value it attaches to treatment and to sickness.' (p. 147)

Access to health care in the UK is generally through the GP service. Accident and Emergency departments, occupational health and school medical services, and clinics for sexually transmitted diseases, for family planning, or for homeless people, are all evidence of the existence of other pathways, but it remains the case that registration with a GP is the normal entrance point to health services. This requires the prospective patient to have a fixed address, and carries a professional expectation of a long-term relationship emerging with the patient and their family which provides the basis for health promotion work. It is a pattern based round the notion of stable communities, in stark contrast to some of the services listed above. Some of these are organized in ways that reflect users' desire for anonymous treatment, and others are attempting to reach individuals who are reluctant users of services, or who have no fixed address and therefore no routine access to service provision.

In a budget-dominated service, improving the health of communities usually means reducing to some small extent the funds available to the hospital- and GP-based health care teams in order to strengthen public health departments. A desire for health promotion may be articulated by individuals who are concerned for their own health, but a dispassionate assessment of community health needs by a public health consultant is likely to highlight the health needs of reluctant users of services. A GP-based primary health care team is focused on the patients registered with the GP. A health visitor or community nurse employed on an outreach programme of health care with a community development agency will be focusing on community-based groups registered with different GPs, or with none. Raising levels of community health can therefore involve challenging the primacy of the GP-based services. Responding equitably to health service users in this situation is a radically different process from a depiction of the health consumer as someone carefully assessing the relative worth of different health care providers, but it is an integral part of responsiveness to need. The tradition of individual care by the GP for a specified list of patients sits uneasily with the tradition of public health medicine and its focus on communities rather than individuals. Deciding priorities involves assessing the values of health professionals who work to different agendas. Collaborating for maximum health gain cannot evade the 'political' issue of deciding whose health gain has priority.

Some health professionals are increasingly involved in health promotion, while others have to treat more sick people ever more rapidly, and both groups of staff have to operate within tight budgets. There are therefore a wide array of professional values that cut across professional boundaries, and interprofessional relations have to accommodate different sociopolitical positions. Beattie (1993) depicts four sociopolitical positions that are linked to different accounts of health: libertarian; reformist; radical pluralist; and conservative. Stainton Rogers (1991) describes numerous accounts of health, that individuals use and discard at intervals. Professional staff as well as patients subscribe to a wide array of changing positions. The pursuit of health and the treatment of illness produces curious philosophical and political alliances and this discourse pervades the health professions as it does the wider public. Professionals have to collaborate across these cultural divisions.

The difficulty of team-work

Many professions are hierarchical organizations in one form or another. Nursing, the paramedical therapies, and social work have hierarchical line management structures and hospital medical staff are in a hierarchical structure until they cease to be 'junior' doctors. Hospital consultants and senior partners in GP practices are exceptions. The way in which health professions are organized as vertical hierarchies is one of the barriers to effective team-working (Mackay, 1993). It is also a pattern that can reduce the likelihood that a practitioner will respond appropriately and immediately to a patient's needs, because of the requirement to check variations from normal practice with senior colleagues. Ward-based teams consisting of doctors, nurses, social workers and therapists find that innovative change often requires authorization from higher up in the line management structure of one or more of the professional groups. Deferring decisions in order to obtain the approval of senior staff injects inertia into teams attempting to respond to the needs of patients. Professional hierarchies become barriers to innovation, as recounted in this section of a research interview with a hospital registrar:

> 'One of the tremendous difficulties that you are faced with in a team [is the] fact of one of the members saying "Well, I'm sorry I can't make a decision about that, I would have to ask my line manager about it." That's very destructive and I think what you need is some commitment from line management, that they are not going to interfere with the running of that team. Because otherwise you can never make a committed decision within the team, you have always got to be nipping out of the room to ask if I am doing the right thing.' (Walby et al., 1994)

Hierarchical structures can be an irritating restraint on innovative teams, but they also offer a refuge when collaboration is difficult to achieve. Demoralized practitioners fall back into familiar patterns of working with colleagues who 'speak the same language'. Mackay (1989) has described inadequate staff support systems in nursing. Adequate staff support is particularly important when organizational change is generating additional stress.

Interprofessional team-working involves forming horizontally organized teams from vertically managed groups of staff. Fig. 20.1 illustrates the situation.

The establishment of clinical directorates is an attempt to strengthen hospital department teams, but the core issue is the presence of responsible professionals who can make autonomous decisions within patient-focused teams. The nurse, the therapist or social worker who has to refer all decisions back to the line manager is not able to participate easily in a flexible team. Medicine has always valued the autonomy of individual practitioners, but until recently nursing has practised a system of careful certification of tasks, with a strongly hierarchical line management system, in keeping with a concept of professionalization that stresses monitoring and professional discipline. The decision by the United Kingdom Central Council for Nursing, Midwifery and Health Visiting (UKCC, 1992) to abandon the extended role system of certification is a move towards a concept of a responsible practitioner who monitors his or her own performance, and has the potential to be a powerful impetus to flexible team-working — provided that hospitals do not replace central regulations for extended roles with parochial versions. Social work demands individual decision-making, but within a detailed and complex array of statutory directives. Coming together to form an effective team means negotiating the work agenda within very different professional frameworks.

Differences may be ignored for a while, but in the final analysis the nature of health care requires clear accountability, so that there has to be agreement as to areas of responsibility. Broadly there are three patterns of interprofessional team-work possible:

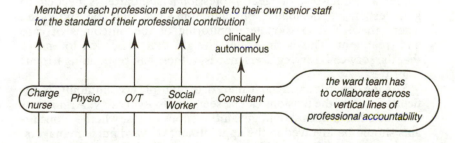

Fig. 20.1   Interprofessional ward teams

- A single profession may have final responsibility for decisions, and thus take a lead role, while other professions accept a subordinate role.
- A second scenario is where there is no agreed pattern, so that there are frequent disputes, and service provision is fractured along the fault lines of professional boundaries.
- A third option is the practice of multiple accountability, to different professionals for different aspects of care or treatment, with power and responsibility moving among professions as dictated by the users' needs.

The first option is one that is traditional in hospital care, and implies a hierarchical pattern of accountability that cannot provide maximum flexibility. The second option can be witnessed in the disputes that occur at the boundaries of medical, nursing and paramedical responsibilities. It is characteristic of interprofessional rivalry where there is incomplete agreement as to the boundaries of responsibility. The third option is a pattern fundamental to the notion of effective collaboration between independent and autonomous professionals. The ideal of multiple accountability is therefore of value to those health professionals who can accept the responsibilities implied by a non-hierarchical working relationship, and who welcome autonomy in order to be responsive to users' needs. Multiple accountability by responsible practitioners gives a greater probability of downward accountability to patients, rather than upward accountability to a line management structure, because there has been an explicit acceptance of individual practitioner responsibility.

The General Secretary of the Royal College of Nursing sees multiple accountability as the key concept in the effective working of clinical directorates (Hancock, 1991). The argument presented in this chapter is that it is equally the key to a capacity to respond flexibly to patients' needs. What it cannot do is to ensure that practitioners use autonomy in order to provide a more responsive service, and not in order to protect their own interests. Professional autonomy within a framework of clear professional standards is needed to give responsive flexibility, but autonomy can only be supported where there is dispassionate monitoring of the outcomes of care and treatment. This is the counterweight that is needed to ensure that the service is serving users' needs, rather than responding to staff priorities.

Moving towards an effective pattern of multiple accountability is difficult. Some of the tensions can be seen almost every day. Arguments over whether nurses should give intravenous drugs, whether consultants should be involved in the appointment of ward nurse managers, what authority GPs should have over the work of community nursing staff, or identifying the exact point when an elderly 'client' of a social work team becomes an elderly 'patient' of a district nursing service, all provide examples of interprofessional boundary conflicts in inflexible health care teams.

Health care teams in hospital: limits to responsive team-work

A study of doctors and registered nurses in five hospitals found that a small majority of respondents felt that doctors and nurses routinely worked well as a team, and all but a small minority reported that this happened sometimes, or on some wards. Differences between specialties were less marked than differences between hospitals (Walby et al., 1994). In their detailed study of the impact of skill mix on the quality of nursing care, Carr-Hill et al. (1992) also found some evidence of a hospital effect, but no consistent difference between medical and surgical wards. The professional management of a ward, and the general management of the hospital, appear to be significant factors, rather than the nature of a specialty.

There are numerous factors that are reported as having an influence on the probability of team-work between medical and nursing staff. The commonplace notion that staff work more effectively together if they are familiar colleagues contrasts with the observation that hospital organization often works in a way that fragments the ward team. There is a level of work pressure above which interprofessional cooperation becomes difficult. Differences in professional culture emerge as conflicts when levels of pressure cannot be accommodated, with doctors needing to maximize turnover in order to achieve waiting-list targets and deal with emergencies, and nursing staff wanting to reach or maintain quality standards and provide a satisfactory level of care. Each group defends their own agenda. Too frequent use of agency and bank nurses, or locum doctors, means that the cooperation that is possible when working with familiar colleagues is absent. A large number of consultants working on a ward, and 'bed scatter' to accommodate the maximum number of patients, are also factors tending to disperse the interprofessional ward team. Interprofessional relations in hospital are therefore dependent on a complex mix of factors often beyond the influence of the team of staff in contact with patients.

Lack of cohesion in a ward team affects the quality of patient care. Information is not exchanged, so care and treatment programmes are inadequately organized. The flexibility that makes maximum use of staff resources disappears, and staff defend territorial boundaries in order to protect their care of treatment priorities.

Primary nursing may have the capacity to protect patients from some of the impact of dispersed professional teams. The study by

Carr-Hill et al. (1992) showed that, in two wards that practised primary nursing, the quality of care was consistently high over all grades of staff. There is a probability that primary nursing improves the quality of information exchange (Walby et al., 1994). Ersser and Tutton (1991) suggest that primary nursing may be influential owing to the way in which it demands clear accountability for nursing care, gives continuity of care, and provides direct communication channels. Primary nursing requires the nurse to accept formal responsibility by being answerable for decisions about nursing care for a named group of patients, and this is a pattern of devolving responsibility for the patient's care down to the bedside, in a way that fits with the 'pursuit of excellence' (Peters and Waterman, 1982).

Health care teams in the community: non-professional colleagues

Another quite different factor that is forcing a change in professional/patient and interprofessional relations is the rapidly developing programme of dehospitalization, and the transfer of many aspects of health care and treatment to the community, and more particularly to the family. The boundaries between health professionals are differently located in hospitals and in the community, and involve different players. Ill people can decide for themselves whether to become a patient of a GP, or a customer of a chemist, or contact a community nurse. Dehospitalization influences interprofessional relations in numerous ways.

The largest difference, though, is that moving treatment and care out of hospitals usually means that the family, or other informal carers, are responsible for a high proportion of care provision, and treatment administration. Home dialysis shows that it is possible to transfer to the community treatment procedures that were at the forefront of technical medicine only a couple of decades ago, when it would have been impossible to conceive that patients could administer dialysis and dispense with routine professional supervision. The increased use of day-surgery shows a similar trend to deprofessionalize some aspects of postoperative nursing care. When families have to function as providers of nursing care, and colleagues of nursing and medical staff, they alter the balance of authority between professionals.

The most obvious transference of responsibility is for providing long-term care and terminal care. Carers are increasingly important partners of professional staff in both these areas of service provision. At the same time, since carers are also themselves potential users of health services, the roles of carers and of patients having treatment may overlap. The distinction between the 'patient' and the 'provider' is becoming increasingly blurred. An elderly person who is caring for a spouse with Alzheimer's disease is a partner of health and social services in providing care, but is also a patient of the GP, and may have a claim on other community health services on his or her own behalf as well. In this situation, setting standards for a 'carer' may also mean simultaneously imposing demands on a 'patient'.

This is not a new situation, in that there have always been patients who are also carers. What is changing is the frequency of caring and the length of years involved in caring at home, the closure of institutional forms of care, and the tightness of budgetary controls. If the 1950s found the boundary between healthy person and patient becoming blurred, the 1990s equivalent is likely to be the boundary between being simultaneously a provider and a recipient of care. Just as reconceptualizing the patient as a healthy person altered the doctor/patient relationship, recognizing the patient as a provider of care alters both the doctor/patient and nurse/patient relationships. The outcome of treatment depends in part on the quality of care given by the informal carer, who is the partner of the health professional. Passing on skills from professional to carer is necessary at times, but making the carer skilled diminishes the skill-based distinction between carer and professional. The old jibe of professions being a conspiracy against the laity has to be entirely laid to rest when the laity are needed as colleagues of the professional.

A significant issue in working with informal carers relates to standard-setting and monitoring. Formalized standards incorporate values that are likely to have different significance to professional service providers and to informal carers. Who sets the standards when a large element of care is provided by the family carer? The notion of being a professional is often inextricably linked to a belief that the professional's standards, where they differ from the lay person's, are superior by definition. The professional who is working in partnership with carers sees a need to monitor the quality of care provided by informal carers, but may feel uneasy in this role. There is a tension in the relationship between informal carer and professional because it sits uncomfortably in the gap between a hierarchical relationship with a junior colleague and a respectful acknowledgement of a patient's or a carer's autonomy. It is easier not to formally agree standards, but this means that aspects of service provision that are deeply unsatisfactory to a carer may continue when they could be adjusted; while from a professional viewpoint, the process of turning a blind eye to poor standards of care may erode standards in a way that has implications for other patients.

In an interprofessional team, packages of care may have to be agreed with service providers from other agencies. Dalley (1993) reports scepticism among community nurses about the existence of interprofessional teamwork:

'The reality of interprofessional team-work was brought into question when discussing how effective health and social services were in identifying and meeting clients' needs. There was widespread agreement that effective team-work was more of a myth than a reality . . . professionals were trained to think in terms of individual cases, e.g. *my patient*, rather than having collective responsibility.' (p. 23)

Measuring professional contributions

The development of an internal health market is tending to reposition the patient within health care in ways that alter the relative influence of different professional providers. A market requires at least 'proxy' consumers and customers, and purchasing can be a powerful stimulus for seeking out patient preferences in a more formal manner. This point is emphasized in the NHS Management Executive document *Local Voices* (1992).

In deciding whether to maintain existing service patterns, or whether to transfer a contract to a different hospital with a better reputation, GPs should be, and often are, assessing how satisfied discharged patients are with the care they have received. Since the publication of *Working for Patients* (DoH, 1989a), and the remodelling of the NHS as an internal market, there has been far greater emphasis on measuring patient satisfaction, evaluating patient preferences, providing information to patients, instituting medical audit, publishing and monitoring quality standards, and establishing local forums to involve local people in establishing health care planning and purchasing decisions.

Given that assessment of outcomes is a legitimate process, it could be expected that the multitude of patient satisfaction surveys produced following *Working for Patients* would have included questions about the efficacy of treatment. In practice it is striking how seldom users have been asked if the treatment they have received has done them any good. Users' views on how services are delivered are sought, sometimes with much enthusiasm, but questions as to the efficacy of treatment and care are far less common. This is partly explained by the fact that patient satisfaction surveys are often initiated by non-medical managers, or quality control directors who are rarely doctors. Treatment is the concern of doctors, not managers, and it is easier to concentrate on assessing satisfaction with administrative and hotel services rather than challenging medical prerogatives. Marketization is promoted as a way of giving primacy to patient preferences, but in smaller hospitals and health authorities the 'marketing' process of obtaining users' opinions may be the responsibility of staff with an instinctive deference to the autonomy of senior doctors — or a sharp awareness that retaining a contract depends on not upsetting a hard-working, but touchy, consultant. An exception occurs in the National Consumer Council's guideline for health service managers (1992), where a flowchart on the stages in service eschews professional niceties in urging managers to '. . . ask users questions that help to measure practical effects such as: were you able to return to work/normal activity? was your pain relieved? did the treatment make you feel better? (not "did you like the service") . . .'

What the NCC is doing here is brushing aside the idea that assessment of treatment is solely a medical concern, to be addressed by clinicians. Users are encouraged in a minor and unthreatening way to assess the work of the health care team in providing treatment, rather than being sidelined into a position where they are only allowed to assess hotel services, or rate the quality of the services provided by the managers, not the core service provided by clinicians. This kind of questioning is a very small intrusion into a medical area. By contrast, the development of medical audit is a significant change. It is an aspect of changing medical organization that places more emphasis on monitoring the work of professional colleagues, rather than respecting the clinical freedom of each practitioner to work to their own agenda; i.e. a move from a collegiate profession to a managed profession. This was initiated as a process by doctors, with the survey of perioperative mortality as a prominent early example, but was rapidly developed following the publication of *Working for Patients*.

Medical audit is an area where it is possible to see the same cultural attitude reflected in attitudes to patient involvement, and to the involvement of other professions. The stance taken by the government in establishing medical audit, that 'the quality of medical work can only be reviewed by a doctor's peers' (Department of Health, 1989b), reinforces the notion of a single profession having autonomy over the work of its members; though this may have been less of a firm policy than a placatory and transient message to encourage doctors to put aside their misgivings about possible management involvement. Nevertheless, and whatever the reason behind it, this kind of statement reinforces a belief that the outcomes of treatment can be best assessed by auditing the work of single professions.

Mallett (1991) compellingly describes the weakness of concentrating on the work of one professional group, and gives examples of the way the multiprofessional health care team is involved in results that are at present the subject of a single profession's audit. Judged by the organization of many clinical audits, the multiprofessional ward-based team is an abstraction rather than a concrete and everyday reality. Individual practitioners and hospital 'Directors of Quality' have developed varied models of practice, but the basic distinction remains that medicine generally organizes audit within its own professional control, while other forms of audit formally encourage interprofessional collaboration. It is difficult to believe that this will not change as audit information compels a greater concentration of attention on how the outcome of care depends on the contribution of a mixed professional team.

Individual consultants do involve other professional groups in medical audit (Walby et al., 1994) but this seems to be unusual. The divide that separates medical audit from the audit programmes of other professions reflects a similar division in the way that complaints are handled within hospitals. Complaints about nursing, paramedical, and 'hotel' services are directed to managers, while complaints about medical treatment go to a consultant. Similarly, quality assurance programmes cut across nursing and management divides, while medical audit is controlled by the medical profession alone. In contrast to medical audit, the Royal College of Nursing's 'Standards of Care' programme specifically states that it is designed to operate within a multidisciplinary framework.

There is evidence of minimal involvement of service users in medical audit, quality assurance, and outcome evaluation. Discussing a survey of London-based medical audit committees and groups, Joule (1992) comments:

> 'The survey . . . finds that users have little access to the first stage of decision making on the selection of topics for audit. Complaints about clinical care are occasionally, though rarely, fed into the audit process. Throughout the next stages of the audit cycle which deal with setting criteria and standards, user involvement is similarly under-developed. At the monitoring stage users are more involved, though in a limited way. Their views are sought on an agenda of issues set by doctors rather than patients, and there is a danger that proxies, such as GPs, are used in preference to asking patients themselves.' (p. 1)

As mentioned earlier, the introduction of the internal market encouraged the use of patient satisfaction surveys by hospitals and GPs. Regrettably, while much of the initial survey work used patients as a source of information, they were rarely involved in identifying problems, setting standards, or assessing practice. Many surveys were bland and generalized, stating the obvious and producing little of worth for either GPs or their patients. The College of Health responded with a patient-centred audit package for GP practices, a 'consumer audit' that gave patients a central role (Dennis, 1991). Once patients are at the centre of an audit process the focus of audit widens to include the work of all the staff involved in service provision. Finely nuanced professional distinctions are not important.

A tendency to professionalize indicators that can only be experienced by users is evident in the design of outcome measures as it is in medical audit, at least partly because suitable measures have not been developed. As Neuberger (1993, p. 2) stresses: 'In all the designing of outcome measures, the users' point of view is not taken into account whereas the practitioners is.' The UK Clearing House for Health Outcomes at the Nuffield Institute may address this omission.

Though nursing or management staff may seek out consumers to give their views, quality assurance circles and initiatives also commonly run independently of user involvement. This is a fundamental weakness. In the end, it is the user of a service who has to assess the quality of what is provided — but as soon as the user's viewpoint is placed at the centre of discussion, professional distinctions diminish in importance. Melia (1993) recognized this after experiencing for herself the contrast between a patient and a professional view of service delivery:

> 'First, I am now convinced (I had long suspected) that we need more ethnographic research on the patient's experience of illness and hospital care . . . Secondly, and this I had not thought much about before, the patient experience of care comes as a package, it is not broken down along professional fault lines. By this I mean that it is exceptionally difficult to focus upon the work of any one member of the team in order to evaluate its effects.' (p. 113)

The development of medical audit is a move away from a form of professional governance that holds each fully trained member responsible for his or her own practice; i.e. a collegiate system. Instead, the profession is moving to a more managerial process, which involves the profession monitoring the work of its members. At the same time that this is happening within medicine, the nursing profession has formally jettisoned its insistence on minutely certificated systems of 'extended role' qualifications, emphasizing instead the need for individuals to accept responsibility for their own practice. These two professions are thus edging slowly towards a common conception of professional accountability. Where there is still a fundamental difference is that the medical profession in hospital and in the community 'owns' the patient.

Ownership of the patient

The concept of 'ownership' of the patient is one that I encountered for the first time while conducting research interviews with nursing and medical staff in the intensive care unit of a teaching hospital. It was used to explain to me what happened if an ICU consultant and a surgical or medical consultant disagreed over the treatment options. Protocol made it clear that the consultant to whom the patient had been referred by the GP 'owned' the patient. So while the ICU consultant could forcefully argue the case for a particular line of treatment, the admitting consultant had the final say.

The concept of ownership of property commonly contains notions of rights to acquire, to use, to modify, and to sell or transfer goods. All of these seem to be wholly alien to patient care, but they have parallels with admission to hospital or acceptance on to a GP list (acquisition); treatment (modifying); and discharging patients from hospital (exchange) or dismissing them from a GP list (disposal). In these senses a doctor can be said to have ownership of patients. Nurses influence treatment decisions but largely through influencing doctors, and in NHS establishments they do not have the right to discharge patients, though they may modify or influence medical practice. NHS nurses do not have ownership. Nor do therapists. This gives rise to some rituals designed to demonstrate medical ownership. Watkins (1987) describes how a medical consultant deals with the situation of having formal ownership of the treatment that a patient receives from an occupational therapist:

> 'One model . . . is to hold case conferences at which members of the rehabilitation professions concerned with particular patients will report on their progress. The consultant will then write these notes into the patient's case notes, and instruct the physiotherapists, OTs [occupational therapists] etc. to do what they have recommended he should tell them to do. This touching ritual emphasizes medical dominance.' (p. 218)

Having absorbed the notion of ownership, I found it a useful way of understanding and predicting some of the cross-currents of hospital and community interprofessional relations. The GP owns the patient in the community and the consultant owns the patient in hospital, and other professions in health care, however significant their role in terms of the outcome of care, necessarily have a subordinate role for as long as the concept of ownership is maintained. A recent discussion paper, *Changing Childbirth* (DoH, 1993), suggests that community midwives should control admissions to 30% of hospital maternity beds. In the terms in which ownership was defined in ICU, this is giving the community midwife 'ownership' of some pregnant women. That it aroused immediate medical unease is unsurprising since this is an overt challenge to the prevailing practice of medical ownership of the patient.

The concept of medical ownership has some advantages for other health professions, since it makes clear who has ultimate responsibility for patient treatment; but it reduces their autonomy, and defines a sharp limit to the exercise of professional responsibility. An initial reaction to the concept of ownership is to state that the patient owns himself, but this is a meaningless argument when patients are seriously ill. The process of acute illness leaves patients dependent on professional codes of practice to protect their interests. Dependence on health care staff is a corollary of serious illness, and generates professional attitudes appropriate for dealing with dependent patients.

Summary

In this chapter I have outlined four areas where interprofessional relations in health care are being modified by changes in the functions ascribed to patients, or changes in the roles that patients are willing to accept for themselves — in health promotion; in the process of devolving authority in hospitals to ward-based teams; in the transfer of services to the community; and through the contracting system. There is also a discussion of the way that ownership of patients by the medical profession sets limits to the autonomy of other health professions. Evaluation of the outcomes of treatment is thought to be the process that will have most impact on the relationship of patients and health professionals, and on interprofessional relationships.

Medical professional dominance has justification when treatment of an acute illness is the primary concern; but different patterns should emerge in the management of rehabilitation, frail elderly patients or chronic disability, where other professionals, or informal carers or patients themselves, may have functional or ethical grounds for claiming control of care management. In a health care team that is responsive to patient needs, authority to make care and treatment decisions should move among professions, carers, and patients as appropriate. Concepts of professional/patient relationships have their origin in various health locations, where professional priorities and organizational structures are necessarily different. In the more health-focused and community-based patterns that are emerging, practitioners need autonomy to be flexible and responsive to patient's needs, and users of services need to have a dominant influence in systems of monitoring and outcome measurement to ensure that practitioners are using their autonomy appropriately. There is still a long way to go.

References

Armstrong D (1993) From clinical gaze to a regime of total health. In: Beattie A, Gott M, Jones L, Sidell M (Eds), *Health and Wellbeing*. London: OU/Macmillan.

Ashton J (1992) 'Health for all': new lamps for old. *Primary Health Care Management*; **2**: (4).

Beattie A (1993) The changing boundaries of health. In: Beattie A, Gott M, Jones L, Sidell M (Eds), *Health and Wellbeing*. London: OU/Macmillan.

Carr-Hill R, Dixon P, Gibbs I, Griffiths M, Higgins M, McCaughan D, Wright K (1992) *Skill Mix and the Effectiveness of Nursing Care*. York: Centre for Health Economics, University of York.

Dalley G (1993) The ideological foundations of informal care. In:

Kitson A (Ed.), *Nursing: Art and Science*. London: Chapman & Hall.

Dennis N (1991) *Ask the Patient: New Approaches to Consumer Feedback in General Practice*. London: College of Health.

Department of Health (1989a) *Working for Patients*. London: HMSO.

Department of Health (1989b) *NHS Review, Working Paper 6: Medical audit*. London: HMSO.

Department of Health (1991) *The Health of the Nation* (Green Paper). London: HMSO.

Department of Health (1992) *The Health of the Nation* (White Paper). London: HMSO.

Department of Health (1993) *Changing Childbirth*. London: HMSO.

Ersser S, Tutton E (1991) Primary nursing — implications for the patient. In: Ersser S, Tutton E (Eds), *Primary Nursing in Perspective*. London: Scuturi Press.

Hancock C (1991) Clinical directorates. *Nursing Standard*, 6 March.

Illman J (1991) Not enough patient power in the waiting room. *The Guardian*; 29 September.

Joule N (1992) *User Involvement in Medical Audit: A Spoke in the Wheel or a Link in the Chain*. London: Greater London Association of CHCs.

Lupton D, Donaldson C, Lloyd P (1991) Caveat emptor or blissful ignorance? Patients and the consumerist ethos. *Social Science and Medicine*; **33**: 559–568.

Mallett J (1991) Shifting the focus of audit. *Health Service Journal*; **101**: (41), 24–25.

Mackay L (1989) *Nursing a Problem*. Milton Keynes: Open University Press.

Mackay L (1993) *Conflicts in Care: Medicine and Nursing*. London: Chapman & Hall.

Melia K (1993) The effects of nursing care: an ethnographic approach. In: Kitson A (Ed.), *Nursing: Art and Science*. London: Chapman & Hall.

Neuberger J (1993) The need to take views seriously. *King's Fund Newsletter*; **16**: (2), 2.

National Consumer Council (1992) *Involving the Community: Guidelines for Health Service Managers*. London: NCC.

NHS Management Executive (1992) *Local Voices*. London: HMSO.

Peters T, Waterman R (1982) *In Search of Excellence: Lessons from America's Best Run Companies*. New York: Harper Collins.

Stainton Rogers R (1991) *Explaining Health and Illness: An Exploration of Diversity*. Hemel Hempstead: Harvester.

United Kingdom Central Council for Nursing, Midwifery and Health Visiting (1992) *The Scope of Professional Practice*. London: UKCC.

Walby S, Greenwell J, Mackay L, Soothill K (1994) *Medicine and Nursing: Professions in a Changing Health Service*. London: Sage.

Watkins S (1987) *Medicine and Labour: The Politics of a Profession*. London: Lawrence & Wishart.

World Health Organization (1981) *Global Strategy for Health for All by the Year 2000*. Geneva: WHO.

21 Patients in interprofessional practice

Eileen McLeod

Introduction

Analysis of interprofessional relations normally focuses on the significance for health care of working relations between professionals. However, this chapter focuses on the significance for health care of working relations between patients and professionals. It argues that patients' participation as co-workers in inter-'professional' health care is essential if practice is actually to promote well-being. The chapter draws on the interim results of a small-scale survey to demonstrate this point. The survey forms part of a project to promote older patients' interests in interprofessional practice and is specifically concerned with referral for hospital social work. The results also help to identify a major factor which impedes placing patients' participation in interprofessional health care on a par with that of professionals.

The aim in focusing on patients' part in interprofessional health care is simply to register its importance in its own right. It is crucial not to disregard the central role of informal carers as well in health care (see Graham, 1992). The importance of this role has had its own struggle for recognition (Finch and Groves, 1983), which still continues (Pitkeathley, 1989, Chapter 8). It is also important to recognize that patients are not all the same and cannot be treated as if they were a homogeneous group. The interplay of social divisions which suffuses every aspect of our experience is present here and gradually being recognized. Activists and commentators have put on record the specific forms of disadvantage that have been experienced in being a patient, as for example in McNaught's (1987) and Eyles and Donovan's (1990) work on racism. The need for patients' differential requirements to be met to avoid discrimination and disadvantage has been spelt out — see, for example, Rees' work on South Asian patients and terminal care (Rees, 1990) and American work on the health care requirements of gay and lesbian older people (Quam and Whitford, 1992). The interaction of different dimensions to inequality such as agism and gender have also been shown to prejudice patients' chances of equitable treatment (Evers, 1981).

Patients as co-workers in health care

The focus on patients as co-workers in health care is not a new one. Indeed, evidence from diverse fields suggests that patients' contribution to health care should be regarded as equally important as that of health care professionals. First, there is evidence that patients are active agents in interactions with health care professionals, and not simply passive recipients or consumers of services. Cornwell (1984) and Donovan (1991), for example, have set out how people as patients have their own paradigms of what constitutes measures which it would be desirable and possible to adopt to promote health. Medical instruction or advice is passed through the sieve of such paradigms and acted on or ignored accordingly. Secondly, a range of initiatives has also recognized that, if health care professionals dismiss the importance of patients' own desires and efforts to maximize their own health, then the professionals' actions tend to undermine patients' psychological and physical well-being. One of the best known examples of work on this issue is feminist action on women's experiences of maternity care. Analyses focusing on women's views of their experiences have established the extent to which various standard practices subject them to avoidable psychological and physical suffering (e.g. Oakley, 1984). This work has fuelled continuing agitation to bring about the optimum conditions in which women's own contribution to labour can be made. This is reflected in the following House of Commons Health Committee report (1992, xcv):

> 'The evidence we have received suggests that the importance of continuity of care needs underlining very heavily for the professionals who are involved in delivering the maternity services of the NHS. Many still demonstrate an insufficient awareness of its prominence among the criteria which women use to judge the quality of the care they have received. Nor have they yet done nearly enough to respond in practical terms to the call by women to be involved as full partners in the decisions made about their care.' (para. 191)

The importance of this principle, even when physical disability and cognitive impairment may have progressed to a stage where the patient is no longer able to take decisions, has also been recognized. For example, the introduction of living wills is an attempt to safeguard patients' wishes concerning the nature of care they will receive in the final stages of terminal illness. These documents record the patient's wishes in advance and their choice of a friend or relative to be consulted in their stead if they wish (Terrence Higgins Trust, 1992).

The significance of patients' contribution to health care has also received some recognition amongst professional health care workers themselves. In the two cases just cited, for example, Wendy Savage, a gynaecologist and obstetrician, has become known for criticism of her own profession along similar lines to the House of Commons Report (Savage, 1990). The British Medical Association has also endorsed the preparation of living wills, recommending the carrying of 'living will cards' to alert doctors that such wills have been made (*The Guardian*, 1992). Such initiatives do not represent a crude drive towards the demedicalization of health care. Instead, they reflect a desire for professional health care that responds to patients' input, as opposed to undermining or dismissing it. This is exemplified in the work of the ME (myalgic encephalomyelitis) Association, which has campaigned for recognition of the need for systematic research into the organic origins of the condition, to counter unproven assertions in public debate that it is a hypochondriacal fantasy (ME Association, 1992).

The work of feminist researchers, and commentators in the field of disability rights, focusing beyond the context of patient–professional interaction, has further revised the relative significance attributed to professionals' and patients' contributions to health care — in two interlinked ways. First, feminist researchers have been prominent in uncovering how the greater mass of health care is not carried out by professionals. They have charted how women as the main informal carers of children, partners and older relatives, or partners and relatives with disabilities, are prime actors in taking action with consequences for health — through the provision of food, clothing, home care, budgeting, social activities and, ironically, negotiation with health care professionals (Graham, 1984). Secondly, commentators on disability rights have set out how, notwithstanding women's efforts as informal carers, people with disabilities themselves are and need to be responsible for ensuring that their needs are met (Morris, 1991, Chapter 6; Oliver, 1990). This perspective, therefore, lends further weight to the idea that the person occupying the 'cared-for' role should be regarded as an active agent in health care.

Meanwhile epidemiological evidence suggests that the work of health care professionals is bound by the same constraint as that of patients (or informal carers) — being mediated by the effects of fundamental social inequalities. It has demonstrated that there is a consistent causal relationship between relative poverty and increased rates of morbidity and mortality. For example, Smith and Jacobson (1988) have reported as follows:

'Almost all health indicators confirm the association between the prevalence of ill health and poor social and economic circumstances. In 1981, the death rate was twice as high in the lowest social classes as in the highest. The expectation of life for a child with parents in social class V is about eight years shorter than for a child whose parents are in social class 1 . . . if manual workers had enjoyed the same death rates as non-manual workers there would have been 42,000 fewer deaths during the year in the age range 16–74 . . . reported rates of chronic illness and days of restricted activity in 1983 were twice as high in social class V as in social class 1.' (pp. 107 and 108).

This relationship is so all-pervasive that the effects of relative poverty supersede those of medical intervention in their influence. The evidence is powerful and can be summarized as follows: 'The relatively minor influence of medical treatment is confirmed by studies which show that geographical differences in the death rate, for all causes combined, are more closely related to socio-economic factors than to differences in medical provision' (Martini et al., 1977; as quoted in Smith and Jacobson, 1988, p. 112). Moreover, even when people behave in ways which can be regarded as conducive to good health, the odds are still unfairly stacked against them by their class position. Among people living in poverty, favoured behaviour — such as not smoking, taking regular exercise and adopting a good diet — produces fewer benefits for their health than for those occupying a higher class position and engaging in the same activities (Blaxter, 1990).

More recently, research has been reported which suggests that the role of inequitable social conditions may be even more powerful than previously indicated. In developed countries, the greater the income differential across a society, then the worse the rates of morbidity and mortality for that society as a whole, not only for those in relative poverty (Quick and Wilkinson, 1991; Wilkinson, 1992). The converse of such a situation is that it is only when measures are taken to equalize income distribution across society that those suffering the worst health — those in relative poverty — will experience any substantial improvement. Wilkinson (1992) makes the point strongly:

'Overall health standards in developed countries are highly dependent on how equal or unequal people's incomes are. The most effective way of improving health is to make incomes more equal. This is more important than providing better public services or making everyone better off while ignoring the inequalities between them.' (p. 5)

Currently the omens for introducing such measures are not good, as the trend over the past decade or so has been for income differentials to widen in Britain (Department of Social Security, 1992).

The mechanisms whereby income differentials have such a treacherous effect on health are not yet fully understood (Quick and Wilkinson, 1991, Chapter 3). However, the picture assembled by epidemiologists suggests that the work of patients, informal carers and professionals for health has two aspects in common. First, it is subject to the undermining effects of relative poverty. Secondly, it is in the interests of all parties that the dire effects of this be unmasked.

Existing evidence therefore seems to indicate that there are good grounds for regarding professionals' and patients' contributions to health care as being equally important. Further evidence to support this point is now presented from research into older patients' participation in interprofessional practice relating to referral for hospital social work.

Older patients' participation and referral for hospital social work

The benefits of access to hospital social workers

As yet, systematic evidence of the outcomes for patients of hospital social workers' intervention is sparse. However, the most comprehensive survey (Connor and Tibbitt, 1988) indicates that hospital social workers do have resources to which older patients need to gain access in the interests of maintaining their health and well-being. In their study, Connor and Tibbitt reviewed the practice of hospital social workers in 'geriatric' specialist hospital units. Where social workers had contact with patients from early on in their hospital stay and the social work staffing levels were high enough for them to pay attention to the following matters, patients benefited accordingly. Patients' and their carers' concerns about the nature and consequences of their condition and its treatment were taken more fully into account by other hospital staff in formulating treatment plans, as a result of social workers acting as intermediaries. Arrangements to avert emergencies at home due to dependants being left uncared for or property unsecured, as a result of unforeseen admissions, were undertaken more promptly. Services essential to managing back at home — such as home care, meals on wheels, day-centre or respite care or the provision of welfare rights information — were either instituted more appropriately, extended or reintroduced more reliably. As a result of such intervention, the likelihood of readmission through onset of further ill-health or relapse was reduced (*op cit.*, pp. 42–62).

Two further studies complement Connor and Tibbitt's findings. Russell's study of a home discharge scheme for older patients in South Wales (1989) found some indications that poor social conditions outweighed the benefits that the aides attached to the scheme could put in, and so raised readmission rates. Factors such as lacking support from close relatives or friends, and suffering '3 or 4 measures of disadvantage' which may involve inadequate heating, no telephone, no inside toilet, financial shortages, were implicated (*op. cit.*, p. 83). However, readmission rates also rose if patients were discharged just before a weekend, when services might not be in place. Patients themselves also identified their main worries on coming home as relating to provision of support services, the emotional adjustment required and the practicalities involved (Russell, 1989, Chapter 3). Both sets of factors indicate that the intervention of hospital social workers would be of benefit. In a study by Townsend et al. (1988), older patients receiving intensive additional support from care assistants for the first two weeks after discharge from hospital were significantly less likely to be readmitted within the next 18 months. The difference in readmission rates was most marked among patients who lived alone and those aged over 85. Again, these are the sort of provisions instituted by hospital social workers.

Obstacles to older patients' access to hospital social work services

Given such indicators of the importance for older hospital patients of access to social work intervention and the fact that, as Victor (1991) has noted, older people are the largest single patient group for most medical specialisms, it would seem to follow that hospital social work services would be in demand by older patients. However, self-referral rates for social work across hospital populations, including older patients, are consistently low. The Social Services Inspectorate's report on hospital social work in England found that 'in practice patients did not usually refer themselves directly to workers in the hospital social services' (SSI, 1992a, p. 15). The same pattern was picked up in the SSI's report on social work in Northern Ireland hospitals: 'Of all referrals to hospital social workers, patients' self-referred in 4% of cases' (SSI, 1992b, p. 42).

In fact the standard means of referral for hospital social work is through other members of the interprofessional care team deciding that such a referral is appropriate and carrying it out. Occasionally this is supplemented by social workers identifying potential cases themselves. In the Northern Ireland study (SSI, 1992b), for example, 76% of all referrals came from medical and nursing staff and 5% were identified by social workers themselves. The incidence of self-referral for hospital social work being low or virtually non-existent is reflected in Bywaters' review of 'case-finding and screening' for hospital social work (Bywaters, 1991). The study weighed the merits of various methods of case-finding initiated interprofessionally or by social workers, against each other, but did not set these against the outcomes of self-referral or initiatives to enhance this. Similarly, Connor and Tibbitt showed that well-staffed social work teams on-site facilitated patients' access to social work services, with beneficial effects. However, a limitation of their study was that they did not interview patients in hospital or subsequently and so did not establish the extent to which their requirements for social work services went beyond those identified by professional staff.

The usual methods of interprofessional referral are either through verbal exchanges or memos between nursing, medical or para-medical staff, or most commonly and most systematically through interprofessional ward meetings (Connor and Tibbitt, 1988, p. 13; Bywaters, 1991; Chadwick and Russell, 1989). Interprofessional ward meetings are typically chaired by the consultant and attended by other members of staff including sister or clinical nurse manager, senior house officer or registrar, occupational therapist, physiotherapist and social worker. Their purpose is for all the professionals concerned with the social and medical needs of the patient to collaborate in reviewing and planning social and medical care and arrangements for discharge. They also serve as the forum where referrals are made to social workers or social workers 'pick-up cases'.

If the interprofessional model of referral could be relied on to meet the requirements of the majority of older patients, it would be unproblematic. However, there is evidence to suggest that this is not the case. Analysis of the internal workings of interprofessional ward meetings by Chadwick and Russell (1989) suggests that they do not function to maximize social workers' take-up of referrals. Instead, social workers along with other professional colleagues tend to negotiate and compete to withdraw from responsibility for taking on new work in the face of a shortage of resources. Neill and Williams' study (1992) of older patients' experience of discharge from hospital provides corroborative evidence of the shortcomings of the interprofessional model of referral, and also — by implication — of the importance of older patients gaining access to social work intervention.

Neill and Williams found that it was standard practice for social workers to obtain referrals through interprofessional ward meetings. However, older patients' need for social work services was either not canvassed, or underestimated in the majority of cases. Their sample was composed of 70 patients aged 75 or older, who had all been referred for home help or home care after a hospital stay of at least three nights. They were interviewed two and twelve weeks after discharge. Only one in three experienced a good discharge according to the criterion of having an opportunity to discuss how they would manage at home. Two weeks following discharge, the majority were found to be in a poor state of health and well-being: two-thirds experienced difficulty with self-care tasks; most still felt unwell and in some degree of pain; about one-third were assessed as possibly depressed. All the older people interviewed were trying to maintain self-care routines. However, they were experiencing the harrowing consequences of not having access to the sort of resources that social work could provide them with, as the following examples illustrate:

> 'A recently bereaved 90 year old man lived alone, was very independent, lonely, deaf and with poor vision. His hip had dislocated at least seven times in recent years and when this occurred he was in great pain and completely immobile. He had no telephone, a home help once each week and no friends or relatives to visit. Putting a light in his window to his neighbour was his only signal that he needed help. He paid his neighbour for this service and for bringing him lunch on a Sunday.' (pp. 119–120)

> 'A woman who had had a leg amputated was confined to a wheelchair and lived alone. Two weeks after discharge she was found to be in pain and depressed. She was unable to reach her kitchen cupboards at all and struggled to reach her taps from her wheelchair because the sink needed adjusting . . . Her bed was too high and her armchair too low . . . This person had no relatives, some contact with neighbours but no regular help at weekends, during which time her commode was unemptied. Her mainstream home help sometimes called, in unpaid time during the weekend, to empty her commode.' (pp. 81–82)

This study is not alone. Indeed, Marks' review of surveys of discharge procedures across the past decade reveals a similar pattern of the majority of patients not being asked by hospital staff about how they would cope at home, and hospital staff grossly underestimating requirements for community support services (Marks, 1992).

My own experience of observing and participating in inter-professional ward meetings, while on placement in a General Services hospital social work team, also raised concerns about whether they functioned uniformly in patients' interests. On grounds of civil liberties they were questionable events. Patients did not seem to know they were happening, they did not participate directly, nor did they have a named person to represent their interests in obtaining social workers' services or not. Moreover, decisions as to whether or not someone was referred for social work could be taken on the basis of stigmatizing and sweeping assumptions such as 'He's not a social problem' or 'She's got a husband'.

Interprofessional ward meetings also seemed to act as a buffer between hospital social workers and patients. In theory they were the gateway to patients. In practice they had a rationing function. If the social worker treated the ward meeting as *the* source of referrals, at the most he or she would have to deal with referrals coming from there. In contrast, if the social worker had direct contact with patients, then he or she risked a ballooning workload or as one social worker put it, 'opening the floodgates'.

As a result of such evidence from secondary sources, and personal observations, I decided to test out whether the current situation regarding older patients' self-referral for hospital social work represented an instance of patients' exclusion from participation in interprofessional practice to the detriment of their well-being, and if so the possible gains of trying to rectify this.

Survey of older patients' participation in interprofessional practice

My survey was carried out as an integral part of my work as an independent adviser to a hospital social work team attached to an acute elderly unit spanning six wards in a district general hospital. The average age of patients was 75 or over. The members of the hospital social work team were interested in reviewing the referral process as they felt patients were not well informed about what social work could offer. Further, they wished to check what criteria other professional staff were using, as they were committed on equal-opportunities grounds to reaching patients from ethnic minorities, and patients with sensory disabilities.

At the outset of the survey, following the pattern in practice more generally, the characteristic means of referral for hospital social work was through weekly interprofessional ward meetings. Social workers did not canvass patients directly on the ward. Brief information on social work was contained in a booklet for all patients to receive on admission. But the information was hard to find and social workers observed that the booklet was not necessarily distributed or read. Self-referral from patients rarely occurred: as one social worker put it, 'Not very frequently, once or twice a month'.

It was agreed that I would interview a sample of patients from two wards (male and female) and the social work team about their experience and views of the referral process, and sit in on a series of ward meetings. The social work team would interview a sample of other professional staff connected with the unit and a sample of relatives and carers to obtain their views on the referral process. On the basis of the results of the survey, it was agreed that the team would decide what (if any) revisions to make to the existing referral process. The following findings are drawn from the interviews with patients and relatives.

Initial results

In theory, the low rate of self-referral could have existed because patients disliked the idea of involvement with social workers. However, it quickly became apparent that patients did not know there *were* hospital social workers on-site, unless they happened to have had previous contact or were currently in contact following a ward meeting referral. (The one exception to this occurred in the third week of interviewing — a man whose father had been a hospital visitor for many years.)

The patient population of two wards, which averaged 24 in number, was interviewed on three occasions, at two-monthly intervals to lessen the chances of duplication. The total numbers interviewed were reduced because patients were not interviewed if they were judged by nursing staff to be too ill or declined on these grounds; if they had combined visual and hearing impairment or severe cognitive impairment; if their ability to communicate was severely impaired following a stroke; or if English was not their first language.

From those interviewed, the numbers not knowing there were hospital social workers on-site were as follows: week 1, 9/11; week 2, 12/14; week 3, 8/15; total, 29/40. So, while the numbers fluctuated from week to week, around three-quarters (73%) of the total did not know of this provision. Patients were also not clear about what hospital social workers did. Those patients who did not know there were hospital social workers on-site, but who offered a suggestion of what social workers did or might do, tended to confuse the identity of social workers with that of home care workers, commenting for example: 'They're good women, they get good dinners' and 'Someone coming in to get the breakfast and help with the shopping'. Even among the seven patients in week 3 who knew there were hospital social workers, two did not know what they did.

Relatives' and carers' views produced a complementary picture. Fifteen who were *already* in contact with hospital social workers completed brief questionnaires asking, among other things, how they had come to know about the existence of hospital social workers and what they did. One had found out from a poster in the hospital, another from a friend of her mother at the time of admission. Otherwise none of the respondents had known as a matter of general knowledge that there were hospital social workers or what they could offer. They had been dependent on being informed of this by hospital or social work staff.

These two sets of findings together provide one part of the explanation of why rates of self-referral are so low. If patients and those connected with them tend not to know about either the existence or the nature of hospital social work resources, there is little chance of them trying to gain access on their own initiative.

This situation might not be worrying on two grounds. First, one must not assume that everyone requires social work intervention. Secondly, interprofessional referral mechanisms — such as principally the ward meeting — might successfully have identified those patients who actually required social work intervention. To test this out, a spot check on the effectiveness of the existing referral process was made. On five separate occasions, at monthly intervals, I interviewed any patients on the two wards (male and female) who had not been referred through the interprofessional team for social work intervention. The exceptions were patients who were too ill to be seen, or had been seen by me already, or — on pragmatic grounds — who were to be discharged that day. I endeavoured to employ the same criteria for referral as those used by the social work team. The bare results are set out in Table 21.1.

The average number of patients on the wards in survey weeks was 22. On average, 13 were referred to the social worker. The existing referral system seemed to be working well in picking up the most serious cases of people who were in an extreme state of danger or deprivation and required immediate residential care. None of the people I interviewed seemed to fall into this category. The proportion of people I interviewed who definitely seemed to require social work contact and had not been referred could be considered small — on average three per week. However, given that the current rate of referral for social work was 3–4 cases per week, this amounted to an apparent need for this rate to be doubled. This result may also have been an underestimate as patients being discharged that day were not interviewed, and patients currently too ill to be seen may have required social work intervention but would not receive it.

Moreover, on average, one person each week not already referred for social work seemed to be grappling with very poor social conditions in trying to maintain their health and well-being. Similarly to the picture emerging in Neill and Williams' study, such conditions both

Table 21.1 Spot check on effectiveness of referral system in survey weeks

	Average number per week
Patients referred to social worker	13
Patients too ill for author to see/discharged that day/seen already	5
Patients seen by author and assessed as needing social work intervention	2
Patients seen by author and assessed as needing check by social worker	1
Patients seen by author and assessed as not needing social work intervention or checking	1
Total on ward	22

caused a great deal of suffering and presaged the collapse of independent living and further deterioration in health, as in the following examples:

Mr A, aged 75, suffering from profound shortness of breath and exhaustion. He lived alone and could now only walk 100 yards maximum. No friends or relatives were close, no home help. He actually had his very specific requirements for home care already worked out — help to collect his pension, medicines and weekly shopping. The shops concerned were ¼ mile away. He also commented 'I don't want to be housebound'. His ideal was for someone occasionally to take him out for a drive in the country.

Ms B, aged 85, had chronic asthma and profound shortness of breath. Lived alone. Generally very anxious, in particular about a repetition at night of the severe chest infection and asthma attack which had resulted in admission to hospital. Had home help twice a week but found she could only go upstairs with great difficulty. Wanted advice on housing. Virtually housebound — only regular outing being taken out to a church meeting once a week. She commented 'I don't like losing my independence'.

Mr C, aged 80. Admitted because of an ulcer and because his diabetes needed controlling. Lived alone. Depressed since the death of his wife 7 years before. Commented 'life is finished'. Very worried about worsening concentration. It meant that reading, which he had previously turned to as his mainstay, was becoming impossible. Also worried about being able to pay his heating bills. He had resorted to living off sandwiches as what he could manage to prepare, given his lack of concentration and deteriorating physical condition. Meals on wheels had been about to start before he came into hospital — needed reorganizing.

Each week I came across at least one patient whose social situation could not be assumed to be safe and therefore needed some checking out through the social worker. Mostly this was because the patient concerned was cognitively impaired and it was impossible to know directly from them whether or not their well-being was in jeopardy. On one occasion, it was through the combined effects of a stroke, the patient (who lived alone) speaking little English and no interpreter having been brought in.

The survey therefore revealed that an interprofessional referral system which excluded older patients' participation on an equal footing — depriving them of information about social workers and direct access to them — posed substantial problems for patients' well-being. In doing so, it lent support to the idea that patients' participation in interprofessional practice on a par with professionals is essential if practice is actually to promote health.

What prevented older patients' participation in interprofessional practice?

The foregoing survey also exposed what was ultimately preventing older patients from participating as co-workers in interprofessional practice concerning referral for hospital social work. This was the underfunding of social services, as one aspect of the general trend against redistributing material resources in older people's favour, to relieve the relative poverty which the majority of older people experience.

The social work team's response to the survey's results and its resource implications revealed that the main factor which kept older patients in ignorance of hospital social work, and thereby excluded their participation in the interprofessional referral mechanism, was shortage of funding for the social services department in question. If the hospital social workers concerned stepped beyond interprofessional referral and opened up self-referral by patients, the survey results indicated that the weekly referral rate would probably double. Also at a conservative estimate, workloads would rise by 25% (see Table 21.1). In addition there would be the demands of the extra time involved in making direct contact with patients.

The hospital social work team's decision to embark on the survey in the first place — without any additional resources — argues against their being work-shy; as does their decision, on the basis of the results, to undertake the following initiative — again without additional resources. Patients, social workers and other staff had identified in the survey that production of an information leaflet, together with face-to-face introductory contact from hospital social workers, was the best means of patients being informed about hospital social workers' presence, what they offered, and how they could be contacted. Although a leaflet and face-to-face contact might generally enhance self-referral, the team also concluded that this could still be discriminatory through excluding or deterring patients in a range of circumstances. Therefore, for example, they agreed that the information leaflet should be translated, indicating also that interpreting facilities were available. The leaflet should reflect a commitment to gay and lesbian patients' rights. The team should also routinely check with the patients themselves, and with their most independent representative, the requirements for social work that patients with cognitive impairment might have. At the time of writing the team had agreed to undertake such an initiative as an experiment for two months, in addition to the interprofessional ward meetings. Its feasibility will then be assessed in the light of an analysis of positive and negative benefits for patients and any increase in demand.

However, a review of the staffing position by the hospital social work team manager revealed why the team could not have considered moving out of the existing interprofessional referral machinery before, and could not do so now on a long-term basis:

> 'The Department (Social Services) has had a freeze on recruitment since last year. The team is 50% understaffed against its establishment figure. We have no money as yet in the form of "a special transitional grant" to implement incoming Community Care procedures. In line with all other sections of the Social Services Department, we have to produce 10% savings across the board.' (personal communication)

The position this social services department is in should not be seen as simply representing its own shortage of resources. It reflects a general trend against redistributing material resources in favour of older people, the majority of whom live in relative poverty. Victor (1991) has stressed that:

> 'Overall 25% of those over 65 have an income at or below supplementary benefit rates and a further 44% live on the margins of poverty; i.e. they have an income within 40% of the poverty level. Within the elderly population, it is the very old (i.e. those aged over 80), women, those living alone, those from manual occupations and the disabled who are most at risk of experiencing poverty in later life.' (p. 39)

While introduced as catering more effectively for the needs of older people (Department of Health, 1989), the implementation of the NHS and Community Care Act 1990 has amounted to the withdrawal of readily funded access to residential care (Marks, 1992). Coincidentally, free hospital care for older people in the form of long-stay beds and the length of stay in acute beds has been rapidly reduced, with no compensatory development of NHS nursing homes (Henwood, 1992). The value of pensions has continued to decline (Quick and Wilkinson 1991). Yet despite this withdrawal of material resources from older people, social services departments have also consistently estimated that they are underfunded for 'care in the community' measures that are being introduced as an alternative to residential provision (Ivory, 1992).

Conclusions

From the exploratory study reported in this chapter, certain clear themes emerge. The findings elaborate earlier ones concerning the importance for patients' well-being of their participation in interprofessional practice, on a par with professionals. First, the study provides further evidence that patients are actively engaged in trying to foster their own health and well-being. Secondly, in relation to these efforts, it indicates that patients' access to crucial resources which professionals hold can depend on measures to promote patient participation in health care on an equal basis with professionals. Thirdly, it suggests that once the principle of patients engaging on an equal footing with professionals in health care is broached, the question of differential disadvantage amongst patients in being able to do so is opened up.

Finally, the study reveals the nature of a major impediment to placing patients' participation in interprofessional practice, on an equal basis to that of professionals. Older patients' low rates of self-referral for hospital social work were brought about primarily because of lack of funding for social services departments. Such underfunding reflected a general trend against the redistribution of material resources in older peoples' favour, to relieve their relative poverty. These were the conditions which locked into place older patients' exclusion from interprofessional practice concerning referral for hospital social work, to the detriment of the patients' well-being.

Therefore, the study unmasks how attempts to promote patients' participation in interprofessional practice in this respect are up against one of the insidious mechanisms whereby the continuation of relative poverty undermines health.

References

Blaxter M (1990) *Health and Lifestyles Survey*. London: Tavistock.

Bywaters P (1991) Casefinding and screening for social work in acute general hospitals. *British Journal of Social Work*; **21**: 19–39.

Chadwick R, Russell J (1989) Hospital discharge of frail elderly people: social and ethical considerations in the discharge decision-making process. *Ageing and Society*; **9**: 277–295.

Connor A, Tibbitt JE (1988) *Social Workers and Health Care in Hospitals*. London: HMSO.

Cornwell J (1984) *Hard Earned Lives*. London: Tavistock.

Department of Health (1989) *Community Care in the Next Decade and Beyond*. London: HMSO.

Department of Social Security (1992) *Households Below Average Income: Statistical Analysis 1979–1988/9*. London: HMSO.

Donovan J (1991) Patient education and the consultation: the importance of lay beliefs. *Annals of Rheumatic Diseases*; **50**: 418–421.

Evers H (1981) Care or Custody? The experiences of women patients in long stay geriatric wards. In: Hutter B, Williams G (Eds), *Controlling Women, the Normal and the Deviant*. London: Croom Helm.

Eyles J, Donovan J (1990) *The Social Effects of Health Policy*. Aldershot: Avebury/Gower.

Finch J, Groves D (1983) *A Labour of Love — Women, Work and Caring*. London: Routledge & Kegan Paul.

Graham H (1984) *Women, Health and the Family*. Hemel Hempstead: Harvester Wheatsheaf.

Graham H (1992) Informal care: problem or solution? *Health Visitor*; **65**:(12).

The Guardian (1992) BMA advocates 'living will' card. 14 November.

Henwood M (1992) *Through a Glass Darkly; Community Care and Elderly People*. London: King's Fund Institute.

House of Commons Health Committee (1992) *Second Report, Maternity Services*, vol. 1. London: HMSO.

Ivory M (1992) Funding announcement heralds major cuts. *Community Care*; 3 Dec.: 1.

Marks L (1992) Discharging patients or responsibilities? Acute hospital discharge and elderly people. In: Harrison and Bruscini (Eds), *Health Care UK 1991*. London: King's Fund Institute.

Martini CJ et al. (1977) Health indices sensitive to medical care variations. *International Journal of Health Services*; **7**: 293–309.

ME Association (1992) *Perspectives*, the magazine of the Myalgic Encephalomyelitis Association, autumn. Stanford le Hope: ME Association.

Morris J (1991) *Pride against Prejudice: Transforming Attitudes to Disability*. London: The Women's Press.

McNaught A (1987) *Health Action and Ethnic Minorities*. London: Bedford Square Press.

Neill and Williams (1992) *Leaving Hospital; Elderly People and their Discharge to Community Care*. London: National Institute of Social Work, DHSS.

Oakley A (1984) *Becoming a Mother*. Oxford: Martin Robertson.

Oliver M (1990) *The Politics of Disablement*. Basingstoke: Macmillan.

Pitkeathley J (1989) *It's My Duty, Isn't It? The Plight of Carers in Our Society*. London: Souvenir Press.

Quam JK, Whitford GS (1992) Adaptation and age-related expectations of older gay and lesbian adults. *The Gerontologist*; **32**: 367–374.

Quick A, Wilkinson R (1991) *Income and Health*. London: Socialist Health Association.

Rees D (1990) Terminal care and bereavement. In: McAvoy BR, Donaldson LJ (Eds), *Health Care of Asians*. Oxford: Oxford University Press.

Russell J (1989) *South Glamorgan Care for the Elderly Hospital Discharge Service*. Cardiff: School of Social and Administrative Studies.

Savage W (1990) How obstetrics might change: Wendy Savage talks to Robert Kilpatrick. In: Garcia J, et al. (Ed.), *The Politics of Maternity Care*. Oxford: Oxford University Press.

Smith A, Jacobson B (1988) *The Nation's Health — A Strategy for the 1990s*. London: King's Fund Institute.

Social Services Inspectorate (1992a) *Social Services for Hospital Patients 1: Working at the Interface*. London: Social Services Inspectorate, DoH.

Social Services Inspectorate (1992b) *An Inspection of Social Work in General Hospitals*. Belfast: Social Services Inspectorate, DHSS.

Terrence Higgins Trust (1992) *What's a Living Will?* London: Terrence Higgins Trust.

Townsend J, et al. (1988) Reduction in hospital readmission stay of elderly patients by a community based discharge scheme: a randomised controlled trial. *British Medical Journal*; **297**: 544–547.

Victor CR (1991) *Health and Health Care in Later Life*. Milton Keynes: Open University Press.

Wilkinson RG (1992) Income distribution and life expectancy. *British Medical Journal*; **304**: 165–168.

22 The patient as pawn in interprofessional relationships

Lesley Mackay

The idea of a 'doctor–nurse game', where nurses surreptitiously advise and prompt doctors, has been tremendously popular. However, the reality of everyday working relationships between doctors and nurses is more accurately presented as a series of performances in which, if the games analogy is maintained, the patient is the pawn. Drawing on findings from interviews with hospital-based doctors and nurses, this chapter looks more closely at the repercussions of these performances for patients, paying particular attention to the care and treatment of terminally ill patients.

Games or performances?

The chapter is based on findings from research into interprofessional relations between doctors and nurses in a variety of specialties in five teaching and non-teaching hospitals in Scotland and England. The interviews with 135 nurses (sisters and staff nurses) and 127 doctors (from consultants to pre-registration house officers) were conducted in 1990 and 1991. The specific findings from the research have been presented elsewhere (Mackay, 1993; Walby et al., 1994) and this chapter will reflect on those findings.

The doctor–nurse game takes place when a knowledgeable and experienced nurse feeds a junior doctor with information so that the doctor looks as though he[1] knows what he is doing when in fact he doesn't (Stein, 1967).[2] Because the patient must not detect any uncertainty or inexperience on the part of the doctor, the nurse

---

1 For the sake of clarity only, 'he' will be used to refer to a doctor and 'she' will be used to refer to a nurse.
2 However, Stein et al. (1990), writing in the USA, have argued that the playing of the doctor–nurse game has declined in popularity as nurses become more assertive. There was little evidence from the research in these five UK hospitals that nurses were becoming more assertive or that junior doctors have tired of being made to 'look good' in front of patients.

ensures that the doctor 'looks good' and does not lose face in front of the patient. The credibility of the doctor is maintained by the nurse at her own expense. The nurse disguises her knowledge and skill. The nurse will continue to be seen as needing to be instructed by the doctor. The point of the 'game', so both doctor and nurse would argue, is to the benefit of the patient.

The games analogy is misleading. Games are played by active participants. In the doctor–nurse game the patient (or at least the 'good' patient) is a passive onlooker, essentially part of the audience. The more useful analogy in looking at nurse–doctor behaviour, particularly as displayed in front of patients and relatives, is that of a performance (Goffman, 1959).

Many other performances are given by nurses and doctors in hospitals. These performances seek to protect the status of, and the respect given to, the doctor. In the outpatient department the attendant nurse does what the doctor asks. She will assist when the doctor asks for assistance. She will usher in the patients when the doctor asks. She will be present at the consultation but she will be silent. She will not offer or even consider offering her opinion during the consultation. She will ensure that the patients are processed for appointments in the appropriate way. The importance of the *doctor's* time and attention is endlessly emphasized. The nurse's voice is lowered, and suitable deference by the patient to the doctor is encouraged by numerous gestures of hand and eye. The nurse acts simply as an attendant. Her skills, training and experience are obscured.

On the ward round, the nurse accompanying the doctor will rarely speak until spoken to by the doctor (although the luxury of having a nurse in attendance on ward rounds is declining in the face of reduced nurse staffing levels and the introduction of primary nursing). She will act as an interpreter between doctor and patient. Should the patient try to say too much, the nurse will shush the patient and promise to return and have a chat later about what the doctor said, but she will not delay the busy doctor's progress. It is the nurse's job to ensure that the ward round goes smoothly and there are no disruptions to a perfect performance. The doctor expects, and the nurse assumes, that the doctor has the leading role.

There are other performances as well as ritual obeisances in the working relationships of nurses and doctors in hospitals which emerged during our investigation.[3] There are rituals in the way nurses and doctors address one another, the topics that come up for discussion, who initiates interaction and many others. As in other settings, there are carefully arranged interactions with finely

3 The research was funded by the ESRC (award no. R000 23 1394) whose support is gratefully acknowledged. The project directors were Keith Soothill and Sylvia Walby. The interviews were conducted by the author and June Greenwell.

tuned performances (Goffman, 1959).

The performances and rituals serve a purpose: that of maintaining the faith of patients. Patients must not doubt the competence or knowledge of those who are carrying out the treatment and care. Thus, the inexperience of the junior doctor needs to be disguised even though that inexperience could be dangerous for the patient. Nurses play a leading role in the way the medical profession is presented to the patient. The deferential stance adopted by nurses puts doctors on a pedestal for patients. The 'pedestal' treatment reinforces the superiority of doctors to patients yet is also seen as a way of maintaining the faith and confidence of the patient.

Maintaining the trust of the patient *is* important. In the world of the hospital, 'medical science' is the God, doctors the priests, nurses the acolytes. The benefits of medical science are not to be questioned. There would be obvious and serious repercussions on the status of the medical profession if questions were daily asked by patients about the efficacy of medical science. Thus, the patient's faith in medical science is fostered and protected.

Many patients eagerly participate in these performances: they want to believe in medical science and that they can be made well again. A 'bad' patient is one who does not believe in the performance: is dissatisfied with his/her treatment, is querulous, questioning and irreverent. The 'good' patient, not wanting to be a 'bother', is grateful, submissive and unquestioning.

However, questioning patients can be given answers, can receive information enabling them to participate in their own health care decision-making process. Quiet and potentially ignorant patients playing at being 'good' can be excluded from active participation in their own health care through lack of knowledge.

Why do nurses go along with the medical profession, perpetuating the profession's pre-eminence and bolstering its members' status and power? Partly it can be explained by the socialization of nurses who are trained in, and nearly half of whom will find employment in, the hospital. Nurse training emphasizes the need to be quiet, discreet and sensitive to those around her. At the same time, hospitals are the arenas established and arranged to display the talents and mirror the interests of the medical profession.

The role of the nurse has developed apace over the decades of this century. Today the nurse carries out many tasks which in the past were done by doctors. Yet the nurse is still in a subordinate position to the doctor. The doctor is dominant in the nurse–doctor relationship.

Nurses enjoy a substantial amount of social prestige yet their status (and pay) is much less than doctors'. However, by working alongside doctors, nurses enhance their own status. Nurses have much invested in their association with doctors. It is, therefore, hardly surprising that the views of nurses are often in accord with those of doctors. Nurses and doctors train in the same environment 'in which prestige, rewards, and professional interest all point in the same direction' (McKeown, 1976, p. 116; see also Mackay, 1989). Doctors also enjoy a superior social class, an aspect of interprofessional relationships which is often neglected. Whether by accent or demeanour the class differences between nurses and doctors can be made apparent. But most of all, doctors enjoy a great deal of *power*.

Doctors have the power to admit and discharge, to prescribe and to perform operations. Doctors substantially determine the workload of nurses by the numbers and type of patients they admit, the length of stay, what tests are done and what observations made.

Nurses are aware and fearful of the overt expression of medical power: the threat of being humiliated by senior doctors on ward rounds. They are afraid of a public dressing-down given in front of patients. Such humiliations are not reserved for nurses alone but are visited on unsuspecting medical students and junior medical staff. The junior doctor may one day be able to 'get his own back'. The nurse, however, has no such salve for her wounded pride: she has learned and knows that she is subservient. Through the public dressings-down the dominance of the senior doctor is maintained and the subordinate role of others emphasized. It is a lesson well-learned and not forgotten by either nurses or junior doctors. The junior doctor, once promoted, will know exactly what behaviour to expect and tolerate from nursing and junior medical staff. So, too, will the senior nurse: the system is perpetuated. Each group knows its place.

Simultaneously, the public displays of power emphasize the doctor's interest in the patient. *His* interest, *his* dedication cannot be doubted when he so assiduously takes to task those who have failed to do what they were asked, or cannot answer a simple question about the patient. By their acts of omission, those who are told off are presented as uncaring. Thus the patient learns that it is the doctor who really does care, and who also knows best.

Professional performances

In the public displays of anger, there is the answering ritual display of deference by the subordinate nurse. The exalted position of the consultant, the need for lengthy training and the expertise of years, are all emphasized when the junior doctor is ridiculed.

There are few benefits and many costs in either the junior doctor or the nurse trying to fight the system. A junior who talks back would not last long, at least within the hospital system. The junior doctor needs his reference, without which he cannot advance. The nurse who talks back will be perceived as a 'cheeky nurse', a trouble-maker. She is a nurse speaking out of turn, not obeying the rules and therefore not to be trusted and whose life will be made difficult by colleagues (Mackay, 1989).

There are many reasons why nurses do not 'speak out'. Nurse training has always emphasized the need for calm, quiet, composed and self-disciplined nurses. It is part of the persona which is highly valued both by nurses and the general public. Nurses learn from their earliest weeks in training that they are to be seen but not heard. Even when qualified, it is extremely difficult for some nurses to express their opinions to doctors (Mackay, 1993). Some feel that the traditional and deferential attitudes perpetuated in nurse training will change with the arrival of Project 2000. However, these hopes may be overoptimistic, given the pressures experienced by graduate nurses (Green, 1988; Kelly, 1991).

Members of the medical profession take great pride in their intellectual abilities and their scientific knowledge. Doctors contrast the high standard of A-levels required to enter medical school with the more modest O-levels required to enter nurse training. It is only once nurses have qualified and gained experience that they muster a measure of confidence enabling them to challenge the opinion of a doctor.

Cementing nurses' unwillingness to offer their opinion is the fear of public humiliation mentioned above. Nurses have no wish to set themselves up for ridicule by speaking 'out of turn': that is, when they have not been spoken to. Speaking out of turn is an initiating activity, not a reactive one. The whole notion of 'speaking out of turn' is one that hinges on power, status and class. Implicit in the concept is the notion of deference, which within hospitals is of the 'due respect' to be given to the medical profession (a respect which is also expected from patients). The traditions of hospital performances ensure that nurses know their place.

Not surprisingly, when nurses have themselves been humiliated, or been witness to a humiliation, they learn to keep quiet. At the same time, the confidence, even the arrogance, of some doctors compounds the ease with which nurses can be put in their place. The 'deafening' display of confidence by some doctors may be one reason why some nurses find it difficult to develop confidence in their own skills and abilities.

The effects of power

Power must be a recurring theme in any discussion of doctor–nurse relationships. Senior doctors *can* publicly ridicule junior staff and nurses because they wield greater power. It is power which is the most potent force in determining the actions and inactions of occupational groups. Nurses have only a negative type of power. They can make life difficult for doctors, especially junior doctors. Nurses can remind doctors, to the extent of nagging, they can seek clarification of simple instructions and they can go by the rule-book. But nurses do not have the power to set the agenda: they have to respond to the actions of others.

The historical traditions of medicine and nursing have their part to play in the 'not speaking out of turn' stance adopted by nurses. Traditionally nurses have been seen as handmaidens of doctors and acting only upon their instructions. If the gendered word of 'handmaiden' is replaced for the more objective and appropriate 'servant', the meaning of the relationship becomes clearer. To serve is to be of service, to be useful, to meet the needs of others. Handmaiden emphasizes the gender of nurses, not their class. A servant relationship is a class relationship.

Nurses have always served doctors in a variety of ways, and still do. Serving does not simply mean preparing the coffee after ward rounds, but setting out trolleys, getting the notes together before the ward round, ensuring that everything is ready and the doctor does not waste any of his (precious) time. Nurses enjoy 'being of service', they want to look after others and it may come naturally to look after 'their' doctors. However, it is noteworthy that there is no indication that nurses want to look after physiotherapists or dietitians in the same way that they want to look after doctors. The nurse cannot bask in any reflected glory from these occupational groups. These things are perhaps changing, but the unthinking action of many nurses is to serve doctors, to smooth things out for the doctor's arrival, to jump when they are told to jump, to follow doctor's orders.

In turn, it is the doctor's patients whom nurses look after, they are not the nurses' patients. Perhaps this helps account for the finding by Mills (1983), that when doctors pronounce 'no active treatment' for a patient the nurses also tend to withdraw their attentions from that patient (see below).

Nurses can actively collude in perpetuating the relationships of subordination and domination between doctors and nurses. Nurses often badger and demand speedy decisions from young and inexperienced doctors. Uncertainty and indecisiveness will receive a sigh of exasperation and the eyes rolled towards the ceiling. The good doctor should not prevaricate, should not have to go and ask someone else, should be certain of his knowledge.

The badgering of young doctors may partly be due to nurses trying to 'get their own back', and redressing the imbalances of power. Nevertheless, the demands of the nurse (and the perceived or real demands of the patient) ensure that junior doctors know they have to exude a confidence and decisiveness they may not feel. The assumed mask of confidence starts to feel comfortable. (That there is a disjunction between this public display and the private persona of the doctor is demonstrated in the high incidence of suicide, alcohol abuse and depressive illness amongst them.) It is a short step from the feigned confidence of the pre-registration house officer to the arrogant approach of some senior medical staff.

Behind these performances there is the reaffirmation of medical science, to themselves and to their patients. There is also a defence by the medical profession when confronted with the challenge to their occupational status which nurses represent. To a large extent, these performances are a display of power, status and the dominance by the medical profession. It is a display of subordination, of inferiority and lack of power by nurses. It is a way in which the nurse displays to the doctor that no challenge to the prevailing order is taking place.

To repeat, the nurse is both victim and willing participant in these performances. She is victim because members of the medical profession enjoy substantially greater power and status than any nurse. She is a willing participant in that she goes along with the medical version of events, of what is right and proper behaviour in the presence of doctors, in front of patients, of what information to tell patients and what not. The needs of the patient to be able to question the doctor, to express fears and reservations, to be given time to establish some rapport with the doctor are not allowed by the nurse (as well as the doctor) in many doctor–patient interactions. There are different justifications available (the busy schedule of the doctor or the inadequate staffing levels); but in truth the interests of the patient are secondary to the continuing working relationships within the medical profession. The patients are outsiders being processed by the system. Patients come and go but colleagues are ever present.

In recent years nurses have been concerned to counter the dominance of the medical profession. There has been a concerted attempt to establish the credibility of nurses as an occupational group by defining their own distinctive sphere of competence and special contribution to patient care. There has been a move to distance nursing from the sitting-next-to-Nellie type of training towards situating training more firmly in higher education (UKCC, 1986). There have been moves for nurses to establish themselves as independent specialist practitioners. There are specialist nurses working in stoma and diabetic care, and there have even been 'nursing beds' (Pembrey and Punton, 1990). Nurses argue that, because of their greater patient contact, knowledge of personal circumstances and relatives, they ought to be consulted in decisions regarding the care of patients. Nurses have a different view of the patient which could act to counterbalance the medical view.

In challenging the dominant position of the medical profession and asserting the value of their own world view, nurses seek to overcome their exclusion from decision-making in patient care. One aspect of this challenge has been the role of 'patient advocate' in which the nurse acts as intermediary between patient and doctor. As patient advocate, the nurse would ensure that patients interests are protected in decisions regarding patient care. In adopting the role of patient advocate, nurses implicitly assert that somehow they are on the patient's side, and by extension doctors are not.

Yet is a patient advocate role possible in an occupation which displays such deference to medical colleagues? Smooth working relationships take priority over patient care. Closing ranks and withholding information from patients means that the potential for patients to enjoy any power or autonomy is correspondingly diminished (Millman, 1976).[4]

Caring for the dying

The performances of the nurse and the doctor take on new meanings when viewed in relation to the care of the terminally ill. It was obvious from our interviews with doctors and nurses that decisions as to when to stop active treatment of terminally ill patients often caused conflict and difficulty. There are no simple solutions in making decisions about patients who are terminally ill. It was generally agreed by doctors and nurses that members of the medical profession tend to want to continue treatment longer than do nursing staff. Medical staff want to do all they can for patients and in no way to hasten their death. Nursing staff want patients to die with dignity and in peace, without unnecessary distress. Lacking final responsibility for the outcome of treatment, nurses may find it easier to say 'enough is enough'. Thus while doctors may wish to fight death to the very end, nurses may be more accepting of its inevitability.

The views of doctors and nurses are not easy to reconcile. The presence of conflict in the care of the dying is welcome *if* it means that careful reflection on the options is taking place. Balancing differing views means that patients will receive optimum care, the options will be debated and considered. The presence of two diverging views safeguards the patient from thoughtless action or inaction.

Although nurses may be angered by actions taken by medical staff, it is not apparent from our data that nurses often confront doctors regarding their decisions to relabel 'patient' to 'terminally ill patient'. Many nurses say they are unable to express anger to a doctor's face. Even the voicing of unsolicited opinions may be difficult, especially for junior nurses. Perhaps these nurses have come to believe in their own performances. Similarly many doctors do not hear nurses' opinions regarding the care of the terminally ill patient. Nurses do mutter

---

4 Of course, there is an equally lethal loyalty amongst members of the medical profession.

amongst themselves and to the more approachable junior medical staff. In corroboration of this, there is less dispute between nursing and junior medical staff about the care and treatment of the terminally ill. There were occasional reports of outbursts and scenes caused by the intransigence of a senior doctor in the treatment of a terminally ill patient. However, it was not apparent that there were many direct cool-tempered confrontations or even expressions of concern made by nurses about doctors' decisions regarding terminally ill patients. Indeed, given some of the performances and charades outlined earlier, it seems hard to imagine how the nurse who is deferential in so many situations could be assertive in another. Nurses might want to look after patients better, but their training, socializaton and traditional relationship with the medical profession combine to make them poor allies for the dying patient. Nurses claim a special relationship with, and knowledge of, the patient. Nurses are vociferous in their assertions that patients must have as dignified and pain-free a death as possible. There is little doubt of the intensity of feelings caused by over-treatment of patients by the medical profession. Yet nurses are often silent in the face of what to them are seen as unacceptable medical decisions. Instead, nurses mutter about their unease or anger regarding medical decisions. Because nurses' muttering takes place out of earshot of the senior doctors who make the critical decisions, these doctors may well be unaware of any disquiet felt by nurses. In effect, through their silence nurses give the appearance of sharing the perspective of the medical profession in the treatment and care of the terminally ill.

How are nurses to defend this silence? What is the point of nurses' special knowledge if it is not to be used for the benefit of the patient? Are nurses' claims to having a special knowledge of patients simply empty rhetoric only to be used in the occupational jockeying for power? Claims to being 'the caring profession' or the 'patient's advocate' must sound hollow to many dying patients.

Many nurses have tried to speak out but found that doctors do not listen to their opinions. Indeed, many nurses speak resentfully of doctors' inability to listen to or seek the opinions of nurses (Mackay, 1993). There is also resentment that doctors do not sufficiently respect nurses or their knowledge and experience. Even if doctors ask for a nurse's opinion it is not always clear that they actually hear what the nurses are saying. It seems that some doctors merely pay lip-service to ideas of communication and team-working. Doctors argue that the quality of nurses is extremely variable and it is hard to know which nurse's opinion to trust. In any case it is the doctor who carries the responsibility and it is his and only his decision. Opinions can be freely given by nurses in the knowledge that they do not bear final responsibility, and so the opinions, by implication, cannot be trusted. Anyway, say some doctors, many nurses do not and will not offer their opinions even when asked.

Patients as pawns

While it is obvious that some nurses do express their opinions to doctors, there is little doubt that many behave passively in front of doctors. (Extremely scathing comments about the failure of British-trained nurses to voice their opinions were made by nurses who had trained in Australasia and North America.) A passive nurse is not a useful ally for a dying or any other patient. The deferential performances and rituals of nurses act against the interests of patients. In protecting the patient's faith in medical science and in the sanctity of the doctor's opinion, the nurse may be actively harming the patient.

Additionally, the performances in which nurses participate act to reduce the confidence of nurses in their own independent action. Nurse training, nursing practice and doctors' behaviour towards nurses all play some part in the level of assertiveness and confidence displayed by nurses. In the same way, medical training, medical practice and nurses' behaviour towards doctors all play some part in the level of confidence displayed by doctors. The 'I don't know, I'll just go and ask sister' mentality, combined with the doctor's need to exude confidence as part of the medical persona, may quite literally be a fatal combination for the patient.

Too often the performance is face-saving behaviour undertaken by nurses on behalf of doctors. It is face-saving behaviour undertaken by the less well paid on behalf of the much better paid. Nurses' career prospects, their status and their power are substantially less than doctors'. Yet nurses have been trained to protect their 'superiors'. Nurses' socialization ensures that, in effect, they are active in maintaining their own subordinate position. They make the doctor look good yet simultaneously deny their own knowledge and expertise. Nurses are in an invidious position in which they have become their own worst enemies.

Overview

The doctor–nurse game was first reported from research in accident and emergency units in the USA (Stein, 1967). Such games may be played in the UK during the pre-registration house officers' first weeks on medical and surgical wards, although they are soon jettisoned in favour of the traditional pattern of doctors telling nurses what to do. The joy when the doctor–nurse game was first 'discovered' — or at least put down on paper by Stein — reflected what nurses wanted to believe. It gelled with nurses' views of the doctor–nurse relationship because it demonstrated that nurses had knowledge and skills which were publicly denied by members of the medical profession. It showed that the relationship was not one of inequality but only of feigned inequality (see Porter, 1991, 1992). This little model of the working relationship has enjoyed a popularity far outweighing its usefulness. In fact, taking the model on board in Britain may have been harmful in creating an illusion of power, obscuring the extent of the continuing dominance of the medical profession. An examination of the many other little performances played by nurses and doctors is arguably of more salience to nurses' participation (or lack of it) in the delivery of health care than the game presented by Stein.

Nevertheless, there are many nurses who seek to challenge the dominance of the medical profession. There are assertive nurses who want to be active participants in decisions regarding the treatment of patients. These nurses have a different view, perhaps a distinctively nursing view of patient care. In order to practise as they would wish they may have to leave the medically dominated world of the hospital to work, for example, as health visitors or as nurses in hospices. In a hospice it is clear that a nurse's need to care holistically can be fulfilled, and it is a world from which the medical profession is still relatively absent (*pace* James and Field, 1992). Within the hospital, the domination by medical science and the medical profession may mean that the needs of nurses to care in a patient-centred way must be denied.

Nurses must think carefully about the performances that are being given in hospitals: they must think carefully about their role and their relationships with patients. In examining those relationships (see May, 1990; Hurst, 1992) nurses may want to challenge them.

References

Goffman E (1959) *The Presentation of Self in Everyday Life*. Harmondsworth: Penguin.

Green GJ (1988) Relationships between role models and role perceptions of new graduate nurses. *Nursing Research*; **37**: 245–248.

Hurst K (1992) Changes in nursing practice 1984–1992. *Nursing Times*; **88**: (12), 54.

James N, Field D (1992) The routinization of hospices: charisma and bureaucratization. *Social Science and Medicine*; **34**: 1363–1375.

Kelly B (1991) The professional values of English nursing undergraduates. *Journal of Advanced Nursing*; **16**: 867–872.

Mackay L (1989) *Nursing a Problem*. Milton Keynes: Open University Press.

Mackay L (1993) *Conflicts in Care: Medicine and Nursing*. London: Chapman & Hall.

May C (1990) Research on nurse–patient relationships: problems of theory, problems of practice. *Journal of Advanced Nursing*; **15**: 307–315.

McKeown T (1976) *The Role of Medicine: Dream, Mirage or Nemesis?* London: Nuffield Hospital Trust.

Millman M (1976) *The Unkindest Cut: Life in the Backrooms of Medicine*. New York: M. Morrow.

Mills W (1983) *Problems Related to the Nursing Management of the Dying Patient*. MLitt thesis, University of Glasgow.

Pembrey S, Punton S (1990) Nursing beds. *Nursing Times*; **86**: (14), 44–45.

Porter S (1991) A participant observation study of power relations between nurses and doctors in a general hospital. *Journal of Advanced Nursing*; **16**: 728–735.

Porter S (1992) Women in a women's job: the gendered experience of nurses. *Sociology of Health and Illness*; **14**: 510–527.

Stein L (1967) The doctor–nurse game. *Archives of General Psychiatry*; **16**: 699–703.

Stein L, Watts DT, Howell T (1990) The doctor–nurse game revisited. *New England Journal of Medicine*; **322**: 546–549.

United Kingdom Central Council (1986) *Project 2000*. London: UKCC.

Walby S, Greenwell J, Mackay L, Soothill K (1994) *Medicine and Nursing: Professions in a Changing Health Service*. London: Sage.

Index